Displacing Human Rights

Displacing Human Rights

WAR AND INTERVENTION IN NORTHERN UGANDA

Adam Branch

OXFORD
UNIVERSITY PRESS

OXFORD
UNIVERSITY PRESS

Oxford University Press, Inc., publishes works that further
Oxford University's objective of excellence
in research, scholarship, and education.

Oxford   New York
Auckland   Cape Town   Dar es Salaam   Hong Kong   Karachi
Kuala Lumpur   Madrid   Melbourne   Mexico City   Nairobi
New Delhi   Shanghai   Taipei   Toronto

With offices in
Argentina   Austria   Brazil   Chile   Czech Republic   France   Greece
Guatemala   Hungary   Italy   Japan   Poland   Portugal   Singapore
South Korea   Switzerland   Thailand   Turkey   Ukraine   Vietnam

Published by Oxford University Press, Inc.
198 Madison Avenue, New York, NY 10016

www.oup.com

Oxford is a registered trademark of Oxford University Press

Library of Congress Cataloging-in-Publication Data
Branch, Adam, 1975–
Displacing human rights: war and intervention in northern Uganda /Adam Branch.
   p.   cm.
Includes bibliographical references and index.
ISBN 978-0-19-978208-6
1. Human rights—Uganda. 2. Civil rights—Uganda.
3. Humanitarian intervention—Uganda. 4. War and society—Uganda.
5. Uganda—Politics and government. 6. Uganda—Social conditions. I. Title.
JC599.U36B73   2011
967.6104'4—dc22   2010049792

9 8 7 6 5 4 3 2 1

Printed in the United States of America
on acid-free paper

To my parents

CONTENTS

ACKNOWLEDGMENTS

Any project like this incurs debts in a number of currencies, most of which cannot be repaid. First, I have to thank my friends and colleagues in Gulu Town and in the displacement camps in Gulu district. In spite of the intense violence and insecurity they faced, they welcomed me when I arrived and, for the last decade, have made this project possible through their friendship, insight, and assistance, often at significant personal risk. This risk also keeps me from naming them—as the book explains, they are often caught between state violence and NGO discipline, and to be associated with a work that tries to challenge both could cause them problems that they do not need. If it were not for these people's friendship, I would have abandoned this project long ago, because that friendship alone is what has given me a stake in what I write about.

One person I will name, because he has made it his life's work to stand up to these risks and because he agreed to be named here, is James A. A. Otto, the Executive Director of Human Rights Focus, Gulu. This book is possible only because of Human Rights Focus, where, as a volunteer and, later, an employee, I was able to work on a variety of human rights issues, during periods of intense fighting and relative calm, while also pursuing my own research questions through constant interaction with those affected by and involved in the war. This relationship also helped to make my research—and myself—accountable on a daily basis to those about whom I was writing. To *Ladit* Otto and the rest of the Human Rights Focus organization goes my deepest gratitude. I have also sought accountability by presenting large portions of what is in this book at various public forums in northern and southern Uganda and in different parts of Africa over the years, and I thank the many discussants and critics at those events.

A number of other friends have helped me along the way. Adrian Yen has been a bridge between life in Uganda and life in the United States, and without his companionship and wisdom for the last twenty-five years I have no idea what would have happened. Martin was there when this book began in Pabbo a decade ago and he and his family have been close ever since. Leslie Grant and Alex Terzich (and Lee), Zachariah Mampilly and Nimmi Gowrinathan (and Cherian), Ham, Robert Wolf, and Andy "Big Man" Ianuzzi have all been part of the research, writing, and everything else that went along with this book. My brother Jordan has given me essential advice and often a place to sleep when I really needed it.

The trajectory behind this book was shaped by a long list of mentors and friends. As an undergraduate in Harvard's Social Studies program, it was under

Joel Greifinger's guidance that a struggle with Adorno gave rise to some of this book's deeper concerns. In Chiapas, Mexico, I want to thank in particular Guiomar Rovira and Mariana Mora, my models of engaged scholarship. It was in Chiapas that Guio explained to me why no one should speak for the Zapatistas, a lesson that I am still trying to abide by today.

In Columbia University's political science PhD program, I had the privilege of studying with Professors Jean Cohen and Mahmood Mamdani. As my dissertation advisers, they offered the extraordinary levels of trust and engagement needed for me to pursue what was a very undisciplinary project. Other people at Columbia who helped me think through the ideas in the book include professors Michael Taussig and Hamid Dabashi, and my fellow-travelling graduate students Bajeera McCorkle, Ron Jennings, and Alex Gourevitch.

In northern Uganda, I was fortunate to be able to follow in the footsteps of three scholars whose generosity, friendship, and encouragement were invaluable, namely, Sverker Finnström, Ron Atkinson, and Tim Allen. Chris Dolan's critical work also helped guide my own study, even though we did not finally meet in person until recently. Along with the seminal work of these four, there was also a diverse community of scholars, researchers, and students working on and around northern Uganda, and this book has profited immensely from conversations and exchanges with them over the years. They include Samar Al-Bulushi, Erin Baines, Chris Blattman, Lydia Kemunto Bosire, Phil Clark, Chris Day, Amy Finnegan, Eric Green, Barbara Harrell-Bond, Professor Leander Komakech, Ayesha Nibbe, Adam O'Brien, Moses Chrispus Okello, Father Joseph Okumu, Fabius Okumu-Alya, Joseph Oloka-Onyango, Michael Otim, Sandrine Perrot, Joanna Quinn, and Kristof Titeca.

I would also like to thank those colleagues and friends I have come to know since finishing graduate school, many of whom have read parts of the manuscript and helped me in refining, revising, or recanting my ideas, especially Jonathan Graubart and Latha Varadarajan at San Diego State, and the British-based intervention and state-building crew, especially David Chandler. The manuscript was given its final touches during my tenure as a visiting research associate at the Makerere Institute of Social Research, Kampala, and I thank MISR and Mahmood Mamdani, its new director, for hosting me and providing such an exciting intellectual environment in which to finish this work. Finally, I want to thank Angela Chnapko, my editor at OUP, whose commitment has made the entire publishing process not only painless, but enjoyable, and also production editor Joellyn Ausanka, whose patience has been a great help.

For their financial assistance, I would like to thank the Columbia University Center for International Conflict Resolution, the Columbia University Institute of African Studies, the Ford Foundation for East Africa, the LSE Crisis States Research Centre, and the UGP Grant Program at SDSU. Parts of this book draw upon previously published articles and book chapters, and I thank the publishers for having granted permission to use those works. Specifically, I would like to thank *Constellations* (Branch 2005a), where parts of chapter 1 appeared; Zed Books, publisher of *The Lord's Resistance Army: Myth and Reality*, where parts of chapter 2 appeared (Branch 2010); *African Studies Quarterly*, where parts of chapter 2 appeared (Branch 2005b); *Civil Wars*, where parts of chapter 3 appeared (Branch 2009); the *Journal of Intervention and Statebuilding*, where parts of chapter 3 appeared (Branch 2008a); the LSE Crisis States Research Centre, which published the working paper where parts of chapters 4 and 5 appeared (Branch 2008b); and *Ethics and International Affairs*, where parts of chapter 6 appeared (Branch 2007).

Finally, and most importantly, I would like to thank my parents for the uncompromising support they have given me since the beginning of this project (including my Dad relentlessly editing every version of every chapter of the entire manuscript)—and, indeed, since the beginning of all my projects. Through their words and examples, our parents taught Jordan and me that justice means treating all people with dignity and calling on others do the same—this book is just my attempt to apply that lesson to a situation in which it seemed badly needed. With profound love and admiration, this book is dedicated, of course, to my Mom and Dad.

Displacing Human Rights

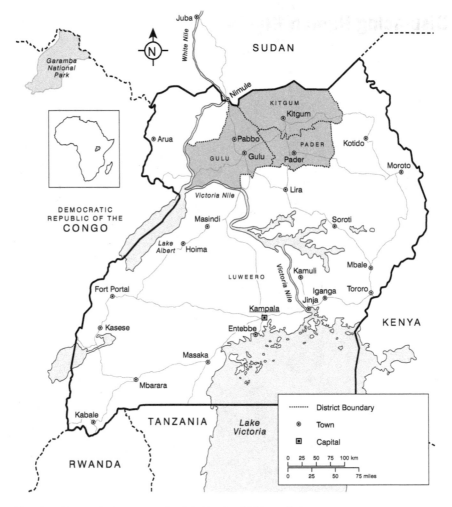

Uganda, with the districts comprising Acholiland in 2004 shaded.

Source: Map prepared by Jonatan Alvarsson.

Introduction

Gulu District, July 2001

Returning to Gulu Town after several weeks in Pabbo camp, where forty thousand Acholi people were living in tiny huts packed into one square kilometer, dependent on relief aid from World Food Program, debilitated by malnutrition and preventable disease, and targeted by the brutal violence of rebels, government troops, and *boo kec* bandits alike, I had two questions that I wanted to ask the Acholi I had met in town the previous month. First, as a political science graduate student, and as a person shocked by what he had seen, I wanted to know how the government had been able to force hundreds of thousands of peasant farmers into camps and keep them interned there for years. What was preventing people, I wondered, from organizing and leaving the camps, returning to their rich lands lying fallow within view of the squalid, overcrowded huts where they were being forced to live, and die? Second, as a Westerner involved in human rights activism, I wanted to know what impact the dozens of Western aid agencies and nongovernmental organizations (NGOs), seen swarming around the war zone in Land Cruisers, were having upon the war and forced displacement. What were they up to, how were they trying to remedy the situation, what good were they doing in the face of all this violence and suffering?

The first question, I thought, was too sensitive for a newcomer to be asking in the middle of an ongoing government counterinsurgency, one that saw all Acholi as potentially suspect, and so I left it for when I knew people better. However, when I asked the second question—not realizing how sensitive it also was—I was given an answer that would guide the next decade of my work. An Acholi acquaintance who himself worked for an NGO put it this way: despite the hundreds of millions of dollars spent by aid agencies and donors in the conflict zone; despite their increasing involvement in economic, social, and cultural life; and despite their incessant declarations that they are promoting peace and human rights—*nothing changes.*

In the years after that, the war expanded, and with the inception of the government's brutal Operation Iron Fist in 2002, forced displacement also expanded, eventually encompassing the entire rural population of Acholiland, almost one million people. International intervention kept pace and grew to include programs for camp management, development, peacebuilding, reconciliation, justice, and even counterterrorism and international law enforcement. During that time, I spent a total of about two years in Acholiland, working with a Ugandan human rights organization based in Gulu Town and also conducting my own research. I was eventually able to inquire into the first question, as well as explore the second further, and the tentative answers to these questions form the substance of this book. In brief, I came to be even more pessimistic than was my acquaintance in 2001 about the impact that foreign intervention was having on the war and on displacement. International intervention, I believe, not only failed to bring about positive change, but also *prevented* such change from occurring, and, at times, it directly and destructively enflamed, enabled, and prolonged the war, displacement, and civilian suffering.

In part, this is not an unprecedented observation: the damaging consequences that the provision of humanitarian relief aid can have for armed conflicts have been documented by anthropologists and political scientists in other war zones. However, the complicity of intervening organizations, agencies, and states in the prolongation and intensification of violence in Acholiland went much further than the diversion of food supplies to government or rebel troops. Indeed, one sort of complicity or another seemed to run through all the forms of intervention I examined, from relief aid, to development, to peacebuilding, to international law enforcement. Moreover, I found that this complicity emerged according to a similar logic in all the different interventions, a similarity I traced to the interventionist human rights discourse that informed and motivated the various interventions, a human rights discourse tied to a specific image of the conflict in Uganda.

African Humanity and Inhumanity

Today, I signed into law the Lord's Resistance Army (LRA) Disarmament and Northern Uganda Recovery Act of 2009. The legislation crystallizes the commitment of the United States to help bring an end to the brutality and destruction that have been a hallmark of the LRA across several countries for two decades, and to pursue a future of greater security and hope for the people of central Africa.

The Lord's Resistance Army preys on civilians—killing, raping, and mutilating the people of central Africa; stealing and brutalizing their children; and displacing hundreds of thousands of people.

Its leadership, indicted by the International Criminal Court for crimes against humanity, has no agenda and no purpose other than its own survival. It fills its ranks of fighters with the young boys and girls it abducts. By any measure, its actions are an affront to human dignity.

Of the millions affected by the violence, each had an individual story and voice that we must not forget. In northern Uganda, we recall Angelina Atyam's 14-year-old daughter, whom the LRA kidnapped in 1996 and held captive for nearly eight years—one of 139 girls abducted that day from a boarding school.

[...]

We mourn those killed. We pray for those abducted to be freed, and for those wounded to heal. We call on the ranks of the LRA to disarm and surrender. We believe that the leadership of the LRA should be brought to justice.

This was Barack Obama in May, 2010, upon signing the bill that signaled the culmination of the LRA's ascendance in American public awareness. Obama's statement engages all the themes of what anthropologist Sverker Finnström has called the "official discourse" on the conflict—the meaningless, criminal brutality of the LRA, the innocent child-victim, and the Western savior—the image that has informed the numerous interventions in northern Uganda.[1] But this image, or minor variations on it, is not unique to the way violence in Uganda is represented in the West. In fact, Africa itself tends to be seen as one large terrain of afflicted humanity, as a continent of mere humans without history, agency, or meaningful political or social life. Their suffering is the suffering of the human, and thus coded as human rights violations, crimes against humanity, or humanitarian crises.

By representing the suffering of Africans as the suffering of humanity, this image allows us in the West to claim to identify with that suffering on the basis of our common humanity with Africans. We Westerners are exhorted—and permitted—to empathize with Africans' abstracted pain from afar, to take their suffering as our own suffering, as an affront to the entire human race, to all of humanity, and thus to us personally. But although the category of humanity provides a supposed foundation for Western identification and commiseration with Africa, and claims to grant dignity, respect, and equality to Africans, it fails to provide any foundation in the Western imagination for agency or action by the African "victim"—he or she is seen as the helpless child, the despairing woman, Atyam and her daughter, to use President Obama's example. Thus, the West's dominant image of Africa, despite its pretence of equality, entails a basic inequality: whereas Africans are mere humans and unable to raise themselves out of that denuded state, we in the West give ourselves the privileged position of both being able to identify with suffering Africans on the basis of a common humanity while also being able to go beyond the mere human and re-assume our political, social, and economic personalities as globally powerful, responsible redeemers. In the Western imagination, therefore, the corollary of being a suffering human—of being an African—is to need outsiders to effect one's redemption, which must be accepted with unqualified gratitude. The corollary of being a Westerner is to claim to act upon the ethical demand made by our common humanity in order to effect that redemption of Africa, it being up to us to determine when Africans need saving and how to provide it, how to give "voice to the voiceless."

Africa is thus deemed to be in dire, perhaps permanent, need of humanitarian aid, human rights promotion, humanitarian law enforcement, or humanitarian military intervention, to be carried out by the West. These interventions base their legitimacy in a dual moral claim—to protect humanity itself while also protecting the actual African victims—and thus present themselves as beyond politics or political reproach. African political or social institutions, whether regional, national, or local, are judged legitimate only insofar as they can protect African humanity, and when those institutions are judged (by the West) to have failed in this task, it putatively becomes up to the West to respond to the moral imperative and save strangers in Africa, to sanctimoniously take upon ourselves the burden of defending Africa's humanity from Africa's inhumanity.

This image, and the fundamental inequality it entails, would remain just another testament to the West's refusal to afford Africa the same dignity it claims for itself, if it were not for the fact that it justifies and informs an immense regime of Western intervention in the continent, including in Uganda. Western institutions and actors have penetrated the highest echelons of the African state as well as the most distant rural village in the name of saving Africa through interventions informed by this particular image. Wherever these interventions occur, and whatever their specific agents or concerns are, I argue that they all share a common paradoxical tendency: Western intervention can tend to impose its own epistemological categories—the human stripped of agency, subject to unaccountable, arbitrary power, seeking an external savior—*on* the situations where it occurs. Intervention can provide a vehicle through which the Western imagination of Africa attempts to impose itself upon Africa, a tendency that can end up intensifying or even creating the very conditions invoked to justify intervention in the first place.

This is the paradox of human rights intervention: that it can entrench, or even give rise to, the very human rights crises it claims to be resolving. I witnessed this paradox appearing dramatically in northern Uganda in two ways. First, human rights intervention undermined popular political agency by repressing autonomous communication, organization, and action, which are the substance of civil and political rights and provide the foundation for democracy. Second, human rights intervention in Uganda also ended up undoing those more basic human rights concerned with human life and wellbeing by unintentionally prolonging and intensifying the conflict and violence. These two paradoxes were intimately related insofar as the negative political consequences of human rights interventions for autonomy and democracy were in large part precisely what led to their negative practical consequences for violence and civilian suffering. In concrete terms, by empowering unaccountable political actors and structures on the local, national, and international levels, by depoliticizing and disciplining those people subject to intervention, and by subverting the efforts by survivors of violence to find peace and justice themselves, human rights intervention set the stage for continued and intensified anticivilian violence and civilian suffering, the very human rights violations of most immediate concern to those intervening. Human rights intervention's political counterproductivity gave rise to its practical counterproductivity.

Behind these counterproductive interventions is a specific human rights discourse that represents rights as being fulfilled through an external agency, not through the organization and action of the rights-holders themselves. Through intervention, the emancipatory and democratic possibilities of human rights are displaced, both concretely and conceptually. In this way, we can see intervention displacing human rights in a series of different realms: human rights are displaced from the political to the administrative, from the popular to the elite, from the autonomous to the dependent, from emancipation to control, from struggle to demobilization.

The consequence is that, instead of fulfilling their stated aspiration of ushering in peace and justice, human rights interventions can converge upon fostering arbitrary power and violence on the local, national, and international levels. Interveners may try to blame this tendency on what they argue are the illiberal, corrupt, and traditional ways of Africans, when, in fact, it stems directly from the lack of accountability that characterizes human rights intervention itself. The irony is that, from the point of view of those subject to intervention, supposedly liberal human rights interventions can end up looking very much like what Western interveners tend to accuse African societies and states of themselves being— illiberal, patrimonial, corrupt, arbitrary, and violent—the very maladies invoked to justify the need for Western intervention in the first place. To understand why violence can exist in various relationships, including collaboration, with human rights intervention, it is therefore necessary to focus on the dimension that is normally excluded from analyses both of violence in Africa and of human rights intervention: politics.

The Contexts of Intervention

The ideological construct of Africa as a terrain of victimized humanity and predatory inhumanity has a long history in the West, stretching back to colonial images of the continent.[2] However, to assess the consequences of its contemporary application through human rights intervention, this construct and the interventions it informs need to be contextualized within Africa's current economic and political dispensation. Most broadly, it is an economic dispensation marked by two or more decades of neoliberal ascendance and donor-imposed structural adjustment, characterized for many states by increasing income inequality and often poverty, continued lack of industrialization, and importance of natural resource extraction. Tens of millions of Africans—including the displaced of northern Uganda—are superfluous according to the global capitalist economy,[3] their roles restricted to being little more than obstacles in the way of large-scale land buyers and raw material for the images of suffering (or "resilience") extracted and marketed by aid agencies, human rights groups, and fair-trade companies. The political context is marked by recent transformations of the African state under neoliberalism: despite the giddy celebration of Africa's "wave of democratization" in the 1990s, the overarching tendencies have been toward the formation of unaccountable, donor-supported, administrative states, state withdrawal from service provision, and militarization, changes that have given rise to popular opposition and, in turn, to various efforts, coercive and consensual, to contain that opposition. Africa's incorporation into the so-called War on Terror has emphasized the most destructive of these trends. These recent developments have occurred in the context of the continued centrality of ethnicized or racialized political identities that were forged under colonial rule and remain embedded in, and mobilized through, sometimes violent processes of state formation, consolidation, and contestation.

In this situation arrive human rights interventions, claiming to bring peace and justice to African populations plagued by violence. A functionalist critique might attribute to such intervention a managerial role of containing the worst depredations of global capitalism, providing humanitarian aid and stability as a welfare scheme of last resort for the most excluded so as to prevent them from threatening the reproduction of the global system. Although human rights interventions do, at times, play that managerial role, at other times they can end up prolonging or causing conflict and upheaval, as the Uganda case exemplifies. Therefore, just as the political consequences of human rights intervention do not conform to intervention's liberal ideology—that is, intervention does not represent the expansion of emancipatory governance globally—neither do intervention's consequences derive from intervention's supposed functionality to global economics or politics. Instead, the political consequences of intervention emerge from a complex and often contradictory interplay of different forces, structures, and interests on local, national, and international levels.

The particular impact of human rights intervention witnessed in Uganda—the entrenchment of unaccountable and antidemocratic social and political forces and the depoliticization of the citizenry so that they are less able to hold accountable those institutions running their lives—although perhaps extreme, reveals possibilities that, I argue, are inherent in human rights intervention anywhere it might occur in Africa. Thus, although I draw attention to the counterproductivity of human rights intervention in Uganda specifically, and recognize that to make claims about the consequences of intervention elsewhere would require comparative studies beyond the scope of this book, I do argue, more generally, that human rights intervention is always open to antidemocratic political instrumentalization and always has the possibility of undermining political autonomy among those subject to it. How these possibilities play out in other situations will depend upon the different political contexts.

At the same time that international and national political structures need to be taken into account as establishing the context for intervention, so too does the political agency of those people subject to intervention, the material upon which intervention seeks to act. Indeed, the consequences of intervention emerge from its constant interaction with the actions and reactions among those subject to intervention. Again, neither the ideology of human rights intervention—that it enjoys universal consent—nor the functionalist critique—that it regulates people to a state of passivity—matches reality. In fact, the transnational expansion and intensification of this particular set of moralized technocratic structures has gone hand-in-hand with the creation and emergence of new possibilities for politics and new expressions of political agency by those subject to the administrative regime. These expressions can take constructive forms, as those subject to intervention, in the face of transnational discipline and violence, reconfigure or refuse interventions in ways that can lead to emancipatory political projects, some grounded in new human rights discourses themselves. However, this is not to say that the ways in which those subject to intervention respond to, resist, or reconfigure intervention will necessarily be emancipatory, inclusive, or democratic. Intervention opens a space in which, and provides a set of resources with which, politics among those subject to intervention can take place—but in doing so, it also establishes limits on what is possible, limits that may be difficult to overcome.

Nevertheless, it is the ways in which human rights intervention may inadvertently provide the tools for emancipatory politics, politics possibly based upon concepts of human rights that imply and depend on individual and collective social and political agency, that will be of central concern to this book. These democratic displacements of human rights, displacements of human rights back onto the terrain of democracy, autonomy, and politics, are important for those subject to intervention because they expand the domain of political possibility among intervention's subjects, but they are also important for those undertaking intervention because they destabilize the position of the Western intervener by demanding that the West recognize what makes people *more than* mere humans and that the West grant others the same dignity it claims for itself. Therefore, the book concludes with an inquiry into the possibility for reconceived human rights discourses that might provide the foundation for a reconfiguration of Western intervention in Africa. I argue that human rights can indeed provide that foundation—but, again paradoxically, only at the expense of the idea of intervention itself.

Today, the situation *has* changed in northern Uganda—in early 2011, the camps have largely been disbanded, the LRA has left northern Uganda, and open fighting there has stopped. The active debilitation of an entire people—what Chris

Dolan termed their "social torture"—has in large part come to an end.[4] What has not ended, however, is the legacy of violence for people, society, and politics. Acholiland perhaps is being reconstructed, but various forms of violence and exclusion continue within Acholi society, particularly around contestations over land and political authority, and continue to characterize the relation between the Acholi and the national government—the very conditions that gave rise to the rebellions and then sustained them for over twenty years. Also, tragically, the violence of the LRA insurgency and counterinsurgency has not ended but has only shifted to Democratic Republic of Congo and South Sudan, with a rising toll of killed and displaced. This development is being used to invite a new intensification of U.S. military involvement promoted by American advocacy groups, whose celebrations of military power are drowning out the proposals for a peaceful solution coming from northern Uganda itself.

Whatever the depth of the changes seen in northern Uganda today may be, the fact that open fighting has stopped and people are at home farming again is definitely a cause for relief and even optimism. It should be made clear, though, that these positive changes were *not* the consequence of Western intervention. Rather, as Ronald Atkinson has documented, they were primarily the product of shifting regional political alignments made possible by the 2005 peace agreement between Khartoum and South Sudanese rebels.[5] Therefore, I would argue, it is most accurate to see these positive changes as having occurred, not because of, but *despite* Western intervention—despite the International Criminal Court's arrest warrants, despite the unrelenting support Western donors have provided to the Ugandan government's militarization and authoritarianism, despite the LRA's placement on the U.S. State Department Terrorist list, despite the aid agencies' reluctance to help people leave the camps, despite the expired seeds and useless machetes the Acholi were given in their so-called return packages. It remains to be seen what the consequences will be of postconflict interventions in northern Uganda and of the newly internationalized and militarized strategy to "finish off" the LRA, questions that are central to the future of peace and democracy in the country and the region.

Chapter Outline

Chapter 1 describes the historical development of contemporary human rights intervention in Africa. The dominant image of Africa in the West—a terrain of permanent human rights crises, in which helpless victims await rescue by international saviors—provides legitimacy for what I term total human rights intervention. Total interventions conceive of themselves as technical efforts to remedy a wide array of problems thought to be internal to African states and societies, such as poverty, social breakdown, psychological trauma, or impunity. Presenting themselves as bringing African societies and states back in line with imagined norms, total interventions are justified through reference to the moral language of human rights. The result is a wide set of technical conflict resolution, peacebuilding, development, reconstruction, and justice interventions undertaken by a wide set of interventionist actors, all claiming absolute moral legitimacy. These interventions can be analytically assessed, I argue, according to two dimensions: first, an *instrumental* dimension, through which interventions' material and symbolic resources are politically instrumentalized to various strategies; and second, an *administrative* dimension, through which interventions bring together international institutions, state structures, and nonstate organizations and actors to discipline affected populations. The chapter ends by showing how human rights intervention can also provide the symbolic and material resources for its subjects to forge new, unexpected forms of political and social organization and action themselves. Chapter 1 thus sets the stage for the rest of the book, which distinguishes between different human rights interventions and draws out the political consequences of each by applying this analytical approach.

Chapter 2 provides a historical account of the politics of the northern Uganda conflict, placing it in its local, national, and international contexts. The chapter begins with the colonial period and follows Acholi political history up to the present in order to demonstrate how internal and national political crises of the Acholi combined to underlie the inception and continuation of the war, and examines the new forms these crises took after the government's mass internment of the Acholi peasantry began in 1996. It argues that a sustainable resolution to violence in northern Uganda will have to be predicated upon a democratic resolution of these political crises, which can only proceed through the inclusive political organization and action of Acholi themselves. The chapter also shows the detrimental impact that the international context has had on the war: Uganda's positive international reputation and its strategic alliances with the United States, the international financial institutions, and European states have given rise to a reductive, moralized understanding of the conflict in which the benevolent but shorthanded Ugandan government needs assistance to protect its population from the evil LRA. Uganda came to be seen as a partner in protecting the human rights of its citizens and not as a possible violator of those rights, and human rights interventions have proceeded on that basis. Consequently, Uganda used international support to intensify the war, increase its militarization, and repress democratic domestic politics. This lays the groundwork for showing how human rights interventions considered in later chapters compounded the political crises of the Acholi and contributed to the war's prolongation.

Chapters 3–7 comprise an intensive study of the politics of specific human rights interventions, mapping out the political effects of a wide range of interventions by focusing both on the distinct logics of different interventions and on their mutual interaction in practice. Chapter 3 addresses the politics of humanitarian relief-aid distribution as it has been reframed within a human rights-based approach. The chapter explicates the epistemology, techniques, and effects of relief aid as they were evidenced in northern Uganda. It argues that, because of the Uganda government's international political relations, it has been allowed by its Western patrons to incorporate relief into its counterinsurgency with highly destructive consequences, most evident in the archipelago of forced internment camps run by the Ugandan military and international aid agencies. The chapter also shows how the administrative dimension of relief aid can discipline the recipients of aid toward becoming passive victims and criminalize those who refuse that aid.

Chapter 4 addresses the politics of societal peacebuilding, an expansive agenda in which interventions claim to build peace by building social order, thus purporting to address a broad set of causes and consequences of conflict. These interventions include activities as diverse as community conflict resolution, psychosocial support, development promotion, civil society building, and women's and children's rights promotion. Whereas relief aid distribution tends to normalize individuals toward a victim identity, I argue that the identities toward which peacebuilding interventions steer their subjects are not denied agency but rather are turned into active, "empowered" agents within the interventionist regime. However, because the autonomous expression of individual or collective agency is coded as deviance, these "re"-constructed identities are to function within externally imposed models of normal society and end up being subject to various forms of discipline and administrative depoliticization.

Chapter 5 is a critique of what I term *ethnojustice* interventions, which claim to promote social reconstruction, peace, and justice by rebuilding traditional society. In northern Uganda, a community of interest has emerged around the ethnojustice agenda among foreign donors in search of African authenticity for their aid programs, the Ugandan state as it looks to undermine its own accountability, and some older male Acholi who have lost authority as a result of the war and face challenges from the new forms of organization that have emerged among women and youth. In this context, the performance of traditional reconciliation rituals, as conceived within the ethnojustice agenda, can end up anchoring the extension of internationally supported, unaccountable power within Acholi society that tries to discipline people into becoming "proper" Acholi within a patriarchal social order. The chapter ends by asking about alternative community-based justice and reconciliation founded on alternative concepts of tradition, which might help ground an inclusive, democratic social order instead.

Chapter 6 examines the politics of the International Criminal Court's intervention in northern Uganda, assessing the claims made by the Court's supporters that it can help realize both peace and justice. The chapter discusses the Court's instrumentalization to the Uganda government's political and military interests and then proceeds to consider the political consequences stemming from the ICC's administrative dimension, specifically from the discourse of the ICC as an agent of global law enforcement. It argues that there is little evidence that ICC intervention can promote either peace or justice in Uganda or more widely. The chapter ends by asking about alternative conceptions of justice and the political projects that may drive them forward, even in the face of the ICC's effort to silence those who dissent from its preferred model of pursuing justice through punishment.

Chapter 7 considers the most recent form of self-proclaimed human rights intervention in Uganda: United States military intervention via its new military command for Africa, AFRICOM. AFRICOM is unprecedented in terms of its embrace of the discourse of partnership, empowerment, cultural understanding, and human security, not only in its proponents' rhetoric, but also to some extent in its activities. The result is that its agenda for Africa represents in many ways a militarization of the total intervention agenda and displays intensified forms of the same pathologies that characterize the latter. The chapter details the potential danger AFRICOM poses to peace and democracy in Africa, with special attention to U.S. military involvement in Uganda and the role of American advocacy organizations in promoting that involvement in the name of peace.

Chapter 8 asks if the West can re-orient its approach to Africa so as to deal with these dilemmas. The chapter begins by sketching a concept of human rights oriented around autonomous political organization, self-determination, and popular sovereignty. It argues for, first, a practice of negotiated disintervention, second, an Africanized practice of coercive intervention where necessary, and, third, what I call solidarity with consequences. All three imply refutations of the Western interventionist model itself: the first calls not for further intervention, but for the end of human rights interventions precisely for the sake of human rights; the second re-locates the agency of forceful intervention internally to Africa; and the third represents a mode of political solidarity premised on the reflexive recognition of common political struggles around common issues that bridge global divides.

A Note on the Research

This book draws on a wide variety of approaches to research, stemming from the interdisciplinary nature of the project. First, it is based on almost two years living, working, and researching in northern Uganda, mostly in Gulu Town, with significant periods of time in the camps. Specifically, I was in Acholiland in June–July 2001, February–June 2003, September–December 2004, and September–December 2005 as part of my PhD dissertation research, and then in February–November 2007 and June–July 2009 to undertake further work and research. The fieldwork drawn on in the book is primarily the product of a long-standing collaboration with Human Rights Focus (HURIFO), a Gulu-based human rights NGO founded in 1994 and under the direction of Mr. James A. A. Otto. That said, the book represents my own opinions and does not necessarily reflect the positions or policies of HURIFO.

The book also draws on the results of two research projects that I directed. First, I was the lead researcher for a project funded by the Ford Foundation of East Africa, run by HURIFO, for which eight researchers lived in displacement camps in every county of Acholiland from May until August, 2007 and conducted well over a thousand interviews and discussions. Second, I led another research project in mid-2007 funded by the Crisis States Research Centre at the London School of Economics, for which two researchers and I conducted over 80 interviews and discussions in and around Gulu Town. Again, this book represents my own opinion and does not necessarily represent the positions or policies of these funding institutions.

Finally, much of the material on the historical period from 1986 to 1997 is drawn from my attempt at a comprehensive reading of Ugandan newspaper articles on the conflict from those years, which I accessed through the collections at Makerere University Main Library and the Centre for Basic Research, Kampala.

1

Human Rights Intervention in Africa

Issa Shivji, in *The Concept of Human Rights in Africa,* argues that human rights—flexible, ambiguous, and often contradictory—can be drawn on to construct a wide array of different discourses that, by emphasizing different rights and agents for the fulfillment of those rights, can mobilize, legitimate, or constitute radically different modes of political practice.[1] Interventionist human rights discourses, for example, which imagine human rights as being realized through external intervention, are only one type among many and can contradict other, noninterventionist, human rights discourses, such as those that base the realization of rights upon democratic political practice. Furthermore, there is significant variation even within the set of interventionist human rights discourses, given the different ways that external intervention can be imagined to fulfill human rights. A major point of Shivji's work—and of this book—is, therefore, to show how emancipatory discourses of human rights can serve to help mobilize and legitimate political action to contest forms of domination that may themselves use the language of human rights.

This chapter traces the emergence of two human rights discourses used to legitimate Western intervention into episodes of violence in Africa, interventions that claim both the pragmatic objective of rescuing victims or bringing peace as well as the moral objective of realizing justice. These particular human rights discourses emerged in response to the dominant post-Cold War image of Africa, an image in which Africa was conceived as a terrain of permanent violent crisis in need of external intervention for its resolution, and thus have helped justify an increasing set of interventions in Africa undertaken by various Western agents. The first form of intervention I explore—what I characterize as *humanitarian rights intervention*—was championed after the first Gulf War by optimistic human rights activists and professionals. They argued that a "new world order" was emerging in which human rights would be upheld through international intervention without regard for state sovereignty. As applied to Africa, this humanitarian rights discourse

emphasized a set of basic human rights, specifically concerned with rescuing populations threatened by violence, to be enforced by the international community by
coercively intervening against predatory African states. This practice of rescue,
however, could not survive its first test in Somalia, and U.S. withdrawal from the
operation there and its refusal to allow increased UN military intervention in
Rwanda left many proponents of international intervention in Africa searching for
a new model.

Consequently, the focus of intervention shifted from rescue to peace. This new
approach revalued the African state and, instead of dismissing it as the enemy of
human rights, claimed to work with it to fulfill human rights and protect populations.[2] Bringing the African state back in was part of a new, broadened interventionist agenda of reforming and reconstructing African societies, polities, economies,
and even psychologies and cultures toward what were considered peaceful and responsible models. It was now a matter of building order in Africa, so that conflict
would be prevented in the future and peace assured. This form of intervention—
what I call *total intervention*—drew upon an expanded human rights discourse, in
which intervention was no longer to fulfill only the basic humanitarian rights of
people in crisis, but a wide array of human rights, from children's rights, to the right
to development, to victims' rights, to the right to mental health, to the right to peace.
As the domain of intervention expanded, so did the set of interventionist actors, and
almost all facets of African life were declared open to intervention in the name of
peace and human rights. This total intervention agenda continues to be dominant
today and is the framework within which the interventions considered throughout
this book take place.

1. The Post–Cold War Image of Africa

Immediately at the end of the Cold War, there was considerable uncertainty over
Africa's position within the new international order. Francis Deng and William
Zartman, for example, while drawing attention to the end of proxy wars in Africa
between the superpowers, could not say whether this would mean a future of
conflict or peace for the continent.[3] By the early-1990s, however, this uncertainty
had disappeared and a dominant image of Africa had been established, primarily
characterizing the continent as a place of permanent violence and conflict. Deng
himself would be an important proponent of this post-Cold War image of Africa,
and his 1996 *Sovereignty as Responsibility* is dominated by images of "brutal and
difficult-to-manage conflicts" and "dramatic cases of chaos and collapse,"[4] among
them "countries like Liberia, Rwanda, Somalia, Sierra Leone, and Sudan, characterized by acute ethnic violence or civil wars and a general disintegration of governance, public order, and personal and national security," such that millions have
been "lost in internecine warfare" in their "failed or failing states."[5] As this section
explains, this dominant post-Cold War image of Africa entails a specific etiology

of these scenes of chaos, collapse, and brutality, locating their origins internally to the continent. In so doing, it absolves the West of responsibility for violence in Africa—but at the same time posits the need for Western intervention to resolve those crises.

AFRICA'S GLOBAL EXCLUSION

According to the dominant image of Africa, the end of the Cold War resulted in Africa's exclusion from international politics and globalization. As the superpowers withdrew their support for their African clients and proxies, it is argued, African states faced material and legitimacy crises, and consequently the wars that broke out in the 1990s are presented as nonideological struggles for wealth and power for their own sake, essentially apolitical reactions to international exclusion.[6] As Kofi Annan puts it, "when the cold war ended, Africa was suddenly left to fend for itself" because "few African regimes could sustain the economic lifestyles to which they had become accustomed, or maintain the permanent hold on power which they had come to expect."[7] According to this image, patrimonial, authoritarian African states faced material crises that led to legitimacy crises, and the struggle for power degenerated quickly into violence.

This argument about superpower withdrawal is often paired with arguments about Africa's exclusion from post–Cold War economic globalization. In an approach most closely associated with Paul Collier and the World Bank, "Africa's rising trend of conflict is due to its atypically poor economic performance,"[8] and because, in neoliberal fashion, Africa's poor economic performance is attributed to its exclusion from globalization, Africa's failure to globalize is represented as the cause of violence.[9] Others have posited Africa's exclusion as being, not from economic globalization, but from social and political globalization. War and poverty are symptoms of Africa's exclusion from the mainstream of world history and are ultimately soluble through its integration into a multifaceted globalization. As Manuel Castells puts it,

> a new world, the Fourth World, has emerged, made up of multiple black holes of social exclusion throughout the planet. The Fourth World comprises large areas of the globe, such as much of Sub-Saharan Africa . . . it is populated by millions of homeless, incarcerated, prostituted, criminalized, brutalized, stigmatized, sick, and illiterate persons.[10]

According to Castells, this "de-humanization of Africa" means that in Africa, "famines, epidemics, violence, civil wars, massacres, mass exodus, and social and political chaos are, in the end of millennium, salient features."[11] Africa becomes the "other" to a supposedly univalent globalization.[12]

Whether conflict in Africa is seen as emerging in the context of international political withdrawal or of exclusion from globalization, the dominant image posits the immediate causes of violent conflict as fundamentally internal to the continent. Kofi Annan puts it succinctly: "there is a growing recognition among Africans themselves that the continent must look beyond its colonial past for the causes of current conflicts. Today more than ever, Africa must look at itself."[13] As Africa collapses, conflict in many cases "becomes virtually inevitable," according to Annan.[14] Africa is portrayed as a terrain of permanent conflict stemming from internal sources that has erupted in the midst of international withdrawal and exclusion—in the "habit of conflict," in one analyst's words.[15]

STATE CRISIS AND VIOLENCE

As African states weaken and collapse due to global marginalization, according to this image, internal conflicts multiply. Political and social breakdown, framed as state failure, are thought to open the way for chaos and violence, and as violence is unleashed upon civilians, conflict is thought to take brutal, prepolitical, forms. In Deng's words, "internal conflicts are the principal source of human suffering, gross violations of human rights, and massive destruction of civilian lives and productive capacity."[16] Boutros Boutros-Ghali also develops this idea in his 1995 *Supplement to an Agenda for Peace*, in which he argues that, since the end of the Cold War, a "rash" of intrastate wars has broken out, "often involving unusual violence and cruelty. The end of the cold war seems also to have contributed to an outbreak of such wars in Africa."[17] These wars are characterized by "a collapse of state institutions . . . with resulting paralysis of governance, a breakdown of law and order, and general banditry and chaos."[18] As a result of this social and political breakdown, Boutros-Ghali argues, these new wars

> are usually fought not only by regular armies but also by militias and armed civilians with little discipline and with ill-defined chains of command. They are often guerrilla wars without clear front lines. Civilians are the main victims and often the main targets. Humanitarian emergencies are commonplace and the combatants and authorities, in so far as they can be called authorities, lack the capacity to cope with them.[19]

Kofi Annan echoes this image of state breakdown and extreme violence, noting that in Africa's intrastate conflicts, it is "the destruction not just of armies but of civilians and entire ethnic groups" that is the target.[20]

The dominant image often dismisses the need to take seriously the motivation for such brutal forms of violence, usually condemning explanation as tantamount to justification. When motivation is sought, it tends to be located in nonpolitical domains, in the individual or collective pathologies to which people are thought to revert in the absence of state order. Ethnicity is perhaps the most commonly cited factor: intrastate violence is "explained" by attributing it to ancient and immutable tribal differences, within which genocidal violence and physical atrocity are always latent. The African state is cast as a mediator among permanent genocidal impulses, and when it fails in this duty, violence is presumed to rise quickly to the surface.

Irrational barbarism is also a commonly accepted motivation for violence in Africa, illustrated well by portrayals of the Lord's Resistance Army (LRA) in northern Uganda, which tends to focus exclusively on the rebels' brutality, in particular their violence against children.[21] Indeed, in most accounts, the rebel group is simply "bizarre," and LRA violence defies understanding, a position that fits well with the essentializing Afro-apocalypticism associated with Robert Kaplan.[22] The mirror image of irrationalist explanations are those that describe violence in Africa as perfectly rational expressions of individual greed, espoused most prominently—and reductively—by Paul Collier,[23] who renders violence equally nonpolitical by locating its origin in Africans' human nature as self-interested utility maximizers. In this framework, as David Keen puts it, apparent "madness" may in fact be a meaningful economic strategy by individuals seeking personal gain, and "even genocide can have an economic purpose."[24]

The dominant image portrays violence in Africa as indigenous and resolutely nonpolitical, with the population caught in the vacuum of state failure among ethnic entrepreneurs, greedy warlords, or psychopaths. The much-evoked brutality of conflicts allows them to be cast in moral terms, such that, as Kofi Annan puts it, "preventing such wars is no longer a matter of defending States or protecting allies. It is a matter of defending humanity itself."[25] Violence in Africa is defined as human rights crisis and civilians as victims of human rights abuses, victimized by a weak state that is unable to protect them or a criminal state that is unwilling to protect them or that preys upon them itself.

THE NECESSITY OF INTERVENTION

Because, according to the dominant image, violent conflict is Africa's indigenous reaction to international withdrawal, international re-engagement is presented as necessary for conflict resolution. Kofi Annan argues that international apathy has had a "particularly harsh impact upon Africa,"[26] which, of all regions, most needs the international community to intervene for the sake of its peace and security. In the past, he argues,

> by not averting these colossal human tragedies, African leaders have failed the peoples of Africa; the international community has failed them; the United Nations has failed them. We have failed them by not addressing the causes of conflict; by not doing enough to ensure peace; and by our repeated inability to create the conditions for sustainable development.[27]

As *Sovereignty as Responsibility* asserts, quoting Boutros-Ghali, "states and their governments cannot face or solve today's problems alone. International cooperation is unavoidable and indispensable."[28] Indeed, for those [people] . . . orphaned by state collapse, the only alternative source of protection, relief assistance, and rehabilitation toward a self-reliant development has to be the international community, both inter-governmental and nongovernmental.[29]

Because most conflicts are internal to states, and state failure or criminalization is the problem, according to this approach, intervention will necessarily run up against, and have to overcome, the sovereignty of African states. Intervention is thus portrayed as defending humanity against predatory African sovereignty.

The international community thereby assumes the moral and practical responsibility to intervene in Africa to resolve human rights crises that Africa has brought and will bring upon itself—but is helpless to resolve itself. This image of suffering Africans in need of Western saviors has a long history, and remains dominant in today's media-driven activism on Africa, most prominently perhaps in the Save Darfur campaign but also in Uganda-focused organizations such as Invisible Children (discussed in chapter 7). The implication of this image is that the West relates to Africa only within a philanthropic model—the West has no responsibility for conflict or violence in Africa, it is only an observer, and so it is only out of charity that the West intervenes to stop violence that, it is assumed, is fated to erupt without international intervention. Africa, as usual, is defined by a lack—an internal deficit or a deviation from a supposedly universal norm to be remedied by outsiders. This dominant image of Africa and the perceived need for external intervention to uphold human rights there underlie both the humanitarian and total human rights discourses, but give rise to a very different agenda for each.

2. Humanitarian Rights Intervention

The first response to this image of African violence was to demand that the West intervene in Africa to rescue African victims whose most basic, humanitarian rights were under grave and immediate threat. This intervention agenda grew out of the exuberance over the UN-authorized military actions of Gulf War I, a war that represented a milestone for many contemporary observers in security cooperation between the United States and the UN. Human rights professionals, academics, and policy makers came together to herald the emergence of what President Bush termed a "new world order" in which, in the words of the U.S. representative on the Security Council, "the hope of mankind of making the United Nations an instrument of peace and stability" would be fulfilled.[30] In this spirit, the Security Council intensified its involvement in Iraq once the Gulf War had ended and passed resolutions used by the United States to justify operations to forcefully protect and deliver relief aid to areas in northern Iraq.[31] In so doing, as many proponents interpreted the event, the Security Council authorized for the first time the use of force in direct violation of state sovereignty in order to protect civilian populations.

The U.S. deployment of military force in the name of human rights was seen by many of these proponents as proving the efficacy of an emergent humanitarian world order in which force could be used to uphold human rights, regardless of sovereignty. Calls began to be heard for the use of force in response to a wide variety of situations internal to sovereign states, most of which did not represent breaches of or threats to the peace under the sovereign state paradigm.[32] As Jarat Chopra and Thomas Weiss argued in 1992, "The erosion of sovereignty and the emergence of a human rights regime converge in the present decade,"[33] and

> [f]our decades have been spent defining human rights, and they are now clearer as a justification for action than ever before. Human rights norms are reaching a point where they can be implemented and enforced.[34]

Or, as Weiss and Larry Minear declared in 1993, "the world is poised between the Cold War and an embryonic new humanitarian order"[35] in which "the international community is groping toward . . . the right to intervene."[36]

This humanitarian rights discourse took as its concern the most basic human rights and made their protection in times of emergency a fundamental aspect of international order. These rights were directly violated by criminal states, or allowed to be violated by failed states, and so this discourse framed the inviolability guaranteed to the state by the doctrine of sovereignty as the main obstacle to human rights. Coercive intervention to provide aid and protection to victim populations, backed up by military force under the aegis of the UN, was projected as the solution—a minimalist, but muscular, cosmopolitanism that would rescue human life in emergencies. As Chopra and Weiss wrote, "one way to circumvent sovereignty altogether is to explore why human rights constitute a legitimate justification for intervention."[37]

It would quickly become apparent, however, that the Council's actions in Iraq had been motivated, not by a new global normative regime, but by the fortuitous convergence of UN interests in proving its efficacy and American interests in driving Iraq from Kuwait while having Council authorization for the operation. The humanitarian rights discourse was, thus, the product of a brief marriage of convenience between the United States, which wanted to establish the legitimacy of its use of force through moral, humanitarian claims, and optimistic human rights activists, professionals, and academics who eagerly seized upon America's instrumental use of human rights and humanitarian language in Iraq and inflated it into an imagined human rights world order in the making.

HUMANITARIAN RIGHTS INTERVENTION IN AFRICA

Many human rights professionals portrayed this emerging "right to intervene" as particularly applicable to Africa, and so the continent came to epitomize the need for human rights intervention in the post–Cold War era. In the words of Chopra and Weiss, the operations in northern Iraq and the possibility of further interventions reflected growing public outrage with African countries—particularly in the Horn—where both governments and rebels had deprived civilians of international succor as part of their war arsenals.[38]

After all, they conclude, "it is finally possible to enforce growing recognition of individuals' rights of access to humanitarian aid, irrespective of their governments' permission," and "20,000 civilians dead in Somalia are adequate testimony to the need for action."[39]

It was Secretary-General Boutros-Ghali who played perhaps the most important role in arguing for the application of the emerging human rights world order to Africa, most famously in his 1992 *Agenda for Peace*.[40] There, declaring that "the time of absolute and exclusive sovereignty . . . has passed,"[41] Boutros-Ghali evoked a model of world order that did not concern itself solely with interstate security, but also with intrastate affairs, and in which the international community would respond to the moral imperative to intervene in human rights crises in Africa, even if no strategic interests were at stake.[42] In early 1992, he even accused the Security Council of being concerned with a "rich man's war" in the former Yugoslavia, while Somalia fell further into crisis without notice.[43]

This fit squarely with the dominant image of Africa as a terrain of helpless victims, the paradigmatic terrain of humanity abandoned or victimized by their states, left with only human rights but unable to uphold those rights themselves. Invoking this basic set of universal human rights allows intervention to claim a legitimacy beyond state-based law or politics, grounding itself in a universal morality that celebrates an abstract solidarity with the figure of the victim. Military force is the guarantee for this practice of rescue that categorically bypasses the illegitimate African state, a state that is irrelevant to human rights protection, only an obstacle to be overcome, its role as a political institution dismissed. Consequently, any action for the sake of upholding the human rights of civilian victims is endowed with exceptionality and a legitimacy that claims to place intervention beyond such political concerns as democratic accountability or the rule of law.

Humanitarian intervention tends to complement its legitimacy claims based upon universal morality with claims based upon the supposed consent given by those to be rescued. The consent of the voiceless victim is invoked frequently—and effortlessly—because the voiceless, by definition, cannot speak for themselves, and so their invocation by their self-appointed saviors, those claiming to give voice to the voiceless, cannot but provide consent to intervention. Proponents may, also, in certain circumstances, point out actually existing local agents calling for intervention—Mary Kaldor's favored "islands of civility" in the midst of brutal "new wars."[44] Despite the ideologization involved in these conceptions, proponents of intervention are correct in that humanitarian rights intervention undeniably enjoys significant consent in many areas of conflict or violence in Africa as people respond to and demand fulfillment of the promises intervention makes—peace, survival, justice, and assistance. By claiming that people everywhere deserve to be assisted or rescued by the international community, the intervention discourse provides the rationale for people subject to violence or state repression to call for intervention themselves, whether voiced as an appeal for NATO bombing, UN peacekeeping, International Criminal Court prosecution, the Responsibility to Protect, humanitarian intervention, or humanitarian aid—the various faces of a single, imaginary global-interventionist agent. As Mahmood Mamdani writes about Darfur, the dissemination of the intervention discourse can give rise to "an internal agency: IDPs [Internally Displaced Persons] demanding to be rescued."[45] Even in places where there is as yet no international involvement, the idea of humanitarian rights intervention can embed itself in the political imagination, transforming people's understanding of their social and political worlds as they see themselves as being subject to morally determined intervention from beyond. The humanitarian rights discourse thereby is able to claim legitimacy, not only by invoking an abstract, universal moral imperative, but also by citing the calls from civilians, politicians, or activists for external intervention, and by presuming the voiceless victims' consent where those calls are not actually heard.

CRITICISM AND CRISIS

The humanitarian rights model of intervention faced vocal criticism since its inception.[46] One major source of controversy has been the possibility many saw for human rights to be used instrumentally by Western states to legitimate military aggression.[47] Against these accusations, proponents of intervention have sometimes argued that human rights itself in fact offers the precise, formal criteria needed to impartially carry out humanitarian intervention. Hugo Slim, for example, argues:

> [T]he emphasis on rights . . . gives humanitarianism an integrated moral, political and legal framework for affirming universal human values. Grounding humanitarian action in rights, duties and laws makes the values of humanitarian work explicit to all and it links humanitarianism directly to justice. This means that humanitarianism is not left free-floating as some generic act of kindness but is rooted in explicit values, precise political contracts, exact military duties, particular types of assistance, functioning courts, tribunals, and truth commissions.[48]

However, the claim that human rights itself can provide formal guidance—or even legal guidance—to decisions about intervention misunderstands the implications of the invocation of human rights. The human rights regime is not on par with a domestic legal regime; instead, it is characterized by deformalization, indeterminacy, and a lack of hierarchy, embodied in a contradictory welter of instruments, documents, statements, cases, and treaties, covering a vast array of subjects and without an authoritative decision-making instance. Legal scholar Costas

Douzinas points out this ambiguity and indeterminacy of human rights, such that "the trust put on lawyers' ability to resolve conflict through the tool of human rights is seriously misplaced."[49] He notes that it is precisely the constant pronouncements about human rights that "create . . . the (false) impression that an enforceable public international law is in the making, which will override the sovereignty of non-compliant states."[50] Because of its lack of formalization, basing an approach to intervention upon human rights allows for a multitude of different justifications, all claiming moral certainty, without providing the grounds for mediation among them, especially when trying to derive answers on something as concrete as coercive intervention. The consequence is that human rights offers resources that can be employed to justify self-interested political action, including military aggression, giving substance to Carl Schmitt's dictum that "whoever invokes humanity wants to cheat."[51]

The humanitarian human rights discourse in particular is subject to easy instrumentalization because of its invocation of crisis and emergency. By proclaiming the need to intervene to protect basic human rights of victims in the midst of emergencies, the justification for intervention is rendered arbitrary and, once invoked, militates against debate or deliberation.[52] That is, in justifying intervention through appealing to the language of human rights crisis, whether in the form of famine, crimes against humanity, massive population displacement, or genocide, an appeal is made to a category that, through its very invocation, rejects on moral grounds any contestation or deliberation; it calls for immediate action and condemns hesitation as tantamount to complicity with violence. The celebration of humanity, with the helpless African victim on the one side and the active and empathetic international community on the other, promotes a moralization of international politics, because the language of human rights can be used by powerful actors to demonize and criminalize certain states and nonstate actors and to sanctify force that is used in the name of ending human rights crises or punishing human rights violators. And finally, any voices questioning the wisdom or legitimacy of the use of violence to uphold human rights are disqualified by the absolute legitimacy of the voiceless victims' demand for intervention, voiced by the Western intervener.

The openness of humanitarian rights discourse to instrumentalization produces a fundamental tension within it, as its claim to universality and impartiality—that all humanity is equally entitled to be rescued by the international community—is consistently contradicted in practice by the political and pragmatic selectivity of intervention and intervention's tendency to fail to realize its stated objectives. This failure of intervention to conform to its ideology is typically dealt with by framing actually existing human rights intervention as evidence of a truly global human rights order *in statu nascendi*. That is, humanitarian rights intervention justifies itself by deferring its realization and rephrasing the gap between selective practice and universal claims as a gap between the present and a necessary future in which intervention will be truly universal.

The consequences of intervention's selectivity, however, proved to be too costly even for its proponents. The crisis of humanitarian rights intervention began with Somalia—an intervention that, at its inception, had been seen as a triumph of the new human rights world order in Africa, proof of the continued convergence between UN legitimacy and the U.S. military. It began with the Bush administration, having its own interests in the region and under pressure domestically, deciding to intervene in Somalia in 1992 at Boutros-Ghali's invitation. The plan was to use overwhelming force under generous rules of engagement to facilitate the distribution of relief supplies.[53] This initial operation, Restore Hope, would be followed by a UN peacekeeping operation, and so, in early December, 1992, the Security Council passed Resolution 794 (drafted by the Pentagon), which gave unified command and control over Restore Hope to the United States. The Resolution explicitly authorized the use of force to address the new wars in Africa, this new kind of "threat to peace and security,"[54] as Somalia became the exemplar of a failed state that was unable and unwilling to protect its own citizenry and thus whose sovereignty was null and void and was open to coercive intervention. The moral legitimacy of coercion to deal with crises internal to states was seen to be further corroborated, and the deployment of U.S. military force authorized by the UN appeared to offer further proof that human rights provided an effective and legitimate global order that transcended state sovereignty.

Reality would quickly re-assert itself, however, and reveal the hollowness of that belief. The popular resistance the intervention provoked in Somalia, and the subsequent deaths of 18 U.S. soldiers once the UN-led operation had taken over from the U.S.-led Restore Hope, largely finished off humanitarian rights intervention for Africa. The deaths were used by the United States to reject the model of UN-led intervention and to insist that military intervention from then on take place with overwhelming force under the command and control of a major Western power, with Security Council authorization a secondary concern. The annulment of the short marriage between the United States and the UN was codified in Presidential Decision Directive 25 (PDD-25), signed by President Clinton in 1994,[55] which defined UN peace operations as merely "one useful tool to advance American national interests and pursue our national security objectives."[56]

The United States' approach to Rwanda proved that PDD-25 was the new rule: as UN commanders called for increased troop strength under an expanded Security Council mandate, the Council refused, principally because of U.S. and British opposition. The genocide began in April, and once its dimensions came to be known, Boutros-Ghali again proposed to the Council to send additional troops, and the United States again refused. The Security Council's refusal to intervene forcefully in Rwanda, seen as caused by Western apathy, was blamed for the Rwandan genocide.[57] In Kofi Annan's words, the Somalia intervention's failure "soured international support for conflict intervention and precipitated a rapid retreat by the international community," leading to "the failure of the international community, including the United Nations, to intervene to prevent genocide in Rwanda."[58] The failure to intervene in Rwanda was seen as proof by proponents of intervention that depending on the convergence of U.S. and UN interests to uphold human rights in Africa—even in the extreme case of genocide—was no longer a viable option.

3. From Rescue to Peace: Total Intervention

The debacle of Somalia, the uncompromising attitude expressed in PDD-25, and the U.S. refusal to enable UN intervention in Rwanda left human rights proponents searching for a new approach to international intervention in Africa, one that would ensure that the tragedy of Rwanda would not happen again. In their view, intervention in Africa would have to be dramatically reconfigured in order to prevent Africa from being abandoned by the international community, a fate that they saw as having devastating consequences. This demand would lead to a shift from rescue to peace, with a new human rights discourse employed to justify the new, expanded interventionist practice.

EXPANDING CONFLICT AND INTERVENTION

Proponents of human rights intervention in Africa understood the "right to intervene" to be too demanding—it demanded that the United States provide military support when called upon by the UN, that the Security Council authorize and enable military intervention, and that intervention be immediate and adequate to emergencies. Once it was clear that the United States would not be guided by the UN nor by human rights concerns more generally, U.S. military capacity to resolve human rights crises could no longer be the centerpiece of intervention strategy. The right to intervene was also too demanding in that it required its critics to quell their suspicions that humanitarian intervention was simply an excuse for Western aggression and meddling. This was matched by an increasing concern that coercive intervention was further undermining the capacities of African states and societies, when it was precisely that weakness that was posited as leading to conflict in the first place. The blunt dismissal of African sovereignty that was the correlate of the right to intervene required too many friends and made too many enemies, at a time when the West no longer appeared to be a friend of human rights intervention in Africa and African states and activists were vocally expressing criticism of the model.

The new approach was to move away from humanitarian interventions—exceptional, coercive interventions that rescued populations under grave, immediate threat—and instead toward what I call total interventions—regularized, consensual interventions that sought peace by reconstructing or reforming social, political, and legal order. Building peace by building order was to happen at the local, national, and international levels, so that past conflicts would be recovered from, present conflicts would be resolved and transformed, and future conflicts would be prevented. It represented an effort to avoid the need for coercive military interventions by preventing situations from becoming massive human rights emergencies in the first place, an intervention strategy that would deal with "future Rwandas" by preventing them from happening.

The expansion and regularization of intervention was based upon an expanded understanding of conflict—no longer were only exceptional cases of mass atrocity of concern, but rather conflict was disaggregated into a wide set of causes and consequences. For example, Boutros-Ghali, in his 1995 *Supplement*, argued that international interventions needed to adapt to the new breed of armed conflicts and "extend beyond military and humanitarian tasks and must include the promotion of national reconciliation and the re-establishment of effective government," tasks that would "demand time and sensitivity," and would be "far more complex and more expensive."[59] He admitted that this would lead to a "vast increase in field deployment," and would also require an expansion of international intervention to the periods before and after conflict.[60]

A similar argument could be heard from Kofi Annan: "crises today, particularly in Africa, have become much more complex, having many dimensions at once and involving many actors;"[61] as a result, "the changing nature of conflict requires new responses."[62] The massive, multidimensional failure of African states and societies requires the response to be equally multidimensional and extensive, according to Annan, and should include interventions before, during, and after conflict, because "the prevention of conflict begins and ends with the promotion of human security and human development."[63] The 1996 *Sovereignty as Responsibility*, the premier statement of this new interventionist agenda, argues that when dealing with cases like Somalia, "the line between food delivery and political order becomes hazy. Regularized state-society relations are required if humanitarian relief is to be delivered to its intended recipients over an extended period."[64] The scope of intervention has taken increasingly expansive formulations: one contribution to the 2001 *Peacebuilding: A Field Guide* explains that interventions can take place at any point on the "peace-conflict-peace continuum," and provides a list of no fewer than 90 "policy tools" in a "toolbox for responding to conflicts and building peace."[65] These include preventing latent conflicts through peacebuilding, conflict prevention, and constructing early warning systems; ending ongoing conflicts through conflict management, conflict transformation, conflict resolution, and peace enforcement; and reconstructing after conflicts through peacekeeping, rehabilitation, reconciliation, and transitional justice.[66]

A particular conceptual framework informs this total intervention agenda. The framework begins with the consequences of conflict, arguing that violence leads to crisis and breakdown in a wide array of different domains. In the political domain, conflict leads to state weakness and failure; in the economic, it leads to poverty and underdevelopment; in the social, it leads to a breakdown of social solidarity and civil society; in the cultural, it leads to a crisis of traditional values and authority; and in the legal, it leads to a breakdown of accountability and a rise of impunity. Next, the total intervention agenda interprets the crisis of order in each domain as causing further violence, as everything from state weakness, to poverty, social anomie, exclusion, loss of traditional values, and impunity are seen as giving rise to conflict. Thus, a series of vicious circles are established, in which a crisis of order in a number of domains is framed as cause and consequence of conflict. Consequently, peace will be established through rebuilding order in those many domains, and peace ends up equated with a stable order itself.

The total intervention agenda declares Africa to be caught in a multi-dimensional "trap" of social, political, economic, cultural, psychological, and legal crises that fuels and is fuelled by violent conflict.[67] The causes of violence are thus internalized to Africa, whether to African states, to specific societies or cultures, or to the continent as a whole. By internalizing violence to Africa, the total intervention agenda imputes a crisis so profound that autonomous action on the part of Africans to escape that crisis is seen as impossible. People, communities, states, the continent itself are trapped in vicious cycles of violence and breakdown that they are incapable of getting out of, and so the initial agency for transformation must come from the outside, through external intervention.

The idea that Africa is caught in a trap that it cannot get out of without external assistance has long antecedents in the colonial period (its proponents have denied its condescending and sometimes racist underpinnings by insisting that they believe that Africa *can* stand on its own eventually—for now, it just needs some help in getting up). Empowerment is the watchword of these interventions, along with its associated concepts of participation, partnership, and capacity building. Africans are to be empowered to solve their own problems and prevent their own conflicts—African solutions for African problems—and external intervention is only to be the catalyst of that process. It is the celebrated "resilience" of Africans that provides the substrate for these empowering interventions, their promise of success. Once responsible order is re-established in the political, social, cultural domains, it is argued, Africa can manage itself. Interventions are justified as temporary exigencies, needed only as long as it takes to get Africa out of the trap and up on its feet. It is no longer a matter of coercing, punishing, or eliminating human rights abusing states, but rather of steering deviant states, societies, and individuals back to a norm of responsible order.

Intervention will thus be primarily normalizing, designed to address deficits internal to Africa and bring Africa and Africans back in line. Of course, this begs the question of what kind of social, political, and cultural orders Africa is to be normalized towards whether in the name of reform or reconstruction. Indeed, to posit peace intervention as promoting "re"-construction is itself an obfuscation, obscuring the fact that any order towards which people and states are being normalized is a new order, one often derived from models posited as normal by Western aid agencies, World Bank development manuals, colonial-era ethnographies, psychologists' training texts, law review articles, humanitarian assistance websites, or American political science professors.

Often, this normalization explicitly claims to be steering Africa toward modern, liberal norms, which are supposed to replace the traditional, illiberal, and thus conflict-prone individuals, societies, economies, and cultures presumed dominant in Africa. For this reason, many proponents and critics alike have characterized the total intervention agenda as one of liberal peace: proponents celebrate the global convergence on liberalism, whereas critics denounce the coercive imposition of Western models and values in the name of a false universalism. However, it is not always the case that liberal models are used by intervention, for, as will be seen with the ethnojustice agenda, there is also a tendency to create norms supposedly specific to Africa in hopes of rendering intervention there more authentic, decreasing resistance, and making peace more sustainable. Nevertheless, regardless of whether normalization claims to lead toward liberal or indigenous African models, these models are still products of the Western imagination, they still are part of a self-justifying interventionist practice, and, as will be seen, their political consequences are remarkably similar.

These normalizing interventions, claiming to steer incapacitated African peoples and states toward responsibility, will thus be primarily technical and administrative. They will be undertaken by self-proclaimed experts who deploy their specialized knowledge and techniques to start the process of empowerment toward peace. The elevation of technique thus leads total intervention to disregard democratic accountability, which is thought to distract from the efficient pursuit of objectives through the application of expert knowledge. It also raises questions about intervention's claims to participation and empowerment because, as critical development scholars have argued, an emphasis on technical administration may restrict participation to taking place within the models provided by interveners. Participation may be hollowed out and amount only to an invitation to conform to norms imagined by experts or to fill an assigned role within incipient technocratic administrations.

Coercive interventions retain a place within this newly consensual intervention framework, because in those cases where prevention fails, rescue by force will still be needed, according to its proponents. Human rights remains the basis upon which the designation between states that require coercive intervention and states that require capacity-building and external support is based. However, even coercive interventions are re-imagined so that they are no longer framed as punishing or eliminating a criminal state, but rather as filling in for a state that has lost its legitimacy. According to this approach, the international community will temporarily assume the mantle of responsible sovereignty while the state can be rescued from the bad hands into which it has fallen, a legitimate state can be reconstituted, and sovereignty handed back. Specific regimes or leaders may be criminalized or targeted, such as by the ICC, but this is in fact framed as supporting African sovereignty and being in partnership with the legitimate African state. As *Sovereignty as Responsibility* explains, coercive intervention is intended "to restore the state's capacity for effective leadership and to bring about a return to responsible sovereignty,"[68] and so all forms of total intervention, whether consensual or coercive, are oriented toward "remodeling the features of governments to live up to their responsibilities."[69]

The total intervention agenda, in sum, has three primary modes through which it claims it will bring peace to Africa: societal peacebuilding, state-building, and international coercion as a last resort. Some forms of intervention, such as the ICC, claim to operate within all three at once: the ICC presents itself as variously empowering victims, building national judicial capacities, and launching prosecutions as a last resort. Others operate within two, such as some contemporary World Bank development interventions which claim to empower society and build state capacity for conflict resolution, and some, such as community peacebuilding or ethnojustice, focus on only one.

The net result is that intervention is justified in domain after domain of African life, as technical solutions are proposed to the various forms of Africa's putative deviance from given norms, each form of deviance a cause and consequence of conflict, and each solution claiming to bring African individuals, societies, economies, cultures, or states back into line with models of properly functioning, normal, responsible models, all in the name of peace. The focus on causes and consequences, on past conflict and future conflict, resolved and latent conflict, on rehabilitation and prevention, means that conflict becomes seen as ubiquitous and imminent, coincident with Africa itself as a terrain of just intervention. Intervention becomes highly self-referential and self-justifying. Objective determinations of what comprises a conflict are dismissed, instead replaced by a vast array of causes and consequences, and conflict dissolves into its putative causes and consequences. Conflict in need of intervention is seen to exist wherever its causes or consequences are found, so any sign of those multiple causes or consequences—poverty, weak states, disease, rights violations, environmental pressures, and so on—is taken as evidence of the need for intervention. Because one or another of these presumed symptoms of conflict can be found just about anywhere, conflict is presumed to be ubiquitous. Because these symptoms are conceived of as internal deficits to be remedied through external intervention, in some cases the lack of intervention itself practically becomes the proof of the need for intervention, and the requirement that actual violence or conflict exist in order to justify intervention is done away with. The result is that almost any place in Africa can be designated a legitimate target for intervention in the name of preventing, transforming, or recovering from conflict or violence.

TOTAL INTERVENTION AND HUMAN RIGHTS

At the same time that all of Africa is declared open to intervention, objective criteria for determining the success or failure of an intervention are lost. This happens in a number of ways. First, the ubiquity and persistence of the causes and consequences of conflict means that, from the perspective of intervention, until everything has changed, it cannot be expected that anything will change. If conflict increases in intensity while interventions are occurring, that is a sign of the conflict's depth and thus of the need for further intervention. By the same token, if fighting diminishes, there is no way to trace the impact of any one intervention to that outcome in such a multicausal context, and so every intervention can take credit for success, while denying credit to others, and insist that it should be expanded further.

Second, the assertion that intervention empowers Africans and builds their capacity, and that those are intervention's ultimate objectives, provides a kind of automatic justification for intervention. Simply by taking place, intervention can claim success because it, by definition, promotes empowerment and builds capacity. Thus, intervention does not need to achieve objective results because its very occurrence is the only result it needs to achieve. And any overt failure can be blamed on the lack of competence and responsibility of the so-called local partners, and thus can also be used to justify further intervention.[70]

Third, total intervention manages to avoid the need for accountability to objective standards, or to its supposed beneficiaries, by mobilizing a new human rights discourse that provides incontestable moral authority for this wide set of technical, problem-solving interventions.[71] To this end, those human rights of concern to intervention are expanded far beyond basic humanitarian rights. If the humanitarian-rights discourse represents emergencies as violations of a few basic rights, especially the right to life, the total human rights discourse represents conflict at all its stages as a wide-spectrum human rights crisis. The dozens of causes and consequences of conflict become coded as human rights issues, and so human rights provides a moral shroud to this vastly expanded set of technical interventions, as each intervention is projected into the moral sphere as a human rights intervention.

This moralization of technical interventions can be performed by citing specific human rights that those technical interventions help to fulfill: interventions for the sake of alleviating suffering promote the right to relief aid, the right to health, to shelter, or to life; interventions for the sake of social order promote the right to development, women's rights, children's rights, or community human rights; interventions for the sake of justice promote victims' rights to remedy or enforce human rights law; state-building promotes a right to democracy; truth commissions fulfill the right to truth; and all interventions help fulfill the right to peace.[72] However, positing such explicit connections is not obligatory: because the connection between human rights and the causes and consequences of conflict has become something of an article of faith, specifications of the way in which particular technical interventions relate to particular rights are rendered dispensable by a proclaimed adherence to a general "rights-based approach." Indeed, sweeping programmatic statements are the norm, such as Hugo Slim's declaration that "protective humanitarian practice now sees NGOs wanting to work for the protection and realisation of the full range of people's rights in war";[73] or the statement by Michael Barfod, a senior officer at the European Community Humanitarian Aid Office, that there is no way we can handle a situation without linking up with human rights issues, without linking up with development, to understand the real impact. We have to be part of the political process leading to peace, that is what we are really there for.[74]

Catholic Relief Services similarly affirms that "when considered through the justice/human rights lens, the mere provision of foodstuffs or medical support is an insufficient response to a humanitarian crisis."[75] A total human rights intervention discourse is articulated as rights are made functional to a technical project of intervention intended to promote social and political order.[76]

The indeterminacy of human rights returns with a vengeance when employed to justify total intervention. Given the vast set of human rights that can be invoked and the vast set of situations into which intervention can be justified, the attempt to answer specific questions pertaining to interventionist practice leads to "confusion about what kinds of rights would be included in a rights-based approach. . . . [I]s there a hierarchy of rights? Do some rights take precedence over others . . . ? Who sets the order of priority?"[77] The indeterminacy of human rights and the contradictions between different rights end up deformalizing the legitimation of interventionist practice further, allowing it to claim moral legitimacy for itself without needing to be accountable to objective criteria or evaluation. Any activity that declares itself as helping to address the causes or consequences of conflict can claim to be part of a rights-based approach and thus partake of the unquestionable legitimacy of human rights and refuse to be restrained by politics or accountability. At the same time, a human rights discourse is established that co-opts a wide range of human rights and declares that they can be realized only through technical intervention.

The end result is the unexpected juxtaposition of technical interventions into narrow domains of social or political life with moralized human rights justifications. Technical interventions end up being divorced from concrete objectives or standards and insulated from criticism, while human rights are embedded in a practice of totalized intervention and the denial of autonomy. Total interventions can claim to be non-political and thus immune to democratic accountability when they invoke their technical side, and to be beyond politics and thus also immune to democratic accountability when they invoke their moral side.

The equation of an intervention's success with its own execution means that often, the only objective measures against which intervention can be assessed are internal.[78] These measures may even amount to no more than intervention's own institutional expansion as measured by beneficiaries reached. This emphasis on numbers of people reached is also encouraged by foreign donors, who demand that NGOs should effectively deliver their "product" to their "beneficiaries"—but since the "product" is as abstract as "human rights promotion" or "conflict resolution," success in product delivery is hard to define other than by the number of people involved. The expansion of activities is taken for proof of their success and so the emphasis on numbers of people as the prime factor in fundraising can even make bribery a wise investment. In the camp setting, NGOs may pay inhabitants to come their workshops and not those of rival NGOs, or they may round up kids on the road and sit them down in front of a video on children's rights, thus fulfilling their benchmark quotas.[79] Total interventions may end up taking their own expansion as their measure of success, and the ends are displaced by the means.

The practical consequence is that total interventions can find a justification for taking place just about anywhere and remaining as long as they want. They can also leave whenever they want and find a justification for doing so—empowerment has been achieved, human rights have been promoted, claims that cannot be empirically evaluated or denied. Interventions become arbitrary when assessed in terms of their self-legitimation—their arrival or departure may have little to do with the actual presence of conflict or peace. Instead, interventionist practice is politically determined, both by the internal politics of aid agencies seeking institutional reproduction and expansion, and the external politics of those who fund interventionist agencies or institutions, steer their work, allow for access, or threaten their projects or existence. Interventions can thus appear, and then disappear without anything having changed, all the while claiming success. Or, in situations in which political forces align behind maintaining intervention in place, such as occurred in northern Uganda for over a decade, interventions can persist over long periods and can end up giving rise to transnational structures of various levels of formality. These structures partake of intervention's administrative logic at the same time that they are steered by the politics behind and around them.

The total intervention agenda itself can be seen as emerging from a distinct set of political forces in the mid-1990s. The West, and the United States in particular, were seeking to avoid entangling engagements in Africa while reserving the right to intervene coercively at their discretion. The new intervention agenda, while framed by its proponents in the human rights field as a strategic response to newly complex conflicts, fulfilled this purpose well by assigning the bulk of intervention in Africa to international agencies, NGOs, and African states and societies, while leaving Western states the option to intervene militarily where they wished, even without Security Council authorization. To undertake this expanded set of interventions, therefore, an expanded set of interventionist actors was needed, who responded by quickly expanding their activities into new domains in order to meet the demand. Boutros-Ghali, for example, saw NGOs as playing "an important role in all United Nations activities,"[80] while Kofi Annan stated that the new peace intervention agenda

> would encompass all partners in the United Nations system, including the Bretton Woods institutions, as well as national authorities, donor organizations, and non-governmental organizations.[81]

NGOs, international agencies, and African states and societies would do the bulk of the work in Africa, and Western states could restrict their involvement to funding.[82] This new interventionist agenda declared that, in order to prevent future genocides, all of Africa should be put under an expansive, intensive, all-pervading regime of Western intervention, but one that required less public, direct, and risky commitments from Western states and more involvement of subcontractors, whether the ICC, regional security bodies, international NGOs, private security companies, or Western-funded organizations and institutions in Africa.

4. Total Intervention in Practice

The political consequences of these expansive, supposedly participatory, and often long-lasting technical interventions, justified through the invocation of human rights, depend in large part upon the particular local, national, and international political contexts in which they take place, along with the particular forms of intervention that are employed. In this last section, I sketch out a framework for approaching those political consequences, presenting the different analytical dimensions through which interventions will be assessed in subsequent chapters.

INSTRUMENTALIZATION

Human rights' potential to be instrumentally deployed as a justification for self-interested intervention has been frequently noted, and total intervention is not exempt from this tendency. Anti-imperialist critics of intervention have drawn attention to this possibility, arguing that human rights intervention can serve powerful political or economic interests, not by promoting peace and stability, but by creating instability, conflict, and violent exploitation for the sake of securing access to natural resources, containing political rivals, or pursuing counterterrorism.[83] Other critics have argued that total intervention can be instrumentalized in the sense that it responds to the needs for global conflict management resulting from the destabilizing consequences of global inequalities of power and wealth. Human rights intervention, even if not itself directly exploitative and destabilizing, according to this position, upholds a fundamentally unequal global order that gives rise to the very violence and crises that it is called in to manage.[84]

The instrumental dimension of total human rights intervention, I argue, includes but also goes far beyond manipulation by the globally powerful, whether states or capital, whether in order to promote stability or instability. Through its use of informal criteria and the language of crisis, and because of its pursuit of partners, the human rights vocabulary can also be invoked by those subject to intervention to gain access to external resources or to steer intervention to their advantage. For example, African states may position themselves as partners of foreign intervention, becoming beneficiaries of sudden increases in finances or power. States can instrumentalize peace operations so that they facilitate counterinsurgency,[85] and governance states can turn their externally built capacity against political opposition. Instrumentalization of intervention by African states can mesh with Western interests, but African states can also instrumentalize intervention to serve their own particular interests in ways invisible to or against the interests of those Western powers supporting it.

Rebel groups, political parties, and other nonstate political, social, and military forces can also instrumentalize intervention and its resources in a multitude of political projects. This phenomenon has drawn most attention through the instrumentalization of humanitarian relief aid by parties to armed conflict, but the politicized manipulation of material aid is only one facet of the broader instrumentalization of all human rights interventions. All interventions offer significant resources, whether intended to directly benefit the objects of administration, such as through food distribution, or to initiate certain changes within society, such as through training and capacity-building programs, that can be marshaled to serve the political or economic interests of various groups or individuals. Symbolic resources are equally important, such as the power that accrues from being labeled a human rights protector or being seen as having access to foreign support. Even those categorized as victims can instrumentalize intervention, securing access to resources or power, and so presenting oneself as a victim can sometimes be a viable strategy.[86]

Total intervention's informal, emergency-centered legitimation, employment of a vague human rights discourse, expansive domain, refusal of accountability, need for local access, and desire for efficacy and legitimacy through participation—all these open intervention to instrumentalization by those with the capacity to do so, which will often be those already exercising arbitrary power and looking to increase it further. Intervention offers resources that can consolidate unaccountable power and so may itself corrupt political institutions. Because of its refusal to recognize its own politics, and because of its claims to absolute moral legitimacy, human rights intervention is open to instrumentalization by political forces on every level in such a way that it tends to give rise to reactionary political consequences. In what Alex de Waal has called the "regressive empowerment of aid,"[87] it is often the least accountable, least legitimate political actors who most effectively instrumentalize human rights intervention.

However, this tendency should not hide the multiplicity of politics enabled by intervention, because the different instances of instrumentalization at different levels can end up going in different directions or even contradicting one another. Actors can steer interventions in directions unanticipated by their sponsors, who may fail to realize the use to which those in the targeted location are applying the intervention. Those subject to intervention may align themselves with broader global political interests behind intervention or may not have any idea of or concern for the broader interests being served by intervention and, in instrumentally accepting it, end up unintentionally serving other political agendas through their own political action.

This instrumentalization of intervention by those subject to it is often unseen, willfully ignored, or simply denied by international interveners and their donors.

Aid agencies may have a strong interest in maintaining such ignorance, as they instrumentalize intervention to serve their own interests—for example, by ensuring the advancement of their own careers or the continued functioning and expansion of their programs and organizations.[88] Where human rights intervention is benefiting a supposedly responsible state or party, scrutiny of the actual effects of aid is deemed unnecessary, and so ignorance is rewarded and admitting knowledge of the negative impact of aid can be detrimental to agencies' interest in gaining more donor funding. Serendipitous conspiracies of denial and distortion can develop around human rights interventions, bringing together the hard interests of aid agencies, donors, and powerful, often undemocratic or violent, national and subnational actors, at the cost of potentially accountable political institutions, the interests of the supposed beneficiaries of intervention, and even peace itself. Human rights interventions occur, are prolonged, and expand through the complex political interactions they give rise to, in particular through their openness to political interests at multiple levels, which may lead to consequences having nothing to do with stated objectives.

ADMINISTRATION AND DISCIPLINE

Coincidental with the political consequences of its instrumental dimension, total intervention also gives rise to political consequences through what I call its administrative dimension.[89] Where the conditions are right, human rights interventions can become the building blocks of lasting administrative structures intended to normalize states, economies, cultures, societies, and individuals in line with given models. The iteration and prolongation of technical, problem-solving interventions and their expansion in space and time, justified through human rights and thus avoiding the need for accountability, end up creating intensive and extensive structures that purport to address the widest range of causes and consequences of conflict. Their deepening involvement with African institutions and individuals leads these administrative structures to become transnational, as African states and societies can be reconstituted through intervention and lasting symbiotic relationships are forged between African and Western actors and institutions, both private and public.[90] Everything from civil-society organizations to political and social elites, intellectuals, grassroots organizations, music groups, microcredit organizations, customary chiefs, and individual beneficiaries may be constituted, re-constituted, or re-oriented through their transnational integration as certain models of state, society, economy, and culture are promoted through intervention.

The net result can be the emergence of an expansive and intensive, but diffuse, set of interventions that is deeply involved, materially and symbolically, in wide domains of African life. These interventions claim the authority to regulate nearly every facet of people's lives and to reconstruct wholesale African societies, polities, cultures, economies, and psychologies. These structures categorically reject democratic accountability, and the pursuit of technical problem-solving can lead to the formation of administrative structures that subvert or replace decision making among those subject to intervention, isolating decisions from political contestation, democratic or otherwise.[91] These technocratic administrative institutions can justify their lack of democratic accountability through reference to the human rights values they claim to uphold. This diffuse transnational administration creates a "sense of mystery and inscrutability" which is "the opposite of the transparency that underpins democracy, [and] is more akin to the transcendental or religious legitimation of pre-democratic political authority," in de Waal's words.[92] The invocation of human rights allows the mystification of this transnational technocracy, its assertion of authority and coercion without any obvious human legitimation, its employment of rites, invocations, and secret language, its intimacy with satellite-steered powers of instant, invisible destruction.

The presence of this antidemocratic, morally justified technocratic administration can be seen, for example, in the way in which basic decisions about who lives and who dies on a mass scale are made without accountability or transparency by the emergency food-distribution system, an inscrutable regime comprising Western state donors, UN agencies, corporate grain sellers, international NGOs, national NGOs, private contractors, government agencies, national or international military forces, food distributors, and others. These unaccountable transnational structures, with varying realms of authority, appear everywhere, from human rights training programs, to development partnerships, to counterterrorism initiatives. African states also are reformed according to this tendency, as those categorized as responsible human rights protectors are deemed deserving of international support intended to build their capacity to protect their populations' human rights. They are steered toward becoming governance states, which focus on effective management of internal conflicts and protection.[93] In other words, instead of democratic government, efficient governance is promoted; instead of democratic participation, management is promoted; instead of popular organization and action, state regulation and control are promoted. There can emerge a totalizing interventionist regime—but this is not to say that this regime effectively achieves its objective of peace, let alone that it succeeds in introducing the radical changes into African states and societies that it claims. In short, because the discourse is totalizing does not mean that it will prove total in practice.

One reason for this is that, as we will see in the case of Uganda, governance states are provided with a set of tools that can be easily instrumentalized by the elites at the core of that state, with consequences that can demolish the technocratic governance rationale itself. On the social level, the failure to be totalizing in practice derives from the way that the creation of unaccountable technocratic structures can lead to diverse and unintended consequences for those subject to intervention. In its pursuit of efficient policy implementation, human rights intervention requires that the population consent to the imposition and participate in the implementation of those externally driven policies. Intervention needs its subjects to, for example, accept material aid, or adopt externally conceived notions of justice, or function within imported notions of normal social order. The problem is that, as proponents and critics alike recognize, universal consent to such interventions is not always automatic. Some people may not be willing to meekly stand in line in the sun all day to receive the ration of grain considered appropriate by World Food Program; others may not want to conform to the models of proper peacebuilders, civil society members, psychologically healthy individuals, or civil servants demanded by intervening agencies; still others may not accept the kind of justice imposed by the ICC. Such resistance tends to be categorically condemned by proponents of liberal peace as antiliberal, and to be categorically celebrated by many critics of liberal peace as emancipatory affirmations of alterity and difference.[94] Regardless of its political meaning (to be considered later), such resistance needs to be dealt with by intervention, which requires that people assume specific identities, whether of helpless victims or of active agents in normal societies, economies, and cultures.

One solution to this overt resistance is to promote participation in intervention. Roland Paris suggests that "peacebuilders could go considerably further than they have in previous missions to incorporate local consultation mechanisms into the apparatus of governance," and he calls for "experimentation with different forms of local participation in international administration."[95] In fact, almost all forms of human rights intervention require some degree of participation, which occurs every time someone attends a community reconciliation workshop, starts a microcredit project, provides testimony to an international court, starts a community-based organization, takes a Prozac pill, stands in line for a bag of grain, or calls for military intervention against their enemies or oppressors. It is in recognition of this that Mark Duffield argues, "Liberal peace aspires to secure stability within the political complexes that it encounters on its shifting borders through the developmental principles of partnership, participation and self-management. People in the South are no longer ordered what to do—they are now expected to do it *willingly* themselves."[96]

However, although its proponents often treat participation as a panacea for the ills of intervention, its consequences are by no means unambiguous. Indeed, critics have maintained that the way participation is formulated within the total intervention agenda renders it not emancipatory but disciplinary and leads it to steer agency within externally provided models that may not match what those subject to intervention genuinely desire or need.[97] This can also give rise to complex and ambiguous situations in which, as Rita Abrahamsen puts it, participation is "voluntary and coercive at the same time, producing both new forms of agency and new forms of discipline."[98] Questions arise over how far participatory intervention can follow its beneficiaries' dictates before running up against its own political and practical imperatives, before the beneficiaries participate to the point that they demand that the intervention turn against the very political interests lying behind it. More positive possibilities have also been noted: participation in one domain, even if restricted, may prompt people to demand more genuine, expansive forms of participation in other domains, including politics[99]—"We want the government to be run the way we manage our co-operative store."[100] The ways in which participation, despite its co-optation by administrative interventions, might be opened up beyond its political and geographical restrictions, thereby challenging the power structures within which it is embedded, will be explored in chapter 4.

Although the development of participatory mechanisms is the preferred way of dealing with resistance for intervention's proponents, many also recognize that at times administrative violence, the coercion deemed legitimate and necessary to force people and institutions to adopt the identities needed to build human rights and peace, will be unavoidable. As Roland Paris explains within his framework for successful state-building, "it *is* paradoxical, and in some respects unfortunate, that international officials must suppress certain forms of political expression in order to build the foundations for a stable and peaceful democracy."[101] In some forms of intervention, such as the distribution of relief aid, administrative violence is much closer to the surface, but violence is present as a supposedly legitimate last-resort option for all human rights interventions. This administrative violence, justified by peace interventions as necessary for their own efficacy, may, from another angle, also simultaneously represent the instrumental, self-interested violence of certain political actors. Violence will thus regularly be two-sided, or multisided, enabled by the discourse of human rights, but serving a number of different purposes in different political strategies.

TOTAL INTERVENTION AND THE AFRICAN STATE

The political consequences of total intervention, assessed in terms of its instrumental and administrative dimensions, will be clearly seen in intervention's impact upon African states and those societies subject to intervention. I briefly consider these here in anticipation of the argument of later chapters. Perhaps the most important African partner in the total intervention agenda is the African state, now absolved for having been the former enemy of human rights and redeemed within the state-building framework as a key factor in preventing and resolving conflict. State weakness is conceived of as a cause and consequence of conflict, and so building states so that they can help prevent, transform, and resolve conflicts becomes part of the pursuit of peace.

To this end, African sovereignty is not dismissed in the name of human rights, but rather intervention is thought of as supporting African sovereignty and remodeling it toward responsibility. *Sovereignty as Responsibility* most completely lays out this agenda, de-emphasizing coercive intervention and bringing the African state back in as a partner in preventing, managing, and transforming conflicts and protecting civilians. Given the generalized crises of African states, it argues, they will frequently need the support of the international community in order to fulfill these responsibilities, and so the international community's assistance in building the capacity of weak African states toward liberal market democracies becomes a principal mode through which Western intervention will take place in Africa.[102] The new interventionist agenda thus moves from a categorical rejection of the African state to a pragmatic engagement with it, in which state weakness is the problem, to be remedied through external assistance. In so doing, sovereignty is instrumentalized to intervention instead of represented as intervention's primary obstacle.[103]

However, in cases of state collapse or regime criminalization, where the state's leaders are deemed unable or unwilling to protect their own population and they fail to request or accept assistance from the international community, or in those cases in which the regime victimizes its people itself, the total intervention agenda makes it the international community's duty to coercively assume the protection role itself, whether in a prevention, resolution, or reconstruction role. This duty, too, is justified by invoking human rights and sovereignty, because, according to *Sovereignty as Responsibility*,

> the international community is the ultimate guarantor of the universal standards that safeguard the rights of all human beings, it has a corresponding responsibility to provide innocent victims of internal conflicts and gross violations of human rights with essential protection and assistance. [104]

In short, "[African] governments are increasingly called on to demonstrate responsibility or risk forfeiting their sovereignty" to the international community.[105] However, as noted already, even coercive intervention is justified as targeting a specific illegitimate regime or individuals leaders so as to restore "responsible sovereignty," and is not, it is claimed, a violation of sovereignty. This is illustrated well by Security Council Resolution 1973 of 2011 authorizing the use of force against Libya. This resolution, while authorizing member states of the UN to "take all necessary measures . . . to protect civilians and civilian populated areas under attack" short of "a foreign occupation force of any form on any part of Libyan territory" (para. 4), simultaneously reaffirms the Council's "strong commitment to the sovereignty, independence, territorial integrity, and national unity" of Libya (preamble). The aerial bombing campaign, according to the resolution, is merely "remodel[ing] the features of governments to live up to their responsibilities," in the words of *Sovereignty as Responsibility*.

Sovereignty as Responsibility bases this framework on a particular definition of sovereignty, arguing that sovereignty "refers not only to the inviolability of a state but to its ability to carry out its functions of government. . . . Normatively, to claim otherwise would be to lose sight of its purpose in the original context of the social contract."[106] It is only by reducing sovereignty to the legitimacy that accrues to the institution with effective protection capacity, its role in promoting so-called human security—a legitimacy that can be equally assumed by national or international institutions—that *Sovereignty as Responsibility* can argue that, when the state fails in its protection role, sovereignty is passed upward to the international community as a "pooled function." Such pronouncements make clear how the report can issue such apparently oxymoronic statements as calling international intervention a "fulfillment of national sovereignty."[107] This externalization of the responsibility for judging state legitimacy also requires the presumption of the failure of democratic political agency.[108] It becomes up to the discretion of the international community to decide when a state is abusing its people to the point where they can no longer act politically for themselves; until that point, it is also up to the international community to deem a state responsible and deserving of support. The people are required to be satisfied with and silent in the face of the international community's judgment and intervention, whether in support of or against their state.

This sets the stage for some African states to be labeled effective human rights supporters, legitimately sovereign, and thus deserving recipients of foreign assistance to build their capacity, which can include military assistance for the sake of "enforcing peace" and eliminating those considered illegitimate military or political actors. However, it also sets the stage for other African states, or really, specific regimes, in the extreme to be denounced as human rights violators, irresponsible, and devoid of sovereignty, and for those acting in the name of the international community to threaten or use force against them in the name of protecting their populations. This is not to say that every Western ally will be termed a human rights protector and every adversary a human rights violator, nor that every state that receives state-building support does so because of its alliances with the West; as addressed already, the politics of intervention are far more polyvalent.

In practice, it will often be a core group of elites at the center of the African state who end up being the beneficiaries of foreign support (as will be seen in Uganda) or the targets of international opprobrium (as is seen, for example, in Sudan or Zimbabwe). In cases of supposedly responsible states like Uganda, the administrative and instrumental dimensions of human rights intervention will converge around the development of an unaccountable group of elites. The same core of elites who are given the responsibility of bringing about donor-mandated changes and effecting donor-driven policies, often over the interests and demands of their citizenries, will be able to take advantage of that unaccountable authority and instrumentalize it to their own ends. In irresponsible states, regime change will be similarly personalized around key figures.

The externally determined responsibility or irresponsibility of any African state can effectively guide the entire range of interventions taking place in and around that state. Interventions in responsible states help build weakened state capacity or refuse funding to groups deemed to be critical of the government. Legal interventions, while claiming impartiality, target irresponsible regimes and support responsible regimes. Humanitarian aid is provided to responsible states but may be refused if it is thought to support irresponsible regimes. In this way, the politicized judgment about an African state's responsibility or irresponsibility can be built into every intervention, as is seen clearly in the case of Uganda.

POLITICS AMONG THE SUBJECTS OF INTERVENTION

The vast range of political possibilities stemming from the agency and action of those subject to intervention will also play a central role in determining the political consequences of total intervention. The primary tendency will be actualized through the administrative dimension, as populations are put under normalizing technocratic regimes. However, instrumentalization also plays a key role, because, while intervention can be instrumentalized in repressive directions by interventions' supposed beneficiaries, it can also be instrumentalized toward more emancipatory ends. When it comes to the subjects of intervention, it can be useful to see instrumentalization as only one facet of a broader phenomenon of the appropriation and renegotiation of intervention and its resources by those subject to it, which can serve a wide range of political and social agendas and projects. So, despite total intervention's tendency toward administration and discipline, it can also provide resources that, when repurposed, can be used by administered subjects to forge new tools of use in their own, possibly emancipatory forms of political and social organization and action.

However, even if its resources are not intentionally redeployed, intervention can still open new spaces and possibilities for those people subject to it. For example, the consent that human rights intervention enjoys can itself provide a basis for political action and should not be interpreted as always representing the uncritical embrace of external intervention or coerced subjugation to external imperatives. Although consent to intervention can indeed lead in depoliticizing directions (Mamdani, in the case of Darfur, associates it with the fading of citizenship and its replacement by a "consumer mentality"),[109] the invocation of intervention's proclaimed ideals by its subjects can, for example, provide the basis for a powerful critique of intervention as it fails to achieve or abide by those ideals in practice.

Even the depoliticizing forms of administration fostered by intervention can unintentionally end up setting the stage for a new "politics of the governed," as Partha Chatterjee puts it, as the administered come together in new contexts and in response to new pressures to associate, deliberate, and act politically, making demands and taking action on local, national, or even international levels.[110] Excluded groups can take advantage of new opportunities to demand political inclusion, and political organizations can adopt human rights discourses that go beyond interventionist models and that legitimate democratic political organization and action.[111] The conditions of the camp itself can produce new possibilities for politics,[112] the "biopolitics" of humanitarianism can provoke emancipatory forms of biopolitical organization in response,[113] or those same biopolitics can provoke a re-engagement with traditional forms of citizenship outside the biopolitical framework.[114] Thus, from these administrative, disciplinary regimes can emerge possibilities for political solidarity and community *among* the victims of violence and subjects of intervention in ways unexpected, unseen, or unwanted by the interveners.

One way this can play out is through a politics of refusal among those subject to intervention, which comprises a rejection of the victim role, of human rights administration and the pacifying function it plays, of its tendency to repress the agency of the administered in the name of efficiency, or of its instrumentalization to repressive local or international agendas. For its part, human rights intervention generally interprets this kind of behavior as deviance, which can lead to demands by interveners for even more extreme, coercive, forms of intervention. Refusal can also be oriented toward specific facets or consequences of interventions, such as when men organize against the effects of women's rights interventions, or when the ICC is rejected in the name of traditional justice. It can also take violent forms, such as food riots or when armed groups target humanitarian agencies.

A variety of forms of resistance to intervention can, thus, emerge, including those that do not resist its disciplinary dimension but rather reject the way intervention is instrumentalized. Rebel groups may attack aid convoys because of aid groups' links to the government, or may attack displacement camps to discourage people from cooperating with those states running the camps. People may protest against aid agencies for their ties to abusive political forces and at the same time demand nonpoliticized and impartial aid provision. The politics of intervention in conflict zones can, thus, give rise to demands *for* administrative intervention, for human rights, for liberal values, or for peace, against the illiberal and violent consequences of supposedly liberal intervention.

This multiplicity reveals the inadequacy of grouping all the different forms of politics among those subject to intervention under the category of resistance, which presumes that the political context of that action is totally defined by that intervention—an impossibility. Intervention will indeed tend to provoke resistance, but resistance is only one dimension of the politics it enables and itself comes in many forms. Moreover, intervention is only one aspect of the vast, complex politics occurring in conflict zones. That said, the capacity for autonomous, meaningful political action among those subject to intervention, in the midst of political and social upheaval and facing significant violence, suffering, and deprivation, should not be overstated. Although recognizing the agency of intervention's subjects is essential, it is important, also, to note that the relation between intervener and subject is not open to any renegotiation, for that relation is always determined by a significant imbalance, the very imbalance that makes intervention possible in the first place. And sometimes, the most prevalent political consequence of intervention can be simply the radical uncertainty it creates for those subject to it. As states, international organizations, private aid groups, contractors, foreign powers, and others all meld together in people's eyes to form an unaccountable administrative regime, it becomes inscrutable to those it administers. As people try to survive and keep their lives going on a day-to-day basis, they do not feel like empowered members of global civil society, but, instead, find themselves in a transnational maze in which they have to do their utmost just to find a way through. From the displaced persons' camp, it is impossible to discern where decisions are being made that are affecting people's lives, who actually holds power, what laws are in force, who will enforce them, of whom to make demands (if such a thing is even possible), or what the consequences would be of doing so. Attempts by subjects of intervention to resist or reconfigure human rights interventions, or even to act politically, are plagued by this uncertainty, which can end up creating among them, not so much a dependency, but a resignation, which can be very dangerous politically, especially in contexts of violence and war. Politics can become reduced to a popular hope for the miraculous as the only possible antidote to the inexplicability of what people face. Again, however, this is only a tendency, and people are constantly rupturing the bounds within which intervention and violence try to keep them.

Therefore, to address the politics of human rights intervention, it is necessary, on the one hand, to address each type of intervention individually, because each utilizes different epistemologies and techniques and leads to different effects, and, on the other, to keep an eye on the overall effect of the total interventionist regime, which can only be done by focusing on a specific historical case. This is the approach I take for the remainder of this book. In the next chapter, I sketch out the political context that I will be investigating, namely, the civil war that occurred in Acholi sub-region of northern Uganda from 1986 until around 2007. In the chapters that follow, I explore a series of different human rights interventions, discerning the logic and possibilities of each, and then showing how those possibilities played out in northern Uganda. I will argue that each tended toward generally counterproductive consequences for democracy, human rights, and peace.

2

The Politics of Violence in Acholiland

The war in northern Uganda is widely represented, both in Uganda and internationally, as a moralized conflict pitting the responsible, but shorthanded, Ugandan government against the evil Lord's Resistance Army, led by the madman Joseph Kony. Uganda is seen as a partner in protecting the human rights of its citizens, and intervention has proceeded on that basis. However, the moralized image of the conflict has led to equally moralized interventions with largely harmful consequences for the people and politics of Uganda. Future chapters chart these consequences, but to understand why intervention has taken the form that it has and has the effects that it does, it is necessary to develop a narrative of the conflict in northern Uganda that refuses the dominant moralized portrayal and places the violence in its historical and political context. To this end, this chapter investigates the political history of the conflict, charting its local dimensions within Acholiland, its national dimensions, and its international dimensions, showing how all three have come together to establish the context for intervention.

Of central importance to a political understanding of the conflict is the role of ethnicity, and in particular ethnicized politics and violence. Ethnicity is sometimes recognized as a factor in the conflict by the policy-oriented reports that dominate the literature on northern Uganda. This literature, however, simply assumes there to exist long-standing ethnic tensions between northern and southern Uganda, and thus ignores how different ethnic identities were constructed historically and became the bases for collective political identification and action. It tends to naturalize ethnic identities and leave unexamined the question of why war, violence, and politics occur within an ethnic framework in the first place, and how that framework itself might be transcended.

Because these processes of political identity formation are tied to the history of state formation, and state formation in Africa has been a process deeply imbricated with global political and economic structures and forces—whether colonial rule of a century ago or the War on Terror of today—it is necessary to start with **45** the beginnings of state formation in Uganda. Thus, the chapter investigates the construction and re-negotiation of ethnic political identity in colonial Uganda, arguing that ethnicity and the state have been in a dynamic, mutually dependent relationship ever since the establishment of indirect rule in the early twentieth century. The postcolonial period would demonstrate just how entrenched ethnic politics had become, as each successive regime, despite rhetoric or even efforts to the contrary, came to depend on and consolidate ethnic politics in its pursuit of power. The resilience of political ethnicity would prove itself again in the succession of rebellions that have wracked the Acholi region of northern Uganda since the National Resistance Army/Movement (NRA/M) took power in 1986; indeed, each Acholi rebel movement represented a different attempt to use ethnic political claims to assert political power within Acholi society and within the national context. This chapter shows how the perpetuation of the political crises underlying the emergence of these rebel groups has allowed the conflict to continue and examines the new forms these crises have taken since the mass internment of the Acholi peasantry began in 1996. The chapter, thus, lays the groundwork for understanding the mechanisms by which human rights interventions, instead of helping to resolve the political crises underlying the war, have compounded them and contributed to the prolongation of the conflict.

1. Colonial Power and Resistance in Acholiland

The indirect-rule state in Africa was a "bifurcated state," containing both a civil power, based in the central state, and a customary power, based in the local state.[1] It combined the despotic power of the central colonial administration with the despotic power of the chief, the central state excluding the colonized from a share in national political power and confining Africans to their "tribes," where they would be ruled by chiefs claiming customary authority. As this section argues, the result was that, under indirect rule in Uganda, ethnic political identity partook of both these dimensions, the national and the internal. Ethnic political identity was embedded in the form that power took in the colonial state, but it also "came to be simultaneously . . . the form of revolt against it,"[2] as those confined to tribes came to use the language of tribe both to demand a place on the national political stage and to contest the supposedly customary power of the British-appointed chiefs.

CHIEFS IN COLONIAL ACHOLILAND

Upon establishing the Uganda Protectorate in 1894, the British objective of collecting taxes and extracting forced labor required an administrative and coercive apparatus that far exceeded what they could staff with their own limited manpower. Facing these practical constraints, and also determined to avoid introducing what they considered disruptive processes of premature modernization to Africa, the

British soon looked to Africans as the local agents of colonial administration. This was made easier in southern Uganda, where the British found, to varying degrees, centralized monarchical political systems and administrative chiefs appointed by the king either existing in competition with or taking precedence over the lineage-based chiefs. It was in the region of Buganda that this structure was most significant, but it also was sufficiently established in the other so-called southern treaty kingdoms that the British did not have to create their own class of administrative chiefs out of whole cloth. That is not to say that the discretionary, despotic authority with which the British endowed their appointed chiefs had antecedents in the immediate precolonial period; rather, in Mamdani's words, "the colonial state really liberated administrative chiefs from all institutionalized constraint, of peers or people," laying the basis for local despotism.[3]

However, within the decentralized socio-political orders of northern Uganda, including the area that would come to be known as Acholiland, this class of administrative chiefs was missing, and there the "colonial imposition could not resonate with any aspect of tradition."[4] At the beginning of the twentieth century, despite an ongoing trend in what would become Acholi district toward a concentration of power in the hands of centralized leadership under pressure from slave traders and Egyptian administrators,[5] the British found social organization there remarkable for the lack of hierarchy and powerful leaders. The first colonial agents described Acholiland as divided into dozens of chiefdoms,[6] in each of which one lineage would provide the chief, or *rwot-moo* (plural: *rwodi-moo*), for the entire chiefdom.[7] However, even the language of *chiefdom* and *chief* is misleading, suggesting a much more centralized political structure than what, in fact, existed. Other lineages within each chiefdom would also have their own *rwodi-moo* to represent them,[8] an authority shared with bodies of elders, spiritual leaders, rainmakers, and others. In the words of Frank Girling, the author of the first ethnographic study of the Acholi (the research for which he carried out in the late 1940s), the *rwot*

> had no coercive machinery for enforcing his decisions. . . . It may even be doubted whether he had decisions of his own which he wished to enforce. The policy of the domain [chiefdom] was the result of the reconciliation of the separate interests of its constituent village-lineages.[9]

As one early administrator put it, it was extremely difficult to find chiefs—as the British understood them—in Acholiland.[10]

Because of the lack of a centralized hierarchical authority, the "pacification" of Acholiland took on a piecemeal, and particularly violent, visage.[11] After the initial period of subjugation, which included mass forced displacement and punitive collective violence, because the *rwodi-moo* were inadequate for the despotic role the British asked of them, the British jettisoned the customary mode of succession among *rwodi-moo* and selected their own chiefs, regardless of their relationship to the lineage-based *rwodi-moo*.[12] The British created chiefs in

Acholiland on the model that they imagined proper African chiefs should be, which would, they believed, help raise the particularly savage Acholi up the civilizational ladder toward the model of the Baganda.[13] The result was that the British-appointed administrative chiefs comprised a system that, as Girling admitted, "has nothing to do with the original indigenous organization."[14] Despite the fact that these appointed chiefs were entirely new, they nevertheless were to rule over the Acholi in the name of Acholi custom, as determined by the British. The indirect-rule regime in Acholiland spoke the language of tribal custom, and, as will be explained later, the resistance against that authority from within would also come to use that same language.

The imposition of chiefs and extraction of taxes and forced labor led to violent resistance. British administrative and military buildings were burned and collaborators and government agents were killed, most famously in the Lamogi Rebellion, the last major instance of collective resistance against the British in Acholiland.[15] By 1920, a regular administration had been imposed upon the districts of Gulu and Chua, and the provincial headquarters of the Northern Province were established at Gulu Town.[16] The powers of the British-appointed chiefs were legally formalized in the Native Authority Ordinance of 1919, which made them responsible to the central government while giving them unlimited judicial, legislative, and executive powers over those designated their subjects.[17] As Sathyamurthy says, the "implication . . . lay in the fact that the chiefs ruled by fear. . . . Government in Acholiland thus became virtually synonymous with police."[18]

Along with the problems they faced in imposing chiefs upon the Acholi, the British also had significant difficulty in convincing the Acholi that they were indeed "Acholi" and not simply members of their disparate clans. There was little or no hierarchy among the different chiefdoms, no "paramount chief" equivalent to the (for the British, archetypal) Kabaka of the Baganda.[19] Girling admits, "There was never, it seems, any real political unity within Acholiland,"[20] and Tarsis Kabwegyere takes this point the furthest, stating that, if the colonial administration of the Acholi did not amount to "the creation of a 'tribe' . . . it is difficult to see what else it was,"[21] a conclusion whose sweeping character has been contested by Ronald Atkinson, among others. Regardless of the extent to which an Acholi identity existed or not in the precolonial period, it is incontestable that the British reified and essentialized an Acholi identity along with other tribal identities, rendering the tribe the dominant political category in national politics. Furthermore, the importance of tribal ethnic identity today derives from its particular mode of politicization and institutionalization under colonialism and in the post-colonial period, so whether or not a coherent Acholi identity existed in the pre-colonial period is of little significance for my argument.

The British set the stage for political competition to take a tribal form on the national level, as northern tribes were incorporated into the Uganda Protectorate as districts, whereas, in the south, the more centralized political communities, in particular the Baganda, were provided certain privileges as they were incorporated as kingdoms through treaties. Once they had done so, the British did not fail to notice the problems that had arisen in northern and eastern Uganda as a result of this imposition of unchecked chiefly power and hierarchical, centralized authority upon people for whom it represented an entirely new institution.[22] The British feared that abuses of power would give rise to opposition from those their chiefs ruled. Governor Sir Philip Mitchell's 1939 *Native Administration: Note by the Governor,* called attention to the problems of trying to establish indirect rule

> where a chief who has no native right to his office is imposed by authority on the people, and then accorded the full support and trust of the British officers, as if he were in fact entitled by custom and heredity to the power which he wields.[23]

In particular, Mitchell feared that unqualified British support would eventually make the colonial administration the target of resistance. The first effort to reduce the appointed chiefs' arbitrary authority in Acholiland had been an attempt in 1937–1938 to re-introduce lineage-based chiefs, that is, to use the mode of succession that had been jettisoned in the 1910s.[24] This experiment was abandoned a few years later, both because the *rwodi-moo* lacked the authority needed to carry out the onerous tasks assigned by colonial rule and because it left out the most important, growing threat to British power, namely, the emerging petty bourgeoisie—the young, educated teachers, traders, farmers, and civil servants.

In order to incorporate both the lineage-based *rwodi-moo* and the petty bourgeoisie and thus avoid domestic strife, Mitchell recommended that those officials responsible for governing "segmentary peoples" introduce "some form of representative institution among the governed," namely, "tribal councils."[25] The councils would not limit the power of chiefs but rather co-opt potential anticolonial elements by giving them a stake in colonial rule.[26] In 1937, Gulu and Chua districts were joined to form Acholi district, and in 1943 local councils with a representative element were introduced at district, divisional, and county levels, bringing together appointed chiefs, unofficial members elected by lineage heads, and leading citizens—that is, the emerging petty bourgeoisie—selected by the district commissioner.[27]

THE PETTY BOURGEOISIE IN COLONIAL ACHOLILAND

The Acholi petty bourgeoisie had its origins in the colonial political economy. From the imposition of colonial administration until the 1930s, the British had discouraged the development of cash cropping in Gulu and Chua districts, preferring to use the area as a labor reservoir for the large farms of the south and for the armed forces.[28] The British tried to reverse this trend in the 1930s and 1940s as an influx of Banyarwanda into the south diminished the need for northern labor,[29] but a number of factors conspired to prevent the development of a profitable cash-crop economy in the north. For one thing, many of the Acholi and Langi migrants to the south had found employment in government service, so that, despite the government program to promote cash cropping in Acholi region, many Acholi remained in the south.[30] Furthermore, Acholi farms remained dependent upon family labor and had few incentives to try to produce cash-crop surpluses.[31] The net result was significant underexploitation of the land, low cotton production, and a small cash economy.[32] As late as the end of the 1950s, colonial officials still perceived Acholiland to be "an area in the development of which commercial enterprise has so far played only a negligible part."[33]

The minimal private sector economy meant that those who did not want to farm cotton looked to the government for opportunities for social and economic advancement. Acholi with requisite education entered the civil service in the district or provincial administrations, became teachers, or went to the south for government or private sector work.[34] As a result, the Acholi had the highest rate of employment of all the peoples of Uganda[35] and were second only to the Baganda in terms of their representation in the civil service.[36] However, even the Acholi private sector, comprising the few traders, hotel keepers, and contractors, "was heavily dependent on government support and regulation."[37] By 1963, there were only 445 African traders versus 7,074 teachers and civil servants in Acholiland, out of a total population of 340,000.[38] Without a large landholding class and without a significant private sector,[39] the petty bourgeoisie in Acholiland was a product of the state, made up mostly of civil servants and teachers,[40] a class dependent upon state resources for their positions. Those Acholi who were without the education needed to join the civil service and who did not want to farm could enter the military or police. The Acholi ended up being overrepresented in both, because of a British policy of recruiting northerners to put down southern rebellions and of the lack of profitable unskilled employment opportunities in Acholiland.[41] This situation thus belies the often-heard narrative that describes the Acholi as having been marginalized under colonialism, with their role restricted to providing military recruits; although the Acholi were indeed found in the security services, more important was their incorporation into the civil service and access to state resources. Marginalization cannot explain the roots of the conflicts in northern Uganda; instead, it is necessary to consider the particular way the Acholi were *included* in the state all the way until the purges undertaken by Idi Amin. For this reason, the exclusion of the Acholi in recent decades has to be seen in the context of the degree of privilege that they formerly enjoyed.

The introduction of councils, especially the district council, by the British provided the petty bourgeoisie with a stage on which to articulate a common political position, while keeping them within institutionalized politics. The 1949 Local Government Ordinance formalized the council hierarchy within each district, and the 1955 District Administration Ordinance gave the councils some authority over appointments within the district administration.[42] In Acholiland the real importance of the councils, however, was not in the power they wielded but in their function as a focal point for the political activity of the emerging petty bourgeoisie and for the community of interests the councils would enable between the petty bourgeoisie and the *rwodi-moo*.

Once political parties entered the scene in the 1950s, the councils proved crucial in their penetration of the north. When the Uganda National Congress (UNC)
and the Democratic Party (DP) began organizing in Acholiland in 1953 and 1955,
respectively,[43] they found a ready-made vehicle for their activities in this local petty
bourgeoisie, which they proceeded to consolidate organizationally and ideologi-
cally. The parties linked national and local in a dynamic relationship: they offered
the national organization that was needed to effect local reform because decisions
on important local issues were only made by the protectorate government. However, this national power was to be built at the local level first, so the power to effect
local change through national action was to be based in rural support. The councils
provided the local institution through which the parties could gain prominence,
make demands of the colonial state, and gain access to a mass base. As Gertzel
points out, during the 1950s, "political activity at the district level was itself largely
nationalist in orientation. It was focused on the district largely because there were
institutions at that level within which the colonial authority could be challenged."[44]
Because of the lack of national-level political institutions accessible to Africans, the
district council

> became an important political arena for nationally-orientated local
> leaders. And those leaders in turn provided the links through which the
> African leadership at the centre could build the support it needed to con-
> front the Protectorate government.[45]

Both the UNC and the DP formed political machines in Acholi district, comprising networks of "educated men, especially teachers and traders, but also junior
government employees such as health assistants and agricultural assistants, and,
undoubtedly, some of the parish chiefs, and young men."[46] The case of the UNC is
instructive: by 1955 several UNC supporters had been elected to the Acholi district
council, and by 1959 they were represented in councils at all levels, and a UNC
district leadership emerged. As Colin Leys explains, the Uganda People's Congress
(UPC) (which emerged in 1960 under the leadership of Milton Obote from within
the UNC and quickly took a dominant role in Ugandan politics) "was generally
stronger at the local level than it was at the centre, which in any case consisted
largely of men . . . who were local notables before they were national leaders, and
some of whom remained heavily dependent upon their local bases."[47]

In order to mobilize rural support, the UNC had to frame issues in local terms.
As Gertzel writes, "Local leadership set out to build grass roots support in this way
by challenging colonial policy and articulating local grievances."[48] Political-party
demands were thus a combination of national and local, joining the call for an end
to British domination in national politics with the demand for an end to the discretionary powers of the chief.[49] This proved successful, and, in response to the consistent articulation of grievances against the British-appointed chiefs, "There was a
genuine popular response to the issues raised by the UNC and this grew steadily
throughout the 1950s."[50] Political-party representatives rapidly gained popularity

among the peasantry: "The UNC leaders were bound to challenge the chiefs for local leadership . . . they appear to have replaced them as the legitimate local leaders in the popular mind with remarkable ease."[51]

The political parties forced the petty bourgeoisie to develop a mass base among the rural Acholi, a constituency to back their demands against the colonial state on the district and national levels. In exchange for this support, the state petty bourgeoisie guaranteed that the interests of the rural Acholi population would be represented to the central government. The political parties catalyzed a community of interest between the Acholi petty bourgeoisie and the rural Acholi, turning the Acholi petty bourgeoisie into the peasantry's link to national politics.

THE EMERGENCE OF ACHOLI POLITICAL IDENTITY

It was within this context—a state-based petty bourgeoisie organized around the district council and demanding consideration on the national stage, and the lineage-based *rwodi-moo* and elders, also organized on an Acholi-wide basis in the council, demanding a moderation of the despotic powers of the appointed chiefs—that Acholi as a political identity with both national and internal dimensions emerged.

First, the national dimension was articulated by the petty bourgeoisie as part of their entry into national politics due to the framework in which national politics was being negotiated in the 1950s. Politics in the Uganda Protectorate had revolved in large part around the "Buganda question," namely, the question of the status of Buganda within the protectorate and then within an independent Uganda. The Baganda elite, who had been the beneficiaries of significant political and economic privilege under colonial rule, at different times demanded political preeminence over the rest of the country, an exceptional degree of autonomy within a unitary state, or secession. To compete with the Baganda on the national political stage, other political elites similarly asserted their own claims in tribal terms to nullify the Baganda's claim to privilege. The petty bourgeoisie of Acholi district adopted this strategy, and came to adopt the administrative ethnic categorization as a natural ethnic identity; they went so far as to demand, through the Acholi district council, a "paramount chief" on the model of the Kabaka of Buganda. The national dimension of an Acholi political identity was thus formed in the dynamic relationship between the educated Acholi class and British administrative strategies in the context of processes of state formation in the Uganda Protectorate.[52] The parties did not moderate this ethnic identification; as Sathyamurthy makes clear, "most of the leaders of UPC were men of district stature, whose loyalties were predominantly to their own tribes rather than to Uganda as a whole."[53]

This assertion of Acholi political identity and unity on the national political stage reinforced the utility of ethnicity as a language of resistance for *rwodi-moo* and elders internally against the despotism of the local state, in particular against the claims to customary power made by the British-appointed chiefs. So, although as late as 1947 colonial administrators could still state that the "urgent trend of modern administration has been to bring the clans together and to make the Acholi conscious of their unity as a single people,"[54] by the late 1950s that consciousness had been effected through the political mobilization of the Acholi on the national stage, and the *rwodi-moo* had articulated their own claim to Acholi tradition to contest the claims of the British-appointed chiefs.

These two forces—the petty bourgeoisie and the *rwodi-moo*—each utilizing a different aspect of Acholi political identity, were brought together on the district council, on the lower-level councils, and, increasingly importantly, in the political parties. These two groups, working together against both sides of the bifurcated colonial state, thus ended up forging a coalition around an Acholi political identity. From the beginning, therefore, Acholi political identity had two dimensions: an internal dimension based around competing claims to an authentic tradition and leadership within Acholi society, at first fought out between the appointed chiefs and the lineage-based *rwodi-moo*, elders, and others; and a national dimension, as Acholi represented themselves as Acholi on the national political stage in order to compete in Ugandan's tribalized national politics. Thus, the political parties, although emphasizing a denominational split within Acholiland between Catholics and Protestants, served as a vehicle for the emergence of a common Acholi identity articulated politically on the local and national levels.[55] With independence and the transformation of Uganda into a one-party state, the appointed chiefs would become part of this community of interest as well, as the UPC would bring all three groups together within its patronage machine.

2. Tribal Politics and Regional Divides: 1962–1986

OBOTE I

Uganda's first prime minister was Milton Obote, a Langi from northern Uganda, who won the post through an alliance between the UPC and the Buganda-based monarchist Kabaka Yekka (Kabaka Only) party. Once in power, however, his relations with the Baganda quickly soured. Controversy remains about the place of ethnicity in politics during what is referred to as Obote I, the period from independence in 1962 until Idi Amin's coup in 1971 (as opposed to Obote II, 1980–1985). On the one hand, many have argued that Milton Obote, first as prime minister and then as president, eschewed ethnic politics in favor of nationalism, anti-imperialism, and, toward the end of his reign, socialism.[56] This nationalist reading of Obote I is refuted by those who argue that Obote in fact did the opposite, and that "central institutions increasingly came under ethnic control under the mask of Obote's official transcripts,"[57] both through patronage distributed by his UPC and through the military, which he increasingly came to rely upon.

This ambiguity can be made sense of if put in the context of the particular way in which the colonial state was established in Uganda. Obote aspired to undo the ethnic political fragmentation that had been created by the differential treatment

of the districts, the kingdoms, and Buganda under colonialism and in the Independence Constitution of 1962, which had incorporated the districts and kingdoms
into Uganda on a fundamentally unequal basis. There were ten federal districts,
concentrated in the north and east, and five kingdoms, all in the south. Four of the
kingdoms were given some autonomy over their internal affairs, whereas Buganda
was given a wide range of exclusive powers. For this reason, tribal equalization
meant very different things in the north—where it appeared to be their guarantee
of equality before the central state—and in the south—where it appeared to be an
attack on constitutionally guaranteed rights.

Obote also looked to regularize and nationalize the local administration so as
to make it a tool of national unification of instead of tribal particularism. He would
aspire, at least to a degree, to create a national civil service in place of the tribally
based institutions that had been inherited from colonialism and, thus, to detribalize the local state. The execution of both these projects would require the fundamental modification of the system of indirect rule that had been forged in Buganda
and then exported throughout the protectorate.

This reform of the local state through detribalization could, perhaps, have
found nationwide support among the peasantry, as the NRA would demonstrate 20
years later, because the decentralized despotism of indirect rule was a burden under
which the Ugandan peasantry suffered throughout the country, and in particular in
Buganda.[58] However, Obote did not try to mobilize support for his project among
the peasantry by basing it upon a democratization of the local state.[59] He failed to
utilize democratic control of the local state at the village level as a motor of local,
and, ultimately, national state reform, and, instead, he located the motor for reform
in the central state and its institutions. The result was that, within his project of
national tribal equalization, instead of finding support for the reform of the central
state in the reform of the local state, Obote used the central state to try to reconfigure both forcibly. To do this, Obote had to transform the central state into an adequate tool for top-down reform of national and local politics, which he accomplished
by centralizing power, creating a one-party state, and building a powerful army
under his control.

To undertake this project, Obote needed a social base for the increasingly
powerful central state. Because he had failed to try to build support among the
peasantry by offering a reform of local despotism, Obote gradually looked for support among those groups that would profit from national political equalization,
and he built support among them through political patronage. To this end, he
disproportionately brought northerners into the central state, both through the
civil service and the military, and he created a patronage machine in northern
Uganda, in particular in Acholiland and Lango, among the northern petty bourgeoisie, the *rwodi-moo*, and the appointed chiefs, organized within the UPC.[60]

This had two major repercussions in terms of ethnic politics. First, in trying
to undo one aspect of the legacy of British colonial rule—the special privileges
accorded to the treaty kingdoms of the south, in particular Buganda—and thereby

equalize tribes politically, Obote ended up introducing a new north-south cleavage into national politics and a new state-based privilege upon that cleavage—the north over the south. At the same time, because Obote did not try to detribalize the local state and left the ethnically oriented structures of power and alliances *within* the districts untouched, he could not help but, in assembling a coalition among northern tribes in support of his project, import into the central state the very intertribal tensions that he was trying to eliminate. Indeed, the individuals he brought in to his national government continued to rely on tribalized structures to maintain their own bases of support in the districts. Obote's project proved counterproductive, not only in that it introduced a regional north-south ethnic cleavage into national politics, but also in that it consolidated tribal political privilege and difference, which had been introduced during colonialism and which he had specifically targeted as inimical to national equalization.

This story was played out in the fortunes of what became the Acholi political class. At independence, the political parties, especially the UPC, had presented the Acholi petty bourgeoisie with significant access to government positions at the national level. There was some differentiation between those Acholi in the national government and those in the district government, but personal ties and dependence of the political parties on mobilization by local politicians meant that the Acholi political stratum remained a coherent group.[61] It had developed, indeed, into a political middle class, but one still dependent on state positions and patronage, with one foot in the national government, whether in elected positions in parliament or in appointed positions in the civil service, in the military, or in the foreign service, and one foot in rural Acholiland, among those who formed their base of support.

As Obote worked to impose what he saw as the solution to the Buganda question—tribal equalization—he built up central state power further and seized his opportunity to challenge the Baganda elite in 1966–1967, when he provoked Buganda into an open confrontation, which he won with significant help from the army.[62] Having defeated the internal challenge to his project, Obote presided over the promulgation of a new constitution in 1967, which abolished the kingdoms, divided Uganda into districts (splitting Buganda into four), and placed all "under the direct and complete control of the central government."[63]

Once again, in order to build support for the expanded powers of the central state, Obote, instead of proposing a democratization at the local level, looked to the north for a base of support. He built that support through preferential access to government positions and resources in the name of national equalization. By the end of the 1960s, with the Move to the Left and some nationalization of foreign industries, the stakes of government patronage had increased significantly. The creation of parastatals led to the emergence of an overwhelmingly Acholi and Langi economic bureaucracy, with the Acholi political class profiting considerably.[64] The outlawing of all political parties save the UPC narrowed Obote's base even further, and by the end of the decade, "all the politicians had given up even the pretence of appealing to the electorate."[65] As Mamdani says, "By 1970, the UPC was but an empty shell, a formal organization whose function was limited to being a pipeline for patronage."[66]

In addition to the expansive, intensive UPC organization, Obote depended heavily upon the security services, a policy that also ended up favoring the Acholi. As Obote expanded the army precipitously, he also entrenched the northern dominance of the armed forces. The army grew from 700 troops at independence to 9,000 at the time of the Amin coup,[67] of which over one-third were Acholi.[68] As he came to forcibly exclude the Baganda from national politics by dismantling the monarchy and putting Buganda under martial law, Obote increasingly had to rely on the security forces.[69] He stacked the barracks with Acholi and Langi troops and built a mostly northern officer corps so as to forge an effective, reliable weapon.

Obote's project of coercive tribal equalization thus ended up giving rise to a new tribal privilege and consolidating tribe as the primary language of politics. Because the Acholi and Langi favored under Obote I were brought into the government as tribal representatives, and because they depended upon their claims to tribal political identity in order to maintain their political positions in the district and on the national stage, Obote only ended up reproducing within the central state the very tribal tensions that he had sought to eliminate. Even though Obote's regime had a regional, northern, basis, those coming from that region still identified themselves as members and representatives of particular tribes, not as northerners.[70] Obote had made tribal political privilege his target, but, because he had not undone the foundation of ethnic politics in the local state, when he went to find support for his centralizing project, he had to go to those very tribal political units he was trying to abolish, so he re-consolidated the tribal orientation of national politics. The result was that Obote's effort at tribal equalization only reversed the national hierarchy, putting northern tribes, in particular the Acholi and Langi, on top and consolidating the importance of tribal ethnic identity within Ugandan politics. At the same time, because he found his support in the north, Obote also introduced a new regional north-south cleavage into national politics. This cleavage, although never providing the basis for a northern ethnic political identity, would, in the early 1980s, provide the ideological basis for the southern ethnic identity central to the NRA rebellion through the articulation of a "Northern question," a matter that became increasingly salient with the continued domination of the country by governments ruled by northerners.

IDI AMIN AND OBOTE II

Idi Amin's coup demonstrated the continued importance of tribal—not regional—political identity in Ugandan politics. Although Obote had managed to forge a strategic alliance between political and military elites of different northern ethnic groups, including Amin, these elites continued to put tribe first. Obote realized this too late, and in the end tried to counteract Amin's growing power by taking two, contradictory, measures: the Move to the Left, which aimed to build support nationally,[71] and an effort to consolidate his own base of power in the army among the Langi and Acholi troops.[72] But as coercion became the state's primary tool, Obote was outflanked by the conspiracy between internal and foreign forces supporting Idi Amin's army faction.[73]

After his coup, Amin declared an end to ethnic favoritism toward the Langi and Acholi and took steps to eradicate their hold on state power. He filled the army ranks with troops from his area of West Nile and purged it of Acholi and Langi; thousands of Acholi and Langi soldiers were killed, mostly in the first months of the regime.[74] He then used the military and other security forces to purge the national civil service of the Acholi and Langi political elite.[75] The substantial redistribution of property by Amin in the wake of the expulsion of Ugandans of Asian descent greatly benefited the army, thus merging the military elite and the state economic bureaucracy.[76]

At the district level, immediately after the coup, Amin had sought to build authority in the countryside by co-opting elders in the districts.[77] However, as the state was militarized further and the army and security services expanded, by 1973 the local government had simply become an extension of those armed forces, as military and police officials displaced the appointed chiefs who had enjoyed significant power under Obote.[78] The local Acholi political leadership and the *rwodi-moo* and elders suffered significant losses as Amin launched a series of violent political purges in Acholi and Lango districts, leading to tens of thousands of civilian deaths. Those local political forces that had benefited under Obote—the political middle class, the *rwodi-moo*, and the pro-UPC chiefs and civil servants— were devastated by Amin's security forces first in 1971, when Amin sealed off the entire north from foreign journalists and massacred his suspected political opponents, and sporadically after that.[79] The last large-scale killings by the Amin regime in Acholiland and Lango occurred in 1977, when government death squads went on a rampage there, killing up to 10,000 people.[80]

Many of the national and local Acholi elite, especially the middle class, who were not killed were driven into exile, giving birth to the large diaspora that continued to expand for decades. The *rwodi-moo* and elders who remained in Acholiland generally withdrew from political life. The Acholi middle class and political elite, lacking a base independent of the state, were easily eliminated by the state, and without these groups there was no independent economic foundation to build a new mediating class between the peasantry and the government. The order that had pertained inside Acholiland was de-stabilized, and the link between the Acholi and the national state was destroyed. This decimation of the Acholi local and national leadership, in particular the political middle class and national political elite, set the stage for the internal and national political crises that would grip the Acholi in the wake of the NRA's victory the following decade.

Amin was overthrown in April 1979 by the Tanzanian Army accompanied by the Uganda National Liberation Army (UNLA), and Obote won the multiparty presidential elections in 1980. Although certain prominent Acholi were incorporated into the new, Obote II, government, there was no return to the massive patronage machine of the Obote I regime, and there was no wide-scale political revival of the Acholi middle class. Indeed, given the years of economic ruin under Amin, the destruction wrought by the Tanzanian invasion, and the newly imposed International Monetary Fund (IMF) austerity measures, there was much less to redistribute.[81] Instead, Acholi were brought into the state principally through the military, and the UNLA officer corps again became heavily weighted toward the Acholi and Langi.[82]

The UNLA, once Obote was in power, had begun by turning its guns on West Nile, as Acholi and Langi militias, under command of UNLA officers, laid waste to Amin's home district, razing several towns.[83] With the inception of the guerrilla war, led by Yoweri Museveni, who had taken to the bush to protest the election rigging (discussed in detail later), the UNLA concentrated on fighting the insurgency in Buganda, and the military became of foremost importance to the Obote II government's hold on power. However, this incorporation of Acholi via the military would not last, as Obote's Acholi-Langi alliance came under pressure and Acholi troops accused Obote of giving officer positions to Langi while using Acholi as cannon fodder.[84] By July 1985, this dissent led to a successful coup by Acholi troops, led by Bazilio Okello and Tito Okello. In an attempt to expand their mass base, the Acholi soldiers forged a new alliance with West Nilers, attempted to create an alliance with the DP, and entered into peace talks in Nairobi with the NRA. However, their strategy did not succeed, and, as will be discussed, the NRA defeated the UNLA and occupied Kampala. Despite the extensive intranorthern conflicts that had characterized the Obote I, Amin, and Obote II regimes, from the perspective of the south, the ascent of the NRA in 1986 marked the end of 25 years of northern rule. It also set the stage for the internal and national political crises that would grip the Acholi in the wake of NRA victory.

THE NRA INSURGENCY AND THE "NORTHERN QUESTION"

Obote won the 1980 presidential election amidst widespread violence and accusations of vote rigging. In response, Yoweri Museveni, according to his autobiography, "decided to launch a protracted people's struggle with the few young comrades whom I had recruited in the 1979 war."[85] Museveni and his small group of fighters, what would eventually become the NRA, carried out an attack on UNLA army barracks on February 6, 1981 and then withdrew to the Luwero Triangle, immediately north and west of Kampala, from where they staged attacks and ambushes on the UNLA.[86]

Museveni and most of his comrades were Banyankole, from Ankole in southwestern Uganda. There was also a significant group of Tutsi refugees within the NRA: two of the fighters who participated in the first attack on Kabamba barracks, Fred Rwigyema and Paul Kagame, were Tutsi, and the proportion of Tutsi in the NRA grew as the rebel forces grew, amounting, eventually, to 3000 of the

14,000 troops when the NRA took Kampala in 1986.[87] The Luwero Triangle, however, had a heterogeneous population, of which the two most populous groups were the Baganda and Banyarwanda migrant workers. Therefore, the NRA's decision to base themselves in the densely populated Luwero Triangle region presented the incipient rebels with a problem: they were unable to appeal to tribal—that is, Baganda or Banyankole—commonality in building the support among the peasantry that would be essential for the protracted struggle they anticipated, both because of the internal heterogeneity of the population in the Luwero Triangle and because of their own lack of tribal commonality with those living there. In the face of this challenge, the NRA built support in Luwero, and then throughout the south of Uganda, through two routes.

First, the NRA built support through the reform of the local state in the areas it controlled. Mamdani has done the most to explicate the meaning of this policy and its legacy in contemporary Uganda. As he says, in launching its rebellion from Luwero,

> [the NRA] was compelled to address the question of building a state power with a difference in its liberated zones. To marshal the support of the peasantry against the Obote II regime, this form of power had to highlight the question of rights of the peasantry in the institutions it created. Its starting point was none other than the replacement of a form of power hitherto unchecked and fused with a system of checks and balances built on a differentiated notion of power. . . . [T]he NRA/M simply abolished the position of the chief. In place of chiefship, it created a system of resistance councils and committees.[88]

Therefore, according to Mamdani, the NRA dismantled the undemocratic power of the appointed chief and replaced it with a multitiered council system, known as the Resistance Councils (RCs) (renamed Local Councils or LCs in 1995). The RC, consisting of all adults in a given area, was endowed with legislative and judicial powers. That Council elected a nine-person Resistance Committee, which had administrative and executive powers, and whose members were subject to recall by the Resistance Council at any time.[89] This proved to be a highly effective mode of building support in Buganda because it was there that the customary chiefly power structure had weighed the most heavily on the peasantry.[90] According to Mamdani's account, the NRA is unique in that it built support, not by appealing to common tribal identity (for there was no such common identity to invoke), but by reforming local power through the establishment of the RC system. As the NRA expanded its control over other parts of Uganda during the civil war and immediately after its end in 1986, they were able to build support throughout the country by extending the RC system throughout the south.[91]

Other scholars argue, however, that this account tells only half the story. The NRA did not go to the bush to effect a reform of the local state but, instead, to carry out a revolution in the national state; local reform was hit upon as an instrument for building support for its national struggle. At the same time that the NRA was struggling against tribalized power in the local state through democratization, it was also struggling against what was represented as northern ethnic power in the national state. Therefore, the rebels also built support in Luwero by putting forth, not tribal ethnic commonality, but common ethnic regional identity, as Bantu southerners united against Nilotic northerners. The rebellion became the crucible in which the north-south divide took a central place in national politics.

The origins of this concern with northern power—the Northern question as A.G.G. Gingyera-Pinycwa has termed it—can be found, according to Gingyera-Pinycwa, in the late 1970s and early 1980s among a group of southern Ugandans, many of whom were in exile, who saw it as necessary to remove northerners from national power in order to establish a new national equalization and to end northern military dictatorship.[92] However, antinorthern sentiment would perhaps have remained an elite bias if it had not served a role in building support for the NRA in Luwero.[93] Therefore, in addition to democratizing the local state, the NRA built support in Luwero, and then throughout the south of Uganda, by framing the revolution in regional terms, as a struggle to throw out the north in favor of the south.

This designation of a northern ethnic enemy resonated with the experience of those living in Luwero and beyond, who had suffered greatly under the UNLA's counterinsurgency. Because of the war, the southern peasantry experienced the power and violence of the central state directly without mediation by the local state. As a result of their disproportionately large presence in the armed forces (especially among the rank-and-file troops sent to fight in Luwero) and of their colonial stereotype of being a martial tribe, Acholi ended up bearing the brunt of this antinorthern sentiment. This was further reinforced by the Acholi-led coup against Obote in 1985, and, subsequently, the most common appellation for UNLA soldiers was simply "Acholi" in many parts of the south.[94]

By positing its armed rebellion in north-south terms, and thanks to the UNLA's often vicious anticivilian violence, the NRA managed to tenuously overcome the challenge posed by Uganda's tribalized political heritage and thus to find an ethnic commonality between itself and the Baganda peasantry, and then between itself and the rest of the southern tribes—as southern Bantu, beyond the tribal ethnic lines that divided them. Furthermore, the deployment of a north-south division may also have helped to resolve other potential antagonisms within the political bloc the NRA was trying to construct, for instance the contested division in Luwero between Banyarwanda "foreigners" and Ugandan "natives." In an attempt to break the alliance forged by the rebels in Luwero between Baganda peasants and Banyaruanda laborers, Obote played that very card and alleged that the NRA represented an alien army, in Finnström's words, "Tutsi or Banyarwandan intruders." Mamdani also cites this tactic, explaining that the Obote II regime "tried to portray that guerrilla struggle as the spearhead of an 'alien' resurgence, a core movement of migrants of Ruandese origin which posed a threat to all Ugandans."[95] The NRA's response was to assert an ethnic identity among the southern Bantu against northern Nilotics, thus possibly framing the Obote II regime and its security services as, in a sense, foreigners themselves—not foreign to Uganda as a nation, but foreign to the south, as inter-lopers who should be driven back to their home on the other side of the Nile.

Obote's effort to frame the NRA as a force of foreign invaders was generally unsuccessful in the south, for, when the war spread beyond Buganda, Obote had to switch gears. From that point on, he attempted to tribalize the conflict by framing it as a war of the Baganda against the rest of the country—which was equally un-successful in dissuading support for the rebel movement in the south.[96] In the north, however, a reversed version of this indigenous/foreign articulation of the war did hold currency, for, even today, the first wave of NRA that entered Acholil-and are often referred to as Rwandese, and much is made of the Rwandan origin of the Deputy Army Commander at the time, Fred Rwigyema, and of rumors of Museveni's Rwandan origins.

Thus, as the north-south framework was utilized by the NRA among the southern peasantry, and, by the end of the bush war, had spread within sectors of their command and of their support base, the war against the Obote II regime was re-interpreted as a war of south against north, which was distilled into a war against the Acholi as the embodiment of northern state power. As the NRA's military struggle gained ground, the Langi-Acholi alliance within the UNLA broke down,[97] and by July 1985 Acholi troops, led by Bazilio Okello and Tito Okello, carried out their coup against Obote. However, lacking popular support and the skill and re-sources needed to rehabilitate the Acholi political elite, the Okello regime soon fell to the NRA after Museveni reneged on a peace agreement signed in Nairobi—the "Nairobi peace jokes" as many Acholi still term them, which they see as a sign of Museveni's duplicity and lack of interest in peace. The rebels took Kampala and sent the last remaining Acholi UNLA troops fleeing north. As a result, when these two military forces—the routed Acholi UNLA remnants with the NRA on their tail—arrived in Acholiland, they faced a population divested of local and national political leadership. In this context, the UNLA's arrival sparked an internal crisis as the surviving Acholi authority structure tried to deal with this new influx of inde-pendent, undisciplined, armed young men. The southern-based NRM govern-ment, which saw the Acholi as its ethnic enemy, compounded this internal crisis by proceeding to repress responsible local leadership. At the same time, the NRA's occupation sparked a national political crisis, as Acholi leaders were excluded from the new NRM government and the NRA undertook a violent counterinsurgency.

3. The Rebellions

As tribal political identity in Acholiland was structured through internal and national dimensions, so did the political crisis of the Acholi partake of those dimensions as well. The internal crisis stemmed from the breakdown of authority

within Acholi society—authority that had been legitimated through the language of
Acholi ethnicity—whereas the national crisis was brought about by the destruction
of the political links that had tied the Acholi to the national state as the Acholi were
excluded from power under the new NRM government on a tribal basis. This section will explain how the post-1986 rebel movements in Acholiland—most importantly the LRA—were responding to both crises at once, as each rebel movement
attempted to impose internal order upon Acholi society by building a constituency
against the NRM around a particular conception of Acholi identity.

NRM POWER AND THE RISE OF THE UGANDA PEOPLE'S DEMOCRATIC ARMY

When the fleeing UNLA and victorious NRA arrived in Acholiland, of the three
dominant socio-political groups that had taken form under colonial rule and during
Obote I—lineage-based authorities and elders, the middle class and national political
elite, and the government-appointed chiefs and administrators—only the first was
left with any internal authority, and even their power had been attenuated under the
regime of state violence. It is not surprising, then, that the arrival of the UNLA
proved to be an event so disruptive that the weakened internal order was thrown
into crisis. Indeed, these fleeing troops were not the political-military elite who had
previously provided the link between the rural Acholi and the central state, and,
except for a few top figures, they had little authority among the Acholi. The UNLA
officers failed to mobilize the Acholi behind them and could only hunker down in
Gulu and Kitgum towns to await the NRA.[98] When the NRA arrived, the UNLA
forces withdrew without a fight, evacuating Gulu and Kitgum Towns by mid-March,
1986. Many UNLA soldiers went back to their villages, and the rest accompanied
their commanders to Sudan.[99] By the end of March, the last pockets of the UNLA
had disappeared from Acholiland, and the NRA had occupied the subregion.[100]

This flood of thousands of undisciplined, armed young Acholi men—the
UNLA returnees—was a significant challenge to male lineage-based authorities
and elders. Perhaps, if a significant Acholi middle class had remained, they could
have together managed the new influx, but, with the internal Acholi political
structure weakened as it was, the new arrivals threw the internal order into crisis.
In response, many lineage-based authorities mobilized the discourse they had
employed since the 1950s, and they tried to secure their position through an appeal
to Acholi tradition. In this way, Acholi ethnicity was reconfirmed as the dominant
legitimate discourse of internal political order, within which aspirants to internal
political authority would have to work.

In a process similar to what is seen today in Acholiland, many lineage-based
authorities claimed that Acholi tradition demanded that the UNLA returnees go
through cleansing rituals, which the lineage-based authorities were to preside
over themselves. Many of these men, as anthropologist Heike Behrend explains,
claimed that

the returnees were the cause of all evil. They had become alien to those who had remained at home. During the civil war, they had plundered, tortured, and murdered, primarily in Luwero, and had become "of impure heart." Because they had killed, they brought *cen*, the spirits of the killed, to Acholi, thus threatening the lives of those who had stayed at home.[101]

The lineage-based authorities laid claim to the exclusive capacity to ritually cleanse the returning soldiers, a power they assumed in the name of saving the Acholi community from the powers of *cen*, thus putting themselves forth as the principal arbiters of internal power. The returnees, however, in large part refused to conform to these demands, and so explosive tensions were introduced into the already fragile internal social and political order.

When the NRA arrived, they fundamentally misinterpreted the situation. They seem not to have understood the political bankruptcy of the Acholi ex-UNLA and not to have understood the alienation of the returning soldiers from significant sectors of the Acholi community. The NRA had cast its enemy in ethnic terms—the Acholi as the consummate northern tribe—and so seems to have presumed that there would be an automatic, natural bond between the Acholi troops and the rural Acholi population. This presumed identity gave rise to the specter of a substantial potential political-military force in Acholiland, so the NRA prepared for a long, difficult fight to win Gulu and Kitgum.[102] Even after it had occupied Acholiland, notwithstanding the ease with which it had accomplished the task, the NRM government continued to act as if it faced an enemy united around ethnicity, not a population torn apart by internal conflict. It seems to have failed to escape the north-south terms in which it had framed its rebellion, and the articulation that the NRA had given the question of national power determined its political-military approach to the Acholi: it proceeded as if it were occupying enemy territory and tried to solve the Northern question for good by destroying the putative ethnically based power of the returning Acholi UNLA.[103] Politically, the NRM excluded the Acholi from national power and suppressed independent local leadership, while militarily, it launched a counterinsurgency without an insurgency. The result was that the NRA/M's wrong-headed strategy gave birth to the very rebellion that had previously only existed in its own mind.

Politically, the NRM government, once in power, faced the same difficulty it had faced as a guerrilla organization: how to secure enough support to govern in Uganda's tribalized political context, made difficult by the its strong ethnic base among the Banyankole in the southwest. The government's response was similar to the response from previous regimes: bring in representatives of other tribal groups in an attempt to ensure their support, in particular the Baganda; espouse a language of national democracy, security, and equalization; and forbid political party activity in the name of national unity. However, again as with previous regimes, these proposals and their implementation meant very different things in the north and the south. Tribal equalization in the south was seen as tribal exclusion in the north, and, moreover, the NRA's vicious counterinsurgency in northern Uganda seemed to belie its promises of national peace and security. The NRM government could not, or chose not, to overcome Uganda's heritage of tribalized, militarized politics, and so the NRM was soon dependent upon the military for establishing a modicum of control in the north, particularly Acholiland. In the south, the government remained dependent on its assertion of common southern interests to retain support among other southern tribes, in particular by invoking the threat of an armed return to power by the north. As the years went on, the NRM state would also increasingly come to be based around a core of military-political-business elites, many of whom were friends, family, or kinsmen of Museveni. This led to a situation in which, on the national level, the NRM reflected its southern base, and Acholi and Langi were generally excluded from political power. The cabinet, for example, was made up of less than 6 percent Luo-speakers, and their appointment to other government positions was similarly disproportionately low.[104] The NRA was composed of over 90 percent Bantu speakers, and the police force saw over three-quarters of its members summarily dismissed.[105] On the local level, the new government refused to deal with respected local Acholi political leaders and instead picked out marginal figures who would cooperate with the new regime.[106] Predictably, when the NRM attempted to establish the RC system in Acholiland, these institutions were perceived as tools of the government, especially as they were widely established without consultation.[107]

Militarily, although Museveni claims in his autobiography that "there was total peace in the north between March and August 1986,"[108] newspapers and human rights reports present a starkly different picture. Stories of harassment and abuse of civilians by the NRA began circulating in mid-April, 1986.[109] NRA orders for general disarmament went largely unheeded, evoking memories of Amin's similar order years before which had resulted in the massacre of disarmed Acholi troops.[110] Reports of looting and rape by NRA soldiers while on "their frequent operations for hidden guns" made their way into the national press.[111] Acholi civilians expressed a willingness to assist in ending the insecurity—indeed, the returnees had brought only disturbance—but complained that it was hard even for them to know who had guns and protested the loss of property to the NRA.[112] When the security situation degenerated in June and armed men began to rob civilians and attack government vehicles, the NRA, blaming the escalated violence on the Acholi as a tribe for refusing to cooperate in collecting guns, stepped up their use of force.[113] Again, the NRA's ethnic lens prevented it from distinguishing between Acholi civilians and the ex-members of the UNLA.

By mid-August, the situation had deteriorated further, and the NRA began broad "security swoops" or "screens," detaining hundreds. Open violence escalated. The most infamous incident was the massacre of over 40 civilians from Namu-okora by the NRA in late 1986, news of which spread rapidly throughout the region.[114] Museveni consistently dismissed allegations of mistreatment, blaming it on the lack of discipline of a few, stating that allegations of NRA human rights abuses were "absolutely rubbish and contemptible."[115] The national political crisis was, by that point, fully in evidence: the Acholi, divested of political leadership, were subjects of a violent military occupation by their own state, which exercised power over them without accountability.

The result was that NRA violence against Acholi civilians—the local manifestation of the national crisis—provided a context in which the internal crisis in Acholiland was temporarily suppressed. Faced with a new external enemy, one that identified all Acholi as its ethnic enemy, the lineage-based authorities and the ex-members of the UNLA were able to come together and provisionally stabilize the internal order through an alliance of political forces around the discourse of Acholi ethnicity.[116] As a result, by August, when three to four thousand former UNLA troops, calling themselves the Uganda People's Democratic Army (UPDA), entered Uganda from southern Sudan, the NRA had alienated the Acholi population sufficiently that the rebels and Acholi lineage-based authorities were able to unite against their common enemy. The need to resolve the national crisis and end NRA violence provided the preconditions for an attempt by Acholi to resolve the internal crisis through a new alliance between previously antagonistic factions around a claim to authority among the Acholi as an ethnic group.

The imagined insurgency that the NRA had been fighting since April became real, the counterinsurgency was escalated, and opposition newspapers were reporting NRA atrocities by September 1986.[117] By December, these accusations had reached the national and international media.[118] Rumors of genocide began circulating,[119] and the NRA allowed Karamojong cattle raiders to loot with impunity as far west as Gulu Town, sometimes participating in the looting themselves, thus destroying one of the bases of Acholi livelihood.[120] As in Luwero, where the national state had made itself known to the peasantry through its military, in Acholiland the new NRM government made itself known through the NRA. As a result, the government's ethnic interpretation of the insurgency led the Acholi to see the occupying army, and the government, in similarly ethnic terms. These terms are predominantly regional—the NRA/M as southern—but have also been tribal—the NRA/M as a tool of a Banyankole or Bahima-Tutsi conspiracy.

The alliance between the UPDA and the Acholi population, mediated by lineage-based authorities, led the rebels to work to gain the trust of the population. They forbade looting, promised compensation for requisitioned property, and conducted meetings in occupied areas to explain their struggle.[121] Most importantly, the UPDA tailored their demands to gain popular support. When they attacked Gulu in August 1986, their intention appears to have been to capture and use it as a base for re-taking Kampala.[122] However, they found little support for these claims to national power. Rather the UPDA found support by responding to the demands of Acholi civilians and promising to stem NRA violence. Consequently, by early 1987, the UPDA had come to phrase their national project in a language of human rights, democracy, and political inclusion, thereby addressing the symptoms of the national political crisis.[123] They called for the fulfillment of unfulfilled NRM promises of democracy and security in the north as well as the south, proposing a political resolution to the national crisis of the Acholi that would have resonance with lineage-based authorities and the population at large.

The UPDA's failure to score significant military victories and the government's exclusively military approach would ensure that the Acholi political crises would end up being further entrenched. The counterinsurgency prevented the development of responsible, experienced leadership on the local and national levels, instead opening the way for politically inexperienced armed groups to take the stage. Thus, as the UPDA failed to resolve the national crisis, the internal crisis erupted again.

THE HOLY SPIRIT MOVEMENT

The UPDA held together until the beginning of 1987, when it began to factionalize in response to several pressures.[124] In a climate of escalating violence, the UPDA had to step up coercion to ensure supplies of food and recruits,[125] and, as a result, the provisional alliance between lineage-based authorities and the UPDA began to break down. The internal social crisis began to make itself felt as the "unclean" young men—now with various factions of UPDA added to the ex-members of the UNLA—again challenged the lineage-based authorities' fragile power. In response, a new force emerged to attempt to mediate this internal crisis through combating the NRA occupation, as a female Acholi spirit medium, Alice Auma, known as Lakwena, proposed a resolution to these renewed internal and external threats. She attempted to resolve the internal crisis by mobilizing a discourse of cleansing that allowed her to assert authority over the UPDA, the ex-members of the UNLA, and Acholi civilians generally. With this cleansed force, eventually to be known as the Holy Spirit Movement (HSM), Lakwena intended to advance upon Kampala and overthrow the NRM government, establishing a new inclusive Uganda, cleansing the country of the violence that was plaguing it. The HSM was to resolve the internal and national crises through a discourse of healing, a project that would later have echoes in Kony's LRA.

Lakwena's project proposed to stabilize the fractured internal order through the creation of a wide constituency founded upon the articulation of a coherent Acholi ethnic identity. The place of Acholi lineage-based authorities within this project is somewhat unclear, but it appears to have been mixed and, among even those who did support her, tenuous. On the one hand, as Tim Allen argues, her spiritual discourse of cleansing presented a challenge to those lineage-based authorities who claimed the exclusive power to cleanse. Thus, by appealing to aspects of Christian imagery that were outside the control of such authorities, Lakwena trumped their claim to be the privileged representatives of the Acholi as an ethnic group and offered a route to cleansing for those ex-members of the UNLA and UPDA who did not want to submit to the authority of male elders.[126] She also could draw support from those who saw the elders as having lost their claim to legitimate authority because they had been unable to stem the violence wracking Acholi society. On the other hand, according to alternative accounts, the response from some lineage-based authorities was positive enough that they helped build Lakwena's significant popular support.[127] It is possible that these lineage-based authorities assisted the healer because they at first saw her, despite the challenge to patriarchal authority she represented, as a useful tool for disciplining the ex-members of the UNLA and UPDA and in calming the general insecurity in the region, thus setting the stage for the reassertion of their own authority. Lakwena also drew recruits from the War Mobilization Committees she established at the subcounty and village levels, which also helped fulfill supply and information functions. Eventually, Lakwena managed to assemble an army of 7,000–10,000 troops.[128] Once again, Acholi ethnicity was reconfirmed as the dominant discourse in which legitimate claims to authority were made as Lakwena presented herself as being able to combat the NRA as well as to cleanse the swelling ranks of impure Acholi and re-establish order within Acholiland, thus addressing the national and internal crises at once. This demonstrates how Acholi tradition or custom, which today is increasingly assumed to be the exclusive preserve of male elders and *rwodi*—an assumption promoted especially by foreign donors—has in fact always been a contested terrain of intergenerational, intergender, and intra-Acholi struggle.

Once her movement was established in Acholiland by late April 1987, Lakwena tried to forge a coalition with the UPDA under her authority. The UPDA's leadership refused, and, subsequently, the UPDA, fearful of losing its civilian base and access to resources, turned on the HSM.[129] Lakwena's forces counterattacked, and she overran a number of UPDA brigades, collecting guns and absorbing troops.[130] As the UPDA factionalized further, and more Holy Spirit movements under the command of other spirit mediums emerged (including the movement that took shape under the command of Kony, which would become the LRA), the fighting in Acholiland intensified between various rebel factions.[131]

The HSM was faced with a dilemma: it claimed to be the agent of a fundamental redemption of Acholiland from impure, violent Acholi armed groups, but it increasingly needed to depend upon violence against the Acholi to ensure its own survival.[132] In this context, Lakwena left Acholiland in a bid to take Kampala and bring about the national redemption she promised. In July 1987, Lakwena's HSM began moving east and south, following the course of the Nile through Lango and Teso. Because the HSM often eschewed traditional military means, they depended upon continuously high recruitment to compensate for high losses. As a result, the ethnic makeup of the HSM became increasingly heterogeneous, testament to the political appeal her movement had throughout the north and east of Uganda.[133] Indeed, the HSM found support in precisely those places where the NRA's arrival had been interpreted as an occupation instead of a liberation, and in places where the government had established RCs, Lakwena ordered the people not to cooperate with them.[134] The limit to this alliance was precisely the border between north and south. As the rebels made it within a few dozen miles of Kampala, they crossed into a southern area where the HSM was no longer seen as a liberator but, rather, as an invading northern army, threatening enough to motivate the peasantry to cooperate with the RCs and Local Defense Units (LDUs).[135] Within a couple of weeks, the HSM had disintegrated in the face of the combined NRA-LDU-civilian defense.[136]

After Lakwena had left Acholiland, violence there between the remaining rebel factions intensified further. Although Lakwena's forces had generally avoided violence against civilians, the fragmented UPDA and the splinters of the HSM terrorized each other's suspected civilian supporters. Additionally, once Lakwena had exhausted the supply of volunteers, those factions remaining had to step up forced recruitment. It was from this environment that Kony emerged. Although at first, Kony may have gained some support, albeit limited relative to Lakwena's, from lineage-based authorities,[137] he was generally confronted with a deficit of volunteers, a population unwilling to support continued violence, and a number of different opponents, many from within Acholiland itself. As a result, Kony had to rely on increased violence against civilians for his group's material and social survival.

In the eyes of the national government, Lakwena had demonstrated the dangerous potential for popular mobilization in Acholiland and throughout the north. Resolved not to let this support develop again, the NRA would, from then on, generally abandon the Acholi to rebel violence, letting rebel groups prey upon the civilian population as a kind of collective punishment by proxy, ensuring that the rebels did not gain civilian support but also doing little to build support among the Acholi population itself.[138] The Acholi were left without any clear leadership or agent of political change. None of the rebel factions had achieved dominance, and the government had only displayed its incapacity and unwillingness to provide protection. Acholi civilians were alienated from the rebels at the same time that they realized that they could not actively support the NRA against them. They were caught in the middle, prevented by the violence of each side from supporting the other.

THE LRA

Two developments took place in late 1987 and early 1988 that would significantly change the character of violence in Acholiland. First, the UPDA dissolved, as those who had not joined Alice Lakwena accepted the government's offer of amnesty, signed on to the Pece Peace Agreement with the NRM in June 1988, or joined Joseph Kony's forces.[139] However, Kony was excluded from the Pece peace talks; setting a precedent that it has often followed since, the Ugandan government had begun negotiations with Kony in early 1988, only to sabotage them at a key moment.[140] The result was threefold: Kony's force was strengthened and became the sole viable rebel group in Acholiland; the incipient LRA appears to have come to see the ex-members of the UPDA who had accepted amnesty and been incorporated into the NRA as having betrayed them;[141] and, judging from later statements by the LRA leadership, Kony and other commanders seem to have become intensely suspicious of government peace initiatives. The Ugandan government, meanwhile, stepped up its violence against civilians, launching a wave of forced displacement in October 1988.[142]

The second development was the establishment of the RC system and the creation of LDUs in Acholiland. RCs had first been introduced into parts of Acholiland immediately following the NRA's occupation, but violence prevented their consolidation until late 1987. In the interim, a significant national debate had transpired over the RC system as it had been set up in the south, specifically around the question of whom the RCs effectively served: the state, the NRM, or the people?[143] In Acholiland, however, there was little question about the function of the RCs. As one critic declared, they "are more or less extraneous to the immediate popular interest and are almost entirely organs of the NRM's/state's local expression and not of the people."[144] Instead of fulfilling their mandated role of providing a check upon the NRA, they facilitated the NRA's counterinsurgency through surveillance and control. To ensure their cooperation, the government frequently purged the RCs of those whom it believed to be sympathetic with the rebels and accused RCs who opposed their violent tactics of being rebel supporters.[145] Furthermore, as the government began organizing LDUs in Gulu in February 1988, mostly from ex-members of the UNLA or the UPDA chosen by the RCs, the RC system became an integral part of the state's military apparatus.[146] The result was that, in Acholiland, the reform of local government created an undemocratic local administration embodied in a hierarchy of agents serving an ethnically exclusive central state. The RCs and LDUs effectively localized the state down to the village level, and this diffuse security apparatus became, in eyes of some, the tool of the state, the NRM, the NRA, and the south, all at once. This meant that the ongoing national crisis—the continued exclusion of legitimate Acholi leadership from the national government and that government's lack of accountability to the Acholi—was localized as well.

These developments—the switch by many UPDA to the NRA, and more importantly the apparent insertion of the foreign occupier into the heart of Acholi society by way of RCs and LDUs—provided Joseph Kony with the opportunity to propose a new and violent resolution to the internal and national political crises. Specifically, the internal crisis merged with the national crisis, as the former was rephrased in terms of the latter, and the external enemy, the NRM, was transposed to the inside of Acholi society in the form of government collaborators, the new internal enemy. Like Lakwena, Kony proposed the cleansing of an internal enemy. However, in Kony's conception, it was not the ex-members of the UNLA to be cleansed, but rather the administrative and security apparatus of the NRM, represented by RCs, LDUs, and others. Internal order would be re-established through the elimination of this internalized external enemy, at the same time that the national crisis would be resolved by eliminating NRM power. The discourse of Acholi ethnicity remained dominant internally because the division between government collaborators and LRA supporters was articulated by the LRA as a difference between "false" and "true" Acholi, which, in turn, opened the way for extreme anticivilian violence against those accused of being false Acholi.

Each of the three rebel movements had proposed different ways of re-establishing internal order by forging alliances between different Acholi factions or a constituency against the external enemy, the NRM. Each used the urgent need to resolve the national crisis and halt state violence as an opportunity to resolve the internal crisis in their favor by laying claim to Acholi ethnic identity. The UPDA had posited an alliance between themselves (that is, the very social faction whose presence had precipitated the internal crisis), lineage-based authorities, and the peasantry in order to combat the NRA. Then, Lakwena had founded her authority upon the claim to resolve what she framed as the key internal cleavage—between the unclean UPDA/ex-members of the UNLA and the Acholi community—through cleansing, and to lead that new purified community against the external enemy. Kony, however, posited a new, more fundamental internal cleavage, one between the genuine Acholi whom he would lead against the government, and those Acholi who had gone over to the government. Because the north-south divide had been imported within Acholi society, to fight the south, part of Acholi society would have to be fought as well. Therefore, anticivilian violence came to be the privileged tool for carrying out this political program, and so much of Kony's violence was intended to destroy those he suspected of supporting the government or being part of the RCs and LDUs, and later of the Arrow Brigades and Homeguards. Kony turned his violence on the internal enemy as the manifestation of the external enemy, on the local state as the representative of the central state. Because that local state used Acholi agents, LRA violence would, from then on, take on an intra-Acholi visage; because violence was being used against those represented as foreigners, as traitors, as non-Acholi Acholi, it could take on a relatively unrestrained character.

Violence was not only used in a targeted fashion against suspected government collaborators, however. Indeed, Kony's conception of an absolute break dividing the Acholi between those who supported the government and those who supported the LRA did not reflect reality, for although the government and the rebels each certainly had supporters, the bulk of the Acholi were stuck between the two sides, unwilling or unable to support either.[147] Therefore, Kony's forces, in a sense, also used violence to try to make their conception of a polarized society a reality. Violence was turned against those who, in the LRA's conception, needed to be convinced to support the rebels. The LRA's campaign of anticivilian violence, therefore, had two aspects, one specifically targeting suspected government supporters and the other widely targeting the civilian population in general in order to bring it under the rebels' authority.[148] Often, the two would be part of the same operation. In early March 1988, for example, Kony and his forces launched a vicious attack on Koch Goma, where a significant contingent of LDUs had been formed, first attacking the LDUs and then burning huts and hacking to death a number of people who refused to join the rebels.[149] Later, Kony's forces would focus their violence on other government-created militia, such as the Arrow Brigades formed during Operation North in 1991. Kony's effort to resolve the internal and national political crises at the same time was to be carried out through violence, and the LRA's extreme anticivilian violence can be understood as an attempt to eradicate the south from inside Acholi society as well as to build support among the peasantry, to force them onto the rebels' side and forge a genuine Acholi under their leadership.

As its violence escalated, the LRA appears increasingly to have based its claim to represent the Acholi, not on what little support lineage-based authorities may have still provided, but on its own claim to spiritual authority that transcended that of the lineage-based authorities. Building on Lakwena's discourse of cleansing, the LRA have employed a religious language to establish the legitimacy of their claim to represent the Acholi.[150] This discourse of cleansing doubtlessly helped supersede the lineage-based authorities' claim to be the genuine representatives of the Acholi, and it provided a further moral sanction for the distinction between true and false Acholi and for the use of extreme anticivilian violence. However, despite certain apparently millenarian statements by LRA commanders (for example, that they were going to kill all Acholi, leaving only 10,000 who would be the basis for a new, purified tribe[151]), the LRA's use of a religious language was more often than not used to build support on a mundane level and so should not be overemphasized. For one thing, the religious discourse has waxed and waned in importance, as the LRA has often framed its goals exclusively in a secular political language.[152] Furthermore, the LRA has, at times, deferred to the authority of Acholi lineage-based leaders, recognizing their role as the arbiters of internal Acholi order. Finally, the LRA's use of violence, it seems, has never been motivated by millenarianism to the extent that it contradicted the political goal of building support for itself and destroying government support—for example, it has never tried to follow through on threats to eradicate the Acholi en masse. The religious language thus appears to have played its most significant role in maintaining support for the LRA leadership among the LRA's fighters. In any case, the LRA represents an attempt to articulate a coherent Acholi ethnic identity and resolve the internal political crisis that emerged from the fragmentation of that Acholi identity by using violence against the national enemy—in both its external and internal manifestation—and thus to resolve the national crisis at the same time.

As Kony's forces stepped up their violence, the population remained unprotected, afraid to report on rebel activity, and NRA violence escalated in turn.[153] Despite the fact that the District Administrator, the Resistance Councilors, and Resident Minister Betty Bigombe all seemed aware of NRA abuses, there was general silence on the issue and retaliation against those who did speak out. The political crisis in Acholiland, the deficit of authoritative leadership, deepened considerably by 1991. As one writer explained, the Acholi "have no one to speak for them. Even the Churches which are supposed to be the voices of the voiceless have become silent now."[154] This pattern of intense violence against civilians lasted in

Acholiland until late 1989, a period that also saw the first episodes of mass forced displacement; As one newspaper reported, the dominant feeling was that "both the Holy Spirit [Joseph Kony] and the NRA are no longer fighting each other but [instead] . . . the civilians."[155]

4. The Entrenchment of the War

OPERATION NORTH AND THE FAILURE OF PEACE TALKS: 1991–1994

Late 1989 and early 1990 saw a period of relative calm, and NRM officials declared the war over.[156] In mid-1990, however, there was an upsurge in violence that continued into 1991.[157] At that point, facing criticism in the south for premature declarations of victory and, according to Behrend, World Bank funding possibly having been made contingent on the re-establishment of peace and security in the north, the NRA went on the offensive, in what was perhaps its first serious attempt to win the war, ending the "peaceful coexistence."[158] In mid-March, a "house-to-house-cordon-and-search operation for remnants of the UDCA" (the name Kony's forces had adopted), was launched, expanding into Operation North on March 27, 1991, when the NRA ended all road transport across the Nile.[159] A few days later, the NRA cut off communications with the north, imposed a media blackout, and seized all radios in the region.[160] Once Acholiland was isolated, the NRA proceeded on two fronts. First, anyone opposing the operation was labeled a rebel collaborator, and dozens of Acholi political leaders were arrested, including Resistance Council members and district officials in the north and national political leaders in Kampala, most notably three Acholi members of the National Resistance Council, Daniel Omara Atubo, Zachary Olum, and Irene Apiu Julu.[161] Second, beginning in Gulu Town and moving out from there to the villages, the NRA conducted a massive screening operation, rounding up and interrogating tens of thousands in an attempt to root out rebels and collaborators.[162] The NRA's brutality in the course of the screening operation still reverberates among the Acholi. Newspapers from the time give details on abuses of detainees, killings, torture, looting, and rapes,[163] and, in the course of my work in Acholiland, I have had the locations of what are said to be mass graves dating from this period pointed out to me.

Museveni and Bigombe categorically denied the accusations of abuse and politically motivated arrests. (To convincingly demonstrate the falsity of the accusations, Museveni pointed out that the minister who had made allegations of human rights abuses against the NRA was on trial for sedition!)[164] The NRA was sanguine as usual: in May, Lt. Gen. David Tinyefuza, in charge of Operation North, labeled it an unqualified success, and Bigombe announced that 3,000 rebels had been caught in Kitgum alone.[165] Bigombe spearheaded the most significant aspect of Operation North: the formation of a new, expanded system of militias known as Arrow Groups to assist the NRA in fighting the rebels. Once journalists were allowed back in, they found that almost all subcounties had Arrow Groups.[166]

Thousands of men, armed with arrows, spears, machetes, and sticks, were mobilized against the rebels with the support of the RCs.[167] The Arrow Groups, reaching much further than the LDUs ever had, were seen by the rebels as an intensified grassroots paramilitary extension of the NRM government.

There is controversy over the degree to which members of the Arrow Groups were forcibly recruited; it is probable that many civilians would have been glad to try to end the violence by participating in the government militias, whereas others would have refused to participate in government initiatives, given the vicious campaign the NRA was undertaking at the time.[168] Either way, for the first time, the Acholi were mobilized on a massive scale in the war effort. This development was short-lived, however. Without warning, the government apparently decided that the Arrow Groups could take care of the rebels alone. They abandoned the mobilized Acholi at the very moment that the LRA stepped up attacks on militia members and their families.[169] The NRA left the Acholi unprotected against an unprecedented wave of atrocities, as Kony's forces began their first massive campaign of collective punishment, including maiming, as they cut off the hands, lips, or ears of those suspected to be working with the Arrow Brigades. Kony's forces went so far as to send a letter to Bigombe announcing that she had "brought death to the Acholi" by telling people to rise up against the LRA.[170]

Bigombe, for her part, further encouraged the creation of the Arrow Groups and tried to justify the abandonment of the militia, arguing that it was the people's duty to clean up the rebels, and so the NRA could now "relax."[171] Tinyefuza agreed and stated that NRA's job was done and that those few rebels remaining would be handled by the Arrow Groups.[172] The dimensions of the blunder were soon apparent. Operation North ended in late July, and by the end of that month the massacres and atrocities had begun.[173] Some Acholi elders and resistance councilors pleaded for the Arrow Brigades to be better armed, but the NRA refused to supply more than a handful of rifles.[174] In September, the *Weekly Topic* asserted that the rebels still numbered between 1,000 and 1,500, concluding correctly that even the cordon-and-search aspect of Operation North had been a failure.[175] By October 1991, as one newspaper reported, "all divisions are in total chaos."[176]

The reason the government abandoned the Arrow Brigades is not clear. Probably it was a strategic miscalculation influenced by the government's impatience to declare victory and to end the military campaign. Those who tend to invoke an NRA/M conspiracy attribute the desertion to a plan to wipe out the Acholi using Kony as a tool.[177] Alternatively, it could be an example of the government's prolonging the existence of the rebels for its own purposes, as it would more apparently do from 1994 onward. In any case, the withdrawal of NRA regulars marked the end of the government's last attempt for a decade to finish off the rebels militarily. At the same time, the eradication of independent Acholi leadership under the guise of eliminating rebel collaborators—accelerated during Operation North—further deepened the political crisis of the Acholi.

Atrocities by the rebels continued unabated until early 1992, but from mid-1992 until late 1993 rebel violence waned. This downturn signaled a new détente between the rebels and the population. The rebels had demonstrated to the Acholi that the government would not or could not protect them and, therefore, that mobilization against the rebels was pointless. In response, the Acholi disbanded the Arrow Groups, and the rebels scaled down their attacks. Violence ebbed to the point that, when Bigombe began peace talks with the rebels in late 1993, they were moving freely in Gulu Town. With the reduction in violence, the Acholi came to welcome the NRA's refusal to pursue the rebels; as one newspaper reported, "The NRA is mostly confined to grass hut barracks in trading centers. Civilians say this is more effective than having mobile NRA units who leave civilians vulnerable to the wrath of the rebels when they move on and who can also misbehave out of the sight of the responsible commanders."[178] In short, by mid-1992, civilians had been included in the "peaceful coexistence" that had transpired between the NRA and the rebels before Operation North. Many hoped that the peace talks between Bigombe and Kony could take advantage of this peace and end the violence for good.

The peace talks, however, were a disaster.[179] After months of negotiations, in February 1994, Kony asked for six months to gather his troops and leave the bush and for a UN observer team to oversee the process.[180] Museveni, in response, publicly announced that Kony had seven days to come out, or he would be annihilated.[181] Kony withdrew from the talks. Museveni declared that Kony was "not a big problem" and sent reinforcements, while the LRA stepped up attacks.[182] As usual, civilians bore the brunt of the onslaught, with one reporter noting "astounding revelations of bizarre excesses by the NRA and the rebels."[183]

The failed peace talks were only the latest symptom of the NRM's local political failure in Acholiland. It had failed to promote democratic reform of the local government, instead establishing a new undemocratic local state through the RCs. Democratization of the local state in Acholiland would not hinge on a de-ethnicization of that state, as it had in the south in the 1980s. Rather, local reform would be a matter of allowing the RCs to be democratically constituted, instead of using them to entrench NRM power at the local level. The NRM's national political failure was also apparent, as it continued to refuse to incorporate genuinely representative Acholi leaders into the national government and had prevented a new political middle class from emerging or returning from the diaspora.

Adamantly denying its political failure in Acholiland, the NRM government, after the peace talks debacle, focused blame on Sudan's role in the conflict. As discussed at greater length later, the Ugandan conflict also became incorporated into the U.S. effort against the Khartoum regime. The United States was providing aid through Uganda to the Sudan People's Liberation Army (SPLA), the southern Sudanese rebel group led by John Garang. In response, and also as part of its regular "militia strategy" against the SPLA,[184] Khartoum began providing increased funding to the LRA. The limited funding the Ugandan rebels had been receiving[185] escalated dramatically, in particular through the pro-Khartoum SPLA-Nasir faction of William Nyuon.[186] The LRA suddenly had better uniforms than the NRA[187] and were often better armed.[188] With his effort to leave the bush stymied, Kony set up permanent bases in southern Sudan in late 1994[189] and occasionally clashed there with Garang's SPLA.[190]

Ever since 1994, the Ugandan government has used the Sudan factor to explain the duration of the war.[191] However, the escalated hostilities in 1994 were not caused solely by Sudanese support. Indeed, the rebels had managed for years without Sudanese support, and, considering the NRA's permissive attitude toward looting, probably could have managed for years more without it. The Sudanese scapegoat allowed the NRM to further demonize the LRA through stories of abducted Ugandan children sold into slavery in Sudan while diverting attention from its own role in prolonging the conflict.[192] It had become apparent that certain sectors within the state wanted the LRA to continue to exist. The war had begun in 1986 in the context of the fear among the NRM that the Acholi were bent on recapturing power. By the early 1990s, however, other interests within the state and army had also emerged around the continuation of the war, as addressed in the next section.

THE ROAD TO THE CAMPS

After the failure of the 1994 peace talks, the LRA once more stepped up its anticivilian violence, concentrating it against suspected government supporters, especially the Resistance Councils.[193] The LRA combined its violence with an information campaign in the villages, explaining that it was Museveni and his advisers who were to blame for sabotaging the talks.[194] In its statements and manifestos, the LRA laid out a political agenda that included demanding the end of the war through negotiations, the national political integration of the Acholi on an equal basis with the rest of the country, an end to government violence against the Acholi, reparations for lost cattle, free elections, and even multipartyism.[195] The LRA's political engagement went so far as to declare a ceasefire for the 1996 presidential elections,[196] conduct political rallies, declare that LRA would participate in the elections, and encourage the Acholi to vote for Museveni's opponent, Paul Ssemogerere, a supporter of peace negotiations.[197]

However, despite the articulation of a political program that resonated with many of the concerns of the Acholi, the LRA never was able to rally sufficient support so as to pose a military threat to the government. For one thing, government violence made supporting the LRA too costly, and the LRA was unable to provide protection against government retaliation. Also, the LRA failed to win victories or to hold territory, which convinced many Acholi that they were not a viable military force. Third, and most important, the violence of the LRA against civilians thoroughly alienated many Acholi. From the perspective of the LRA, the parameters of government collaboration among civilians were uncertain, so the LRA tended to cast too wide a net with its violence against suspected government supporters. As a result, many people felt unfairly targeted, which became particularly relevant with the formation of the camps. At the same time, because of the wider context of the violence—namely, the government's counterinsurgency and the LRA's inability to prove its viability—attempts by the LRA to build support through the use of violence generally came to naught. As a result, the LRA's violence was the main obstacle in the way of its acquisition of significant popular support; indeed, many Acholi, especially the youth, made it clear that if it were not for Kony's program of violence, they very well might have supported the LRA.[198]

At the end of 1995, there was a series of highly publicized attacks by the SPLA on LRA positions in Sudan.[199] By December, Bigombe and Museveni had again declared the definitive end of the LRA.[200] This euphoria lasted only until February 1996,[201] when Kony's troops re-entered from Sudan.[202] The Ugandan press went on the offensive against Museveni and those who had declared victory over the LRA.[203] As violence escalated dramatically in March, Museveni's response was again to reject peace talks and to promise that "we shall deal with them by mid-April."[204] Violence did not abate, as the LRA executed several massacres to prove their continued viability, and the Uganda People's Defence Force (UPDF) (the post-1995 successor to the NRA) employed helicopter gunships against rebels and civilians.[205] There was an LRA ceasefire in the run up to the 1996 elections, but with Museveni's victory, Kony called off the ceasefire and again stepped up his attacks.[206] Museveni responded by sending Salim Saleh to the north, who announced the inception of a new offensive and then total war against the LRA.[207]

Once more facing pressure over his premature announcements of the war's end, Museveni turned to a new strategy. In September 1996, the UPDF began forcibly displacing and interning the Acholi in what it euphemistically termed "protected villages" or "protected camps."[208] The internment camps' total population stood at a few hundred thousand by the end of 1996 and grew to over one million by 2004.[209] Although many government officials and members of Local Councils (LCs) (the Resistance Councils had been renamed Local Councils in the 1995 Constitution) took refuge in the camps for their own safety, the majority of the Acholi went to the camps in response to a wide-scale campaign of forced displacement by the UPDF involving intimidation, murder, and the bombing and burning of villages.[210] After the formation of the camps, the UPDF announced that anyone found outside of the camps would be considered a rebel and killed.

At its inception, displacement into internment camps could have made sense within a counterinsurgency military strategy since clearing out the countryside would cut off rebel resources and give free rein to UPDF mobile units. One UPDF officer put forth a slightly different but still militarily reasonable (although morally dubious) explanation for the camps, comparing them to the bait with which to catch the LRA: "The depopulation of the villages removes the soft targets and logistics for the survival of the rebels. They would lack food, information, and youth to abduct and people to kill. Desperation would drive them to attack the Army in the camps. That will be their end."[211]

However, the possibility that the camps were part of a military strategy was quickly belied by the UPDF's actions: the army failed to protect the "protected camps."[212] In fact, with its military attention increasingly focused on Zaire,[213] once the camps were formed, the UPDF began withdrawing soldiers from the north, leaving the Acholi unprotected by the regular army. Even the few UPDF soldiers who did remain rarely responded to rebel incursions.[214] In place of the UPDF, the government accelerated a program, begun the previous year, of training homeguards, again under the direction of Bigombe.[215] By February 1995, up to 12,000 Acholi civilians had been given basic training and arms.[216] Relative to the threat faced, Homeguard numbers were dismally inadequate,[217] but, despite this, the government used them as an excuse not to provide regular military protection to the camps.[218] The failure to protect the camps provides even more evidence suggesting that the Ugandan government had little interest in defeating the LRA.

Devoid of protection, the camps did not serve a military purpose for the Ugandan government.[219] Instead, as I explain in the next chapter, the camps' political consequence was to prevent Acholi political organization that might hold the UPDF accountable, demand the end of the war, or provide a base of opposition to the government. Whereas in the late 1980s, anticivilian violence by the government was in response to the fear that the Acholi were the support base for the rebels, by the mid-1990s, a reversal took place and the accusation of being a rebel collaborator became a convenient way of eliminating independent political organization in the north. Anticivilian violence came to be used, not just to prevent the population from building political ties with the rebels, but also to prevent the population from organizing to demand an end to the war.

Displacement into camps also led to increased rebel violence. Like the Arrow Brigades before them, the undertrained and underarmed Homeguards became an easy target for the LRA and incited the LRA to further retaliation. Displacement made the parameters of government support even more uncertain, as the LRA frequently accused all those in the camps of being government collaborators and attacked civilians they found outside the camp. The LRA consistently demanded the dismantling of the camps and the return of the Acholi to their lands, at times launching intense attacks on the camps, burning them down, and calling on people to go back to their villages.[220] In one case, over 200 civilians were killed in Atiak in April 1995; after defeating the Homeguard, the LRA announced, "You Acholi have refused to support us. We shall now teach you a lesson."[221] Indeed, the LRA would regularly defeat the Homeguard and then punish the civilians they were guarding, while the UPDF refused to intervene.[222] It appears that the formation of the camps made resource acquisition, if anything, easier for the rebels. Indeed, there was so little protection and the rebels would loot and abduct so easily that some Acholi suggested giving food and medicine to the rebels so that they would stop looting.[223]

The politics of the camps and the role of aid agencies in sustaining them is considered in the next chapter.

NRM POWER AND THE CONTINUATION OF THE WAR

On the national level, by the mid-1990s the NRM had consolidated its power over the re-built Ugandan state.[224] Militarily, it had, through a combination of military force and buying off rebel leaders, dealt with most of the 27 or so rebel groups that had arisen in the late 1980s.[225] (The LRA, of course, remained.) Legally, the NRM consolidated power by way of its 1995 constitution, which laid the foundation for Museveni's next two terms and for the "Movement political system," a "no-party democracy" based supposedly on individual merit and devoid of sectarianism.[226] Financially, the NRM had obtained regular access to significant levels of foreign aid, aid that, as will be discussed later, was used to fund the NRM's political patronage machine. The core group of elites around Museveni had consolidated, controlling key positions in the military, the government, the NRM, and the economy, and they were often tied to the president through family, friendship, or tribe.

Understanding the centrality of this core of elites to the power of the Ugandan state helps clarify the political function of the war in Uganda's national and international politics and helps explain why the war lasted as long as it did. For most of the duration of the conflict, the dominant argument used to explain why the war had dragged on was that the Ugandan government, despite its good faith efforts, had simply been unable to defeat the LRA. The government and donors tended to blame Sudanese support to the LRA: according to Major Shaban Bantariza, former UPDF spokesman, the NRA had finished off the LRA by 1992, but the latter was then resuscitated by Khartoum.[227] More critical observers focused on the incapacity of the UPDF, suffering from a lack of training, poor morale, involvement in Congo, and, especially, corruption, to explain the inability to defeat the northern rebels.[228] In response to such criticism, Museveni tended to blame the donors themselves for Uganda's military incapacity because of the restrictions they tried to place on Uganda's defense budget.

However, evidence points to the possibility that the prolongation of the war was not due to the government's inability to defeat the LRA but rather to its unwillingness to do so. Although the Sudan factor doubtlessly made the military campaign more difficult, the massive diversion of military resources and troops to the Congo and the government's permissive attitude toward corruption also clearly contributed to the persistence of the conflict. The military would fail to follow up on victories and fail to engage the rebels both in their overall strategy and in individual skirmishes. Peace talks, moreover, were repeatedly undermined by members of the Ugandan military and government. With these facts in mind, some analysts and critics of the Ugandan government have attributed the continuation of the war not to Uganda's lack of military capacity, but to its intention to maintain a contained war in the north for its own political purposes.

Possible political benefits of the war for the Ugandan government can be found on a number of levels. First, on the local level, many Acholi argue that the government maintained the war as revenge for Acholi violence against the civilian population of Luwero during the NRA's civil war, or that it is part of the "grass-hopper" approach, letting Acholi rebel groups survive so that the Acholi would kill themselves off. Whatever the merit of those arguments, it is certain that the war prevented any effective political organization among the Acholi that might have challenged Museveni's hold on power.[229] If this was the case, the government had placed itself in a bind: the longer the war continued, the more antigovernment resentment built up among the Acholi and the greater potential challenge they posed to the government, thus the more they had to be violently contained.

Maintaining the conflict also helped the Ugandan government maintain support throughout the south. The LRA was cast as the northern enemy, a representative of previous regimes waiting to return and visit its savagery on the south. As Andrew Mwenda says, "the war became an important political instrument to literally blackmail the people in the south to support the NRM."[230] It provided a convenient way to disqualify and to shut down political opposition, as the war against LRA "terrorists" established "a crisis environment that enables the government to justify measures that would be unacceptable in different circumstances."[231] Political dissent was silenced in the name of counter-terrorism:[232] for example, vocal Acholi Members of Parliament were regularly accused of being "friends of the terrorists" by Museveni himself or by other members of the Movement government.[233] The treason trial of presidential contender Kizza Besigye, in which the government persistently tried to establish Besigye's connections with the LRA, was a particularly glaring example.[234]

The war was also important in terms of allowing Museveni to consolidate control over the most important foundation of his government's power—the military. The war justified the continued expansion of the Ugandan military and its presence in northern Uganda.[235] On a financial level, the petty corruption and war profiteering engaged in by military officers served the purpose of giving them a stake in the Museveni government. Profits could be gained by maintaining dead or missing soldiers on the payroll and pocketing their wages (the "ghost soldiers" phenomenon),[236] looting resources in southern Sudan, and land-grabbing in northern Uganda.[237] However, the profits to be reaped in the northern Uganda war were minimal compared with the stakes in the wars in Sierra Leone, Angola, or elsewhere.[238] The importance of the war to the government's power was therefore less through the decentralized profiteering it enabled among officers, and more a result of the importance of the defense budget to the NRM government. Defense is the only part of the Ugandan budget without significant donor—or parliamentary—oversight, and, thus, it represents the pot of money that the government can most easily tap into in order to fund its political patronage machine.[239] Corruption within defense spending thus plays a fundamental role. This form of centralized corruption may be threatened by the decentralized corruption represented by lower-level war profiteering, such as through ghost soldiers, which may help explain President Museveni's occasional public efforts to end such practices.

This points to the intricate relationship between the donors and the power of the Museveni regime. As will be addressed in detail in the next section, the continuation of the war provided the means through which Museveni maintained discretionary control over the defense budget and continually expanded it despite donors' protests.[240] Museveni has been particularly successful in tying his war against the LRA to U.S. interests in the region by serving as a conduit to the SPLA in southern Sudan, framing his war against the LRA as part of the War on Terror[241] and, most recently, expanding the UPDF presence throughout central Africa in the name of providing protection for civilians against the LRA. As a result, the United States has put pressure on other donors to allow Museveni to continue increasing military expenditure.[242] Most donors, not wanting to damage Uganda's reputation as a model of development, have tended to conveniently ignore the conflict.[243] In short, the Ugandan army's economic interests, the government's political interests, and American, European, and World Bank interests converged to create a situation in which none of the players saw any benefit in ending the war. All the parties with political or economic power—Museveni, the UPDF, the United States, the other donor governments and institutions—aligned themselves so that the continuation of the war either served their purposes or, at least, did them no significant damage— the price for which was paid by Uganda's civilians.

5. The International Context: Neoliberalism and Counterterrorism

Despite depending on donor funds for over half its budget during certain periods (and a total of $31 billion since 1986),[244] and being unable to survive more than six months without donor funding,[245] the Ugandan government managed to divert a significant portion of its budget to defense over donor protests, invade and occupy eastern Democratic Republic of Congo (DRC) with devastating consequences, come to the brink of war with Rwanda, viciously shut down political opposition, rig elections, amend the constitution so as to allow Museveni to be president for life, engage in massive and systemic corruption, and fail to make a serious effort to end the war in northern Uganda either militarily or through negotiations. This situation challenges the predominant view of African states' status in the post-Cold War era, according to which, as one analyst puts it, "The world's poorest countries, particularly in sub-Saharan Africa, have seen the substance of their sovereignty almost disappear."[246] Whereas African states are often thought to lose power—and especially discretionary power—in the era of neoliberal conditionality, the case of Uganda shows the need to amend this view in the age of sovereignty as responsibility.

Although losing control over much of its budget and facing the need to meet donor demands for austerity, privatization, and decentralization, the core group of elites at the center of the Ugandan state has been able to steer these foreign-driven projects to their own political and economic advantage and to build significant unaccountable power through those means.[247] This has been realized through three distinct, but overlapping, tendencies. First, Uganda, often personified in President Museveni, has managed to cultivate its reputation as a success story of neoliberal economics, good governance, and AIDS policy—Uganda's reputation as a "responsible" state—in order to silence donor criticism over certain less savory aspects of the regime's policies, including massive diversion to the military budget. The war in northern Uganda played an essential role in this process of building Uganda's reputation. Second, the Ugandan military-political-business elite has aligned its agenda with the U.S. agenda in the region, most starkly visible in the U.S. support provided to Uganda as part of the War on Terror. The result is the traditional double standard of U.S. foreign policy: while it speaks the rhetoric of democracy, it continues to fund authoritarian client states that serve U.S. interests in Africa. Third, the very nature of donor-imposed policies and reforms is that they require a group of unaccountable state elites in order to be pushed through. Thus, this empowered group of unaccountable elites, the tools of often supposedly liberal interventions, can use that newfound capacity to serve their own agendas in ways that can end up blatantly contradicting the stated objectives of donor reforms.

UGANDA'S REPUTATION

Uganda's reputation is tied strongly to Museveni himself.[248] By the mid-1990s, President Museveni, along with Presidents Laurent Kabila of DRC, Paul Kagame of Rwanda, Meles Zenawi of Ethiopia, and Isaias Afwerki of Eritrea, had been picked by President Clinton as one of the "new leaders of Africa" who would lead the "new African renaissance sweeping the continent."[249] Museveni was singled out as a "beacon of hope" by Secretary of State Madeleine Albright,[250] and has cultivated close personal relations with a number of European politicians. The United States in particular has been important in maintaining donor support for Museveni, and, despite occasional reservations expressed by individuals within the U.S. administration or Congress, Museveni has managed to retain important political support from significant sections of the U.S. establishment.[251] A statement on the United States Agency for International Development (USAID) web site epitomizes Uganda's international image: "Uganda has been a model in the fight against HIV/ AIDS, poverty reduction, and economic reform, and is a strong ally in the war against terrorism."[252]

However, the strength of Museveni's personality only goes so far, and two other factors have boosted Uganda's reputation and made it easier to divert significant funding to the military: Uganda's supposedly just war against the LRA and its embrace of neoliberal restructuring. As to the first, The LRA's rebellion is widely seen as an exemplar of incomprehensible African barbarism and is framed in unambiguous moral terms. This "official discourse," as Finnström calls it, has consistently downplayed, if not ignored, government violence, while focusing on the LRA's brutality, in particular its violence against children.[253] In most accounts the rebel group is, in a word, bizarre, and LRA violence simply defies understanding. Media reports tell of a rebel army of abducted children led by a self-proclaimed spirit medium in an attempt to overthrow the government of Uganda, using violence against their own people without any apparent reason. These accounts purport to sum up LRA motivations in the endlessly iterated declaration that "the rebels have no clear political agenda but have said they want the country governed in accordance with the Christian Ten Commandments."[254] Uganda, as a "responsible" state in need of assistance to defeat an absolutely evil, criminal, terrorist organization, thus avoids having to be accountable for the consequences of the support it receives—any criticism of the joint Ugandan-international effort against the LRA is condemned as complicity in the violence itself.

Uganda's reputation among donors has also been ensured by its image as a success story of economic neoliberalism. This has played an important role in helping the Ugandan government ensure that any donor criticism of its human rights record or its militarization will be short-lived and that Uganda will be able to continue to use donor funding at its own discretion. Museveni's willingness to subject Uganda to neoliberal orthodoxy has been a result of his political pragmatism. Immediately after taking power, the NRM was hesitant to accept IMF or World Bank loans on account of the strict conditionalities attached to them.[255] However, faced with a desperate need for foreign exchange and unable to acquire it from the Soviet bloc or Arab states, the NRM government accepted the lenders' conditionalities and received an IDA economic recovery credit of SDR 50.9 million and an African Facility credit of Special Drawing Rights (SDR) 18.8 million in late 1987.[256] Since then, Uganda has been the regular recipient of increasing multilateral and bilateral aid from donors to help with the process of economic reform.[257]

The result has been that, measured by the international financial institutions' favored standard of macroeconomic growth rates, for many years after 1987 Uganda saw significant economic development, featuring an impressive 6.5 percent annual growth.[258] This put Uganda at the top of the World Bank's list of successful cases of neoliberal economic development in Africa.[259]

> When the NRM assumed power in 1986, Uganda's standing with the international donor community was very low, because of its long record of economic mismanagement and human rights abuses. However, it established fresh credentials with the launch of its Economic Recovery Programme in 1987, backed by a two-year structural adjustment facility with the IMF of SDR69m (US$89m). During the following decade Uganda built up a reputation for financial discipline and economic competence that was second to none among less-developed countries, and further arrangements with the IMF were made in the late 1980s and throughout the 1990s.[260]

There are several facts, however, that cast doubt on the accuracy of Uganda's presumed status as a model of development. First, there is a question of whether the growth rates are due to economic reforms or are the unsustainable epiphenomenon of the extremely high levels of foreign aid enjoyed by Uganda. As the *Economist Intelligence Unit* states,

> The trade balance has traditionally posted a large deficit, and this has increased gradually since the National Resistance Movement (NRM) came to power, reaching nearly US$700m in 2003—an indication of the extent to which Uganda continues to attract donor assistance to fund its import bill.[261]

Moreover,

> The remarkable economic recovery that has been achieved since 1986 would not have been possible without substantial injections of foreign aid. Aid has been essential for the long-term rehabilitation of infrastructure and productive resources, for new development projects, and for short-term balance-of-payments support.[262]

A similar concern is voiced by William Reno, who writes that "creditors present Uganda's export performance as evidence that policies stressing poverty reduction through economic growth via increased trade and investment really work in very poor countries,"[263] when, in fact, increased export numbers are the result, not of sustainable economic restructuring, but of resources—especially gold—looted from the DRC by the UPDF.[264] Thus, he argues, it is not economic reform that has led to Uganda's high growth rate but rather foreign aid and war-related commerce. Ugandan economist Jossy Bibangambah points out what he calls the "Ugandan paradox": "on the one hand there is impressive economic performance and on the other there is deepening abject poverty, human depravation, vulnerability and inadequate social services," in short, the contradiction between "macro-level performance and micro-level realities."[265] These microlevel realities are all the more jarring when regional discrepancies are taken into account. Indeed, the north of Uganda has seen a significant increase in poverty since the early 1990s, even as poverty was decreasing or remaining stable in the rest of the country. By 1999, 65 percent of those in the north were under the poverty line, three times as high as in the central region.[266]

Questions over the reality of Uganda's economic growth are generally ignored by the international financial institutions and the donor community, as they focus exclusively on high GDP growth rates and do not look into the source of those figures. In this way, donors have found in Uganda the model of development in Africa they need to prove the efficacy of their policies. As Reno puts it, "Creditors... claim Uganda as a seemingly successful HIPC [Heavily Indebted Poor Country] client that can be used to set a higher performance standard for other countries included in this programme. 'If Uganda can do it, no other government has an excuse.'"[267]

In the words of Sam Tindifa, the director of the Human Rights and Peace Center at Makerere University, "Museveni has been a guinea pig for the World Bank and the International Monetary Fund. Of course no one will say it is not working, it will dent their success story, and they have to have a success story."[268]

Museveni and the elite around him recognized that the donors had staked their own reputations on Uganda's continued positive economic performance, a performance that is made possible only through high levels of aid and, often, exploitation of foreign resources. Donors are wary of doing anything that might threaten that reputation and put the efficacy of their own policies into doubt. Therefore, while donors extended their control over most of the budget, they left the military budget under Museveni's discretionary control, which the regime uses for political consolidation. Andrew Mwenda explains, "Museveni found that he had bought himself independence and discretion to pursue his preferred military and political agendas," and so "the more donors gained control of the policy and budget process, the more Museveni called for increased defense spending"; despite donor complaints, "Museveni always won; the donors always lost."[269] The defense budget has consistently increased under Museveni, from $42 million in 1992, to $110 million in 2001, to $260 million by the end of the decade.[270] According to Reno, by the late 1990s, "Museveni's outside backers [were] trapped: back away from Museveni's regime and expect disorder and a roll-back of reforms, or support him and his patronage politics and facilitate the UPDF's continued involvement in Congo."[271]

Although donors frequently criticize the Ugandan government for using aid in ways that contradict donor agendas, their protests uniformly die out, and the high levels of foreign funding continue. A 2005 newspaper report verifies this:

> Uganda will in the new financial year spend a massive Ush351 billion ($200 million) on defence in spite of protests from donors. In the middle of the 2002/03 financial year, the government diverted 23 per cent of the budgets of all its departments to the army, which was fighting wars in the north and southwest of Uganda as well as in the Democratic Republic of Congo. Donors, who funded half the budget, protested against the real-locations to no avail. Last year, the donor community led by the World Bank threatened to cut aid to Uganda when former Finance Minister, Gerald Sendaula, proposed a 19 per cent increase in defence spending to Ush365 billion ($208.5 million). Although donors refused to endorse the 2004/05 budget, defence got the money.[272]

Since the mid-1990s, Uganda has enjoyed an influx of foreign aid amounting to 80 percent of its development expenditures and has been the beneficiary of a number of generous donor initiatives.[273] For example, in April 1998, it was the first country to benefit from debt relief under the Heavily Indebted Poor Country Initiative,[274] and, in June 2005, Uganda was in the first group of countries to be slated for a full multilateral debt write off.[275]

In this context, as numerous analysts have made clear, the dominant image of the LRA conflict plays the essential role of providing an internationally acceptable justification for this expansion of the military budget. No donor wants to be seen as preventing Uganda from using the military force needed to protect its population from the LRA, an accusation the Ugandan government levels at those donors calling for decreases in military spending. Given the centrality of the military budget to the Museveni regime's hold on power, and the centrality of the LRA conflict to justifying that military budget, the key importance of the war to the regime becomes apparent. Today, as the LRA has left northern Uganda, the Ugandan government uses the need to hunt the rebels down wherever they are, along with its role in peacekeeping in Somalia, in order to justify this expanding military budget. The War on Terror has only exacerbated these tendencies.

THE WAR ON TERROR

Militarization by the Ugandan regime has been promoted or at least allowed by the U.S. government since the mid-1990s. This has been in response to Uganda's willingness to serve a key U.S. ally in the region, in particular in the political and military campaign against the Khartoum government and then, since 9/11, in the War on Terror. Sudan was placed on the list of state sponsors of terrorism in August 1993, and by 1995, Anthony Lake, President Clinton's National Security Adviser, had articulated the "Frontline States" policy toward Sudan: "We will be working with other governments in the region to see how we can best contain the influence of the Sudanese Government until it changes its views and begins to behave in accordance with the norms of international behavior that we think governments should follow."[276] President Clinton, on November 3, 1997 signed Executive Order 13067, declaring that

> the policies and actions of the Government of Sudan, including continued support for international terrorism; ongoing efforts to destabilize neighboring governments; and the prevalence of human rights violations, including slavery and the denial of religious freedom, constitute an unusual and extraordinary threat to the national security and foreign policy of the United States, and hereby declare a national emergency to deal with that threat.[277]

Since the mid 1990s, Western media have reported that the United States has provided military aid to Uganda that the latter was to provide to the SPLA, although the United States has consistently denied such reports.[278] Uganda's role of being a conduit for U.S. military assistance to South Sudan may stand to increase again depending on the outcome of the referendum there in 2011.

Since 9/11, Uganda's role as a proxy in the U.S. campaign against the Sudanese government has been incorporated into the War on Terror. On December 5, 2001, Colin Powell announced that the LRA had been placed on the State Department's

Terrorist Exclusion List.[279] Very soon after that, the Ugandan government and the U.S. government began linking their respective Wars on Terror—that of the United States against global terror and Uganda's against the local terror of the LRA.[280] This designation of the LRA as a terrorist organization only further exaggerated the predominant image of the conflict and made a negotiated political solution more difficult.

Although the United States cut military support in the wake of Uganda's invasion of DRC in the late 1990s, by the early 2000s, the United States was directly contributing to the Ugandan military in the name of helping Uganda's War on Terror. In an embarrassing encounter in 2003, the minister for the presidency, Gilbert Bukenya, publicly thanked the new U.S. ambassador, Jimmy Kolker, for having given Uganda $3 million to fight the LRA. As the newspaper reported,

> Before Bukenya could give details, Kolker interjected, saying it was not necessary to do so. "What is important is that the partnership between Uganda and the United States shall continue especially in the sectors of peace and security, poverty reduction, trade and economic development and the fight against HIV/Aids," Kolker said.[281]

In July 2003, President Bush announced an antiterrorism package of $100 million to help fight terrorism in Uganda, Kenya, Ethiopia, Djibouti, and Tanzania.[282] In a 2004 BBC interview, General Charles Wald, head of U.S. operations in Africa, implied that the United States was assisting the UPDF militarily against the LRA, stating that, "It's not just moral support, but some things need to be kept a bit more private."[283] This assistance would culminate with the inception of AFRICOM in 2008, discussed in chapter 7. In exchange, Uganda was the only East African country to openly support the U.S. invasion of Iraq, and it even offered to send troops in the early days of the war. The persistence of the LRA allows the Ugandan government to remain a U.S. key ally in the War on Terror, with all the benefits that follow from that designation. Furthermore, the United States needs Uganda's military to be under the control of the unaccountable elites at the center of the state so as to ensure that popular demands for peace and an end to Ugandan military involvement— whether in northern Uganda, in DRC, or in Somalia—are ignored or silenced.

Since the termination of open fighting in northern Uganda in 2007, the Ugandan government has been diversifying its military role, justifying increased military spending as needed to pursue the LRA in central Africa and to provide support for the African Union peacekeeping mission in Somalia. The latter provides Uganda its trump card to silence criticism of its military's activities. For example, when a leaked UN report in September 2010 detailed the UPDF's commission of war crimes and crimes against humanity in DRC, the Ugandan foreign minister's reaction to the leak was swift and to the point: "Such sinister tactics undermine Uganda's resolve to continue contributing to, and participating in, various regional and international peacekeeping operations."[284] The Ugandan government thus lets the United States know that if it is going to continue acting as America's military proxy, the United States cannot raise questions about the UPDF's activities elsewhere.

BUILDING STATE CAPACITY, DESTROYING ACCOUNTABILITY

The way in which the United States depends on a group of unaccountable state elites in order to carry out foreign-directed military policies is only one example of donors' broad dependence on unaccountable elites as the local agents of intervention.[285] This dependence is the result of the fact that even the most self-proclaimed democratic or liberal reforms demanded by donors remain external demands to be put into place, not through democratic organization and action, but through top-down implementation. Thus, regardless of the content of such donor-demanded policies, they will be antidemocratic in their form. Sometimes donors are explicit about the need for unaccountable elites to push through policies—for example, the World Bank's infamous 1981 Berg Report that argued that "African governments, therefore, must be willing to take firm action on internal problems"[286]—but mostly, in today's era of "good governance," donors tend to disavow the antidemocratic basis of external imposition of policies and stress instead capacity building and partnership.

Donors' preference for unaccountable state elites is particularly conspicuous in economic policy.[287] Economic reform required a group of unaccountable technocrats at the core of the Ugandan state who would serve as the executors of unpopular structural adjustment policies and needed insulation from popular protest by the coercive powers of the state. In this situation, both those implementing these policies and those given the task of protecting them from popular discontent, can take advantage of their externally buttressed authority to pursue their own agendas as well. For the military-political-business nexus around Museveni, this has amounted mostly to the pursuit of personal enrichment and the consolidation of power through patronage and an expanded security apparatus.

The result has been a massive gap between the stated liberal objectives of these policies—whether good governance, electoral reform, economic liberalization, or anticorruption—and the political consequences stemming from their unaccountable, state-driven implementation. In this vein, Mwenda and Roger Tangri conclude that "donor reforms have reinforced rather than reduced the propensity of political leaders to use the state and its resources to maintain themselves in power."[288] The paradox of liberal state-building intervention becomes stark. Donor policies intended to reduce corruption only fuel it further. Good governance promotion increases patronage politics. Decentralization centralizes power in the hands of the executive who gains the discretion to decide where to create new administrative units and thus new channels for patronage. The leeway given to the Ugandan government to fight a just war against the LRA sets the stage for the invasion and looting of the DRC and the militarization of Uganda. Donor policies do indeed undermine the "substance of sovereignty"—in the sense of popular sovereignty, while empowering the unaccountable state elites who are the donors' local agents.

RESOLVING THE CRISES, ENDING THE VIOLENCE

The consolidation of unaccountable state power through Western intervention exposes an international dimension to the political crises underlying the war in northern Uganda. As long as donors continue funding the Ugandan state in such a way so as to entrench the unaccountable elites at its center, democracy will suffer, militarization will proceed, and violence will be imminent.

It was during the phase of mass displacement from 1996 onward that the political crises of the Acholi reached their apogee. Internally, what legitimate order and authority had existed before the war had been decimated by over a decade of anticivilian, antipolitical violence by both sides, violent forced recruitment, and general devastation. The camps made this even worse by removing the Acholi from their sources of livelihood, splitting up families and clans, and throwing many people into a state of despair and physical debilitation. Nationally, the fact that the government was able to violently displace and intern over a million people into wretched displacement camps with total impunity and with the assistance and acquiescence of donors signaled that the national political crisis had intensified dramatically, a crisis rooted in the lack of a legitimate Acholi political class, their exclusion from the national government, the imposition of unpopular state agents in the local administration, the silencing of independent Acholi voices, and the failure of the Acholi diaspora to engage meaningfully in Ugandan politics. These crises were intensified once people were interned in the camps, where, as discussed, state and rebel violence did much to shut down politics. However, as I argue in the coming chapters, violence by itself was not sufficient, and it was only with a vast regime of human rights intervention in the camps that effective political organization failed to emerge and the crises remained unresolved.

As it happened, resolving these crises turned out not to be a necessary condition for the end of the war in northern Uganda, because the end of fighting came about through a temporary reconfiguration of regional politics in the wake of the 2005 Comprehensive Peace Agreement between Khartoum and the SPLA and the LRA's subsequent shift from Uganda into neighboring countries. However, I maintain that the kind of democratic political organization and action that is necessary to resolve these crises would also have had a good chance of bringing the war and displacement to an end. Furthermore, I argue that as long as the crises remain, the conditions for a return to open violence also remain, through either the return of the LRA, the emergence of a new rebel group, or an upsurge in state violence against the Acholi around issues such as land.

For this reason, today's peace in northern Uganda should not lead people to forget about the need for political reform—that is, the end of the fighting does not mean the end of the crises. Rather, today's peace should be seen as providing the opportunity for new, more inclusive and democratic political configurations to come about within Acholi society and within Uganda. That said, however, today the internal crisis may perhaps have become more difficult to resolve as the social upheaval and efflorescence of the pseudo-urban space of displacement has been replaced by a return to villages and, with it, an effort to re-impose patriarchal authority structures. Nationally, however, today may offer an unprecedented opportunity to initiate a new pursuit of political and social justice. The end of fighting in Acholiland and people's return home from the camps has undone what seemed the exceptionality of the Acholi situation and has revealed that the crisis of the Acholi is also the crisis of the rest of the country. While the state increasingly employs a militarized indirect-rule mode of social control, dividing Uganda up into ever-more tribes, each identified with a different administrative district, the question arises of whether opposition politics will continue to take an ethnic character as well, or if the common crisis people face will lead them to reject divisive tribalization and come up with new modes of national political identity and organization.

Today's situation may also help solve the international dimension of these political crises. The international crisis faced by Uganda's people will not be resolved internationally. Donors have demonstrated that they are perfectly willing to promote unaccountable and arbitrary power and are determined to refuse any responsibility, let alone accountability, for the consequences of their actions. Instead, the international crisis will only be resolved through national democratic action, through democratic demands by organized African citizenries for an end to the most recent form of destructive Western interference in Africa, taking their states back from the hands of unaccountable African elites and the foreign donors who help keep them in power.

But this is today, now that the LRA is gone and almost all Acholi have left the camps. The rest of the book returns to the period of war and intense displacement, the early- to mid-2000s, when political violence, combined with human rights intervention, precluded the kind of political organization or action that would have been required for people to demand peace, promote political change, or go home.

3

Humanitarianism, Violence, and the Camp

In the most unambiguous portrayals, the provision of humanitarian relief aid is presented as a nonpolitical antidote to violence—even if only a temporary one—offering a "bed for the night"[1] for those "victims of bad causes"[2] who have, it is asserted, multiplied rapidly in today's upsurge of brutal conflicts and "new wars."[3] It fulfills, it is claimed, a commitment to a basic set of human rights that must be respected without regard for political calculation. This politically and morally unambiguous account, however, invites questioning. As will be seen in the Uganda case, when humanitarian aid is provided within a moralized conflict, its politicization is made easy:[4] assistance to the "good" side is endowed with absolute legitimacy, so that those providing resources aid avoid accountability for its possible negative consequences,[5] while violence against the "bad" side is justified as humanitarian.[6] The moralization of humanitarianism, combined with aid's inherent fungibility, allows it to be instrumentalized to political and military agendas and means that humanitarianism can end up being politically and practically counterproductive, worsening the crises and conflicts it claims to be ameliorating.

This chapter will argue that it is not only the instrumentalization of humanitarian aid, but also its administrative dimension that can lead to negative political and practical consequences. Humanitarianism can silence its supposed beneficiaries, subjecting them to intense discipline in the name of efficient aid delivery and leading to depoliticization. However, because this depoliticization can never be complete, humanitarianism can end up provoking political resistance, in response to which it comes to depend on administrative violence against its beneficiaries to promote its own efficacy.[7]

This chapter provides an account of the political and practical consequences of humanitarianism in northern Uganda, demonstrating how it ended up in a sustained collaboration with state violence. This collaboration was concretely anchored in the archipelago of forced displacement camps, which, at the peak of the war, contained the entire rural population of Acholi subregion, about a million people. I will argue that these internment camps were able to exist only because of, first, the violence of the Ugandan state which forced people into the camps, prevented people from leaving them, and repressed political organization, and, second, the intervention of international humanitarian aid agencies, which ran and sustained the camps for over a decade. In this context, I argue that humanitarianism served not only to enable the Ugandan government's militarization and violent repression of dissent, but also to depoliticize the population and thus prolong and intensify war and violence, with devastating consequences. State violence and humanitarianism each depended on the other for its own viability, as the regime of state violence against the Acholi in the camps was only possible because of the intervention of the aid agencies, and the aid agencies' administrative management strategy was only possible because of their direct and indirect reliance on state violence.

1. War and the Instrumentalization of Humanitarianism

Aid agencies' need to access vulnerable populations can provide the context for the instrumentalization of relief aid: as those with power make themselves the local arbiters of international assistance, aid agencies can face the dilemma of providing aid to in-need populations at the price of strengthening warring parties.[8] One notorious case was in the southern Sudanese civil war, where the Sudanese People's Liberation Army (SPLA) and the Khartoum government both commandeered aid for their own consumption and politicized re-distribution.[9] Aid agencies, for their part, tend willfully to ignore this instrumentalization or try to excuse it as an unavoidable, unfortunate side-effect of assisting needy victims.[10]

The Ugandan case demonstrates how the incorporation of humanitarianism into a moralized human rights agenda, according to which the responsible Ugandan government was seen as the good side in the conflict, opened humanitarianism to an even more intensive and systematic instrumentalization than that which results from the need for access alone. In Uganda, it was not the aid agencies' need for access, but the Ugandan government's international alliances and reputation as a responsible state that allowed it to blatantly instrumentalize humanitarian aid, with devastating consequences. Aid agencies in northern Uganda did not face the dilemma of needing to cut deals with the government to guarantee access to suffering populations. Rather, the agencies found it convenient to cooperate openly with the government's counterinsurgency to the point of enabling its policy of mass forced displacement and internment, which itself *resulted in* the humanitarian crisis. Subsequently, any criticism of the role of aid agencies was muted, since no one had an interest in demanding that the government be held accountable for mass forced displacement or that aid groups be held accountable for their complicity. Therefore, it is a mistake to see the collaboration between aid agencies and government violence in northern Uganda as an unfortunate side effect stemming from the delivery of desperately needed aid. Rather, aid groups were deeply involved in creating the conditions for the humanitarian crisis, and neither the government's violence nor the aid agencies' intervention would have been possible without the other.

THE ORIGINS OF FORCED DISPLACEMENT

In September 1996, the government began what would prove to be a policy of long-term mass forced displacement and internment in Acholiland. The UPDF drove hundreds of thousands of Acholi peasants out of their villages and into camps through a campaign of intimidation, murder, torture, and bombing and burning entire villages, as discussed in chapter 2. After the formation of the camps, the UPDF announced that anyone found outside of the camps would be considered a rebel and killed. Although the government euphemistically called the camps "protected villages," they were most accurately identified as internment or concentration camps, given their origins in forced displacement and the continued government violence used to keep civilians from leaving. The total population of these internment camps stood at a few hundred thousand by the end of 1996, but by the mid-2000s had grown to around a million, encompassing nearly the entire rural population of Acholi subregion.

Forced displacement had devastating consequences for the interned civilians.[11] Whereas humanitarian aid was only occasionally needed before 1996, with mass displacement and internment the population became dependent on relief aid. The inadequacy of that aid, however, and the squalid conditions in the camps led to a massive humanitarian crisis, with excess mortality levels reaching approximately 1,000 per week by the mid-2000s.[12] Moreover, the camps were tragically unprotected, and accusations that government soldiers failed to protect the camps, refused to respond to LRA incursions, and thus turned civilians into easy targets for the LRA, were heard regularly from camp inhabitants.

Despite a record of extreme anti-civilian violence by both sides, as explained in the last chapter, dominant international portrayals of the conflict have tended to cast it in unambiguous moral terms, celebrating the Ugandan government and demonizing the LRA. This portrayal has been in the interests of the Ugandan government and its Western donors, but it is also in the interests of aid agencies, as I explain in this chapter. Through it, the Ugandan government legitimates and funds its militarizati   on, the media sell gory images of incomprehensible barbarism in Africa, Western states protect their East African ally, the World Bank retains its African success story, and aid agencies are able to collect funds through marketing the suffering of abducted children and pour in aid to support the Ugandan government's military campaign, even as they absolve themselves of the need to be accountable for the consequences of their actions. The irony, of course, is that the internment camps were, by far, the greatest cause of children's—and adults'—suffering in northern Uganda and, if anything, made abductions by the LRA easier.

FORCED DISPLACEMENT AND INTERNMENT

When the government began the displacement of the northern population in September, 1996, it appears to have done so without much thought about the duration, sustainability, or broader effects of interning several hundred thousand people and not providing them with food, water, medicine, shelter, or protection. People in the camps were left stranded, without means of acquiring food or supplies, and they were told to build their own shelters within demarcated areas. Already, by the end of October, 1996, the destructive effects of displacement on the civilian population had become apparent and were being reported in the national press. An article in *The Monitor* revealed that Gulu district was "losing more lives through secondary effects of the war than the war itself," most of those effects proceeding directly from displacement.[13] The camps were, within a month of their inception, turning into a serious political scandal for the government.

More important, however, was the fact that the people who had been displaced were themselves rendering the government's strategy unsustainable by refusing to remain in the camps. Many displaced people preferred the relative safety and security of their homes and were leaving the "protected villages" spontaneously, willing to stand up to the threat of government violence in their villages rather than resigning themselves to starvation in the camps. This was noted early on by the UN. As a Humanitarian Situation Report explains:

10. . . . The attention of the international humanitarian agencies has recently been focused on the question of "protected villages." The local authorities characterize these as places, often close to UPDF posts, where people have spontaneously gathered together for their own protection. Displaced people interviewed in Gulu, however, report that UPDF soldiers told them that they would be regarded as rebels if they stayed in their home villages. Leading politicians and soldiers are on record as saying that protected villages will be an important part of their strategy to isolate rebels and deny them food, freedom of movement and the ability to re-group.

11. Although a number of sites are reported each to have attracted several thousand people over the past few weeks, there are also reports that many of these people are already returning to their homes. Certainly, displaced people interviewed at a site designated by the authorities in Gulu expressed a reluctance to stay where they were; having found no food, water or sanitation facilities at the site they were talking about returning home. Several people said that they felt unsafe in the sites, one of which is already reported to have been attacked by the LRA.

12. Whether or not protected villages develop over the coming weeks will also depend on the ability of aid agencies to provide the services which are lacking, and certainly beyond the means of the local authorities.[14]

The government soon realized what the UN had pointed out, that, without the intervention of aid agencies to provide assistance to the camps, their policy of displacement would be a failure. People were refusing to stay in the camps, and violence was not enough to convince them to stay. Consequently, the government began to request food aid from World Food Program (WFP). By November, 1996, WFP reported that the Ugandan government had asked that it help feed up to 200,000 displaced people.[15] At the same time, aid agencies began to undertake registration and other logistical tasks required to establish the camps.

Some international relief agencies had had a presence in northern Uganda since the inception of the war, but there are few reports of any aid activity oriented toward providing relief to the Acholi civilian population until after the advent of large-scale displacement in late 1996.[16] With the forced displacement of several hundred thousand peasants into ad-hoc camps in a matter of a week, a massive humanitarian crisis among an easily accessed population suddenly became imminent, and aid agencies began to prepare for a greatly increased role. Obviously, the Acholi case differs from what are thought of as typical situations of displacement, in which people flee their homes for their safety; in Uganda, people wanted to stay at home for their safety but were forced into internment camps by their government as part of an explicit counterinsurgency strategy. As a result, there was some debate among the agencies about whether they should intervene in this situation of forced displacement and internment, because intervening might make them appear complicit with the government's military campaign.[17] However, anxiety was quickly quieted as some of the most influential agencies led the way by providing large quantities of material aid to the displaced, and others quickly followed suit, assisting in organizing the camps and registering the inhabitants.[18] Indeed, the same qualities that made the camps attractive to the Ugandan government—a concentrated, easily surveilled, accessed, and controlled population—made them particularly attractive to aid agencies. Equally important was Uganda's image as a responsible supporter of human rights and the sanctification of its war against the LRA, which meant that its military campaign could be supported by donors and aid agencies without question and the consequences of that support would be immune to criticism. The camps simply represented too profitable an opportunity for aid agencies to pass up, and by December 1996, according to the UN,

> The World Food Programme is trying to supply emergency relief food to Gulu, and is currently planning a programme for 100,000 people in Gulu town and Kilak, Nyowa, Omoro and Aswa counties (as and when they can be accessed) as well as in the Masindi-Karuma area. In Gulu town the organizations distributing the food are World Vision, Oxfam/Accord, the Church of Uganda and the Catholic diocese. . . . MSF-Holland is helping the health authorities to monitor the health situation, as well as assessing and assisting the water situation in Gulu town. UNICEF is funding

vaccination activities in accessible areas and has provided tented schools for Gulu town, while the ICRC and ACF also have teams on the spot.[19]

The aid agencies' intervention effectively defused popular opposition to forced displacement. The presence and assistance of the aid agencies, the provision of some of the needed resources, and the potential that that provision would increase abated the spontaneous movement of people out of the camps. If the relief agencies had not intervened, it appears that the government simply would not have been able to sustain the camps through violence alone and people would have continued leaving the camps and going back home. However, once the humanitarian infrastructure had been deployed and movement out of the camps had been halted, forced internment became a viable long-term strategy—so much so that it expanded precipitously.

After 1996, the presence of relief agencies increased significantly in the north, as did the extent of displacement. Indeed, it seems that the government came to expect aid agencies to intervene to support those who it displaced and was therefore more willing to use mass displacement as a strategy than it would have been without humanitarian aid. In 2003, the consolidated appeal by humanitarian relief agencies working in northern Uganda amounted to $148.1 million, of which $123.6 million was received, and over half of which went to buy and distribute food to the displaced;[20] over one hundred organizations participated in the appeal process.[21] At the same time, the government's policy of forced displacement expanded to encompass the entire rural Acholi population.[22] By 2007, according to the International Development Committee of the British Parliament, running the camps was costing donors no less than $200 million per year.[23] In addition to providing relief aid, the humanitarian agencies increasingly provided an entire rudimentary civil administration in the camps, rendering them increasingly permanent. In the mid-2000s, the aid agencies launched a "camp management" strategy and parceled out Acholiland, subcounty by subcounty, among themselves, all in the name of rendering the camps more sustainable. Evidently, the aid agencies had forgotten that the only sustainable solution was to let people go back home. They also failed to see that the very premise that camps should be made sustainable declared acceptable the suffering of the million people forced to live in them.

A MORAL DILEMMA?

Some have argued in the agencies' defense that they faced a moral dilemma in having to decide whether to provide aid to the camps or not—specifically, that they were faced with two morally bad choices: one, to provide aid to the camps and save lives, but in doing so to support the government's possibly illegal counterinsurgency; the other, not to provide aid and thus to keep their hands clean of the government's unsavory policies, but at the cost of thousands of civilian lives. In the face of options like these, it has been argued that to decide not to provide aid for the sake of keeping one's hands clean is morally unconscionable.[24] Nicholas Stockton cites this type of dilemma in his defense of the delivery of relief aid to camps of displaced Rwandans in eastern Zaire in the mid-1990s. He condemns those aid agencies that refused to deliver aid to the camps, complaining that:

> [H]umanitarian protection was quite deliberately suspended and tens of thousands of people were sacrificed on the altar of a convenient combination of political correctness and short-term financial expediency that seem to underpin the "new pragmatists," "do no harm" and "local solutions" policies.... The only likely result is that the victims of war will have their sentences enhanced.[25]

A 1999 internal World Food Program report[26] explicitly tried to frame the decision to provide aid to the Ugandan camps as just such a tough, but ultimately justified, choice, citing the "tension" that "remains between the government's broader political concern to control the population (for example, through the protected villages/camps) and the potential co-opting of the aid program to this end."[27] The report goes on to explain that:

> There is a difficult balance between the provision of humanitarian assistance and the implicit sanctioning of illegal action. This was nowhere more apparent than in the formation of the "protected villages," effectively sanctioned by WFP through its close collaboration with the authorities in providing assistance and advice on registration, locations and common services . . . The programme [of forced displacement] as a whole was not designed around protection concerns, other than the general assumption (not necessarily proven) that camps were safer than outlying villages . . . WFP may have too readily fallen in line with government policy, in effect becoming both provider and legitimizer of a villagization policy.[28]

The last sentence is revealing because, in trying to frame the choice faced by aid agencies as a moral dilemma, the report provides evidence contradicting that claim. The report admits that civilians accrued no benefit from staying in the camps and laments that WFP had agreed to cooperate with "illegal" forced displacement despite "the lack of reasonable steps taken by the authorities first, to minimize displacement and second, to create conditions in which it can be brought to an end as quickly as possible."[29] It concludes that WFP in fact had the option of acting to help bring forced displacement to an end instead of collaborating with and enabling it:

> some local authorities were keen to pass by-laws demanding the early return of IDPs. If this had been explicitly linked to a WFP "food return package" and the demand for access to areas of return, the focus of the programme may not have been on food-dependent camps but on a more fluid and responsible approach to the cycle of displacement.[30]

That is, WFP could have assisted civilians *by remaining independent* of the government counterinsurgency but chose not to. There was, in fact, no moral dilemma, as WFP's own report makes clear, because the interests of the civilians themselves would have been best served if the aid agencies had refused to help create and sustain the camps. Instead, the agencies cooperated with a brutally anti-civilian and, by the report's own suggestion, illegal counterinsurgency policy.

It should also be noted that, although the aid agencies provided enough food and supplies to keep people in the camps by making life in the camps possible for most people, they did not provide enough to prevent what became a massive humanitarian crisis, with excess mortality levels of 1,000 per week. Thus, in sustaining the camps, the aid agencies not only enabled the government's counterinsurgency but also created the conditions for the humanitarian crisis that would ensue. An equilibrium was quickly reached in which conditions in the camps were not bad enough that the displaced went home en masse but not good enough to prevent the chronic physical debilitation of the Acholi population and the slow destruction of Acholiland. Thus, because the humanitarian crisis was the product of displacement into the camps and because the camps could only be sustained due to the massive presence of relief agencies, the logical conclusion is that the relief agencies, instead of ameliorating a pre-existing humanitarian crisis, helped create one where it had not existed and did not need to exist, and then contributed to its perpetuation. The result was assured because Uganda's reputation as a responsible state prevented any scrutiny of the effects of intervention, even though in intervening, the relief agencies made the long-term internment of the entire rural Acholi population a viable strategy for the Ugandan government, at the cost of tens of thousands of civilian lives. It is in this context that Chris Dolan argues that, "like doctors in a torture situation," the aid agencies "appear to be there to ease the suffering of victims, but in reality they enable the process to be prolonged by keeping the victim alive for further abuse."[31]

Once people had been in the camps for several years, the solution to the problem of forced displacement became more complicated, given that homesteads were ruined, granaries looted and destroyed, fields overgrown, and water sources blocked. Furthermore, having been in the camps for years, preyed on by UPDF and rebels, people were understandably nervous about security back at home. There was also the issue of the debilitation—physical, psychological, cultural, and social—that people in the camps had been subjected to, which had reduced their very capacity to undertake the effort returning home would entail.[32] Thus, as Dolan reports, "research findings consistently indicated that although people in principle wished to return home there would be no immediate exodus from the camps whatever changes occurred in the policy context."[33] Just withdrawing aid outright in that context—which would have been a viable option in the early days of displacement in 1996—no longer was, because it would have led to an even more massive humanitarian disaster. However, this in no way exculpates the aid agencies for their policy of camp management; rather, it makes clear the alternative policies they could have adopted instead, which would have ended the ongoing humanitarian crisis without sparking a new one. The best alternative policy, always available but never tried by the aid agencies and donors, would have been to continue providing aid, but aid tailored to helping people return home—return packages, seeds, water source rehabilitation, and so on. This could have been combined with coherent public pressure on the Ugandan government to let people go home—as Acholi peace and human rights groups were calling for—and to provide the transitional security people felt they needed in order to return and exercise their freedom of movement. The aid agencies and donors, however, never did anything of the sort, and even when criticism of the camps began to be heard in the mid-2000s, UNHCR still refused to demand that people be allowed to go home and shifted instead to calling for camp decongestion, that is, a movement to smaller, more "sustainable," camps.[34]

POLITICAL CONTROL AND REPRESSION

Over the course of the war, the government used the presence of the aid agencies not only to contain the civilian population physically, but also to control it politically. One way it did this was to politicize aid distribution so as to shut down opposition in the camps. Camps seen as opposition strongholds were told that aid would be withdrawn unless they supported certain candidates in elections.[35] The position in charge of aid distribution in each camp was ensured to be filled by a government supporter, and the government allowed aid agencies to deliver relief aid only to those camps that it had approved.

The internment of people in camps also enabled a regime of violence by the government against the Acholi, intended to eradicate political organization and opposition. Once the camps were formed, the government stepped up political repression against the population, employing the UPDF, the Homeguard, and other paramilitary forces to that end.[36] Those in the camps who protested their continued internment, government abuse, or the lack of security faced violent repression by state security services, including arbitrary arrest, torture, and even death.[37] Paralegals and human rights activists were particular targets; as one paralegal living in a camp explained, "when you want to speak freely, the government accuses you of being a rebel."[38] Local elections also occasioned state violence; in one case, a prominent local government official in conjunction with a UPDF commander organized a paramilitary group to ensure that a key election would go their way through a campaign of violent intimidation.[39]

The role of the security forces, once the camps were formed, was not to provide protection to the camps but to repress those in the camps who might organize to protest their internment or poor conditions. Devoid of protection, the camps did not serve the claimed military purpose of separating the Acholi from the rebels but rather the political purpose of preventing political organization among the Acholi that, in the short run, could hold the UPDF accountable or demand the end of the war or, in the long run, could become a base of opposition against the current government.

Humanitarianism ended up legitimating the government's counterinsurgency in other ways as well. Because the government was seen as the only legitimate armed force in the conflict, in the words of a World Bank officer, the aid agencies depended on the "good graces" of the UPDF for their protection.[40] World Food Program food distribution convoys, for example, travelled with UPDF armed personnel carriers, scores of troops, and an array of heavy weaponry. Aid groups reported having to pay UPDF officers to provide them with protection or to ensure that the aid delivery goes smoothly.[41] The aid agencies' need for administrative violence became a justification used instrumentally by the government for its further militarization of the north and the orientation of its budget toward counterinsurgency infrastructure.

Humanitarianism also allowed the Ugandan government to tap into U.S. military support and allowed the U.S. government to provide military aid to a key regional ally. As far back as 2003 there were reports that the United States was to provide military assistance to ensure the provision of humanitarian assistance and to establish humanitarian corridors to the camps for aid delivery.[42] As chapter 7 will address, this U.S. military presence has increased dramatically in recent years, justified as helping protect civilians from the LRA.

The official discourse on the conflict, however, silenced any criticism of aid agencies' role in enabling the government's counterinsurgency. Supporters of the aid regime would declare the existence of a humanitarian emergency and invoke the desperate plight of victims in order to accuse critics of being insensitive to, and even complicit with, victims' suffering.[43] The humanitarian enterprise shifted the very terms in which displacement was framed so that violence and death—which in fact resulted from the government's policy of forced displacement—was seen as a purely humanitarian problem to be solved by foreign aid agencies through their moral commitment to helping civilian victims of the LRA. The fact of displacement itself could not be questioned; no longer was the solution to disband the camps and allow the Acholi to return home, but to provide more aid to the IDPs. The humanitarian incursion normalized forced internment and effaced the possibility of challenging it as a war crime or crime against humanity. The imposition of an administrative aid regime, which itself depended on the invocation of exceptionality for its own legitimacy, ended up normalizing violence and suffering within its discursive categories.

The category of the IDP itself contributed significantly to this process.[44] IDP is a neutral, nonpolitical designation, conflating those displaced due to natural disaster, those voluntarily fleeing to government-controlled areas to avoid rebel violence, and those forcibly displaced by their own government. Thus, the IDP designation occludes the reason for displacement, leaving it unquestioned, and turns displacement into something that is to be resolved, not through return home, but through technical humanitarian intervention to ameliorate IDP suffering. In so doing, it transforms people from citizens living within their own country and thus deserving of certain constitutionally guaranteed rights into an identity that implies only the provision of charity by foreign humanitarians, without even the minimal legal guarantees provided to refugees. The Ugandan government profited immensely from this humanitarianization of forced displacement through the IDP discourse, as it erased the reasons for displacement from the debate and moralized, depoliticized, and externalized responsibility for dealing with displaced civilians to the so-called international community through aid provision.

2. Humanitarian Administration and Discipline

State violence in northern Uganda, I have argued, attempted to contain, control, and depoliticize the Acholi population by interning them in camps and exercising direct political coercion over them, an agenda that would not have worked without the instrumentalization of humanitarianism by the state. The management function of humanitarianism, its administrative dimension, is described in this section with an eye to explaining how humanitarianism ends up promoting the same outcome among interned civilians as does government violence, namely, containment, control, and depoliticization. The result is mutual dependence: just as state violence could not achieve this outcome without humanitarianism, neither could humanitarianism achieve effective population control and efficient delivery of aid in the face of popular resistance without state violence.

Humanitarianism is an administrative regime that combines macrolevel surveillance and direction with microlevel discipline in order to efficiently provide aid to victim populations. In order for it to efficiently distribute aid according to the humanitarian imperative of promoting statistically defined life, the humanitarian regime needs to contain, control, and discipline populations so that they passively accept that aid. In practice, this means that the aid industry not only sees people as helpless victims, but also *needs* people to be those very helpless victims and ends up disciplining them toward that identity.

This understanding of humanitarianism is based loosely on Michel Foucault's discussion of "governmentality," according to which the state's ability to steer a population toward an optimization of life through macrolevel techniques cannot take place without ensuring that the individuals that make up that population are normalized so as to be responsive to this steering and regulation.[45] Thus, a microlevel disciplinary regime coordinates with a macrolevel regulatory regime in the overall "governmental" process of population administration toward the end of optimizing life—but in the transnational humanitarian relief regime, optimization never reaches higher than a minimum threshold of survival, and often not even that.[46]

HUMANITARIAN REGULATION

The regulatory dimension of the humanitarian regime is informed by a certain epistemology and operates according to a certain logic. Humanitarianism employs a language of emergency, in which an emergency is a problem that is too profound and too paralyzing to be solved except through outside intervention.[47] This legitimates a technical approach on the part of intervention based on expert knowledge: specifically, the humanitarian epistemology translates the effects of violence into population statistics and then intervenes to bring those statistics back in line with a given norm. The dominant approach of relief-oriented humanitarianism is thereby directed toward improving the biological attributes of a statistically defined population and is informed by an epistemology that represents violence and suffering caused by war and displacement in those statistical terms: number of people displaced, size of camps, the population's aggregate nutritional and health status.

By representing the violence and suffering caused by war and displacement in statistical terms, relief-oriented humanitarianism legitimates technical intervention by relief agencies because the agencies alone possess the expert knowledge supposedly needed to rectify statistical deficiencies.[48] Thus, humanitarian interventions are designed to improve statistical outputs and are driven by the imperative of maximizing the efficiency of interventions so as to maximize survival. As violence is technicized by its interpretation through a statistical epistemology, so the solution to the violence is similarly technicized.[49] All the while, humanitarianism's dedication to the abstract category of "humanity" and its claim to be promoting human rights allows relief agencies to declare that their work is nonpolitical, universally applicable, and morally incontestable.

To achieve the macrolevel regulation of populations, the relief industry requires expansive surveillance regimes. This surveillance system is tuned to sense the first stirrings of humanitarian crises and to track the movements of populations as they react to violence, to map their flows as they move across the land.[50] There is an increasing employment of high-tech surveillance tools, such as GIS, that are coordinated with electronically linked global networks of relief agencies, human rights groups, and reporters.[51] There is also an effort at present to formalize surveillance and reporting in early-warning systems through the dissemination of a set of criteria which, when met, trigger action by international agencies and relief organizations, reducing response time.[52] States are brought into these early-warning systems through the incorporation of specialized offices into transnational regulatory complexes and through their participation in regional security arrangements.[53]

Once a humanitarian crisis is detected, its scope judged sufficient for international action, and funding made available, the logistical infrastructure is deployed. Relief organizations insert themselves into population flows and set up relief centers that are to attract displaced people, populations are re-territorialized in locations the aid agencies consider safe, and camps of aid recipients, whether refugees or IDPs, take shape.[54] Alternatively, as occurred in Uganda, aid agencies move into displacement camps already established by the warring parties. Once in the camps, aid groups carry out a series of "needs assessments," measuring the population against certain biostatistical norms. Great importance is put on fine-tuning the needs-assessment process, thus avoiding larger questions by fetishizing technical accuracy through statistics. The population becomes visible as a mass, allowing targeted interventions to alleviate the worst hunger, to address certain diseases, and to bring the population back in line with the norm of survival. As Liisa Malkki puts it, the camp becomes a "technology of power" that helps "to constitute 'the refugees' as an object of knowledge and control."[55]

The state can end up disaggregated, with its elements incorporated into the transnational humanitarian surveillance system and thus divested of their political dimension. In Uganda, for example, in the name of greater efficiency, the Local Council system has, in large part, been bypassed by the humanitarian regime in favor of the new position of "camp commander."[56] This single person, responsible for the distribution of aid within the camp, is the principal local agent of the transformation of the population into statistics. In addition, a myriad of committees is established dedicated to the collection of information and intended to better secure the overall regulation of the population.[57] These committees, like the camp commander, are divorced from the Local Council system; if anything, members of the LCs are incorporated as surveillance tools, their role as popular representatives unimportant. When government officials are incorporated into these administrative committees oriented toward efficient aid delivery in conflict areas, they are given equal standing with international NGO officials.[58] In fact, all are ideologized simply as "stakeholders." These committees are driven by the exigencies of international surveillance and regulation and end up being accountable primarily to the donors funding them.

Aid agencies need the people comprising these statistical aggregates to passively accept the aid they are deemed to require. In order to distribute relief aid most efficiently, humanitarian agencies need a docile population that will accept the level of aid provided and will not disrupt the distribution of aid in the camps—in a word, they need victims. Because relief agencies need the beneficiaries of aid to be incapable of doing anything about their own condition or of articulating their own demands, they help to turn the population into those requisite victims by forging a microlevel disciplinary regime whose effect is to infantilize individuals and render them helpless, thereby allowing the population to be managed through macrolevel regulation. Humanitarianism's technically required epistemology is tenuously imposed on reality through discipline and, ultimately, through violence.

HUMANITARIAN DISCIPLINE

The helpless victim is the microlevel corollary of the macrolevel statistical approach, the model toward which individual beneficiaries of aid are disciplined. As Barbara Harrell-Bond explains, "Outsiders view African refugees as *helpless*; as needing outsiders to plan for them and to take care of them."[59] This failure of recognition leads to a practice that silences those humanitarian beneficiaries, dehistoricizing and depoliticizing them. As Malkki describes, humanitarianism focuses on masses and groups, on women and children embodying helplessness, and thus implies that they "need protection, need someone to speak for them."[60] People are seen as representing "a bare, 'mere', common underlying humanity," and become "a merely biological or demographic presence."[61] Béatrice Pouligny has called attention to this prevalence of the victim identity, noting that "the lines of analysis followed by intervention are mostly based on the figure of the victim—the civilian—passive, and seen as an undifferentiated mass."[62]

This victim epistemology translates into a disciplinary practice, as Harrell-Bond was one of the first to argue. She explains, "There is much evidence that the treatment meted out to refugees by too many of those delegated to help them is such that it can only be described as 'inhuman,'"[63] and involves a large degree of "discipline" to "infantilize" the population.[64] She describes the process of conducting "needs assessments":

> Because numbers are essential for appeals for international funding, extraordinary efforts are taken by UNHCR and NGO partners to conduct "accurate" censuses. Methods involve herding refugees into enclosures and night swoops on camps. As one manual on registration advises: "Spot checks involve an actual head count and are best carried out at unsocial hours like midnight or dawn when the majority of people will be in their houses. You will need a large number of staff to go round counting every person."[65]

Jennifer Hyndman also provides a trenchant critique of these practices, describing how UNHCR focuses its energies on managing what it calls "difficult" populations through physical containment and control.[66]

These processes could be seen during World Food Program food distributions in the Ugandan internment camps. The distributions I accompanied were highly regimented, with several feeding centers set up in each camp. The people were divided up by parish, village, and then household, with lists of names that WFP had made up based on previous needs assessments. The heads of households were divided up and made to stand in line for hours to receive their ration of corn, beans, and oil. Accompanying the food trucks at all times were armed personnel carriers and large contingents of Ugandan troops. In the name of efficiency, people were made to fill out cards, stand in line all day, maintain silence, not get out of line at risk of a scolding, a blow from a stick, or the loss of food. They were forced to obey whistles and barked commands, and they had to assemble immediately when the trucks arrived and then disperse after receiving their allotment. As the population was regimented further, more demands for discipline were made on them in the name of increased efficiency.

This performative discipline is matched by pedagogical discipline. For the population to be kept in a state of satisfaction with the level of services allotted them, it is necessary that they be prevented from organizing and demanding a level of service provision that accords with their own desires. Because aid groups have a monopoly on service provision, the poor are taught to re-orient their attention away from the state and toward the "international community." But this international community is fundamentally unaccountable to the populations it claims to serve and refuses to respond to, and in fact will often withdraw in the face of, popular political organization or protest. As the only organizations offering services, relief organizations teach communities to be satisfied with what is offered. At most, people can make ineffectual appeals to the international community for more charity. The politics of survival and welfare is transformed into access to handouts from the "international community," mediated by organizations with no accountability to the population, operating within a philanthropic paradigm in which the decision about the just level of material well-being is removed from the population and invested instead in the opaque international structure. The need to take into account the demands voiced by beneficiaries is denied by the very logic of intervention, which defines problems and solutions ahead of time and only asks the technical question of how to achieve those goals efficiently.

These disciplinary strategies inevitably involve processes of subjectification, often toward control and depoliticization.[67] As Harrell-Bond argues,

> It should not be surprising that once refugees move under the aid umbrella their perceptions and behaviour change. Numerous signals remind them that they are now being cared for by others. . . . As UNHCR "children," refugees have little choice but to completely surrender autonomy and freedom of action.[68]

As a result, a transnational administrative apparatus emerges that is anchored at the local level within individual subjectivities, forms of organization, and institutions, disciplining individuals and groups in the service of macrolevel regulation. By trying to turn people into victims, humanitarianism effectively helps to contain, control, and depoliticize them, undermining their agency and voice.

This depoliticization is furthered by the uncertainty that reigns in these places of violence and humanitarianism. From the perspective of the aid recipient, as Alex de Waal has noted, the international aid bureaucracy appears more akin to a form of charismatic authority than rational authority.[69] To the governed, the aid delivery system is inscrutable and hidden; its decisions proceed from unknown sources, it responds to unknown exigencies and logics, it operates on the terrain of the miraculous, a *deus ex machina* without any attributable cause. Finnström has called attention to this "existential uncertainty" characterizing the lived experiences of Acholi in the conflict zone, which the aid distribution system exemplifies. On basic questions, such as when aid deliveries will arrive, the aid agencies would often purposefully keep people ignorant, the rationale being that it would prevent rebel attacks on the food convoys. People in the camps were unsure about where the aid came from—some thought perhaps the government, others the United States (because American flags were stamped on many of the bags of food and oil tins), while others believed foreigners or foreign countries in general. Indeed, as the only white person along on some food convoys, at times I would be stopped and have a particular grievance brought to my attention. From the camp, the only obvious form of authority was the violence of the Ugandan military, which constantly accompanied food distribution. This uncertainty can lead to resignation among the population in response to the incomprehensibility of a regime that provides only basic needs for survival, an outcome that serves the interests of the state as well in maintaining helpless, incapacitated populations. But it can also lead people to come up with active strategies for reasserting some control over their lives in the face of state violence and humanitarian discipline, as I address in the next section.

3. Resisting the Victim Role

No matter how much aid is provided, it can never fully satisfy people's desires and often not even their needs, as testified to by the high mortality rates in the Ugandan camps, where disease and malnutrition were rampant and basic survival was never assured. Aid was offered merely as the best thing the displaced could hope and wait for. But even in cases where enough aid is provided to maintain human life, the passivity the distribution regime demands and its systematic denial of the dignity and agency of its beneficiaries would still render it subject to resistance. The result is that the identity of the helpless victim imposed by humanitarianism will always be tenuous and subject to rupture. Because the disciplining of people to a state of total passivity is impossible with the tools and techniques of humanitarianism alone, resistance by the civilian population ends up requiring direct forms of coercion, a kind of administrative violence.

RECONFIGURATION, REFUSAL, AND COERCION

The need for coercion that goes beyond the discipline imposed by the aid agencies' humanitarian practice is made evident at those times when people reconfigure the resources provided by humanitarianism or even refuse humanitarianism itself. That is, recipients of humanitarian aid will react against the circumstances in which they find themselves—facing violence, squalor, and the inadequate provision of assistance—and act in ways that rupture the victim identity. Humanitarianism, however, tends to interpret this kind of autonomous behavior as deviance.[70] For example, people may try to acquire food aid through personal connections or sell what they have been given; this is coded as corruption. People may take part in demonstrations or protests against the inadequacy of aid or the mode in which it is distributed; this behavior is generally dismissed as rioting. People may also try to acquire aid outside the routes established by the aid industry, either individually—coded as stealing by the humanitarian epistemology—or in groups—coded as looting—or by joining armed forces—seen as tantamount to loot-seeking, greedy rebellion.

An illustrative instance of this in northern Uganda occurred in 2007, during the period when people had started leaving the camps and going home. People required basic information about if, when, and where aid agencies or the government were going to provide the minimal assistance needed to re-start their lives—machetes, a few seeds, and help in rehabilitating water sources. Moreover, they wanted to know how much longer food distribution would continue in the camps. The aid agencies did nothing to meet these demands for basic information by people wishing to leave the camps; indeed, not a single displaced person I spoke to during that time had any information about how much longer food would be provided, and so they were left guessing, based on rumors and speculation. People were unaware of any meetings or other opportunities to obtain information from or provide input to the aid agencies.[71] This failure to provide information made it extremely difficult for people to plan their return home. This uncertainty led to resignation and frustration among some, but it led others to employ strategies to deal with the information deficit. One such strategy was to maintain two basic homes, one in the main camp and one in a transition site, with the idea that it would help increase the chances that they would receive any assistance at all. This strategy was then condemned by aid agencies, who accused these people of double registering, attempting dishonestly to receive more than their fair share of aid. Later, when some international agencies cited supposed dependency among the displaced as an obstacle to return, they revealed yet another self-serving failure of understanding on the agencies' part: people were slow in moving home because of the failures of the aid agencies to provide information or minimal needed assistance, not because of the agencies' effectiveness in providing aid in the camps. However, people kept moving home anyway despite the total lack of information needed to plan their return.

Aid and its disciplinary demands can also be refused outright. Hyndman describes how, in 1994, Sudanese refugees in Kakuma refused to subject themselves to the humiliation of headcounts, tore down the headcount enclosure, and kidnapped the staff conducting the headcount, justifying their actions by proclaiming that "the rounding up of people into fenced lots did not respect basic human dignity and reminded them of the slavery of their people under Arab rule."[72] In Uganda, less dramatic but equally significant processes were seen. For example, in late 2004, there was a cholera outbreak in one of the biggest internment camps in northern Uganda. Médecins Sans Frontières intervened, erecting a cholera treatment center, and other NGOs helped establish a basic water purification process. Although the camp inhabitants went along with these procedures and the outbreak was brought under control, they also held firmly onto their own interpretation of the cause of the cholera outbreak: the food, specifically the sorghum, distributed by WFP.[73] People refused to eat the sorghum, and rumors circulated that it had been poisoned as part of a genocidal plot.[74] Rumors of genetically modified corn being provided by the United States have also led to popular refusal of aid elsewhere. People were not demanding more food or more benefits from the humanitarian agencies but were rejecting them and their benefits outright.

A related event occurred in another camp in northern Uganda in October 2005, when, it was reported, the inhabitants collectively refused the food delivered by WFP, refusing to line up and obey the discipline forced on them by WFP and its implementing partners. Later, the story became less clear, as other reports claimed that the inhabitants of the camp had simply been out in the fields when the trucks came and so were unable to assemble.[75] Regardless, the camp inhabitants were eventually forced by the district officials to apologize publicly over the radio to WFP. As Harrell-Bond puts it, "Since they [the agencies] are guided by a moral virtue . . . [a]nd, since the objective is to do good, it is inconceivable that recipients will fail to be grateful."[76] Whatever the truth of the event, it remains that the initial account of the outright rejection of humanitarian aid provoked a great deal of sympathy and support from people in the camps and in town, revealing the resentment among much of the population toward the treatment meted out to them by the humanitarian agencies and the willingness of the interned to, in certain situations, refuse the benefits of that administrative regime and its victim identity.

These forms of resistance represent a challenge to the humanitarian regime, challenges that it cannot deal with alone. Aid agencies can threaten to withhold aid, but this is often an inadequate disincentive, and, as a result, humanitarianism ends up depending on extradisciplinary, administrative violence to control this resistance and deal with this putatively criminal, deviant behavior as people refuse to submit to the aid agencies' disciplinary demands. This becomes particularly evident when aid agencies, in distributing relief, depend directly on the violence provided by the military forces accompanying them. They will, formally or informally, pay for protection from local armed factions: they may bring in foreign mercenaries (euphemized as private security corporations) to protect aid shipments[77] or, in the extreme, they may call for international military intervention.[78] In Uganda, a constant UPDF presence accompanied food delivery, not only to guard the transport of food, but also to ensure the good behavior of the camp population during distribution—that is, to protect aid *from* its beneficiaries. The World Food Program itself admitted this in its 1999 report, stating that "the role of convoy soldiers after a while became that of ensuring orderliness at distributions, rather than safe delivery along the road. . . . This was not only inappropriate . . . but also underlined the WFP-government-army axis in the eyes of recipients."[79]

This collaboration reached the point in northern Uganda where aid agencies and government violence were indistinguishable in the eyes of many Acholi. As Sverker Finnström explains,

> When a truck of the World Food Programme (UN) drove through Gulu town loaded with armed and uniformed government troops . . . people related it to the wider international context, where the United Nations and the international community are said to be allied with the Ugandan

government but also with political actors such as the United States and
the rebels of Southern Sudan.[80]

The open collaboration between the Ugandan military and the aid agencies
gave rise to more brutal forms of resistance by armed opposition. For example, the
LRA at times attacked and burned down the displacement camps, seeing them as
a key element in the government's counterinsurgency, in order to try to convince
people to leave them. The rebels also, in October and early November 2005, carried out a series of attacks on humanitarian aid workers in northern Uganda and
southern Sudan,[81] accompanied by an ultimatum to the aid agencies demanding
that they withdraw their international staff from the field or become targets. The
LRA consistently criticized the collusion between aid agencies and government
and even accused WFP of being involved in the government's genocidal plot by
distributing poisoned food.[82] The aid agencies' response typically was to demand
more forceful protection and increased intervention, which in turn was used by
the Ugandan government to justify further militarization. The consequence was
that the aid agencies' claim of neutrality was put into question by their cooperation
with the Ugandan authorities, as was, therefore, their protection from attack under
humanitarian law.

The aid agencies also relied on state violence to silence any potential organized opposition they might have faced in the camps. Because the Ugandan government violently targeted autonomous organization that emerged in the camps,
any sustained organization that could have made demands of the humanitarian
agencies was also shut down as part of the larger campaign of political repression.
Humanitarianism depended on violent state repression for its own ability to operate without encountering protest or opposition from those being managed in such
desperate conditions, at the same time that it perpetuated those conditions and
facilitated that very exercise of violence through its instrumentalization by the
Ugandan state.

THE HUMANITARIANISM-VIOLENCE COMPLEX

In sum, a mutual dependence emerged in northern Uganda between government
violence and humanitarianism, most notably in the management of the internment
camps. At first, when the camps were formed, it was less the disciplining effect of
humanitarianism than simply the provision of material resources that made the
camps viable—that is, without the initial intervention, people would probably have
ended up going home, and there would have been no camps at all. In this way, the
Ugandan government quickly instrumentalized the provision of resources in order
to make the camps sustainable and to make the long-term displacement of the
Acholi peasantry a feasible strategy. Once people found themselves in the camps,
without protection or adequate resources for survival, this provision of minimal
aid became double-sided: it could serve as a pacificatory and disciplinary tool, but,

also, its very inadequacy might become a focal point for popular mobilization and demands. Therefore, state violence was integrated as a necessary component of the humanitarian enterprise in order to address this latter problem.

This collusion helps make sense of why, given the tens of thousands of people assembled together in small camps facing similar conditions, organized opposition to these conditions—either against internment, against government violence, against the lack of protection, or against the inadequacy of humanitarian aid—did not arise that could have rendered the camps unmanageable. The failure to organize derived in large part from the political crises faced by the displaced Acholi population, the lack of legitimate political authority—but this does not answer why new authority did not emerge in the camps. It also had to do with, as Dolan explains, the debilitation of the Acholi in the camps. However, I argue that it found its primary source in the mutual dependence of government violence and interventionist discipline—not just the discipline of humanitarianism, but also the depoliticizing discipline imposed by the peacebuilding and justice interventions considered in future chapters. Together, violence and discipline prevented the eruption of unmanageability among the displaced, kept the political crises from being resolved, and prevented effective organization and action on the part of the camp inhabitants. The result was that the humanitarian crisis was sustained and calls for intervention were reproduced. In short, government violence alone was not enough to keep people in the camps and under control, because turning the internment camps into prison camps would have required a security regime far in excess of what was present, and humanitarianism alone was also not enough, because humanitarian aid was inadequate and there was an intense desire among people to go home in order to escape the humanitarian crisis of the camps. Both were needed.

The complementary combination of the instrumental and administrative dimensions of humanitarianism—the instrumental dimension by which the state acquires external support for its counterinsurgency and the administrative dimension by which people are disciplined to victimhood—can, thus, in certain circumstances, help create the very conditions among the population whose existence is invoked to justify humanitarian intervention in the first place. Humanitarianism and violence can together promote the reduction of subjects toward victimhood, an existence without social or political relationships, and, in so doing, through a bootstrapping operation, tenuously bring into existence what it sees as the conditions for its own intervention into the domain of the mere human, conditions that did not exist prior to its intervention. The assertion that the relief agencies in Uganda were simply responding to an existing state of affairs on its own terms—taking emergency measures and saving human lives in a context in which the domain of meaningful politics had already been left behind through depoliticizing violence—confuses the consequence of intervention with its cause. In sum, through the instrumentalization of aid and the disciplining of the population, humanitarianism can help give rise to the very conditions that legitimate its

intervention, namely, displaced, victimized populations facing unaccountable violence. In Uganda, this translated directly into the perpetuation of the camps and
the humanitarian crisis caused by displacement into the camps.

Those who are subject to violence by their own state to the point that they are
expelled as refugees or interned as IDPs, and thus find themselves divested of
their legal and political standing, can find that divestiture entrenched and normalized by aid agencies. Indeed, aid agencies and the government shared more
than just a common interest in maintaining the camps in Uganda. They shared an
underlying epistemology, seeing the population as helpless victims on whom they
were free to use their techniques of choice, the camp being the preferred institutional form for realizing these projects. The only potential force that had an
incentive to break the system, end the war, leave the camps, and go home, were
those who had had their capacity to organize toward that end undermined
through terror and philanthropy. By the efforts of the government, the rebels, and
the relief agencies, people are normalized toward victimhood, unable to effectively confront the perpetrators.

Some analysts, especially those drawing on the work of Giorgio Agamben,
have argued that this collaboration between state violence and humanitarianism
in depoliticizing displaced populations can end up triumphing totally in practice.
Agamben's concept of the political is transferred to the global level, and humanitarianism, it is argued, reduces people to the bare human and places them in a
space of exception to be either regulated or killed. Often, the very possibility of
politics among those subject to intervention is rejected. As Mariella Pandolfi puts
it, humanitarian governance has meant "rendering the human being no longer as
a citizen, but as a bare life."[83] Jenny Edkins maintains that displacement camps in
Africa become "a permanent space of exception" in which "victims only appear as
a form of life that can be saved (bare life), not as people . . . who still have political
views."[84] As a result, according to her, humanitarianism and violence cancel the
possibility of politics by creating a space of permanent exception, and camps
become "a zone of indistinction where the possibility of the political disappears."[85]
Some of those who see resistance as possible at all, such as Peter Nyers, argue that
it can occur only on the terrain of "bare life" itself, for example when detained
refugees end up "responding in a decidedly noncivil and nonhumanitarian
manner. Their lives stripped bare—indeed, constituted as bare life—they have
devised strategies of resistance that highlight the politics of their caged bodies,"
through hunger strikes, self-mutilation, and self-immolation.[86] Lost is that action's
connection with political organization and struggle against concrete forms of
domination and inequality.

However, I have argued that, even though humanitarianism and violence can
operate together highly effectively, they are not effective enough to cancel politics
entirely. They cannot entirely encompass and neutralize the surplus of thought,
organization, and action that results from people trying to make meaning and
live their lives in the camp, exercising their agency individually and collectively

in ways unpredictable to and unable to be captured by humanitarianism and violence. Perhaps the total eradication of politics without remainder was the case in the death camp, but to extend the logic of the death camp to displaced people's camps, as some writers following Agamben have tended to do, is unwarranted. In many cases, the new congregation of the camps cannot help but give rise to new politics.

In northern Uganda, although some displacement camps may have indeed been bereft of overt politics, others saw political life continue—albeit within narrow limits. For example, the largest camp in northern Uganda, Pabbo, was the site of significant political ferment, which included the resistance occasioned by humanitarianism itself. Because the camps represented large concentrations of votes, political struggles were seen around local and national elections. Complex political relations existed among government informers, rebel informers, militias, and former rebels. Peacebuilding interventions set the stage for the emergence of new political actors and struggles among elders and youth, and men and women. There were struggles among different spiritual authorities, around the non-Acholi living in the camps, and around the presence of foreigners including SPLA agents, American marines, aid workers, land speculators, and researchers. But the sustained political organization needed to challenge forced displacement and the regime of violence never emerged.

Humanitarianism and state violence tend to contain, control, and depoliticize— but through these very practices they cannot help but open new spaces for politics in the camps. As a result, a complex, political life can emerge, which is both limited and enabled by people's internment through state violence and international humanitarianism. It is on this terrain of the camp that the other human rights interventions oriented toward order, peace, and justice took place, as discussed in the coming chapters.

4. Accountability and Participation: Solutions?

The situation in Uganda represented perhaps a worst-case scenario, one in which, at the outset, relief aid was not only unnecessary, but enabled an illegal policy of forced mass internment and caused a humanitarian crisis. There are other situations of humanitarian crisis, of course, in which relief aid *is* clearly needed. In this last section, I argue that the tragically counterproductive consequences of relief aid, such as seen in Uganda, may be avoided, and that humanitarian work can perhaps be made more productive generally, if it is made accountable, both under international law and to those it is claiming to serve. Human rights and international law can provide tools to guide this form of accountability, which should be premised, I argue, on specific modes of participation. In terms of aid delivery specifically, I would argue that participation can be an element in the positive reform of intervention (something that will not be the case in forms of intervention considered in future chapters).

LEGAL ACCOUNTABILITY

Aid agencies' collaboration with forced displacement in Uganda raises the need to hold agencies legally accountable under international humanitarian law. Although the Ugandan government would be considered the principal to any crimes committed in the course of forced displacement, because it could not have carried out forced displacement and internment without the assistance of the aid agencies, the agencies could be considered accessories to those crimes, and to fail to demand that they be held liable for that complicity before the existing law of war will only encourage the worst forms of humanitarian impunity.

The Ugandan government policy of forced displacement and internment could comprise a number of crimes under international humanitarian law, specifically when measured against three standards pertaining to forced displacement of populations during wartime: the mode of displacement and internment, the rationale for displacement, and the conditions of the displaced.[87] First, displacement in Uganda was initiated and sustained through egregious government violence against the civilian population, which represents grave violations of human rights and humanitarian law, in particular Common Article III to the Geneva Conventions of 1949. Specifically, Common Article III prohibits "violence to life and person, in particular murder of all kinds, mutilation, cruel treatment and torture." Second, the Geneva Conventions allow for displacement of the civilian population only in order to protect that population or in cases of military necessity.[88] In Uganda, the population was not protected—if anything, it became an easier target for rebel violence—and there was no clear military imperative for such a policy, which lasted over 10 years in many places, far beyond what any imperative military reasons could demand. Third, the Geneva Conventions state that: "Should such displacements have to be carried out, all possible measures shall be taken in order that the civilian population may be received under satisfactory conditions of shelter, hygiene, health, safety and nutrition."[89] None of these conditions were met by the Ugandan government. Finally, there are the tens of thousands of deaths and the devastation of Acholi society and economy that resulted from the prolongation of the policy of forced displacement, possibly comprising a crime against humanity.

Because the Ugandan government's policy of forced displacement and interment in camps could be a war crime under the Geneva Conventions and possibly a crime against humanity, parties that knowingly acted in such a way so as to assist in keeping people in the camps may be complicit in those crimes. This is an emerging area of international law, but it would seem reasonable that the fact that the aid agencies and UN knew that providing aid and assistance to the Ugandan government would help keep people in the camps, knew the violence that went into forcing people into the camps, and knew that people were trying to leave the camps to go home, would perhaps be sufficient to establish their criminal complicity.

Demanding legal liability through prosecutions, lawsuits, or even through "naming and shaming" could have a number of benefits beyond the Uganda case. By striving to make those who call for and carry out humanitarian interventions accountable for the consequences of their actions, calls for intervention may become more considered, and, in cases of instrumentalization of relief aid by states, the invocation of humanitarianism would no longer shield aid agencies from prosecution under international law. If they know that the aid agencies will not allow them to do so, states may be less likely to blatantly instrumentalize relief aid.

Several arguments might be made against holding aid agencies legally liable. First, there is the question of intentionality—that individual aid workers have only good intentions and so do not deserve punishment. In response, I would maintain that the lack of intention to commit a crime does not necessarily absolve one from legal accountability for the criminal consequences of one's actions if those consequences are known. Also, legal liability will not send the those truck drivers or doctors carrying out humanitarian policies to jail—principles such as command responsibility can help ensure that low-level employees are not used as scapegoats to absolve those who are actually setting policies and making decisions. Legal liability will encourage all aid workers to be more conscientious about how they get involved and perhaps provide them with the space needed to speak out against or refuse to participate in what they may themselves see as counterproductive or illegal interventions. By promoting reform, legal liability can help make the consequences of interventions conform more closely to aid workers' good intentions, a benefit to them as well.

A second argument against legal liability is that humanitarian action cannot be concerned with consequentialist reasoning because it must be focused on the duty to respond as best it can in the face of an incontestable moral demand for assistance.[90] If aid agencies have to worry about being held legally liable for the consequences of their interventions, the argument goes, they will end up risk averse and not acting in cases of genuine need. Moreover, it is asserted, such consequentialist reasoning is impossible because the complexity of humanitarian crises precludes accurate predictions as to the consequences of aid. I would respond that, first, consequentialist reasoning needs to be a part of decision making by aid agencies because things can *always* get worse, and intervention may very well make things worse. Admittedly, humanitarian crises are complex and all consequences cannot be known, but this does not preclude legal liability for those cases in which negative consequences were known or could have been reasonably expected. Second, if such legal accountability makes aid agencies more risk averse and more careful with their interventions, this may perhaps help to counter what Alex de Waal has called the "Gresham's Law" of humanitarian assistance, whereby the most responsible aid agencies are pushed aside by the least scrupulous. Hard international humanitarian law exists and should be enforced, including against its own self-proclaimed champions.

DEMOCRATIC ACCOUNTABILITY AND PARTICIPATION

Although no aid agency has offered itself up for legal liability, many humanitarian aid practitioners have made at least a rhetorical commitment to being accountable to their beneficiaries: Jan Egeland, for example, has declared that "our ultimate accountability as humanitarians is to the people we serve."[91] This has translated into little change in practice, however, if by accountability we mean formalized mechanisms by which aid recipients are provided with complete information, are able to judge aid agencies' performance, and can impose sanctions. To date, there has been no proposal to establish concrete mechanisms to formalize accountability beyond a rhetorical commitment to self-regulation, and, as Alex de Waal makes clear, "internal mechanisms for evaluation and accountability . . . are not adequate," because "accountability without sanctions is meaningless."[92] If any accountability mechanism is to be genuine and effective, he argues, it must be "democratic, founded in law and must have real sanctions and penalties to impose."[93] This failure to provide concrete formal mechanisms perhaps should not be surprising, because intervening agencies and their state and nonstate partners certainly do not see it in their interests to be democratically accountable, let alone to face the possibility of sanctions. All parties involved in humanitarian aid delivery rely on the invocation of vague moral obligations to justify their activities, a freedom that would be threatened if they were held accountable to the people whose human rights they claim to uphold.

Although formalized accountability has remained at the rhetorical stage, initiatives to promote beneficiary participation have proceeded significantly in practice in recent years. For example, Principle 7 of the Good Humanitarian Donorship Initiative requests "implementing humanitarian organisations to ensure to the greatest possible extent, adequate involvement of beneficiaries in the design, implementation, monitoring and evaluation of humanitarian response." UNHCR has begun similar projects, and even Bill Clinton, in the wake of the Indian Ocean tsunami, declared that more cooperation with local structures was necessary.

The push for participation is both moral and pragmatic, invoking the respect of human rights and better efficacy; as Groupe URD puts it, "Participation inevitably takes time, but this time is easily compensated for by gains in efficiency, adaptability, relevance and acceptability."[94] One early and prominent argument in favor of ensuring the participation of local organizations in the interventionist enterprise was put forth by Mark Duffield and John Prendergast, who propose providing aid to states or rebel groups that are genuinely interested in upholding the population's human rights. According to them, the Emergency Relief Desk's effort to deliver aid into the nongovernment areas of Eritrea and northern Ethiopia managed to create "partnerships with indigenous relief agencies" through the civilian departments created by the rebel Fronts.[95] Because the rebel groups were accountable to the populations they fought for, Duffield and Prendergast conclude that the promotion of their capacity was ultimately in the interests of human rights, peace, and efficiency.[96] According to this model, where states or armed organizations are recognized as human rights defenders, they can participate directly in interventions and aid can go directly to them to build their capacity. However, where there are no "good guys," where all political and military actors are predatory, interventions should seek the participation of and help promote, not political actors, but civil society organizations.[97] In this way, it is argued, participation in humanitarian aid can both make aid more effective and help in the process of capacity building toward peace in a war-ravaged society.[98]

Today, the focus among aid agencies is often less on assisting rebel groups than on developing participatory and partnership relations with war-affected communities, and a number of handbooks have been produced on promoting this type of participation in humanitarian action. Some critics have argued that these initiatives remain superficial: "while it was pretty well accepted on paper that beneficiary participation in the evaluation of assistance programmes is a desirable thing for a range of reasons, it still took place rather infrequently in practice."[99] Others argue that aid agencies will not voluntarily give up their power and only integrate participation into certain limited phases of projects as a cost-saving measure or as an effort to absolve themselves of responsibility for failed interventions by attributing that failure to local incompetence.

Proposals for humanitarian participation, however, also have their critics. One argument against participation is that it will detract from effectiveness and thus harm people's human right to humanitarian aid. This is based on the idea that beneficiary participation necessarily subjugates aid distribution to imperatives that are alien to its own logic of the efficient promotion of survival through specialized expertise. It is the humanitarian faith in expertise, whether the technical standards and codes of conduct or the voluntaristic genius of the aid worker and her space to experiment and take risks as leading to the most efficient delivery of aid, that gives rise to the assumption that participation may, even if minimally imposed, impinge on the efficient promotion of survival. This argument takes on a moral dimension when the rights of victims are invoked. Victim demands for participation may be rejected in the name of the victims' own rights, as they may make demands that, according to aid agencies, are against the victims' own interests. As one humanitarian agency official explains, "We must hold to this right and these principles, even if others, including at times claimants themselves, might not give them priority."[100] For example, by refusing to provide education to a displaced community, which that community had itself demanded, and instead providing access to clean water, "we were being accountable to the claimants by means of adherence to the principle of the right to life."[101]

Calls for participation are also sometimes dismissed by invoking the figure of the helpless victim whose very incapacity necessitates foreign assistance. As Austen Davis argues,

> Ultimately, we should be primarily accountable to victims. However, the idea that this means that we need greater community participation is a

dangerous over-simplification. The degree to which a humanitarian worker can be accountable to people in societies that have been destroyed from within is questionable.[102]

Again, it is the humanitarian worker as genius that is invoked to resolve humanitarianism's dilemmas: "We must remember that victims are victims," and so it is up to the "political savvy of aid workers," not the political judgment of the beneficiaries, to steer humanitarian action.[103] Fiona Terry expands on this, arguing that aid agencies are dealing with

> victims of abuse that has left them powerless to meet their own needs. To imagine that they will organize of their own volition to oppose the people who came to assist them is not only utopian, it ignores the real source of their distress. It is not the aid agencies which overlook the dietary preferences of victims that pose the greatest constraints on effective relief, but local power-holders who in most cases cause the suffering. . . . Placing the onus on the victims to identify the problems of humanitarian action shifts responsibility away from aid agencies; it does not make them more responsible for their actions.[104]

A third critique is that, because even the most basic forms of community involvement in aid distribution involve political questions about decision making and representation, any kind of participation will have the tendency to empower unaccountable, exploitative authorities. As Terry writes, "Aid organizations seek to identify 'leaders' to act on behalf of the refugees, thereby imbuing certain individuals with legitimacy and power over their 'constituency.' . . . [T]he people who control the aid control the refugees."[105] Her quotation marks reveal Terry's dismissal of even the possibility of nonexploitative, legitimate leadership among beneficiary populations. An associated problem is that participatory initiatives that do manage to reach the vulnerable can threaten established, often violent, power holders, so participation may be too difficult or too dangerous for conflict situations.[106]

These three challenges to participation and democratic accountability—that participation and accountability diminish effectiveness, that powerless victims cannot participate, and that they may counterproductively empower the exploitative and violent—demonstrate, not a need to abandon participation, but rather a need for a democratic approach to participation. First, the debate over effectiveness suffers from a serious deficit of independent evaluations of the results of participatory initiatives—although the negative repercussions of a lack of participation can be clearly seen in specific cases, such as in Uganda. Second, the presumption that those caught in the middle of violent upheaval are powerless, even if only during an emergency phase in which people truly are helpless victims, has been subject to intense critique by the work of academics and activists for decades now.[107] And third, although negative politicization is certainly a legitimate concern, it does not speak against democratic accountability and participation per se, but rather against inadequate efforts to promote those goals. The orientation of participatory initiatives should not be toward determining which groups will be the local agents of massive influxes of foreign resources but instead toward fostering formalized, public mechanisms that can regulate the work of aid agencies. These mechanisms would be characterized by publicity, transparency, and inclusion, would be legally constituted, and would work along with existing formal local and national political structures.

In broader terms, the threat that unrepresentative, corrupt, or illegitimate actors or political forces will hijack participatory political structures is a danger faced by *any* participatory political system, whether electoral democracy or local councils. The problem of self-interest usurping legitimate representation is the constitutive problematic of all political life, therefore, its presence within the question of humanitarian participation should not lead to a rejection of participation but rather to a recognition of the need both to set up institutions that are less exposed to instrumentalization and to create an atmosphere of publicity and transparency that will deter such antidemocratic possibilities from coming to pass. This form of democratic participation would also diminish the potential for humanitarian agencies to be complicit with wide-scale and grave violations of the human rights of the very people they purport to serve, thus diminishing the need for post facto legal liability. In northern Uganda, for example, if the aid agencies had been responsive to the civilian population instead of to the Ugandan government, the agencies would have, instead of helping people stay in the camps, helped them stay at home.

This project can be founded on a human rights discourse that focuses on formal guarantees of rights to freedom of association, to information, to organization, to opinion, and to participation—precisely the rights that are considered superfluous in contexts of conflict or disaster. Such a project cannot be brought about by aid agencies, however, despite their stated commitments to participation or rights. Instead, initiatives would have to be undertaken by organizations and institutions independent of aid agencies, groups whose work is in community organization and education, not in aid distribution. Their work could be similar to the work larger labor unions do when they provide technical advice, assistance, and resources in local labor struggles. They would work to make needed information available to displaced populations and to establish formalized transparency arrangements with aid agencies and would provide the technical assistance needed by displaced people so that they can articulate and make demands of international NGOs and governments. These initiatives would help provide the resources and space needed by displaced people to realize their freedom of association, opinion, and organization without being shut down by government or aid agencies. Such initiatives can also help channel information from displaced populations in the South to other groups in the South as well as to audiences and activists in the North. In those cases in which aid agencies have been complicit in crimes or guilty of repeated violations of human rights or humanitarian standards, these initiatives can help work toward the legal accountability of aid agencies through the use of national or international legal mechanisms.

This would help provide the tools that displaced people need to make the demands that they themselves see as appropriate, even if—especially if—those demands are not compatible with aid agency or government policy, if those demands represent challenges to policies of displacement and internment. Such initiatives can also serve to make the displaced themselves more realistic and politically responsible about what they demand. Instead of making vague appeals to the "international community" for intervention, the displaced would have the information needed to better understand the system that is governing them, what they have rights to demand and have rights to do, and perhaps even how to change things.

4

Peacebuilding and Social Order

Humanitarian aid was the most spectacular, and most spectacularly counterproductive, form of human rights intervention in northern Uganda. Starting around 2000, however, and especially after Jan Egeland's visit in 2003, another array of interventions became part of the landscape there: so-called peacebuilding. Peacebuilding is a concept that can admit to a multitude of meanings and a wide range of practices, from development, to education, microcredit, community-conflict resolution, human rights promotion, psychotherapy, civil-society promotion, and traditional reconciliation. Although most often associated with postconflict intervention, peacebuilding has also been conceived as including interventions that can take place at any point in a conflict, justified as being concerned with latent, existing, or recently ended violence.[1] In northern Uganda, although some intervening agencies pretended that the conflict had already been resolved and that northern Uganda was in a postconflict, reconstruction phase, most simply tailored their wide array of peacebuilding interventions in the camps to the context of ongoing violent conflict. There, an ever-expanding menagerie of international NGOs and aid agencies carried out peacebuilding interventions that, espousing the rights-based approach, emphasized participation, empowerment, and capacity building.

Societal peacebuilding interventions, as noted in chapter 1, purport to address the causes and consequences of violence by reforming and reconstructing the targeted society. They see violence as leading to social crisis, which in turn is thought to cause further violence—the "cause and consequence" formula. Social breakdown can be interpreted through a number of lenses, depending on the particular form of intervention: the peace-through-development agenda interprets violence as causing and caused by underdevelopment; the community-reconciliation agenda interprets violence as causing and caused by a breakdown community cohesion; the traditional-reconciliation agenda interprets violence as causing and caused by a breakdown of traditional culture, and so on. Intervention thus is directed toward rebuilding social order, where a stable social order is equated with peace and social disorder is expressed as a deficiency in any one of a number of different domains. Each peace-building intervention is imagined as rebuilding social order by externally compen-sating for these particular internal deficiencies, while these essentially technical interventions draw legitimacy from an expanded human rights discourse.

Societal peacebuilding interventions tend to internalize the causes and ef-fects of violence to the community of victims, attributing it to deviations on the part of groups or individuals. It is assumed that individuals and communities, trapped in a vicious cycle of violence and social, cultural, or psychological break-down, are incapable of autonomous action, and so the initial agency for social transformation will have to come from the outside. Breakdown is assumed to have left only the victim, and intervention is to proceed by building a new social-ized subject upon that basis to function within a peaceful, normal, social order. Although the distribution of humanitarian aid attempts to discipline individuals toward victimhood and the elimination of agency, because any agency on the part of the displaced threatens the efficient distribution of aid, societal peacebuilding conceives of victims as transcending that status and, through intervention, be-coming socially, economically, psychologically, and culturally healthy beings.

The consequence is that peacebuilding can discipline people by interpreting autonomous expressions of agency as deviance—as conflict, as psychological trauma, as human rights violations, as refusal to submit to authority, as antisocial, anticul-tural, antitraditional behavior—and attempting to steer their agency into its own models of law-abiding individuals, peacebuilders, participants in development, civil-society actors, youth, women, or even proper tribespeople. In this way, peacebuilding leads to the creation of more intensive, extensive, and robust administrative systems that are to function through the agency of the redeemed victims themselves.

These many intensive and extensive interventions had their paths to imple-mentation made smooth by the political crises afflicting the Acholi; indeed, the lack of significant local or national Acholi leadership, the co-optation of potential leaders by the interventionist structures, and the concentration of the increasingly desperate Acholi peasantry into camps made northern Uganda a useful guinea pig for experimentation by international agencies. The World Bank's NUSAF, AFRI-COM's involvement, and the International Criminal Court's investigation of the LRA were all explicitly formulated by their implementers as cutting-edge and even experimental. For this reason, human rights interventions into northern Uganda have significance beyond this specific case because they may serve as blueprints for future interventions in Africa and elsewhere.

1. The World Bank in Northern Uganda

The World Bank has been a major donor to Uganda since the late 1980s, and its aid programs to northern Uganda—Northern Uganda Reconstruction Programs I and II—have been among the largest. These interventions need to be understood in the context of the World Bank's changing strategies over last three decades. Since the 1980s, the World Bank, although not shifting its rhetorical commitment to growth through the free market, has experimented with a host of supplements to this market-based strategy that comprise different ways of managing the popular protest and social dislocation caused in large part by the policies mandated by neoliberal orthodoxy. Thus, the general failure of Bank policies to promote economic growth[2] has been matched in importance by the Bank's concomitant experiments in social and political engineering.[3] The state, for example, has occupied a changing place in the World Bank's strategies of social control, from the coercive role asked of it in the 1981 Berg Report, to its marginalization in favor of NGOs as the chosen agents of neoliberal reform in the early 1990s, to its revaluation as a key component of conflict resolution and market promotion in the 2000s.[4] As a result, the policies and programs that go under the name of development, with regard to Africa, have undergone a number of dramatic shifts and continue to be reformed.[5]

The most recent phase entails a highly expansive agenda for intervention in the name of development, as the World Bank has embraced the language of participation, human rights, and good governance. While some critics dismiss this language as mere rhetoric, I argue that these supplemental policies must be taken seriously because they are being put into place and having dramatic social and political effects, structuring subjectivities, social relations, and states. The expansiveness of today's development agenda lies precisely in the failure of World Bank policies to promote development: as the economic growth and poverty alleviation predicted by the World Bank consistently failed to materialize, the World Bank internalized to Africa the reasons for this failure by blaming it on problems within previously unaddressed sectors of African state or society and then proposed new interventions designed to address those sectors.[6] By constantly expanding its etiology of underdevelopment while keeping it internal to African states and societies, the Bank has justified its intervention into ever-wider domains of African life, seeking to engineer new areas in the name of establishing the necessary preconditions for economic development.[7]

Development ended up dissolved into other categories. At the same time that the preconditions of development were universalized and universal interventions were legitimated, development itself was emptied of objective content against which to measure the success or failure of the World Bank's prescriptions. In its 2000 report, the Bank equated "development" with four ill-defined "circles of cumulative causation," which included a jumble of social, economic, and political problems, all tied together in a mutually reinforcing system as causes and consequences of development.[8] "Circles of cumulative causation" imply no clear causality and no clear starting place; thus, everything was responsible for the failure of economic development, so everything would have to be changed before anything could be expected to change. Africans were told not to expect economic growth until there had been revolutionary transformations in all domains of life, driven by Western intervention. The Bank laid the groundwork for it and its partners to engage in new experiments of social, political, and cultural engineering in an effort to manage the population in its poverty, all in the name of development, without ever having to show evidence of success.

This section details the reorientation of World Bank development policy for Africa toward conflict resolution and peacebuilding since 2000 and the consequences that agenda has had for Uganda as it has informed interventions into the north. The conflict-resolution dimension primarily concerns building the capacity of the Ugandan state to manage conflicts; this has led to the expansion of its administrative dimension and the promotion of an unaccountable "governance state," in Graham Harrison's phrase. It has also provided resources to the state that could be instrumentalized by the military and political elites at its core, and so the constitution of an administrative state went hand-in-hand with increasing militarization and securitization.[9] The peacebuilding dimension concerns society and is designed to manage a population in crisis using the full array of peacebuilding tools and techniques. In Uganda's case, this was embodied in the Northern Uganda Social Action Fund (NUSAF), which Fredrick Golooba-Mutebi and Sam Hickey characterize as a paradigmatic case of "inclusive neoliberalism" and the participatory approach to development interventions.[10] By the 2000s, "development" for Uganda was being reduced to building state security in the context of totalizing societal interventions. The means had become the ends, and development was divorced from poverty alleviation and even from economics, all in the name of peace.

THE WORLD BANK IN 2000: STATE-BUILDING AND CONFLICT RESOLUTION

In accordance with Africa's dominant image, the World Bank in the 1990s came to identify the continent as a terrain of permanent violent conflict. Conflict, it argued in its seminal 2000 report, *Can Africa Claim the 21st Century?*, represented the primary threat to economic development, resulting in "huge direct costs and incalculable indirect costs, including the destruction of physical infrastructure, loss of institutional capacity and social capital, and flight of financial and human capital."[11] Consequently, the management of conflict was made the centerpiece of the Bank's new development strategy. Evoking the standard peacebuilding formula, the Bank argued that not only do conflicts "perpetuate poverty," they also are perpetuated by poverty, "creating a vicious circle that can be reversed only through special development efforts—including long-run peacebuilding and political reforms. With success in these areas, countries can grow rapidly, and flight capital can return."[12] To this end, the World Bank declared, "*Improving governance and resolving conflict* is [sic] perhaps the most basic requirement for faster development."[13] The conclusion was that "socially fractionalized societies—like most in Africa—require careful management."[14]

Can Africa Claim the 21st Century?, therefore, incorporated state-led conflict resolution and societal peacebuilding into its development agenda. Conflict resolution, it argued, would be realized primarily through a "re-built" state, a reversal of the Bank's generally antistate orientation of the late 1980s and early 1990s.[15] Reflecting a general trend toward state-building, the Bank in 2000 argued that "effective policies for Africa must . . . both strengthen the economy and contribute to the formation of effective states,"[16] for "Africa's recent economic history can be seen as a process of marginalization—first of people, then of governments."[17] However, what the Bank saw as bringing the state back in was not a "re"-construction, but was rather a new construction, the creation of a state form focused on security. As the report admitted, "the question of providing security for the state and its people is at the center of the debate on political reform in Africa."[18]

The World Bank's "effective state" found its raison d'être in the resolution of existing wars and conflicts and in the prevention of potential conflicts through conflict management and effective security provision. According to the Bank's vision, state security services would be integrated into regional collective security bodies, which would bind national security services within regional and global norms. As the report declared, "because effective collective security arrangements depend on the national security forces that comprise them, attention must be given to creating coherent and efficient national security structures."[19]

Uganda, given its international reputation and its willingness to undertake harsh restructuring measures directed by donors, qualified as just such a potentially effective state in the Bank's eyes, if only given the requisite external assistance, in particular to suppress the conflict in the north. The suppression of the insurgency was additionally important for the Bank because it did not want to be seen to be involved in a conflict area. It is telling that the World Bank, in its official documents, consistently either termed northern Uganda a postconflict situation or simply ignored the presence of continuing armed conflict.[20] Some Ugandan officials outside the main World Bank office admitted confidentially that the Bank had glossed over or chosen to ignore the armed conflict. One project officer in northern Uganda told me that if the north had not been framed as a postconflict situation, the "technocrats" would not have let NUSAF go through; another official in Kampala agreed, stating that NUSAF had been "written under the assumption that there will be a postconflict situation very soon."[21] Any admission that there was an ongoing conflict in northern Uganda was systematically excised from the Bank's documents. According to one aid agency's report:

> A consultant who asked to remain anonymous was contracted by the World Bank to write a report, *From Conflict to Sustained Growth and Deep Reductions in Poverty*, for its May 2004 Shanghai meeting. He insisted on writing a section on the conflict in Uganda, maintaining that Uganda could not be classified as a "postconflict country." When this section was deleted, he asked to have his name removed from the report.[22]

Furthermore, the fact that the government's two most significant operations against the LRA—1991 Operation North and 2002 Operation Iron Fist—occurred right before the inception of the two major World Bank-funded reconstruction projects for northern Uganda—Northern Uganda Reconstruction Programme (NURP) I and NURP II/NUSAF—raises questions about the possibility that officials within the Bank tacitly premised the provision of reconstruction aid on the Ugandan government's termination of the conflict through military means.[23] Regardless of these possible arrangements, the overall logic of the Bank's intervention agenda is that the "re"-built state takes on the function of terminating and managing internal conflicts so as to create postconflict situations into which the Bank can intervene without being accused of interfering in politics or in ongoing conflicts. As was documented in chapter 2, the Bank, along with other donors, did, indeed, regularly look the other way as the Ugandan government diverted its budget into military spending and expanded the war in the north.

However, the Ugandan government did not use that increased defense funding, enabled by donors, to win the war in the north militarily, but rather to serve other purposes at home and abroad. The consequence of allowing Uganda to use budgetary support to fund its militarization was that the Bank's state-building agenda translated, not into conflict resolution, but into the construction of a security state and the prolongation of war and violence in and around Uganda. As factions of the Ugandan government have seen the security apparatus, consecrated by the Bank, become a useful tool for realizing their own political interests, the containment of the war provided an airtight excuse to the government for expanding its military budget with donor assistance, even over donors' occasional remonstrations. The unaccountable elites at the center of the Ugandan state, who the World Bank depends on to push through its economic policies,[24] end up taking advantage of that external support to carry out their own agendas, even if those agendas contradict the stated objectives of the donors themselves. This is another example of the paradox of liberal interventions: good governance interventions create corruption, which is then condemned as an inherent cultural or social characteristic of the people the interveners claim they have come to save.

UGANDA'S NUSAF

Along with this securitized state-building agenda, the World Bank has also put in place a societal peacebuilding agenda, one whose primary purpose was to maintain social order using all the tools of participatory peacebuilding. According to the Bank's 2000 report, in Africa "efforts must also be made to address the socio-political problems that caused the war and to develop institutions that encourage economic growth, equitable distribution of resources, and political inclusion."[25] Therefore, the Bank oriented its initiatives around the disciplinary discourses of psychology, family, and community as well as the discourse of African tradition, as modes of normalization and social management in the service of development. In addition to addressing these issues, which it framed as the root causes of poverty and conflict, there were also the tasks of reconstruction and reconciliation,[26] and so the report proposed supporting "activities ranging from demobilization and reintegration of former combatants and resettlement of refugees to demining, emergency relief, food aid, and economic rehabilitation, including infrastructure repair."[27] The financial crises of postconflict states allow the donor community to claim the exclusive responsibility for funding these operations, according to the Bank, and so the report put forth international and regional assistance as being central to the success of peacebuilding. The World Bank's expanded development agenda reflected the expanded peacebuilding agenda, as there was little left out of the Bank's domain; every area of life, whether political, economic, social, psychological, familial, or environmental, was made potentially subject to foreign intervention in the name of peacebuilding and development. As the 2000 report modestly put it, "postconflict reconstruction requires a comprehensive approach."

The consequences of these totalizing interventions and of the changing meaning of "development" are put into relief by Uganda's NUSAF, From 1992 until 2000, the World Bank provided significant funding to NURP I. NURP I has been the target of significant criticism, mostly around the corruption it fueled, its inefficiencies, and its lack of results.[28] Since 2002, the Bank has funded NUSAF, a major component of NURP II. NUSAF, cast in the mold of *Can Africa Claim the 21st Century?*, was designed to correct the failings of NURP I, mostly through more community participation and more attention to building so-called social capital instead of economic infrastructure—that is, to promoting social order in the name of development while avoiding the need to be accountable by objective standards.[29]

According to the NUSAF Project Appraisal Document, in northern Uganda "development has been stifled by both local and international cross-border conflicts as well as inter and intra-tribal conflicts."[30] Therefore, NUSAF will "tackle poverty and bring about development through participatory community efforts that utilise community value systems, which are particularly strong in the family, clan, and cattle-rearing culture found in northern Uganda"; this is represented as part of the stated effort to ensure that the north can "catch-up with the rest of the country's development agenda and programs."[31] The implications require some analysis.

First, echoing *Can Africa Claim the 21st Century?*, the Bank claims in the NUSAF Project Appraisal that "insecurity in the Northern Region has become both a cause and consequence of poverty."[32] Or, as it is phrased in the NUSAF "Community Reconciliation and Conflict Management Handbook," prepared by the Office of the Prime Minister, "peace could be considered a public good that provides an enabling environment for sustainable development. Peacebuilding is a precondition for poverty reduction" and is essential in "preparing them [the war-affected population] for participation in other development processes."[33]

The Bank's explanation of the root cause of the northern Ugandan conflict focuses predictably on underdevelopment as well. As the Project Appraisal Document makes clear, "The relatively poor districts in Northern and Eastern Uganda have not benefited sufficiently from economic growth and reforms. . . . The historical imbalances in the development of the North have led to increased poverty and conflict—which is both politically motivated and tied to livelihood insecurity of the communities."[34] Or, as the Office of the Prime Minister put it:

> Conflict is both a consequence and cause of poverty in the North. Peacebuilding therefore is about resuscitation of community social capital to increase cohesiveness. Social cohesiveness is central for community empowerment in the North. The increasing poverty level in the region is mainly the result of insecurity, which invariably has resulted in much weaker institutional capacities of formal systems in the region. For communities to effectively participate and own the processes of their development and implement their visions . . . restoration of self-confidence and community cohesiveness is critical. NUSAF provides a vehicle for community dialogue and leadership development so that individuals can establish and/or promote peace.[35]

The Bank thereby finds the root cause of northern Uganda's relative poverty and underdevelopment—and ultimately of the conflict as well—in a deficiency internal to the north itself, namely, the north's lack of capacity to utilize the resources for development.[36] The positing of the current conflict as a response to a history of relative economic deprivation is unsubstantiated, as is the effort to frame the north's current relative economic deprivation as caused by problems internal to the north. The World Bank has to rewrite Ugandan history in order for its interpretive scheme to fit and to be able to blame on the Acholi peasantry what is in large part a failure of the Ugandan government, the international order, and the World Bank itself to foster the political and social preconditions for peace and development in the north.

Once northern underdevelopment erupted into conflict, the Bank argues, violence and underdevelopment became united into a familiar vicious circle. The medium for this mutually reinforcing interaction is social breakdown or the lack of social capital, and since the cause of conflict and underdevelopment are internalized to the Acholi, the solution is to rebuild social order so that the north can resolve conflict and use development funds effectively. Thus, the purpose of NUSAF is to "create an enabling environment for economic growth and structural transformation"[37] and to "support sustainable social, cultural, and economic growth."[38] This represents a participatory development strategy, one in which a healed, cohesive community is to be mobilized and given form through its engagement in development.

Rebuilding social order entails two reconciliation agendas: one supposedly traditional and one nontraditional. The traditional agenda involves using tribe as a disciplinary discourse, reflecting the focus on ethnicity in *Can Africa Claim the 21st Century?* That report expanded "civil society" beyond NGOs to include "traditional councils of elders, ethnic mediators, [and] contemporary religious and secular organizations,"[39] and even proposed the devolution of state power along ethnic lines.[40] Ethnicity as a disciplinary tool is an important element of NUSAF, as addressed in the next chapter.

What the Bank termed non-traditional modes of social reconciliation were also important in NUSAF, one aspect of which was the training of hundreds of community-reconciliation and conflict-management promoters and the distribution of funds to several hundred communities "supported by reconciliation-related NGOs."[41] A massive, microlevel regime of social discipline for the sake of peace and development was to be created, training Acholi to undertake social, familial, and psychological peacebuilding interventions, the consequences of which are discussed later.

NUSAF also commits substantial funding to more orthodox local development projects in the name of bringing peace: building schools, digging wells, setting up medical centers, providing grinding mills, and supplying microcredit for small businesses. A number of other NGOs in northern Uganda, especially the larger ones such as World Vision and Norwegian Refugee Council, also invested significant amounts of money in building this infrastructure for social and economic development. Indeed, I did not find a single so-called internally displaced school in the camps that was not funded by foreign donors or NGOs. However, in the context of mass displacement in northern Uganda, these camp infrastructure projects can end up being complicit with the counterinsurgency in much the same way as the distribution of relief aid to the camps is complicit. They teach people to look to the international community for basic services, while helping to make the camps more lasting by building a rudimentary social and economic infrastructure within them. Promoting this kind of "development" in the Ugandan war zone, and especially in displaced-people's camps can end up prolonging the existence of the camps and diverting people from the government's responsibility for keeping them interned.

Another important part of NUSAF has been its vulnerable-groups support initiative:

> Through a participatory process, vulnerable groups in the region will be identified and supported to develop interventions that contribute to improvements in their livelihood. Activities under this component would include rehabilitation and expansion of training facilities to provide vocational skills; sponsorships for youths to undergo vocational/life skills training (masonry, carpentry, tailoring, blacksmiths, welding, etc.), provision of tool-kits upon their graduation to work on sub-projects, [and] financing new and ongoing income generating activities.[42]

NUSAF is not alone in undertaking these projects with so-called vulnerable groups; indeed, an significant number of NGOs and international agencies were involved in providing microcredit, grants or livelihood support to women, youth, orphans, former rebels, the disabled, and other categories. In particular, in the case of youth, there is a clear managerial dimension to these programs: those sectors of the population most likely to join the rebels or otherwise disturb social order are given the opportunity to learn trades—but trades that, at best, may provide a small income and at worst are useless in the context of continued economic breakdown and displacement. The Bank has tailored its distribution of funds not to projects that could realistically lead to economic development or broad-based poverty reduction, but rather to initiatives that will give enough money to threatening sectors of the population to keep them from disturbing a peace that exists only in the World Bank's imagination.

Even when grassroots-development projects do not focus purely on vulnerable groups, they still can serve a depoliticizing function, in large part through the promotion of microcapitalist self-help entrepreneurship and of NGOs as the chosen vehicles for promoting that agenda. As far back as 1989, the Bank had argued that "experience suggests that the management of primary services could be placed with decentralized agencies—local government, local communities, or NGOs."[43] NGOs and community-based organizations would execute projects generally free of charge; the effect was for the poor to re-orient their demands away from the state and toward the international community through local aid agencies.[44] The politics of material well-being was to be transformed into access to foreign handouts, mediated by NGOs, which had the task of teaching the rural poor that they did not need state assistance but rather should look to themselves and, at the margin, to the international community for capital,[45] which is equally in the interests of the aid agencies, looking to expand and legitimate their activities, and the Ugandan government, looking to withdraw further.

The participatory structure through which NUSAF was to operate drove on this tendency. The Bank explains that a "lead NGO" will be responsible for each project at the district level because the district government does not have the capacity to regulate the large number of new projects. As a NUSAF officer in Kampala explained, each project is carried out by a parish-level committee that is elected by the communities, receives funding directly from the World Bank, and implements projects with the assistance of NGOs.[46] By doing so, he noted, the Bank wants to make development more "participatory" and to privilege the "informal" over the "formal" so as to "depoliticize development." What is actually being depoliticized, as Golooba-Mutebi and Hickey incisively explain, and as critics of "participatory development" have argued since the 1990s, are those people who are supposed to participate and thus be empowered. For one thing, the idea that the massive structural causes of poverty in the north could be effectively addressed by shifting the agency for transformation to the displaced Acholi peasantry is absurd and absolves those truly responsible for and benefiting from those structures. By blaming a lack of social cohesion and insufficient entrepreneurialism on the part of the Acholi for poverty in the north, the World Bank economists somehow consistently miss the role that the long history of collusion between donors, capitalists, and the Ugandan political elite has played in underpinning poverty. The Acholi peasants who are asked to participate in NUSAF, however, do not miss this dimension of their economic situation, and so, as Golooba-Mutebi and Hickey report, "ironically, the community-driven approach fails to fully resonate with the priorities of local people, who are painfully aware of the huge scale of the development challenge facing the north."[47] Their final assessment is that NUSAF "may actually have exacerbated the tendencies that contributed toward this situation in the first place."[48]

Depoliticization can also characterize NUSAF's effect on local government. Specifically, the Bank goes around the Local Council (LC) system in the distribution of funds and the implementation of projects because the LCs have the tendency, according to the Bank, to "politicize development." The Bank's strategy thus tends to entrench an unaccountable administrative system and open that system to politicization at the expense of politically accountable local government. For one thing, NUSAF undermined the LC system even further, which, however compromised it may be, nevertheless is an existing institution with a potential for popular political participation. LCs were included only as surveillance tools and sources of information, and significant power over resources was, instead, given to community committees that would receive funding only if the World Bank deemed them suitable and if they were under the trusteeship of NGOs, creating administrative systems that were unaccountable to the population but accountable to foreign donors. At the same time, due to the informality and lack of transparency that went into World Bank decisions about who gets funds, this system provided a potential means through which the Ugandan government could control the distribution of resources and punish political opposition. Despite the Bank's assurances that they were depoliticizing development, the opposite appears to have sometimes been the case: numerous people reported that they have been unable to gain access to NUSAF funds because they are known to be opposed to the government.[49] So the merging of development and peacebuilding within participatory strategies can promote depoliticization through an increased orientation toward outside donors and through the undermining of political institutions and capacities, at the same time as it provides new resources for political instrumentalization by the government. In the case of Uganda, such forms of restricted, depoliticizing participation are the antithesis of the kinds of inclusive, expansive participation that would be needed to address the internal or national crises.

2. Rebuilding the Community

COMMUNITY CONFLICT RESOLUTION

Just as the peace-through-development agenda took a very real problem faced by the Acholi—material impoverishment—and then, terming that problem a cause and consequence of the conflict, attributed it to a deficiency within Acholi society to be remedied through external intervention, so does the community conflict resolution agenda take a problem faced by the Acholi—violence—term it a cause and consequence of conflict, and then attribute it to a deficiency within Acholi social order. Normal social order is understood to be nonviolence and the mutual respect for human rights among camp inhabitants; therefore, intervention is to reconstruct Acholi society and bring peace by promoting the respect for human rights among the victims themselves.

Some community conflict resolution interventions utilize a technical discourse of conflict resolution developed as a subfield of public policy and management. It is disseminated through workshops run by international organizations and is incorporated widely into the activities of NGOs, often because of the ease of acquiring international funding for conflict resolution projects.[50] In one such workshop I attended, participants were instructed that the violent conflicts afflicting their communities should be transformed into nonviolent deliberations and negotiations. Every conflict, whether the war in Acholiland, disputes over cattle in Karamoja, or the activities of rebel groups in Kasese, was subsumed within the same conceptual scheme: two actors are represented as competing over a scarce resource and, unable to solve the collective-action problem themselves, they turn to violence. The role of conflict-resolution interventions, according to this model, is to convince the two sides that they would both be better served by sharing the resource instead of fighting over it.

This model is useless for understanding the war between the LRA and the Ugandan government. More importantly, when it is disseminated and informs interventions into the camps, it can become counterproductive. A good example is a secondary school justice and peace club I visited, one of dozens of such bodies established in the camps at the instigation of foreign NGOs and often with the assistance of foreign funds. As the organizers of the club explained, their purpose is to "sensitize" their students about nonviolent conflict resolution and then to help their students carry out activities to sensitize the camp population as a whole through plays and songs teaching people that peace is better than war.[51] They teach their students how to resolve conflicts nonviolently, and they were especially adamant about convincing students to avoid strikes, which, they said, could lead to violence, as there had been a series of strikes and riots in Ugandan schools around that time. This kind of conflict resolution, informed by a technical approach in which all conflicts are equivalent and can be resolved through intracommunity deliberation and mediation, reframed the need to end LRA and government violence as the need to resolve and prevent conflict among the camp inhabitants themselves by preventing their participation in all potentially conflictual activities. The causes of the violence in Acholiland are internalized to the Acholi themselves, who are seen as victim and perpetrator. These interventions ignore violence between the government and the LRA, violence by the government against civilians, and often violence by the LRA against civilians, effectively reducing all three to violence between camp inhabitants themselves. They turn the overall conflict and the multiple forms of violence faced into intracommunal conflict and violence. Because violence is seen as caused by the breakdown of

Acholi society, the answer, its is concluded, is for Acholi society to be rebuilt by promoting human rights, community reconciliation, and conflict resolution—through sensitization. Once again, the victims of structural problems far beyond the reach of community reconciliation initiatives are blamed for those problems and given the responsibility for solving them in the name of a participatory, rights-based approach.

These interventions, carried out by a wide range of NGOs in the camps in the name of peacebuilding, are thus dedicated to resolving overt violence by putting to an end forms of contentious organization or action that may potentially lead to violence.[52] The effects of these interventions are ironic: many of the activities that the peace committees were mobilizing against—such as strikes, protests, or confrontations with authorities—were, in fact, precisely those activities that could have allowed the people in the camps to develop a way of challenging their internment. That is, people were being normalized away from practices of unmanageability or from undertaking possibly conflictual or contentious modes of organization and action. Instead, they were normalized toward identities and forms of organization whose point is to empower people to actively manage, by themselves, the conflicts that emerge as a result of living in inhumane conditions in a camp. Community conflict resolution can, in this way, end up teaching self-pacification to a community in crisis, teaching it to draw on its own resources in resolving the conflicts that erupt in the camps due to the continued nonresolution of the broader structural injustice and violence people face. It replicates the neoliberal logic underlying participatory development interventions, one of promoting self-management and depoliticization in the name of celebrating resilience and agency.

The government and NGOs, meanwhile, are put forth as the mediators of these intra-Acholi conflicts, for, along with sensitization, peacebuilding interventions also often involve the component of capacity building. Each person, through this particular human rights discourse, is instructed to displace the blame for violence onto fellow camp inhabitants and then to ask the government and NGOs, the instigators and propagators of the overall regime of structural and direct violence, to resolve the problem as supposedly impartial arbiters. NGOs become the agents helping to promote community self-management, people are reoriented away from the cause of their suffering, and contentious collective activity is dissuaded in the name of peace. This particular articulation of the human rights discourse lacks the potential for reorienting people toward practices that could organize a challenge to the camps or for promoting forms of organization that might help in resolving the underlying political crises. Human rights are incorporated into a program of self-management, in which foreign intervention provides the tools with which the community is supposed to pacify itself.

This approach is also evident in some women's rights interventions. For instance, a UNICEF report, "Suffering in Silence: A Study of Sexual and Gender-Based Violence," gives recommendations on how to lower the rising rate of sexual and gender-based violence seen in northern Uganda.[53] It notes that

the three most common forms [of] sexual and gender based violence
identified in Pabbo camp, in order of reported frequency, are found to be
the following: [1] Rape and marital rape perpetrated by UPDF, husbands
and strangers. . . . [2] Child sexual abuse, defilement and incest, perpetrated by uncles, friends, teachers and soldiers. . . . [3] Physical assault,
perpetrated by intimate friends, soldiers, strangers and spouses.[54]

To deal with these forms of violence, the report recommends more awareness
among NGOs and other service providers about the particular needs of sexual-
violence victims, greater coordination among agencies working on issues of violence against women and children, and community sensitization on sexual
violence. This would include:

> Strengthen[ing] awareness creation/sensitization activities in the Sub-
> County. This should begin right from the Sub-County officials down
> to the camp leaders, zonal and ward leaders. Sensitization workshops
> should be organized for all concerned stakeholders including NGOs; so
> as to create opportunities to develop strategies for SGBV [sexual and
> gender-based violence] related activities. This will help to improve the
> conceptualization of the current SGBV awareness and victims support
> project and strengthen coordination mechanism for SGBV activities in
> the camp [sic].[55]

This report reveals the logic behind this articulation of the peacebuilding
agenda. First, the report identifies violence by camp inhabitants against other camp
inhabitants as the most significant form of violence against women. It ignores the
violence that went into forcing women (and men) into the camps in the first place
and the regimes of violence maintained both by the LRA and by the Ugandan government to keep women and men in the camps, except for a cursory reference to
rape by the UPDF. It ignores the massive daily suffering experienced by women as
a result of living in the camps, without sufficient food, supplies, or medicine. As a
solution, the report suggests sensitization, in other words, teaching camp inhabitants to not be violent toward women. Of course, there is significant violence within
the camp population, a consequence of large numbers of people living under
conditions of extreme deprivation in extremely close quarters. Because of this, the
peacebuilding regime does respond to real problems experienced by the camp
inhabitants—but it then teaches camp inhabitants to define this violence among
themselves as the full extent of the violence they face, to blame themselves for the
violence, and to see the solution to violence and the conflict as residing in their own
embrace of less violent and less conflictual activities and attitudes. Again, it plays a
managerial role, reorienting people away from those responsible for the larger
problems and toward blaming themselves. In Uganda, this approach ignores the
fact that the direct and structural violence faced by women would not be solved by
any amount of sensitization as long as people were forced to remain in the camps.

Children's rights sensitizations can also abide by a similar logic and display similar depoliticizing and counterproductive tendencies.[56] There is a special emphasis on children's rights in northern Uganda, in part because of the ease of getting funding for children's rights projects, derived in large part through the way in which the war in Uganda has been defined around children, whether former LRA recruits or the so-called "night commuters."[57] For example, one of the largest international NGOs operating in northern Uganda was promoting human rights by conducting children's rights workshops for every primary and secondary school teacher in the camps.[58] In these workshops, teachers were taught to inform their students and parents about children's rights—the right to go to school, to a safe environment, to recreation, and so on.[59] As with the other peacebuilding interventions, this program of promoting children's rights was misdirected. By teaching teachers to teach parents and children about the rights that children hold, they presume that it was within the ability of children, parents, and teachers themselves to effect the realization of these rights. The sensitization courses ignored the daily violence faced by children as a result of the camps and the ongoing war. It is nonsensical for NGOs to lecture parents and teachers on the rights of children while those children are under threat of abduction by the LRA, not protected by the UPDF, and forced to stay in camps by the government, camps run by the NGOs themselves.

Thus, although some of the actions that are being disciplined out of existence by community conflict resolution are clearly destructive and without political potential, others—such as the upsurge of youth and women against older men; the refusal of returnees to submit to authority; the participation of youth in strikes, protests, or more militant actions—do represent modes of autonomous political action and, perhaps, the beginnings of the construction of new forms of effective political organization. The total inadequacy of human rights sensitization interventions, the way in which they eviscerate collective action of its political potential—of the potential to actually end the war and help people go home—the effacement of ends by empty means, and the frequent absurdity of these interventions is captured by a short photo caption from *The New Vision*:

> Ernst Surr, the Warchild Holland project adviser, Gulu LC5 Chief Norbert Mao (second right) and children march on the streets of Gulu town during the launch of a five-day peace concert on Tuesday. The event, organized by Warchild, I-Network, Cry Uganda, the Uganda Communications Commission and MTN [a multinational telecom company], is aimed at enlightening children on the role of the media in peacebuilding.[60]

CHILD SOLDIERS IN THE INTERVENTIONIST IMAGINATION

Many international organizations, from UNICEF, to Human Rights Watch, to Invisible Children, have focused on the violations of children's rights represented by the forced recruitment of youth by the LRA. The rescue of child soldiers has been the centerpiece of a host of fund-raising campaigns, and some international actors have even made the release of child soldiers by the LRA the precondition for peace talks. The entire conflict is often seen through the lens of children's rights, which focuses attention once again on violence within Acholi society, specifically the violence of the LRA in recruiting fighters. A certain concept of children's rights then informs interventions that claim to effect transformations within Acholi society. However, as with the forms of intervention just considered, these can also have counterproductive consequences by disciplining out of existence putatively coerced or deviant forms of organization or action on the part of youth and by promoting "normal" identities and behaviors that in fact lack political capacity and may entail their own forms of coercion.

These forms of child-centered intervention are premised on what Laura Edmondson calls the "master narrative" of the LRA: that it comprises absolutely evil perpetrators—those men who abduct, maim, kill, and enslave children—and their innocent, helpless child victims, who are in need of redemption through intervention.[61] This distinction is often blurred in practice, for example when UPDF operations declare those LRA killed as "terrorists" and those captured as "abductees." However, the more fundamental issue is that this portrayal fails to capture the complexity of the experiences of either those designated victims or those designated perpetrators, either when they were with the LRA or once they have returned from the rebels. The question of the perpetrators will be addressed in chapter 6;[62] for now, I want to focus on those designated victims.

Edmondson, in her analysis of World Vision's art therapy work with girls who have returned from the LRA, argues that the aid agency makes the young women perform drama that, by portraying their time with the LRA as unambiguous suffering and their time since leaving the LRA as redemption, does epistemic violence to the girls' experiences in both worlds, which are imbued with significantly more ambiguity than interveners will admit in their desire to "market trauma." This can end up having important psychological and political consequences; as she quotes another analyst: "during the process of reintegration and rehabilitation, far too often, we suppress and undermine skills and strengths that have enabled these girls to survive in the first place."[63]

Similar patterns can be found in the image of child soldiers informing interventions intended for their rehabilitation. By representing child soldiers as helpless victims, as the children's rights epistemology requires, human rights organizations ignore the evidence that many male youth with the LRA, UPDF, and Homeguard are not unwilling victims and may instead be expressing their agency by actually choosing to remain with armed forces because, to use the human rights language, they find their rights better fulfilled there than as civilians in the camps. Some Acholi working in northern Uganda have remarked to me that many young men in the LRA, once past the abduction itself, actually come to want to remain with the rebels because they are glad to leave the permanent insecurity, hunger, and boredom of the camp.[64] This ambiguity is being explored further in a number of studies,[65] such as the one by Ben Mergelsberg. He presents the male former LRA abductees he knows as "young adults with certain capacities, a sense of independence and self-esteem, and more or less clear reasons as to why they were fighting with the LRA." They had been in two worlds, and "both worlds have their pleasant sides and both worlds can be terrifying."[66]

The possibility that young men are themselves fulfilling their own ideas about their rights by remaining with or even joining the rebels, despite the violation of the international human rights standards concerning child soldiers it entails, is not acceptable within the children's rights discourse, which cannot countenance that international instruments, supposedly representing the best interests of children, may be contravened by children themselves through the expression of their own agency.[67] The children's rights discourse cannot admit that children may choose to be child soldiers for what they perceive as their own good in response to a situation so desperate that they would rather take up arms than sit and suffer in the camps. By focusing almost exclusively on the LRA, this approach also normalizes the regime of government violence that gave rise to the situation in which children decide to join or remain in armed organizations and obscures the political crises underlying the war.

This focus on LRA child soldiers as helpless victims has a number of detrimental consequences. For one thing, it distracts from the violence experienced every day by the displaced, including displaced children. Chris Dolan makes the point that the focus on abducted children has "diverted attention from the extreme needs of the children who live in the affected districts of northern Uganda as a whole"—the 99 percent of children—living in conditions forced on them by the Ugandan government. He points out that this focus has furthered the interests of NGOs, which have found an easy money-raising issue and an easy way to mobilize support internationally, and the government of Uganda, which has used the issue to demonize the LRA. The focus on the children's rights of those youth with the LRA, he concludes, "has done little either to help resolve the conflict or to create a climate conducive to longer-term peace and stability."[68] More recently, rescuing child soldiers has become a primary justification for military action, in particular U.S. military involvement, as promoted by the U.S.-based lobby group Invisible Children and others, discussed in chapter 7.

However, it has negative consequences also for those designated traumatized victims, as trauma has become a popular lens for seeing northern Uganda. In 1998, the Government of Uganda and UNICEF carried out a psychological survey of the population of Acholi, the Northern Uganda Psycho-Social Needs Assessment. The report gave several reasons for its significance: as it explained, the war had "broken down the very fabric of civil society," and "traditional customs which brought community people together to discuss problems and implement solutions jointly are no longer followed." This situation of social breakdown resulted from the fact that people, especially children, had witnessed "psychologically wounding events."[69] In response, a number of NGOs in Acholi took up psychosocial support programs as part of their broader conflict-resolution and peacebuilding agendas.[70] Because former LRA fighters are often deemed to be the most traumatized, and because aid agencies assume that they will become violent again without treatment, this group may be specially targeted for psychosocial interventions.

The irony of this approach is that, as Christopher Blattman shows, these former members of the LRA are a group that is not helpless but rather is often highly politically mobilized and engaged.[71] Moreover, as Mergelsberg emphasizes, the problems faced by "returning LRA fighters cannot be separated from the general problem of a population living in the extreme conditions of the IDP camps."[72] Thus, when former LRA fighters react against the conditions in which they and their fellow Acholi find themselves in the camps, they are not showing destructive symptoms of their exceptional trauma but rather are expressing their rejection of the circumstances in which the government and aid agencies are keeping them. They are expressing sentiments common to all of Acholi society, but sentiments on which they, because of their experiences with the LRA, may have a greater motivation and confidence to act. Therefore, former LRA reacting against the common conditions of enforced displacement, poverty, and repression, while potentially being a source of leadership in the community, may be the ones who are most likely to be termed traumatized, the political expressions of their agency medicalized as symptoms of trauma, and provided therapy to discipline that behavior out of existence or given psychopharmaceuticals to eliminate such behavior chemically.[73] Trauma is portrayed as cause and consequence of conflict, and the behavior that youth in the camps display, such as a lack of respect for authority, whether governmental, nongovernmental, or "traditional," must be eliminated through therapy; the children must be made into "normal," productive members of Acholi society. Behaviors that might be able to lead to change are disciplined away, and potential Acholi political leaders are to be counseled and medicated into not contesting the war or its consequences.

Interventions that regard former members of the LRA as a vulnerable group in need of special treatment in order to prevent them from returning to conflict may also simply backfire. In interviews, many ex-members of the LRA expressed resentment and frustration with NGO projects, sometimes with great vehemence.[74] Many returnees only agreed to be interviewed once they were convinced that my research team and I were not with an NGO. In one former LRA fighter's words, "had it been that you introduced yourself as working for an NGO, we were not going to give you an audience. We are fed up with them, they are eating our blood." Indeed, it is ex-members of the LRA, the very category of people that many NGOs use to justify their fund raising, who often feel the most abused and exploited by their supposed saviors. As one woman who had returned from the LRA put it, "The help NGOs do give is just a cover-up for their interest in making personal fortunes out of our suffering." Many ex-LRA returnees were eager to relate detailed stories about how they felt they had been exploited or cheated by NGOs,[75] made to sign for goods they never received, and photographed repeatedly by whites without getting anything in return. One cause for significant frustration was that child-sponsorship NGOs refused to give returnees the addresses of their American sponsors so that they could write to their sponsors themselves and report their mistreatment at the hands of NGOs. One group of male ex-LRA combatants described feeling so betrayed that, in a moment of bravado, they told the researcher that they were considering going back to the bush, getting their weapons, and taking revenge on the NGO that they felt had exploited them. The recent spontaneous emergence of what have been termed peer groups among former members of the LRA represents a more productive mode of refusing the way NGOs conceive of them, their categorization as "vulnerable groups,"[76] and the depoliticizing and ineffective modes of behavior encouraged by NGOs. Former members of the LRA are organizing themselves in order to improve their conditions, rejecting NGOs and the representational violence they feel has been done to them. In short, the discipline of children's rights interventions is by no means totalizing or even, much of the time, successful, and in many cases it provokes as much resistance as it contains.

WOMEN'S RIGHTS IN ACHOLI

Women, another supposedly vulnerable group, have also been subject to an array of specialized interventions in northern Uganda. Women's responses to these women's rights interventions provide another example of resistance to the disciplinary nature of intervention and of the renegotiation of human rights discourses in an emancipatory direction. This women's rights discourse articulated by Acholi women has been used to confront the violence and deprivation they face as a result of the war and displacement. In contrast to the self-management through "sensitization" that is often promoted in the name of women's rights, women themselves have undertaken a different kind of women's rights mobilization in response to their own experiences, needs, and demands, one oriented around women's organization and access to legal remedy. It also represents a different vision of peace, one built not on normalization towards an imposed model of social order, but premised upon the demand for increasing political and social inclusion, confrontationally if need be. Social order and peace are not ensured through management, but through constant internal contestation, and this women's rights agenda thus represents an autonomous response to the crises of Acholi society.

The use of women's rights emerged in the context of the changing roles women experienced during displacement.[77] The physical setting, whether in camps or in towns, represented a general collapse of the spatial ordering that had regulated Acholi society. Whereas previously families were separate from each other, clans were in distinct areas, women and men were separate, and children were separated according to age, under displacement, everyone was thrown together. For example, clans were scattered, which made meetings difficult and reduced the powers of clan authorities who could no longer enforce decisions, having lost their ultimate sanction, namely, banishment from the clan and stripping away of the right to land.

This disruption introduced new difficulties into women's lives, and most women interviewed pointed out how the camps had had a significantly negative impact in terms of their quality of life and the hardships they had to endure.[78] "I did not find anything good about camp life, it is a curse and punishment. Returning home is my wish as long as there's peace, much as we will start from scratch because we have lost almost everything apart from our lives," said a woman in Awach camp, voicing a common response. Because many men had died, joined armed organizations, abandoned their wives, or turned to alcohol abuse, women in large part were left with the primary responsibility for providing for their families, which had often expanded to include a number of dependents in addition to their own children. Food rations and nonfood-item distributions were inadequate, so women were faced with the additional need to earn money to feed their families and to buy basics such as soap or clothes. The level of violent abuse suffered by women at the hands of men was also extremely high in the camps, in large part due to a breakdown of traditional male roles and corresponding rampant alcoholism.[79] Camps were the context for a regime of intense direct and structural violence against women.

As a woman commuting to Gwengdiya transition site said, "Camp life has changed many women: they have learned to shoulder responsibility amidst poverty and pain." However, many women also explained how it was precisely this need to shoulder additional responsibility in the context of the camp, where they were in a public space with other women with new opportunities for earning money and gaining education or training, that had given rise to certain positive changes in their lives that they would like to retain even after the end of displacement. At the same time that men, and especially male elders, saw their authority and status within Acholi society wane, women, and to a lesser extent youth, saw their authority and status rise precipitously in camps. Before displacement, women related, they lived in relatively isolated family homesteads, spaced out enough so that the male ideal of being "chief in one's own house" could be realized. As a middle-aged woman in Gulu Town explained, "we [women] were very far apart in the village. We did not have groups or come together like we do now."

Displacement not only caused significant physical hardship and suffering for women, but also brought women together in a way they had not been before. Combined with resources provided by government and international agencies, this created the context in which women could forge new forms of associational life amid the devastation of camp life. Perhaps the most noticeable result was the emergence of women's groups, mostly for economic empowerment through rotational work schemes—*kalulu pur*—or loan schemes—*kalulu cente*. These were often combined with cultural activities, such as music, dance, or drama, and served the additional purpose of providing women with a space in which to come together and discuss their problems. Some groups were started through interventions by aid agencies or by the government, but many of them received no external support. The women's group proved to be a rapidly multiplying social form as each group that was created served as a catalyst for other groups in the dense camp setting. Indeed, many women who were not in a group expressed their desire to join one in the future.

In addition to the benefit of women's groups, some displaced women also cited the relative independence, in particular from husbands and fathers, that they had in the camps. Economically, women had gained access to loans, both individually and collectively. They could run small businesses and retain possession over the proceeds, and many expressed satisfaction at having learned to sell agricultural produce and save the money. Women pointed out the number of women who are now in positions of authority, especially in the local government system. Women were achieving new education through training by NGOs and government on health and other issues. Again, many of these developments were seen as resulting from strategies employed in the struggle to feed families in the camps. Nonetheless, many women saw these developments as positive. As an older woman in Pabbo said, although "women's experiences in camps have not been good, some have gained power through women's rights." Women's rights helped provide legitimation to the kinds of organization and action that women were undertaking themselves in the context of displacement.

Women's rights appear to have emerged as a common discourse in Acholiland in the 1990s, and to have become more important in the camps, brought there in particular through government and Western NGO initiatives. This kind of women's organization does not seem to have a long history in Acholiland; in my research, I found only one group, Labonge Lworo ("Without Fear") in Ogwil, Pader, which had come together in the early 1990s specifically to help women socially and economically. As members of the group explained, they formed "because women were naturally considered shy. We could not speak in public and we were kept behind doors. So we came together in this group to change the way that people thought about women. We wanted to strengthen our assertiveness, and be together with each other, and also entertain people."

In the intervening period of social and political upheaval, however, women's rights became a prevalent discourse. It was a widespread sentiment among women that, as a woman in Palaro said, "It is not only men that have rights, women are human beings and so also have rights." What women meant by women's rights was rather specific. The word commonly used for *rights* in Acholi is *twero*, literally meaning "having the ability or authority" to do something. When the phrase *twero pa mon* ("rights of women") is used as the translation of *women's rights*, it thus bears connotations of women's authority or power. In this way, a group of women could speak positively about women's rights but then complain of people "misusing" women's rights, either taking them as a guarantee of personal license or as an excuse for imposing illegitimate authority. One group of women raised the case of a female politician who, during campaigns, showed up with armed bodyguards to a rally. It would be hard to understand how this could be construed as a misuse of women's rights without taking into account the association of *twero* with authority in Acholi.

Women's rights, as explained by a women's group in Laguti, include the right to political participation and leadership, to economic activity and business, to own money and property, to education, to associate and form groups, to express themselves, to employment, and, very importantly, to legal remedy when men try to violate their rights. "These rights are good because they make us independent not dependent on men," one woman in the Laguti group explained. However, another woman in the group pointed out unhelpful aspects of women's rights promotion: for example, a radio program on which, according to the women, freedom of dress was encouraged, or T-shirts that were distributed in the camp on which a figure of a woman and of a man are pictured with an equal sign between them. According to this women's group, these interventions only provoke men, belittle important aspects of Acholi culture, and end up giving women's rights a bad name.[80] For Acholi women, women's rights can have many different dimensions and meanings, and they clearly distinguished between a foreign-sponsored version of women's rights versus an Acholi version of women's rights that made sense and was legitimate within traditional Acholi cultural context.

The pseudo-urban environment of the camps and the discourse of women's rights provided the opportunity for women to respond to the crisis and also to try to rectify aspects of traditional Acholi culture they found unjust. Many women, while expressing their general approval for women's roles in Acholi culture, also expressed their opinion that certain aspects of those roles should be changed, or that certain negative aspects that had receded with war and displacement should be done away with permanently. Most often cited were the practices of pulling teeth, scarification, and certain food restrictions. However, some women also made clear that, as an older woman in Mucwini put it, "I agree with most of Acholi culture except the issue of being so submissive to men that makes us be just like slaves." This sentiment stems from a common practice in Acholi society, in which wives are exchanged for bride wealth and then brought to the man's family. As a result, unmarried women may be seen as a source of wealth to the family but not really part of it because they are going to leave once of a marriageable age. On the other hand, women who marry into a family may be represented as having been paid for by the men through bride wealth, and thus seen as lacking authority within the husband's clan.[81] At the extreme, one woman in Palaro explained that she felt that in current Acholi tradition there is the idea that "a woman is married into a family and so has no power there: she cannot have any rights; she is almost like a slave, or like property." As a result, both unmarried and married women may lack a strong claim on authority within the family or clan and be generally dependent on husbands, fathers, brothers, or male clan elders in resolving disputes or in accessing land.

In this context, women are using women's rights to transform what is seen to be Acholi tradition from within. There was no inherent divide between human rights and Acholi tradition, according to these women. In fact, women's rights represented a terrain for struggle *within* Acholi society and tradition.[82] Many Acholi women, as opposed to some of the people promoting their own version of traditional justice, considered in the next chapter, explained that tradition is not a closed, petrified set of customs and practices, but rather is open to constant contestation and renegotiation from within. Indeed, Acholi women are both using their own reconfiguration of women's rights as a way of transforming Acholi tradition, while refusing some of the articulations of women's rights promoted by Western agencies that attempt to transform Acholi culture from the outside in what they see as counterproductive directions.

Not surprisingly, this increasing authority of women and the question of women's rights has provoked significant resentment from many men, in particular older men. Acholi men tended to blame government and foreign NGOs for promoting a desire among women for more authority than what they had had in the village, and many men treated the issue of women's rights with undisguised disdain. From one extreme point of view, all women's rights represent an illegitimate attempt by women, encouraged by government and NGOs and backed up by LCs and police, to usurp male authority and impose themselves as equal to or superior than men. As a male elder in Palaro said, "if women are to possess rights, our homes are doomed." A group of male elders in Gulu Town concurred, saying, "Women have been so spoiled because of women's rights." They have become "big-headed," and a situation has emerged where "men have become women and women are men."

From this perspective, the very idea of women's rights as authority goes against the idea that women are paid for in marriage and thus become a kind of property of their husbands. As property, according to some men, women cannot possibly have a claim to authority over men, and women's earnings are, from that perspective, in fact the earnings of her husband as a return on bride price. There was also a widespread accusation among men that women's rights are to blame for increased domestic violence in the camps: the reasoning is that, because women now think they can do anything in the name of women's rights, they provoke their men into beating them.

Some men have even articulated their own discourse of women's rights as a way of refusing the increase in women's authority. A male elder in Anaka camp explained that the current understanding of women's rights is mistaken. Women do indeed have rights—understood as authority—in the village, namely their customarily defined rights over the kitchen and over preparing and serving food. The assertion of other rights is a violation of men's rights, he explained. More common, however, is for men to invoke a discourse of Acholi tradition when seeking to meet the challenge of women's power, as will be addressed in the next chapter.

In the face of this backlash, women often insisted on the importance of legal remedy for abuses of their rights by men, in particular through the special police constables, or SPCs. Indeed, *contra* claims by men that women's rights have caused domestic violence, many women explained that women's rights, when backed up legally by SPCs, had instead reduced domestic violence. The reputation that SPCs rapidly earned in the camps of being a friend to women put into relief the significant gap in legal redress for cases of domestic violence. The intercession of SPCs in cases of domestic violence led some men to complain that women were going to these authorities for cases of domestic violence instead of taking the cases to family and clan structures first. As a man in Awach explained, also invoking the language of rights himself, the SPCs are "violating men's rights to control their women." The SPCs have also been reported to provide help in some cases where women's husbands tell them to hand over the proceeds from their business on penalty of divorce or a beating. The popularity of SPCs among women demonstrates that family and clan structures were inadequate from the point of view of many women for dealing with violence and other abuses of their rights.

In sum, this particular struggle over human rights within Acholi society in no way represents a clash between what are conceived of as international women's rights and men's local, traditional efforts to refuse those rights. Instead, both women and, to a lesser extent, men are explicitly invoking concepts of rights—or more accurately, of *twero*—as they understand them within Acholi culture and tradition: women's rights as understood by women having to do with the opening of opportunities through new forms of community among women and access to legal remedy, and women's rights understood by men as the authority over a certain limited household domain. In so doing, both women and men were creating alternatives to, and sometimes explicitly rejecting, the modes through which many foreign organizations were promoting women's rights in Acholiland, but using the resources provided though governmental and international intervention to wage political struggles on their own terrain. In so doing, they are seeking to build their own ideas of peace.

3. Civil Society in the War Zone

Civil society is often thought to be inherently bound up with human rights, both as the institutional expression of certain rights, such as association, opinion, and organization, and as a safeguard against the abuse of human rights by the state. Its role in peacebuilding is also often seen as essential, representing as it does a domain of non-violent politics opposed to the violence of armed groups. Northern Uganda has seen the dramatic expansion of organizations that go under the title "civil society" since the late 1990s, a result of capacity-building and civil society-promotion activities by aid agencies and donors and also of the fact that thousands of Acholi are employed by the scores of international aid agencies that operate in northern Uganda.[83] These capacity-building and empowerment initiatives are supposed to help create structures and leadership within Acholi society so that it can reconstruct itself and build its capacity for peace. However, the optimistic predictions for the political and social potential of this civil society are misplaced when it comes to this aid-driven sector. The main problem is that this is an aid-based civil society, which is not surprising given that the massive financial aid inflow into an area with minimal agricultural production, no industry, and total displacement led to the development of an economy almost entirely determined by foreign funding. The focus in this section is on the politics of this aid-based class, the educated, mostly younger people in the camps and in town who are directly or indirectly connected into global flows of funds and who have become the agents of the transnational human rights-intervention regime.

NONPOLITICAL CIVIL SOCIETY

This regime of Acholi aid workers and organizations whose capacity is being built in the name of participation and local sustainability is a key part of the transnational intervention regime and has as its primary function the administration of camp populations. However, the main consequence for members of that group itself is not their empowerment but rather their own disciplining into nonpolitical forms of organization and action as their own projects, aspirations, and scope for political action are closed off. Thus, this apparent upsurge of civil society has not been the condition for positive political transformation, and this civil society has been unable to secure even the population's minimal requirements for biological life. This civil society has been unable to hold the government accountable for the establishment of the camps, to demand the dismantling of the camps, to end government violence against the Acholi, or to push successfully for peace negotiations. It has stepped into the shoes of the missing Acholi middle class, gone since the 1980s, but has been unable to carry out any of the political functions of that class. Why this existing civil society has been unable to make even the most rudimentary demands of the government—that it stop killing its own people—must be considered, not only for the sake of explaining the situation in northern Uganda, but also because it may generally problematize those forms of organization that go under the rubric of civil society and are celebrated widely by donors, academics, and policy institutions today as instruments of peacebuilding or democratization.

The problem is that the body of organizations and associations and those processes of deliberation and communication that exist in northern Uganda and which are generally framed as comprising the fabric of civil society are without many of the components—such as social movements—that, in other instantiations of civil society, can endow it with political and democratic potential. Those components of civil society that do exist in northern Uganda, because of their dependence on external support instead of internal constituencies, end up themselves taking a form that is without political or democratic potential. Those Acholi who are part of civil society—the aid-based class—are disciplined into political inaction, both in terms of national politics and in terms of local politics. Actually existing civil society in northern Uganda is a superficial phenomenon, without autonomy or popular constituencies and dependent on foreign funds. If this set of organizations, institutions, and practices that exists in northern Uganda is to be called civil society, then it should be specified as a resolutely nonpolitical form of civil society and should not be ideologized as having the potential to promote democratization or to demand accountability from the state. The implication is that civil society promotion as part of peacebuilding, as it unfolded in northern Uganda, could help resolve neither the humanitarian crisis nor the underlying political crises.

The autonomy of this aid-based civil society is undermined in a number of ways. For one thing, the set of organizations and associations that exist in northern Uganda exclude those components of civil society that tend to give it political potential. To take the definition of civil society provided by Jean Cohen and Andrew Arato in their *Civil Society and Political Theory*, civil society with political capacity partakes of two dimensions: one, a dynamic moment embedded in processes of popular "self-constitution and self-mobilization," in particular within social movements, and the other, an institutional moment that consolidates the gains made by the processes of autonomous organization and action.[84] In northern Uganda, this first dynamic moment is absent from what goes under the name civil society. The organizations and associations that exist are not products of the institutionalization of social movements or autonomous collective action; they *begin* as professionalized and institutionalized, because professionalism is a prerequisite for access to foreign funds. These organizations only subsequently try to build a constituency, which can only amount to a group of beneficiaries. Mamdani brings out the repercussions of this reversal, arguing that,

> No matter how undemocratic a popular organization, its constituency is its formal membership . . . but this is not the case with NGOs, which are mainly inspired by a philanthropic perspective . . . Its constituency (beneficiaries) are never members of the NGO. . . . Being outside the formal membership of the NGO, the constituency is structurally precluded from waging any struggle for rights. . . . It is the spread of an anti-democratic culture.[85]

The absence of the dynamic, self-mobilizing, and self-constituting dimension of civil society in northern Uganda, most conspicuous in the absence of social movements, points to the second reason actually existing civil society there lacks political potential, namely, because the organizations that do exist derive their support from access to external funds instead of from internal support. Civil society in Acholiland is not a terrain of voluntary associations but of professional associations. Those who make up this new Acholi aid-based class, the core of civil society, generally live in Gulu or Kitgum Towns, have postsecondary education, are fluent in English, and often have spent significant time abroad. They may run their own indigenous NGOs or staff large international NGOs or UN agencies. There are few employed, college-educated Acholi in Acholiland who do not work for a foreign NGO or a foreign-funded NGO, or who are not otherwise dependent on donor funds. In the face of violence, a closed political arena, and economic disintegration, foreign funds and NGOs offer the only apparent way for these Acholi to make money or hold positions of authority. As a result, the accountability of these organizations, which are parasitical on the war and the humanitarian complex, is to donors, and their goal often is, not to give voice to the demands of the Acholi peasantry, but rather to expand their own activities according to the exigencies of peacebuilding.

This civil society, thus, does not partake of liberal qualities of transparency, inclusivity, and deliberation, but is, instead, often seen as a terrain of entrenched corruption, as supposedly liberal peacebuilding interventions turn out to be anything but liberal in practice. There is considerable resentment of NGOs, especially in Gulu Town, often because of what many see as the corrupt and partial manner through which assistance and jobs are provided. One common accusation is that, unless one has a relative on the inside of an NGO, one will not benefit.[86] People cite cases in which money or goods—such as bicycles, start-up capital, or school fees—are promised but then not provided, or even are signed for by the supposed beneficiaries but then never delivered. Furthermore, people are hesitant to raise the problems of NGOs publicly out of fear of retribution: "NGOs are only giving to their relatives and the real needy are not getting anything. So people are afraid to talk about it because they know that if they do they will not be helped," explained a young woman in Gulu Town. Indeed, once people have seen the internal workings of NGOs from close range—large houses, plush Land Cruisers, running water and electricity (as Zoë Marriage puts it, many Western NGO workers "live like ministers or militia leaders")[87]—and have had experiences trying to get jobs with NGOs and failing, their resentment may be such that they flatly reject NGOs and their perceived exploitative behavior. "I don't want to talk about NGOs: they are thieves and benefiting a lot out of our problems," said a young woman in Gulu. Of course, these same characterizations are normally heard from Western NGOs in describing African political and social systems, used to explain the need for Western "liberal" intervention!

In short, the elements of a democratic civil society are simply not present:

> [W]ithout *active* participation on the part of citizens in *egalitarian* institutions and civil associations, as well as in politically relevant organizations, there will be no way to maintain the democratic character of the political culture or of social and political institutions.[88]

Civil society in Acholiland is not voluntary but professional, does not have active participation of citizens, and is not egalitarian but is restricted to those who have the requisite connections.

The process of building constituencies—amassing beneficiaries—is often, in similar fashion, dependent on money instead of on deliberation, further undermining the political potential of this civil society. In order to gain access to foreign funding, a prospective NGO director first needs to identify an issue that donors are likely to fund, then set up an NGO, then find beneficiaries, exactly the opposite of the constitution of social movements. The public debate fostered by this civil society is similarly politically impotent. NGOs are taught to use the expert language of conflict resolution and peacebuilding as part of receiving funding—the language of "capacity building," "stakeholders," "sensitization," "networking," "facilitation," "good governance," and other such empty terminology. Indeed, this NGO-ese, often a degraded form of the already none-too-lofty language of American business management, becomes the new language of power. It unites the highest levels of the World Bank and UN with NGO-based civil society with the community "facilitator" in the refugee camp, and it increasingly makes its way into all forms of communication, replacing terms that have a political relevance with administrative terms that obscure the politics behind them—the ubiquity of the IDP label is one major example. This ersatz civil society focuses on activities such as holding workshops, seminars, and conferences, and, of course, on networking itself, activities that reaffirm a discourse that asks questions and gives answers phrased in, and supplied by, international NGO jargon. Its own expansion becomes its objective, the means replace the ends, and networking becomes a self-evident justification for existence. Through the dissemination of this expert language, these empty, depoliticizing, disciplinary concepts permeate the very fabric of communication and social life.

In sum, superficially it may appear that there is an active civil society in northern Uganda, participating in public deliberation, promoting state accountability and democratization. However, although the right actors seem to be present and seem to go through the motions of what civil society organizations are supposed to do, they, their deliberations, and their demands are hollow, lacking constituencies and political power. Dependence on foreign funding leads state and civil society, because both are independent of political support from the population, to put on a grand act for donors, the first pretending to listen to civil society, the second pretending to carry on a public debate, both with the intention of acquiring more funding and prolonging their own institutional lives, promoting their self-interest. In general, in a context like Uganda, where foreign-funded human rights, development, capacity-building, and conflict resolution organizations are spreading rapidly—but none base their power on popular constituencies and there is no incentive to challenge the state—there is little chance that this form of civil society can promote political reform. Indeed, this kind of civil society can deepen and expand indefinitely along with a deepening and expanding authoritarian regime.

THE RIGHTS OF THE AID-BASED CLASS

Young, educated Acholi working for this depoliticized civil society face a dilemma. Many tend to resent their treatment by foreign staff and their lack of voice in foreign NGOs. In private settings, some Acholi staff accused NGO foreign staff of neocolonialism and racism. However, given the minimal private sector, the few jobs available in the civil service, and the discrimination practiced against Acholi in the south of Uganda, many young, educated Acholi simply have no other choice than to work for NGOs or other international agencies. Ironically, in working for the human rights interventionist regime, they themselves lose many of their human rights and find themselves disciplined and depoliticized.

Disciplining begins with the labor market itself. Complaints abound that the process of getting a job with an NGO is unfair and abusive. Nepotism and corruption are frequently cited to be a part of recruitment and hiring. Women especially can face serious sexual abuse and exploitation in trying to find and retain jobs. There is a surplus of qualified potential NGO employees in town, and it is not uncommon to receive a hundred applications for one NGO national staff position, almost all of which will be from university graduates. Furthermore, university education in Uganda is increasingly tailored to the NGO job market: courses in such vocational topics as logistics management are increasingly popular, courses that are primarily of use in the NGO context. Therefore, especially with the opening of Gulu University in 2003 and the exponentially increased intake of students at Makerere, the number of Acholi university graduates with expectations of finding work in the NGO sector has grown constantly. This is in the context of extreme youth unemployment, which reaches as high as 80 percent. As a result, NGOs can fire employees with impunity, subject workers to harsh demands and poor conditions, and remain impervious to worker dissatisfaction because there is always another university graduate desperate to take the job.[89]

As part of foreign aid organizations, young Acholi often feel systematically excluded from decision making. There is no pretense of internal democracy in international or in many national NGOs. As one national staffperson put it, "national staff are treated [by foreign staff] as work horses and not consulted for any decision by the organization." There is a widespread sentiment that international staff simply do not trust national staff, do not listen to them, and often do not treat them with respect. National staff reported being given short contracts, often only a few months at a time, and frequently finding themselves under probation or being fired for unclear offenses. As another person put it, "Our experts just love bullying national staff. They have the perception that blacks are stupid and that because they are giving money to Africa they have the right to rule over us." Some evangelical Christian NGOs have reportedly gone so far as to demand that employees be "saved"—that is, convert—if they are to work there. Acholi workers often see these directives as evidence of foreigners' intention to assert power over Africans. As one staff member said, "The whites do these things purposely so as to contain everything under their control and achieve their desires, and also to impose their authority and to leave the national staff confused." This is reflected in the very titles commonly used to divide up NGO workers: "international staff" versus "local staff" with an entire regime of privileges that go along with the former. Perhaps using the more accurate "temporary guest worker" and "citizen," respectively, would be a salutary change.

The surplus of potential national staff, often eminently replaceable in the eyes of the foreign staff, makes for a situation in which, in one man's words, "NGOs' response to criticism from national staff is always negative. You'll either be fired or warned." Many staff reported their fear at raising even basic issues about working conditions, such as the lack of a lunch allowance during fieldwork. Complaints abounded that international agencies failed to respect national labor law or workers' rights more generally.

Due to job insecurity, there is significant fear among national staff that prevents them from speaking out, let alone from attempting to organize. One male national staff member explained that "there is limited freedom of expression for national staff with NGOs." Another told us, "We have not tried to do anything because of a lack of job security with NGOs. The NGOs can create something against you once they realize you want to stand up for the truth and pin them: then you are dropped like rotten fruits." Some Ugandan NGO workers, while in support of an NGO national staff organization, or at least a public forum in which problems could be aired and solutions proposed, noted serious obstacles to such a forum, including fear of retribution, intimidation, and the fact that those national staff with high positions might sabotage initiatives in order to build favor with foreign staff. This shows again the paradoxical consequences of intervention, as young Acholi workers feel the need to employ liberal human rights to contest and resist the illiberal abuses and human rights violations of supposedly liberal peacebuilding interventions.

The consequence is that, despite the size and organizational depth of civil society in Acholiland, young educated Acholi are generally extremely politically disillusioned.[90] "We are second-class citizens," said one NGO employee, a sentiment that was echoed repeatedly, and the Movement government was often seen as a tribal and partisan cabal that considers the Acholi, and especially educated Acholi such as themselves, to be a threat. Their political frustration in the face of government oppression and exclusion is compounded by injunctions among NGOs against political activities by national staff. As one man put it, "most if not all NGOs are not political and so local staff who are politically active are always shown the exit." Interviewees noted that the sanction against politics among NGOs leads to the neutralization of political potential among young, educated Acholi: "One could be endowed with leadership and political talent but because of the NGO policies, one's talent goes unrealized." Some of the major UN agencies, such as WFP, were seen by some people as progovernment, even in their hiring. This is not a surprise, given the long-standing cooperation between WFP and the Ugandan government in the northern war and given the fear on the part of most international NGOs of raising the government's ire and losing their lucrative contracts and projects.

The political frustration among this aid-based class at present is a clear symptom of the ongoing political crisis in Acholiland. In the past, it would have been this very group that would have provided the key political link between the Acholi and the national government. Instead, the most enterprising and active Acholi, whether in town or in camps, are appropriated by the international intervention regime and turned into relief coordinators, research assistants, and petty administrators. Through civil-society capacity building, this group is politically neutralized and the political crisis is only prolonged. This new Acholi civil society is not filling in for a "retreating state," but rather filling in for a missing middle class, and in doing so, suppresses the emergence of a political middle class by disciplining its members to become the agents of a transnational technocracy. Unlike the original Acholi middle class, which, as representatives of the peasantry to the government, had the power to make demands and hold the state accountable, this new civil society lacks this capacity. Thus, it seems unlikely that it will contribute to the resolution of the internal or national political crises of the Acholi. Neither was it able to catalyze organization that would demand the end of the camps or their adequate protection: this civil society cannot mobilize mass action, as they would lose their funding if they organized strikes, riots, or even nonviolent confrontations. Moreover, NGOs lack the popular legitimacy that would endow them with this mobilizational capacity. But all the while, this class, as the local agents of human rights interventions, plays a key role in sustaining the regime of popular discipline. If this is to be termed "civil society," it represents the extreme of nonpolitical civil society; perhaps it would be preferable to reserve the category "civil society" for those forms that display at least a modicum of potential political or democratic capacity.

4. Participation and Its Limits

In this chapter, I have endeavored to show how societal peacebuilding interventions misconstrue the cause of the conflict and the political crises of the Acholi and seek to re-establish peace and order based, not on the legitimate or democratic social or political forces, but on models imported by the peacebuilders. These models and the self-proclaimed empowering, capacity-building, and participatory interventions they are embedded in give rise to forms of organization that do not have the potential to challenge the regime of displacement that people live under. Instead, they end up repressing autonomous forms of organization and action among the Acholi that could contest violence and displacement. The consequence is that many peacebuilding interventions managed the possible eruption of unmanageability among the displaced and thereby indirectly perpetuated the humanitarian crisis and the camps. By trying to impose a reified social order through discipline, these interventions also prevented the emergence of democratic social orders based upon contentious political and social organization and action, precisely what would be necessary for the internal and national crises of the Acholi to be resolved.

As was seen in the contentious politics around women's rights, however, these disciplinary interventions can be rejected or reconfigured by those subject to them.

Women were using women's rights to demand inclusion within Acholi society and thus address the internal crisis in a democratic fashion. What has been less apparent is how human rights have been reconfigured to address the national political crisis and directly challenge war, displacement, and political repression. Human Rights Focus has documented government violence since the mid-1990s but is not geared toward a broad popular constituency, whereas the Acholi Religious Leaders Peace Initiative, the one group that has the potential to be a strong force for peace and justice, given its natural constituency in the churches, generally failed to mobilize its potentially massive constituency in an effective way. Nevertheless, it is clear that human rights, when reconfigured by those who are claiming those rights, has the potential to help mobilize and legitimate inclusive processes of democratization.

PARTICIPATION AND UNDERSTANDING

The irony of peacebuilding is that it uses the language of participation and empowerment to justify these fundamentally disciplinary and normalizing interventions. I have noted how participation ends up being reduced to participating in ways allowed by the intervention and adopting roles and identities provided by the intervention. Because each peacebuilding intervention interprets conflict as being caused by a specific breakdown internal to the affected society and then tries to resolve the conflict by resolving that problem, if such limited interpretations of violence do not make sense to those subject to intervention, the proposed solutions—for people to participate within models of individual and collective identities that are deemed normal—no matter how supposedly participatory, will make little sense either. Instead, they will be seen as attempts to convince people to consent to identities, practices, and forms of organization that do not address, and may even do violence to, the full extent of their own experiences of suffering, violence, or repression. For example, when the ICC Prosecutor unequivocally declares that ICC intervention will bring peace and justice to a war-affected society, or when people living in a government-run internment camp are made to participate in NGO-run children's rights sensitization workshops in the name of peace, or when Acholi are told that their poverty is the result of insufficient entrepreneurship on their part, the disjuncture between the promises of peace and justice and the consequences of intervention becomes starkly obvious, as it does when interventions collaborate with violence or when those interventions themselves violate human rights. As a result, although some people may choose to participate in interventions within the given limits, others will resist or reject them because they are being told to do things that they do not want to do and that do not make sense to them.

This raises the question of whether peacebuilding can institute forms of genuine participation so as to foster and build upon, instead of shut down, agency and independent initiative among war-affected communities. Béatrice Pouligny, for example, has argued that intervention can be reformed in a truly participatory direction by basing itself on "intensive field investigations" and on an effort to think of those involved in conflicts, not as victims or perpetrators, but as "authentic actors."[91] This would have to happen "over a period sufficiently long to allow for the establishment of a relationship of confidence with the people concerned" and to allow interveners always to question the understanding they have of situations.[92] Intervention would thus require lengthy stays in conflict zones, learning languages, and extensive engagement with members of the community, not merely seeing them through identities such as "IDPs," "the poor," "victims," or "beneficiaries," so as to allow people to represent themselves instead of imposing alien identities on them. As Pouligny argues, this would require that interventions, instead of constructing nonpolitical subjects and organizations, orient themselves toward working with sites within the community that are trying to challenge violence through political organization and action on their own terms. The "needs assessment" phase would be reoriented toward discerning who is working for peace, and intervention would be transformed from a disciplinary practice to a practice that learns from its subjects and then works with them.

However, even where human rights intervention attempts to abandon its limited, preassigned interpretive schemes, establish relations of genuine communication and understanding with subjects of intervention, and then act on that understanding in solidarity with legitimate social and political actors, there remain two sets of problems that make genuine participation in intervention difficult. The first problem is that the fundamental inequality and lack of accountability that characterize the interventionist encounter lead it to be undermined by the difficulty of, as Gayatri Spivak puts it, hearing the subaltern speak—or, in this case, hearing the "beneficiaries" speak.[93] Interveners, however great their commitment to listen to the beneficiaries, always retain the freedom to hear whatever they choose to hear without having to face consequences for possible misunderstanding. The interveners may hear the subjects of intervention offering consent, when in fact the consenting voices are ultimately those of the interveners themselves.

In practice, this means that, in pursuing genuine participation and empowerment, interveners will face a never-ending process of trying to decide who represents whom, whom to listen and respond to, and negotiating a path through apparently equally valid claims, when genuine participation would require that interveners be able to accurately discern the political context into which they intervene. Tough questions arise: in focusing on a certain marginalized group, such as women, how do interveners know that they are not erasing relations of inequality or exploitation within that group?[94] How do they know they are not missing the ways in which apparently marginalized groups are, in fact, participating in political decision making, though in informal or less obvious fashions?[95] The obstacles to understanding open intervention, not only to inefficacy, but to blatant forms of instrumentalization, without any form of accountability to regulate those consequences. "Local partners" may end up dominated by outsiders and others without legitimacy, whereas those who work with interveners, if those interveners prove unresponsive, can lose the political support of their constituencies.[96] Consequently, interveners may end up promoting unaccountable, illegitimate organizations and actors through the pursuit of participation.

Intervention can also skew practices and ethics of self-representation among those subject to intervention.[97] In something of an interventionist "observer effect," simply by showing up to assess a situation, interveners inescapably have already changed political calculations, incentives, and structures among those subject to intervention.[98] Local and national civil and political organizations that were democratically legitimate and accountable before the appearance of outsiders will have a tendency to re-orient themselves toward external interests and agendas once intervention becomes a possibility. Once an intervention begins, groups that are having their "capacity" supported by external agencies can end up changing their orientation, as organizations and leaders become habituated to making appeals to unaccountable international bodies for assistance instead of making appeals to existing political authorities or creating inclusive, self-sustaining organizations that draw support from a popular constituency with which to effect their demands.[99] Finally, the power that aid agencies embody may also lead people to assent to their interventions publicly but then undermine them once out of sight of the aid agencies.

THE POLITICS OF PARTICIPATION

The second problem is that there are fundamental political limits to participation. These limits derive from the fact that, in any situation, there will be certain forms of inequality, power, violence, or oppression that human rights interventions cannot challenge. This is not because intervention is perfectly functional to global power, but because human rights interventions are beholden to and work in the context of so many different kinds of political power, inequality, and domination. There will always be certain forms of power and inequality that interventions simply cannot challenge without undoing their own basis for existence, whether locally, nationally, or internationally. If they do try to challenge those limits, interveners will lose funding, local partners, government support, or access to populations. They will be expelled, become targets for coercion and repression themselves, or be labeled terrorist supporters and dealt with accordingly.

When human rights interventions ask people to participate in building peace, human rights, justice, or material well-being, they assign people the task of changing structural conditions far beyond what can be changed by, say, a few villagers assembled in a workshop. People may respond by making demands according to their own experiences of suffering and violence that go beyond or directly contradict the kinds of projects or assistance that intervening organizations, regardless of their commitment to participation, can provide, whether for practical, political, or ideological reasons. As a result, voices among participants that challenge international forms of inequality and exploitation may be silenced or ignored; those making what are seen as revolutionary, extremist, nationalist, socialist, or violent political claims will be accused of opposing liberal human rights and be disqualified; those raising broader systematic issues that can only be dealt with through forms of collective action far beyond the participatory project will be derided as unwilling to participate; and those who point out the complicity of intervening agencies or donors with political repression or violence will be ignored or violently silenced. Decisions concerning the legitimacy of demands made by beneficiaries are contingent on those demands not challenging the power inequalities and forms of domination that interveners depend on and may even support. In this way, opening intervention to genuine participation may represent, not a redemption of, but a danger to, the interventionist framework.[100]

So as long as popular participation is made, through coercion and consent, to conform to the political limits behind intervention, it may actively end up preventing people from effectively addressing the political problems they face, as the focus on local participation hides broader relations of domination. As Majid Rahnema puts it, "For the modern construct of participation, a person should be part of a predefined project . . . in order to qualify as a participant," and so participation becomes a way of channeling, containing, and rendering unrisky the kind of demands for political change that people themselves are driving forward.[101] This produces absurd situations, such as the World Bank and AFRICOM claiming to undertake participatory interventions while they militarize states and undermine the foundations of participatory democracy. Genuine participation, therefore, may very well involve the rejection of those participatory interventions themselves. These forms of imposed participation also shift the blame for the failure of intervention to its subjects, blaming the victim when things do not change based on the assumption that it is their responsibility, as partners, stakeholders, or participants, to find solutions—solutions, however, for which the only tools that they are allowed to use are totally inadequate.

Each human rights intervention will, through the forms of normalization it undertakes to realize its own exigencies, end up steering individuals and groups toward identities that cannot challenge certain forms of violence, repression, and inequality that they face, whether local, national, or international. When demands for participation run up against intervention's political and practical context, intervention must turn to administrative violence to silence such dissent. This alignment of human rights intervention with broader political interests can occur in a number of ways, from halting and serendipitous, to explicit and collusive, to evolutionary and systemic. In Uganda, human rights interventions, in pursuing their own ends, ended up providing tools useless against the forms of domination people faced, and so ended up naturalizing that violence, domination, and inequality, putting it beyond question or contestation. This tendency will again be on display in the traditional reconciliation agenda, addressed in the next chapter.

5

Ethnojustice: The Turn to Culture

Since the mid-2000s, the promotion of traditional reconciliation and justice has been a major growth industry in northern Uganda, as increased foreign funding has been made available and numerous foreign agencies and donors have launched initiatives. Uganda is by no means an exception; such interventions are found throughout Africa, and the increasing interest in African tradition as part of the peace agenda is part of a broader turn toward culture in development, justice, state-building, and counterinsurgency.[1] In the words of Roger MacGinty, there has been a well-warranted "renaissance in the concept of 'the indigenous,'" and "the concepts of 'traditional' and 'indigenous' . . . offer possible advantages of sustainability and participation, the 'elixir' that orthodox approaches to peace-making seek to attain."[2]

This turn to culture represents the newest attempt to institute genuine popular participation in peacebuilding as a way of improving the legitimacy and efficacy of international intervention. This attempt is based on the idea that in certain parts of the world, the most important, authentic identities are cultural identities, particularly traditional, customary, or tribal identities, and so participation should take place within this cultural framework or risk being rejected as alien impositions.[3] Africa has long been understood by the West as a land of tribes, so it should not be a surprise that Africa finds itself at the cutting edge of this multifaceted turn toward cultural intervention. Like the instrumental identification and use of African tradition during the colonial period, today African tradition is again imagined and deployed instrumentally for the sake of promoting peace and justice, and it is important to inquire into the political and practical consequences of this specific mobilization of tradition. Indeed, the history of Western instrumentalization of imagined concepts of African tradition as the basis of indirect-rule colonialism should itself give pause to those promoting this new phase of peace intervention.

The invocation of culture and tradition in the service of peace represents an effort by interveners to transcend the problems they see as arising from the attempt to impose liberal Western models on "illiberal" places like Africa. However, the existence of a fundamental opposition between traditional cultural interventions and liberalism is not universally agreed on.[4] Many proponents of the traditional justice agenda argue that traditional justice in fact represents an indigenization of universal human rights standards and adheres to the same values and human rights protections as more orthodox forms of Western justice, but in a culturally authentic African idiom. Regardless of whether they are seen as aligned with or in contradiction to human rights standards, the irony is that the political tendencies of these supposedly Africanized interventions can be identical to the tendencies of supposedly liberal human rights interventions: namely, instrumentalization and administrative discipline. That said, the deployment of culture within peacebuilding remains in its infancy, so the contours it takes and the relation that emerges among neoliberalism, security, and culture more generally will be an important subject of study.

Traditional reconciliation and justice interventions tend to frame the breakdown of war-affected societies as a result of the collapse of traditional values and social harmony, the disappearance of ritual practices that enforced such harmony, and the loss of authority among elders and other traditional leaders. Thus, the breakdown of war-affected society, where that society is defined as traditional, is, following the typical peacebuilding formula, cause and consequence of violence. Traditional reconciliation and justice interventions are to help rebuild this lost authority structure so that it can preside over reconstructed traditional societies. Africans are to be empowered and helped back up on their feet—as tribes, under customary chiefs. I term this the *ethnojustice* agenda, in which the fulfillment of justice is equated with the establishment of a traditional social order.

This chapter begins with the first major articulation of a traditional reconciliation agenda for the Acholi, namely, Dennis Pain's 1997 report, *The Bending of Spears: Producing Consensus for Peace & Development in Northern Uganda.*[5] Building on Paulin Hountondji's critique of ethnophilosophy, I then describe the ethnojustice discourse, through which I provide a critique of a more recent, influential report, the 2005 *Roco Wat i Acholi: Restoring Relationships in Acholi-land: Traditional Approaches to Justice and Reintegration.*[6] *The Bending of Spears* and *Roco Wat* have helped provide the underpinnings to a number of traditional justice and reconciliation projects that are being promoted today by donors, spanning everything from discovering lost chiefs, building a palace for the so-called Acholi paramount chief, providing development funds for redistribution by the Acholi council of chiefs, and providing money for reconciliation rituals.

1. The Bending of Spears

Dennis Pain's 1997 report purports to give an account of the "traditional authority structure" of the Acholi, which he derives from a wide array of sources ranging from nineteenth century explorers' accounts to Pain's conversations with Acholi elders, all of which are put forth as representing expressions of a single traditional Acholi identity.[7] In Chris Dolan's words, the report is "littered with cultural and political land-mines" and "perpetuates/creates a highly sentimental picture of Acholi culture rather than really attempting to assess either the extent to which that picture is accurate or whether the cultural institutions identified are up to the task of bringing peace to northern Uganda."[8] At the heart of Pain's account is his assertion that among the Acholi, conflicts were traditionally regulated and resolved by the *rwodi-moo*, or traditional elders: "The principle of conflict resolution in Acholi is to create reconciliation which brings the two sides together," he writes, and involves both paying compensation for harm done and ritually drinking a "bitter root extract drink," known as "*mato oput.*"[9] In the current conflict, as in any conflict among the Acholi, Pain asserts, the *rwodi-moo* should meet and decide on a route for its resolution. Then, Pain confidently proclaims, "as with any idea in Acholi, if the proposal is good, all will accept and Acholi can then speak with one voice."[10] As he puts it,

> Acholi traditional resolution of conflict and violence stands among the highest practices anywhere in the world. . . . The practice of reconciliation lies at the heart of a traditional approach to "cooling" the situation and healing the land and restoring relationships, far beyond the limited approaches of conservative western legal systems and a formal amnesty for offences against the state. . . . All Acholi know that because of atrocities, particularly against children since 1994 . . . all involved must go through *mato oput* reconciliation.[11]

But today, according to Pain, this traditional order and the reconciliation it enabled have suffered a "social break-down," in particular a "collapse of traditional networking and values" in which "the elders have failed to take on the responsibility which they should have taken."[12] Thus, the breakdown of traditional social order is the cause of the current war, which is represented as an intra-Acholi conflict that unfortunately had been allowed to escape the limits traditionally imposed by elders. He quotes one *rwot* as saying that "what the rebels are doing is so strange—never known in Acholi experience."[13]

Pain argues that, because the LRA come from every clan and because the LRA has attacked every clan, reconciliation must take place among all clans. As he writes, "all clans (and subclans) are both victims and perpetrators," and so, since all Acholi are equally victims and perpetrators in the war, "the Acholi must be given the chance to amend the wounds among themselves. This must be done traditionally by the community."[14] Pain internalizes the conflict as an intra-Acholi problem and at the same time universalizes it among the Acholi. The war is thus reduced to an internal social crisis brought about by the breakdown of traditional authority, to be resolved through rebuilding traditional Acholi order.[15]

Pain invokes peacebuilding's "cause and consequence" formula, going on to argue, not only that the breakdown of traditional authority has caused the conflict, but also that the conflict has in turn furthered the breakdown of traditional authority. In particular, he draws attention to the alienation of the LRA from the rest of the Acholi. This alienation has made it more difficult to resolve the conflict through traditional means: "The consequent marginalization of the LRA/M from the Acholi has left them isolated and has thus helped perpetuate the war since they cannot expect to be welcomed back into Acholi with open arms."[16] However, Pain states, "although the rebels are seen to have rejected society, if society now establishes the means of reconciliation, the rebels will accept that authority."[17] The national and local politics of the conflict are reduced to the breakdown of Acholi culture embodied in a patriarchal regime of elders and chiefs, and so the resolution of the conflict and the underlying political crisis are reduced to the acceptance of the LRA back into Acholi society. By this logic, the promotion of traditional reconciliation practices will allow LRA victims to accept the rebels back and will give the LRA the confidence needed to return. Because it is an intra-Acholi conflict, Pain implies, it is only by reconstructing the Acholi as an ethnic group that the conflict can be resolved.

A similar approach can be found in the "Community Reconciliation and Conflict Management" component of the World Bank's NUSAF. As the Bank explains:

> Traditional approaches include holding reconciliation meetings and/or negotiations between clans and/or tribes; supporting inter-tribal dialogue including visits to other districts; cleansing of reporters and/or returnees.... These approaches will ... build strong ties (integration) within and between war-torn societies that are needed to cope with transitional shocks and thereby regenerate community safety nets; facilitate intra-and inter-clans and tribal linkages needed within and among the sub-regions.[18]

It continues,

> Peacebuilding initiatives by the traditional leaders supported by civic organizations constitute the lynch-pin for survival in the insecure areas by enhancing integration and social cohesion among the displaced and vulnerable.[19]

The emphasis on traditional authorities was pronounced among the officers in charge of NUSAF, as the traditional conflict management component required that the Bank frame the conflict as tied to the breakdown of ethnically defined social order. As one World Bank official explained, to rebuild traditional authority it would be necessary to resolve the conflicts among the 50 or so clans and subclans in Gulu and in Kitgum,[20] an opinion that conformed to the Bank's standard practice of failing to recognize the ongoing civil war against the Ugandan government.

As addressed in chapter 4, although it is true that there has been a significant loss of authority by male elders as a result of the war and displacement, to reduce the national and internal political crises of the Acholi to that loss of authority is unwarranted. When that misconception informs interventions, it can have reactionary political consequences. Pain and the World Bank ignore the violence used by the LRA and the government against each other and ignore the violence of the government against civilians, in favor of focusing on LRA violence against civilians, defining it as intra-Acholi violence. This reduction leads to two significant misinterpretations of the internal and national political crises of the Acholi.

First, it reads the current internal crisis as an extension of and in the terms of the crisis that was existent in the late 1980s—that is, between returning Acholi soldiers and Acholi elders. It ignores that that crisis in the late 1980s could have only taken place in the context of a preexisting breakdown of internal authority, namely, the decimation of the Acholi political elite, which left the elders the only authority figures in Acholiland. It ignores that the discourse of traditional authority was strategically mobilized by elders in the late 1980s because it was the best choice available to them in their struggle against the new arrivals, and it takes that discourse at face value, as an expression of a timeless, legitimate Acholi tradition. Pain dehistoricizes the conflict of the late 1980s and frames the current crisis in its terms: he sees only a cleavage between the LRA, as the most recent generation of rebellious, violent youth, and the Acholi represented by Acholi elders as arbiters of tradition. By reading the current crisis in terms of the rupture of a genuine Acholi tradition by deviant youths, Pain sees the resolution of the current crisis as necessarily occurring in those terms, that is, through the reconciliation of deviant rebels with the singular Acholi culture.

Second, on the national level, the crisis faced by the Acholi simply cannot be resolved by reconstructing the chiefly order, because the current crisis is also the product of the decimation of the Acholi political middle class, which served as the local mediator between national political power, whether parties or state, and the peasantry. A rehabilitation of this political class would be a prerequisite for the inclusion of the Acholi in the national government. It also ignores the fact that the LRA itself frames the current crisis not in terms of its deviance from Acholi culture, but rather in terms of the political penetration of the Movement government into Acholi society, and the division of government collaborators from the genuine Acholi. Although most Acholi reject that dichotomy, many would accept the salience of a cleavage between those who are progovernment and those who are independent, a political cleavage that is ignored by the traditional reconciliation agenda.

In addition to the benefits derived by donors in pursuit of African authenticity, and by older male Acholi in pursuit of their lost authority (addressed later), the promotion of traditional authority can also be of significant benefit to the Ugandan government. The government made efforts to co-opt the newly established, and foreign-supported, paramount chief, Rwot Acana II, whose unaccountable authority makes him a good candidate for government manipulation. In the early 2000s, the government, in particular President Museveni, was attempting to turn

Acana into the main mediator in peace efforts, I was informed by a government official close to the negotiations. The government has already had some success in co-opting the lesser chiefs, according to some members of the political opposition; in the words of one man openly opposed to the Movement government, many chiefs were "in the pocket of the government."[21] Once again, it remains to be seen whether this cadre of chiefs supported by foreign donors and the government will be able to establish legitimacy within Acholi society or if their dependence on external funds and lack of a popular mandate will make them tools of outsiders seeking political control or economic benefits—the issue of land will be central to the latter, as there are already reports of these chiefs serving as the middlemen for unpopular large land purchases by investors.

The rest of this chapter inquires more deeply into the theoretical underpinnings of this traditional reconciliation agenda, especially as it has been articulated within a justice framework, and the political consequences of promoting it through external interventions. I argue that it can serve to increase and consolidate the unaccountable power of certain groups within Acholi society, principally older men, while also enabling a disciplinary project by men against those cast as deviant within the traditional reconciliation agenda, mostly women and youth. To do so, I begin with a critique of the concept of traditional justice itself, which I derive from Beninese philosopher Paulin Hountondji's 1976 classic, *African Philosophy: Myth and Reality*.

2. Ethnophilosophy

In *African Philosophy*, Hountondji coins the phrase "ethnophilosophy," which he identifies as "a defined thought-pattern and a permanent temptation of Africanist discourse" (vii).[22] I engage with Hountondji's critique of ethnophilosophy in order to designate and analyze what I term ethnojustice, an agenda that focuses on promoting social order through so-called traditional justice.

THE ELEMENTS OF ETHNOPHILOSOPHY

Hountondji begins with what he considers the seminal text of ethnophilosophy, the 1945 *Bantu Philosophy* by the Belgian missionary Placide Tempels. According to Hountondji, *Bantu Philosophy* is "an ethnological work with philosophical pretensions" (34), which "aimed to reconstruct a particular *Weltanschauung*, a specific world-view commonly attributed to all Africans, abstracted from history and change and, moreover, philosophical, through an interpretation of the customs and traditions, proverbs and institutions—in short, various data—concerning the cultural life of African peoples" (34). Hountondji explains how, at first glance, Tempels' motivation may appear generous, since it was in part an attempt to debunk the prevalent belief in the African "primitive mentality" (34) and to insist on the systematic nature of African thought. Tempels strove to elicit, from ethnographic data, a coherent, singular worldview, which he identified as genuine philosophy, of equal complexity, and capable of dealing with the same questions as European philosophy: "At first sight, then, Tempels' object appeared to be to rehabilitate the black man and his culture and to redeem them from the contempt from which they had suffered until then" (34).

However, according to Hountondji, the ethnophilosophical approach did not represent a true redemption of autonomous African thought, because it represented that thought to be a singular worldview, in which Africans unconsciously and unanimously believed and in which individual Africans had no voice. "Africans are, as usual, excluded from the discussion, and Bantu philosophy is a mere pretext for learned disquisitions among Europeans. The black man continues to be the very opposite of an interlocutor; he remains a topic, a voiceless face under private investigation, an object to be defined and not the subject of a possible discourse" (34).

This is because of the way in which the ethnophilosopher constructs African philosophy. African philosophy, according to ethnophilosophy, is not the product of discussion and debate among Africans. Instead, when philosophy is applied to Africa, Hountondji explains, it is supposed to designate "merely a collective worldview, an implicit, spontaneous, perhaps even unconscious system of beliefs to which all Africans are supposed to adhere" (60). Thus, it can be reconstructed as a single, coherent system only by the professional ethnophilosopher. The outcome is that ethnophilosophy privileges the Western voice and silences the African voice, which is deemed unable to articulate its own beliefs:

> The white scholar's discourse is based here on the black man's silence, and this, in turn, is the outcome of a long historical process that remains unquestioned. As a result, the ethnographer does not meet any resistance while submitting the Bantu people to all sorts of conceptual manipulation (xviii).

Unsurprisingly, Tempels' work, and indeed ethnophilosophy in general, "is not addressed to Africans but to Europeans," and particularly to colonizers and missionaries.

One consequence of the ethnophilosophical approach is the myth of what Hountondji calls *unanimism*, namely,

> the illusion that all men and women in such societies speak with one voice and share the same opinion about all fundamental issues. This implies the rejection of pluralism, the sweeping away of all internal contradictions and tensions, the denial of the intense intellectual life, and the extreme cultural richness associated with these societies (xviii).

This "myth of primitive unanimity," Hountondji further explains, implies "that in 'primitive' societies—that is to say, non-Western societies—everybody always agrees with everybody else. It follows that in such societies there can never be individual beliefs or philosophies but only collective systems of belief" (60).

Hountondji extends his critique by addressing *The Bantu-Rwandese Philosophy of Being,* by the Rwandese priest Alexis Kagamé, as an example of ethnophilosophy produced by Africans, which

> has been built up essentially *for a European public.* The African ethnophilosopher's discourse is not intended for Africans. It has not been produced for their benefit, and its authors understood that it would be challenged, if at all, not by Africans but by Europe alone. Unless, of course, the West expressed itself through Africans, as it knows so well how to do (45; emphasis in original).

Part and parcel of ethnophilosophy, whether by Europeans or Africans, is a certain image of African society and African "tradition." As Hountondji explains, because it espouses unanimism, ethnophilosophy posits an "immutable, ahistorical and inert" African "tradition" and social order (77), based on the "refusal to accept that a non-Western society could contain a plurality of opinions that might conceivably diverge" (78). It employs "the ideological conception that non-Western cultures are dead, petrified, reified, eternally self-replicating and lacking any internal capacity for negation or transcendence" (165). As a result, the ethnophilosopher believes that "in a 'primitive' society thought never has any real subversive effect" (80), and that there is universal, consensual, spontaneous conformity to a singular social order. There are no revolts or resistances from within; this leads to "the same pervasive ideological assumption: in a non-Western culture, change can only come from outside" (164). To the ethnophilosopher, such change is usually identified with Westernization, and thus a harmful falling away from pure "tradition," based on "the exclusive valorization of a simplified, superficial and imaginary blueprint of cultural tradition" (162).

Hountondji dismisses this fiction and dismisses the way in which "traditional African civilization . . . is used to mean 'pre-colonial African civilization,'" an equation that implies a disjuncture between precolonial, supposedly pure, and unchanging African "tradition" and colonial and postcolonial, supposedly Western, and non-"traditional" cultural forms and processes (161–162) and, on that basis, attributes absolute legitimacy to the supposed contemporary representatives and manifestations of "tradition." Hountondji's response is to reject the putative singularity and unconscious character of African thought and African "tradition." He calls on philosophers to, "instead of 'African traditional thought,' consider 'African *traditions* of thought'" (xxiv; emphasis added), where those traditions are themselves plural, contrasting, and conflictual, and not identified with a singular worldview based on a pure, unchanging precolonial essence. In fact, Hountondji argues, in describing such a worldview, the ethnophilosopher is only, if anything, identifying the dominant practical ideology of a given society, which is then projected as the universal worldview for that society.

THE POLITICS OF ETHNOPHILOSOPHY

This analysis leads to Hountondji's social-political critique of ethnophilosophy. He asks "why certain Western authors, followed (and this is more serious) by African authors, should from a certain time onwards have felt the need to look for such a collective world-view in the secret recesses of the mysterious African soul" (76). He argues that Tempels' text, and ethnophilosophy generally, serve specific purposes for Europeans and for Africans. First, they serve the psychological needs of Europeans who want to believe in a kind of equality of African philosophy. As Hountondji concludes, this has led to a situation in which "in present conditions the dialogue with the West can only encourage 'folklorism,' a sort of collective cultural exhibitionism which compels the 'Third World' intellectual to 'defend and illustrate' the peculiarities of his tradition for the benefit of a Western public" (67), satisfying their exoticist desire to hear the subaltern speak in dulcet tones.

Ethnophilosophy also served a more expressly political purpose, entwined with "the profoundly conservative nature of the ethnophilosophical project itself" (57). For Europeans, Hountondji explains, ethnophilosophy is a tool to help discover, within African culture, opportunities and channels for European penetration for the sake of civilizing Africa. As he says, European missionaries and colonizers wanted to "find a psychological and cultural basis for rooting their Christian message in the African's mind without betraying either" (59), and so ethnophilosophy provided a way for colonizers to engage with what was construed to be the authentic African mind and character.

Ethnophilosophy also had political support from within Africa because of the changing purposes it served, made possible because ethnophilosophy "could be objectivized and manipulated at will" (78). In his own context, Hountondji explains that "ethnophilosophy has a positive function to fulfill as a powerful opiate." Whereas before, some strands of ethnophilosophy had served to help in the African "restoration of self-confidence" in the face of colonialism (171), now "the function of ethnophilosophy has changed: it is no longer a possible means of demystification but a powerful means of mystification in the hands of all those who have a vested interest in discouraging intellectual initiative because it prompts not living thought in our peoples but simply pious rumination on the past" (171). As a reified ideology, it becomes an instrument in the hands of rulers, "an ideological placebo," used to silence intellectual discussion and dissent. Therefore, he argues that debunking the "myth" of ethnophilosophy is "inseparable from political effort—namely, the anti-imperialist struggle" (44).

Accordingly, this struggle should be pursued by promoting philosophical debate and discussion among Africans, based on a redefinition of African philosophy that recognizes the plurality of African thought. The minimalist redefinition of African philosophy offered by Hountondji would term that philosophy "African," which is taking place within the continent or is conducted by Africans. Thus, the "traditional" is eviscerated of its essentialism, and "so-called modern African philosophy is also a tradition of its own" (xxiv). He goes on to state that,

> African philosophy does not lie where we have long been seeking it, in some mysterious corner of our supposedly immutable soul, a collective and unconscious world-view which it is incumbent upon us to study and revive, but that our philosophy consists essentially in the process of analysis itself, in that very discourse through which we have been doggedly attempting to define ourselves (33).

The result is that African philosophy is the conscious activity of Africans embodying a vast plurality of different traditions and modes of thought: "Admit, then, that our philosophy is yet to come. Take the word 'philosophy' in the active, not passive, sense. . . . It can exist as a philosophy only in the form of a confrontation between individual thoughts, a discussion, a debate" (53). He concludes with a program of action for philosophers: "the first thing to do, then, is to organize such discussions in the midst of the society where the birth of these sciences is desired" (67). The next section explores how these elements of Hountondji's analysis can be used to designate and critique another ethnoscience: ethnojustice.

3. Ethnojustice in Theory

Ethnojustice is a discourse that combines elements from ethnography and from the study of law and morality to describe what it claims are traditional systems of justice of non-Western cultures. In describing a traditional system of justice, ethnojustice purports to describe a single, coherent, positive system that is presented as being universally, consensually, and spontaneously adhered to by all members of that culture and that, even if in abeyance today, remains valid and should be revived. I will argue, however, following Hountondji, that contrary to what ethnojustice asserts, genuine peace and justice will not be found through the imposition of an inert, authoritarian order on African societies, but will emerge through the ongoing and contentious process of including more groups, interests, and voices in the deliberations over the shape of those societies—in a word, through democracy.

ACHOLI ETHNOJUSTICE, OR, HOW TO BE ACHOLI

A paradigmatic ethnojustice text concerning the Acholi is the 2005 *Roco Wat i Acholi: Restoring Relationships in Acholi-land: Traditional Approaches to Justice and Reconciliation*, funded by the John D. and Catherine T. Macarthur Foundation and by the Royal Embassy of the Netherlands.[23] Although there are other accounts of traditional justice in northern Uganda, I want to analyze a single key text so that aspects of the analysis and critique might help illuminate other ethnojustice texts and interventions in Uganda and beyond.

The purpose of *Roco Wat* is "to provide an initial assessment of how traditional rituals and ceremonies could be further adapted to address the crimes committed during the 19-year old conflict in Uganda" (1). To this end, it seeks principally to "identify and describe: a) Justice from the perspective of Acholi traditional culture; [and] b) the processes and mechanisms of traditional justice" (7). In doing so, it endeavors to establish that traditional justice is just as genuine a system of justice as "Western justice" and meets the requirements of Western justice and human rights. To this end, the report cites "the equivalences of traditional mechanisms to judicial mechanisms—such as the concept of precedence and ground for appeal— in order to illustrate its potential to act as an alternative justice mechanism" (4–5). That is, the ethnojustice discourse presents Acholi "traditional justice" as a local articulation of universal standards of justice and human rights.

According to the report, the core of Acholi traditional justice is embodied in the title itself, *Roco Wat i Acholi*, that is, "the restoration of relationships," which "captures the essence of Acholi approaches to justice" (2). Therefore, the Acholi traditional system of justice is particularly apposite now:

> After nearly two decades of conflict, social relationships and trust within a traditionally communal culture have been severely degraded. Consequently, so has Acholi culture, and the prominent role cultural leaders (Chiefs, Elders and *Mego*) once held in society. Due to mass displacement, youth have little opportunity to learn about their history or culture (2).

For this reason, the report frames the recently created body of Acholi chiefs and elders, Ker Kwaro Acholi (KKA), as key to this process of reviving traditional justice mechanisms in order to help restore relationships in Acholiland. *Roco Wat* intends to begin the project of the positivization and formalization of so-called Acholi traditional justice by collecting and writing down practices, rituals, and ceremonies, which are to proceed in tandem with the empowerment of KKA as the privileged body that will apply this formalized traditional justice system.

As with ethnophilosophy, the ethnojustice of *Roco Wat* does not allow Acholi themselves to fully articulate their own traditional justice system, for, as the report admits, the term *traditional justice* "has no direct translation in Luo" (14). Instead, it is up to experts and outsiders, with the assistance of Acholi academics and elders, to compile and formalize the traditional justice system as a coherent whole, subsequent to which it will be up to outsiders to help revive those traditions among the Acholi. Although *Roco Wat* recognizes that some elders have considerable knowledge of the traditional justice system, it also implies that they still need additional instruction, and it notes that outside organizations, funded by foreign donors, are conducting "leadership training on traditional practices" (31). The situation of the youth is even more deplorable from the ethnojustice perspective; indeed, "one Elder remarked that the younger generations *do not know how to be Acholi*" (22; emphasis added). The strangeness of foreign organizations teaching elders how to be proper Acholi elders is compounded by the fact that elders are then to teach recalcitrant youth and women how to be proper Acholi. In this sense, many women and youth, according to ethnojustice, are not even aware that they need their traditional culture revived, so alienated are they from their essential traditional identity. This, as we will see, is a recipe for a potentially disciplinary project, one based on the silence of actual Africans in favor of the "true" traditional Acholi identity elicited and promoted by foreign NGOs and donors, together with select local partners.

THE UNANIMISM OF ACHOLI TRADITION

So what are the characteristics of this Acholi traditional justice system, according to the ethnojustice discourse? First, ethnojustice relies on the putative absolute break introduced by British colonialism. What existed before colonialism was supposedly a pure Acholi culture, a timeless, unchanging essence of Acholi identity and practice. In this spirit, *Roco Wat* repeatedly refers to "how traditional justice was once practiced in Acholi prior to colonialism" (9). The report explains that it derives most of its information from Acholi informants, asserting that there are "a wealth of informants—namely, Acholi Elders—who can recall traditional justice as practiced within villages when they were young, and how such practices were affected by the introduction of British colonial administration" (4).

Roco Wat displays the ethnojustice tendency to equate a pure, essential cultural identity, termed "traditional," with the precolonial, and to oppose it to the impure colonial and postcolonial society, which has been infected by Western ideas and practices. Reductive characterizations of both are present: "Traditional justice in Acholi culture was described by informants as restorative rather than punitive, seeking to repair social harmony of a community, rather than establish individual innocence or guilt" (16). Again, "Historically, compensation and rituals were highly employed to promote restoration of relations. Today, traditional courts have largely been replaced by the state" (10). Also, the Acholi traditional system, it is asserted, was based on the "consensual" arrival at decisions that would help the entire community (16), whereas the "Western" system is one based on the rhetorical skill of lawyers, not the truth (18).

This invites historical critique. First, the idea that a pure, self-regulating, harmonious Acholi culture existed throughout the precolonial period, in which a pure Acholi traditional justice system held sway, has little evidence to support it.[24] It ignores what many have described as the invention of the Acholi as a tribe by the British, but, even if a precolonial Acholi identity did exist, it also ignores the century of extensive, violent conflict and upheaval that preceded the advent of British colonialism, a period, not of primitive harmony and cultural purity, but of destructive foreign incursion, slave raiding, and internecine warfare with modern weaponry.

Second, because the British colonial administration was regularized in northern Uganda by 1920, despite the assertion that a wealth of informants could recall the precolonial justice system, it is probable that, aside from centenarians, most informants were in fact recalling the system of native courts and councils established by the British themselves, not the precolonial system, reflecting the tendency to mistake British tribal administrative categories and institutions for precolonial cultural order. These historical equivocations allow the report to assert the fundamental ethnojustice distinction between, on the one hand, the traditional, precolonial, nonstate, communal, consensual, and restorative and, on the other, the Western, colonial/postcolonial, individualist, and punitive, which supposedly disrupted this earlier harmonious traditional justice system.

Roco Wat explains that the Acholi system of traditional justice has a normative dimension when seen from the internal perspective, specifically a "spiritual approach to justice" (3), and has a functional dimension when seen from the external perspective, because "in traditional Acholi culture, justice is done for *ber bedo*, to restore harmonious life" (14). In traditional Acholi culture, according to *Roco Wat*, belief in and consent to this justice system and the social order it supports is unanimous, because all Acholi value the unity of the Acholi, or the clan, before they value themselves. The typical Acholi, then, believes absolutely in the spiritual world and in the punishment that the spiritual world sends down when rules are violated. This adherence to the spiritual/moral order ends up being beneficial for the Acholi community as a whole as well as for each individual Acholi, because that social order is taken to be superior to individual interests. The system forms a closed circuit, in which the judgments made by the spiritual world, enforced by male elders, beneficially support the social order unanimously endorsed by the Acholi.

Ethnojustice thereby tends to reduce the spiritual domain to being functional to the reproduction of a petrified social order. It does so by rendering the spiritual domain positive, that is, capable of being formalized in writing and codified in a series of specific normative rules and prescriptions. I will address this presumed functionality of a positivist spiritual domain to social order later, because it turns out that this version of the spiritual promoted by the report is functional to a very specific and partial social order. First, though, I want to note the problem with the positivization of the spiritual itself, specifically, in this case, the codification of ritual. As Tim Allen explains, when positivized, rituals "will lose their flexibility, and will no longer have all the many resonances and associations of lived ritual actions. They will have status that is at least partly based on their externally supported authority. They will become privileged rites, and, most likely, the preserve of certain figures of male authority recognized by the government."[25] Indeed, the spiritual is a realm of surplus, a domain from which the potential for social or political rupture can always emerge. The idea that it can be contained in positive form without remainder, in a form that makes it perfectly functional to existing social order, that its surplus and capacity for disruption can be repressed or excised, is a fiction, a fiction that those in power often want to propagate. As I explain in the next section, numerous examples can be found within Acholi society of the inherently disruptive dimension of the spiritual and of ritual practice and of the way in which those with power try to excise that dimension and render the spiritual positive, coherent, and reified for their own purposes, a project with which the ethnojustice discourse is complicit.

4. Ethnojustice in Practice

ETHNOJUSTICE AS A DOMINANT IDEOLOGY

Following Hountondji, we would expect that this putatively unanimous adherence to Acholi traditional justice and to the social order it upholds is, in fact, a mystification of a situation in which one particular version of traditional justice is part of a dominant ideology and upholds the power of a specific group. This begins to emerge as we consider the tension in *Roco Wat* around the figure of the male elder informant. Throughout the report, as noted already, male elders are presented as the privileged repositories and guardians of tradition and the exclusive mediators with the spiritual world. At one point, the report states that elders are "considered closest to *Jok*" (11), and it explains that, prior to the current war, elders were in charge of carrying out "a series of rituals within village settings and household compounds in order to appease the ancestors and ensure the moral order was upheld" (11). According to *Roco Wat*, elders and *rwodi* had the exclusive role of regulating Acholi society through their access to the spiritual world.

The interesting thing about the role of male elders in *Roco Wat* is that they also seem to be the only Acholi capable of seeing the traditional system of justice from the external perspective as well as from the internal perspective, that is, as capable of seeing how traditional justice serves to reproduce social order by using the language of the spiritual. Thus we find, in *Roco Wat*, an Acholi elder bluntly declaring that

> All rituals . . . are meant to inculcate good behaviour. . . . for good behaviour to be entrenched in Acholi, all acts of misbehaviour are linked to the spiritual world. Anyone who acts contrary to established norms displeases our ancestors and rituals should be performed to appease them (11).

Some of the Acholi male elders quoted seem almost cynical about the way that the administration of spiritual justice is a tool of social order, a social order in which they have a privileged position.

Indeed, the privileging of male elders in the report, seen in light of elders' own understanding that enforcing spiritual order represents the enforcement of a disciplinary social project, gives rise to a different picture of Acholi culture: not one of spontaneous, universal, and consensual adherence to spiritual dictates for the good of the Acholi as a whole, but rather one of enforcement of a certain set of norms, couched in a spiritual language, by male elders and others claiming the mantle of chiefship who claim exclusive access to that spiritual domain in order to ensure the reproduction of their preferred social order. This cannot help but explode the myth of primitive unanimism and give to this version of Acholi traditional justice a different visage: that of a dominant practical ideology serving the interests of a dominant or formerly dominant group. The ethnojustice discourse is based upon assertions of both the primacy of male elders and the unanimism of the Acholi, and, in practice, it is the latter that loses out and must be imposed by the former.

Therefore, in addition to the positivization of the spiritual that the ethnojustice discourse effects, it also effects a reification of justice and social order, excising from each its inherent plurality and possibility for rupture. In fact, neither the spiritual, the moral, nor the social are the positive, singular, and unanimous domains that ethnojustice insist they are, and they cannot exist in the closed, mutually supporting circuit that ethnojustice claims to identify. Each is a terrain on which there is contradiction, conflict, and struggle between dominant and nondominant opinions, ideas, and projects. It is in this spirit that Hountondji demands "additional investigations into the wide range of nondominant, marginal, and even adverse ideologies" that co-exist with any dominant practical ideology (xxiv).

THE PLURALITY OF THE SPIRITUAL AND THE SOCIAL

Given the stakes of the ethnojustice project in northern Uganda and the political and social context in which it takes place, it is perhaps not a surprise that some male elders would employ the ethnojustice discourse as their language of power and as a route to external support. Indeed, ethnojustice is explicitly phrased in terms of "reviving" traditional authority, and in the case of *Roco Wat*, the power of the KKA. This is because, presently, the lineage- and clan-based structure of patriarchal, generally gerontocratic, male leadership, which had held significant internal authority in Acholi society at various times over the last century, has been thrown into crisis by the war and displacement. Male Acholi elders and chiefs have largely lost their power of social regulation and political leadership, and although men have seen their authority and status within Acholi society wane (as discussed in the last chapter), women, and to a lesser extent youth, have seen their economic, social, and political authority and status rise. These latter groups have benefited from new business and educational opportunities, human rights interventions, and new associations made possible in the environment of displacement. So, ethnojustice represents an opportunity for older men to assert their power under the mantle of tradition and to dismiss challenges to that power as nontraditional and nonauthentic. In noting this, I do not mean to imply that the authority formerly enjoyed by male elders was ever the unanimous, consensual authority imagined by ethnojustice; instead, at most it was the dominant ideology. However, at present it is doubtful that it is even a dominant ideology, or that its proponents are the dominant group in society; therefore, ethnojustice may amount to a project of constructing male power justified as "re"-constructing a still-legitimate order from the past. It is a typical peacebuilding project, where peace is equated with a specific social order, this time under the control of male elders.

The lack of consensus among the Acholi on the version of the spiritual and the social promoted by ethnojustice is very apparent even in recent Acholi history. Indeed, against what ethnojustice asserts, the spiritual domain has offered a wide scope for alternative and counterhegemonic ideologies among the Acholi, most notably in the form of spirit possession and the work of *ajwaka*. The Holy Spirit Movement and LRA itself can be seen as embodying counterhegemonic spiritual claims in part against the power of male elders. The spiritual is a terrain on which women and youth have asserted claims to power and authority beyond that of the male elders, and it is by no means the exclusive preserve of those elders, as ethnojustice would have it. *Roco Wat* briefly recognizes these potentially disruptive dimensions of Acholi spirituality, but denies them in favor of the male elder-dominated vision of spirituality. As to *ajwaka*, *Roco Wat* explains:

> Often, when the source of *cen* is not readily apparent, Elders may consult one another and the affected family or sub-clan to determine the circumstances that must be addressed. If this fails, Elders will often call on diviners, or healers, *ajwaka*. . . . They are believed to have a strong communication link to the spirit worlds, and ability to heal those afflicted. In Acholi-bur, one Elder described *ajwaka* as a last resort when Elders, Rwodi, or courts of law fail (13).

Ajwaka are reduced to the ancilla of male elders and chiefs and of the dominant social order, and their disruptive is power ignored.[26] This ignores the autonomy of *ajwaka*, and it also ignores the fact that many *ajwaka* today come from outside Acholiland, and thus may draw on the spiritual to articulate national or even cosmopolitan identities and projects.[27] Ethnojustice instead imposes the tribe, under the customary power of the chief, as the essential political and social unit, ignoring how the spiritual may rupture not only the power of the male chief but also the boundaries of the tribe as the key collective identity. Ethnojustice seeks to retribalize conflict and political identity in the name of justice and social order, when it is a movement towards the national that is desperately needed to overcome the legacy of violence.

As for the spiritual dimension of the LRA, *Roco Wat* recognizes that the LRA conducts spiritual rituals but dismisses them as being only superficially "similar" to those of the Acholi: "According to several interviewees, *cen* did follow fighters returning to base camps and required rituals *similar to* Acholi to cleanse them. Former LRA Commander Michael Opio described one ritual involving the slaughter of two sheep that *resembles* Yubu Kum rituals in Acholi" (50; emphasis added).[28] Even though the LRA are mostly Acholi themselves, the rituals they carry out, according to ethnojustice, are only superficially similar to those rituals of the real Acholi. Thus, ethnojustice denies the authenticity of the spiritual in the hands of women, youth, and dissenting men, and denies the legitimacy of their use of the spiritual as a source for alternative projects of social order.

The domain of justice is a terrain of social struggle in northern Uganda at present and is in no way reducible to being functional to a certain patriarchal model of social order. This is seen with the contestation over what justice should mean in the wake of the war. *Roco Wat*'s insistence on the "consensual" nature of all "traditional" Acholi justice should draw our attention to how that consent is enforced and at whose expense. The monopolization of justice and reconciliation by an externally supported male authority structure, dictated by ethnojustice, fails to address the fact that different groups within Acholi society, in particular women and youth, might have their own particular demands for justice. Furthermore, these demands may be centered around alternative spiritual mechanisms or have nothing to do with the spiritual at all, oriented instead toward formal, state-based legal processes, nonspiritual community-based processes, or other alternatives. As a result, ethnojustice has the potential to silence those who do not identify with this revived male authority and its version of the spiritual it claims to uphold.

Women, for example, could be prevented from deciding for themselves what justice means in response to their own specific experiences during the war. Women have faced particular kinds of violence on a massive scale not experienced by men, and it is unreasonable to assume that women would agree to male elders deciding what justice means for them, or to assume that women would be satisfied with men deciding that the perpetrators of violence against women should simply be forgiven, as male elders may very well do under the mantle of tradition. Men may be satisfied with a negotiated, ritualized solution among themselves that does not involve punishment or compensation, whereas women may not be willing to accept that as a just solution at all. The imposition of such justice could create a peace among men built on a reinforced regime of gendered violence.

In short, community-based justice cannot be reduced to a male-dominated version of traditional justice because the community itself, especially now after two decades of war, is in no way reducible to those who would claim traditional authority (not that it was before the war either). Acholi society, like any society, is not a homogeneous, coherent whole, and Acholi traditional justice as identified and celebrated by ethnojustice is only one practical ideology supporting a claim to power by one group, legitimated through an appeal to a singular tradition and Acholi identity. It is promoted at the expense of alternative traditions of spiritualism, justice, and social and political order *within* Acholi society, some of which may even draw on discourses of human rights.

THE POLITICS OF ETHNOJUSTICE

This discussion raises the question of the political effects of ethnojustice in northern Uganda. *Roco Wat* favorably reports that,

> participants at the Consultative Workshop agreed that Acholi culture was in decline, and in need of revival, especially for youth. Ker Kwaro Acholi

and its supporters should embark upon a cultural revival through the recommendations below, which should be supported by donors and the Government of Uganda (74).

The motivation is clear: to channel donor funding to the promotion of "traditional authorities," who can lead a cultural revival and, through mechanisms of traditional justice, restore social order among the Acholi, as an alternative to Western systems of justice through punishment. It is an empowering, participatory project, where Acholi are empowered to participate as proper, "responsible," Acholi under the authority of chiefs. As with all ethnoscience discourses, this is oriented principally toward a Western audience—in this case, toward donors.

This is also the course of action proposed by Pain, who suggests that the work of the elders be facilitated by NGOs.[29] The planners of NUSAF similarly envisioned two thousand "interventions targeted at traditional institutions," which would promote social order by reviving traditional authorities, in particular chiefs and elders. The official at the Prime Minister's office for NUSAF explained that the World Bank was fostering interclan meetings and dialogue in order to help the process of reconciliation between the LRA and the Acholi.[30] He said that they had hired a number of NGOs and individuals to identify the traditional leadership. In response to a question about the existence of such leaders, he stated, "of course communities have leaders," who comprised a "whole hierarchy" up to the highest levels, the paramount chief. As a NUSAF official in Gulu explained, the Bank is not limiting their intervention to helping *rwodi*, but rather is working to consolidate all the traditional "centers of power that are already there."[31] To this end, the Bank was in the process of identifying and categorizing clans and subclans so as to rebuild authority structures at all those levels. The official unfailingly expressed the project in terms of re-establishing "his power," namely, the discipline of the father, clan chief, or elder, as a means of reversing the breakdown of internal order and authority among the Acholi.[32]

The ethnojustice discourse serves purposes for the West similar to those described by Hountondji. It is a cutting edge of global interventionism, one that pushes the bounds of human rights so as to describe new channels for Western penetration into Africa. Instead of enabling the civilizing mission of missionaries and colonialists, as Tempels' work did, ethnojustice enables what is imagined as the empowering mission of NGOs, international agencies, and donors in the violent and traditional parts of the world. Ethnojustice also appeals to the Western audience because, like ethnophilosophy, it bases its legitimacy on a claim to represent and work with genuine African identity and difference, to treat Africans with dignity as Africans, and to avoid imposing Western ideas and models on them: to paraphrase Hountondji, it attempts to find a cultural basis for rooting their message of peace, justice, and human rights in the African's mind without betraying any of them. However, because ethnojustice understands Africans as possessing unspoken worldviews on which they agree in ethnic unanimity, then, of course, it cannot but impose a Western model of society and justice on Africa—a model that does not represent idealized Western institutions, as some liberal interventions do, but rather represents the Western *imagination* of African institutions. This is a model that can be given voice by Africans, as donors fund workshops and conferences where their findings are guaranteed their desired imprimatur of authentic African approval through the medium of "sitting allowances," per diems, and promises of funding.

Ethnojustice, when it informs interventions, does more than try to facilitate the imposition of a certain form of order on Africa and appeal to the Western taste for exoticism and authenticity. It also has powerful political effects on the local and national levels. On the local level, as mentioned, traditional justice is instrumentalized by male Acholi as an opportunity to build their faltering power through foreign support, which could lead to a disciplinary project. As Erin Baines puts it, "although local mechanisms emphasize reconciliation in a way that punitive approaches do not, it could potentially increase violence rather than restore relationships."[33]

Indeed, although some revival of traditional authority seems to be widely supported among Acholi, there is controversy over just what that authority will comprise, and what its domain will be, in the postwar period. Among women and youth, especially those in town a return to the idealizations of prewar order advocated by many male elders, would be neither practical nor just. For their part, however, elders and many men tend to project a comparatively vast increase in their authority once back in the village in a bid to correct the corruption introduced into Acholi society during displacement. During interviews, in the most extreme versions, elders explained how they saw themselves as taking a dominant and all-encompassing role in social regulation in the postconflict period by dealing with everyone from ex-rebels, thieves, government informers, prostitutes, and foreign women to troublemakers, generally.[34] This revival of their traditional authority, men and elders explained, would take place by imposing discipline at the family and clan levels through warnings, fines, corporal punishment, and, if all else fails, expulsion from the clan and curses in the name of genuine Acholi identity.

Therefore, there is a possibility that postwar Acholi society could see a coercive project carried out by men, especially men with family or clan authority, designed to eliminate what they see as the corruption that had infected Acholi society during the war and displacement. Although men generally explained that they would not punish people for what they had done in the camps, and that it would only be those who continued to misbehave in the village who would be disciplined, as the transition out of the camps began in 2007, strict rules were already being imposed in some places to keep certain people out of the villages. For example, in one camp, the clan elders had assembled and told the men that if they brought Congolese women back to the village, the men would be refused land and expelled from the clan. A wide range of those seeking to return to the village could be subject to this kind of harsh discipline, or even excluded from clan affiliation and land access through revived family and clan meetings. Independent or assertive women or youth, those with unclear ancestry, those with foreign connections or relations, or simply those deemed undesirable or vulnerable could be disciplined or excluded through accusations of contravening Acholi tradition or Acholi laws. Ex-LRA may face even more acute problems, as will be addressed later. There is thus the potential for violence and upheaval within Acholi society around this kind of systematic exclusion of certain categories of people from clan membership and land possession.

The potential for tough discipline or exclusion by male authorities has a prominent gender dimension, stemming from the patrilocal, patrilineal nature of Acholi society. Although firm adherence to patrilocal and patrilineal norms is often disrupted at present as a result of the war and displacement, this only increases the potential negative impact of their purposeful re-imposition by male authorities on women and youth. Indeed, among men, the re-establishment of traditional authority was often framed explicitly in terms of undoing the power gained by women and youth in the camps and imposing the power of men and elders over these formerly subservient groups.

In the words of one group of male elders, "the rules in the village are different" from those in town or in camps. Because women have "forgotten" the rules and even how to do their basic duties, these men argued, women will have to be "trained" again in their proper roles and duties, "reminded" of village life. Men admitted that women might not be ready to accept these roles, and so it would take a concerted effort, a group of men from Kirombe Custom subward explained, by men at home, and then by elders and chiefs at the village and clan level, to make sure women conform to the rules of the village. As a group of men in Laguti put it (to a female Acholi researcher), women will be re-instructed, "just like teaching new oxen how to plough."

This project could involve physical violence: older men explained how women could be caned for refusing to work or to cook, for refusing to have sex with their husbands, or for breaking other social norms. Caning and other punishments can take place within the family or else at the clan level, administered by the husband or by clan enforcers. Thus, while the acute level of violence against women seen in camps, much of it due to alcohol, will probably be reduced as people become occupied with farming and other jobs, there is a possibility that physical violence by men against women could continue under another guise, namely family or clan discipline. As a result, women's public space and the social and economic opportunities they enjoy with it, as described in the previous chapter, may be erased as women are confined to the private world of the home, whereas the public space of men will re-open through social interaction within the lineage and clan.

Men were not unanimous on the need to "retrain" women. Indeed, many men explained that they would be happy to accept their wives' new roles as business women and leaders, and some noted that women had even been given seats on councils of elders in Bobi and Alero. For their part, women recognized the variation among men's attitudes, and often explained that their ability to maintain their businesses, property, associations, education, and skills would depend greatly on the individual husband. But for the most part, women appeared to be expecting many men to try to re-impose their authority. As a group of women in Gulu Town said, "men are always telling women that, you wait, you are feeling good in town because you are protected." Although women declared their hope that their husbands would accept their new economic and political roles back in the village, they also recognized that this might not be the case.

For many women, this represented a significant injustice. As a group of women in Madi Opei explained, the custom of not letting women speak at clan meetings and not letting them have a role in decision making should be done away with. After all, they continued, since it was women who had kept men and even Acholi society itself alive during the years of displacement, why should they now be silenced and ruled by the very men who abandoned their responsibilities? Why should men "re-instruct" women once back in the village, instead of women instructing men as to how things will be?

Ex-LRA returnees, in particular those youths who are the most marginalized or unwilling to conform to the demands of older male authorities, could also face difficulties under the imposition of an ethnojustice agenda. A guarantee of community acceptance mediated by male elders may be enough to convince many ex-LRA returnees to accept that authority, but this is by no means certain. Indeed, tensions between male lineage-based authorities and armed young men have been one of the roots of the wars that have plagued northern Uganda for over two decades, so there is no historical precedent that would imply that ex-members of the LRA will necessarily submit to this authority. Moreover, there is no guarantee that traditional authorities will not use that authority *against* ex-members of the LRA whom they see as undesirable or who are without firm family or clan connections. Many ex-members of the LRA expressed their desire for government protection and regulation of land issues in the village because they did not trust the capacity or intention of clan authorities to ensure their protection or fair access to land. In short, fear of revenge, the refusal of ex-LRA to submit to male authority, and the possibility that those male authorities may exclude certain ex-members of the LRA from clan membership and access to land meant that ex-LRA members, especially those who had been in the bush the longest and those without strong family relations, could end up facing discipline and exclusion, with dangerous consequences for peace and justice.

Therefore, the externally funded ethnojustice project could enable a wider project of imposing disciplinary male authority on an Acholi society where that male authority lost much of its legitimacy decades ago. This could amount to another kind of "transitional justice," a private project carried out by men to redeem what they see as a deeply corrupted Acholi society, an agenda that would ride on the coattails of the more public transitional justice agenda promoted by foreigners and the Ugandan government. However, because it would represent peace built on the backs of women and youth, there is the potential for further crisis within Acholi society around the exclusion of certain categories of people from clan membership and land possession.

On the national level, ethnojustice can have significant appeal for states involved in political violence. Uganda exemplifies this: it seems likely that the Ugandan government is interested in promoting Acholi traditional justice precisely because traditional justice may guarantee state impunity. Indeed, rituals presided over by male lineage-based Acholi authorities are simply inadequate to deal with crimes and human rights violations committed by a modern state.[35] Such authorities have no jurisdiction over non-Acholi and lack the coercive power of national courts. Also, traditional justice is premised, in large part, on admission of crime, and, under the present circumstances, it seems unlikely that the government would be willing to admit what it has done. Therefore, if promoted exclusively, traditional justice could provide the government and army with impunity for the crimes they have committed in the course of the war. Ethnojustice also fails to take into account the international dimensions of the war, including the role of the donors in funding Uganda's militarization, and the role of the aid agencies in collaborating with forced displacement. The assertion of a uniquely Acholi traditional justice further tribalizes the conflict and can make national political justice even more difficult.[36]

CHALLENGES TO ETHNOJUSTICE

"The process of reviving traditional justice is not an easy task," *Roco Wat* admits (3), and at one point the report does indeed recognize that the imposition of a gerontocratic, patriarchal order on contemporary Acholi society might not be an unmitigated good. This recognition, however, is dealt with in a way that reveals again who the true agent of traditional justice in the ethnojustice discourse is: the international community. *Roco Wat* notes the fact that physical punishment of women and youth through beating is a widely prevalent aspect of the traditional culture being promoted by older men—a traditional justice that supposedly rejects justice through punishment as Western. Indeed, this brings out the very different standards that apply to women and youth and that apply to men in the ethnojustice discourse, and it belies the claim that traditional justice is restorative and nonpunitive: women and youth can be "traditionally" subject to punishment, physical violence, expulsion, even fatal curses by male elders, whereas men's transgressions—or really a certain category of men's transgressions of interest to male elders—will be dealt with through the lofty language of reconciliation, forgiveness, and restorative justice.

In fact, *Roco Wat* at times seems aware of the possibility that violence may claim legitimacy in the name of tradition. It notes that "concerns over the representation in KKA have been raised" and that KKA's executive council, despite its two women representatives, is a body of men with "traditional views on appropriate gender and age roles." Here, the report seems to be using a different, less unambiguously positive, use of the word *traditional*. The report continues,

> During a consultative workshop hosted by the researchers in mid August, a few Elders revealed their frustrations with the growing awareness of women and youth rights. At times they argued that the expansion of these rights threatened and prevented them from carrying out their "traditional roles," such as disciplining a woman through beatings. This does not represent the majority of cultural leaders, but it does raise the concern that not all cultural norms or practices should be revived (32–33).

In this short passage, male elders suddenly no longer are the unquestionable guardians of a unanimous, benevolent tradition, and the report's placement of quotation marks around "traditional roles" appears an attempt to distance itself from their more distasteful claims. However, this recognition on the part of the ethnojustice agenda does not lead to a questioning of the concept of tradition itself or the project of reviving traditional institutions. Instead, a petrified vision of tradition is retained, of which a few parts will not be revived because they do not meet with the sensibilities of the international community. It does not prompt the consideration that perhaps the entire ethnojustice project is a gendered project. Instead, it reveals the unspoken mentality behind ethnojustice: it is the right of outsiders to decide which traditional practices will be revived and which will not, so as to ensure that traditional justice really does conform to human rights standards. However, because ethnojustice is a foreign-funded project, one in which foreign organizations are designating the "anointed" *rwodi* and are teaching the Acholi how to be Acholi, maybe this should not come as such a surprise. Ethnojustice represents the revival not of Acholi tradition but of the British tradition of indirect rule in Africa in which Africans were to be civilized as tribes; as Allen puts it, "efforts were made to do the same thing rather more systematically in the past, when 'tribal' customs were incorporated into the indirect administration of the British protectorate through government-appointed chiefs and other local agents."[37]

It should be noted that the external promotion of this form of traditional authority does not enjoy unanimous support even among men. Some men see the project not as the redemption of a corrupt Acholi society, but as part of that corruption itself. Foreign sponsorship of traditional authority has provided supposed chiefs with the opportunity to grab land and enrich themselves with the protection of KKA. Whites and their money are seen as promoting dependency among the Acholi, turning Acholi against Acholi within the NGO job market and creating a new breed of "*Acholi matar*," or "white Acholi." Foreign agencies are accused of paying people sitting allowances to participate in workshops and sensitizations, a practice that has corrupted the traditional Acholi practice of sitting and meeting to resolve problems without concern for monetary compensation. So there are certainly those men who see ethnojustice, not as a revival of traditional Acholi society with external assistance, but as corrupting Acholi society even further.

Following Hountondji, what is needed are not the minor concessions made to women and youth dictated by donors to the KKA, but rather a discussion among all the active political and social forces in Acholi society, a discussion in which the current real balance of power is recognized, a discussion that does not take as its starting point the need to establish the putatively traditional power of male elders. This would require the refutation of the discourse of ethnojustice, its myth of primitive unanimism, and its assertion of a timeless, ahistorical cultural identity. It would require the admission that internal plurality, conflict, and contestation have always characterized Acholi society, and the recognition of the many traditions found *within* Acholi society pertaining to the spiritual world and to justice. Finally, it would require recognizing the national and even cosmopolitan dimensions that justice may take, which can be found articulated in sources as diverse as the Ugandan constitution, discourses of *ajwaka,* and the Rome Statute of the ICC.

In short, there are many African and many Acholi traditions of justice. Some may find their origins in the precolonial period, others find their origins in the colonial, and others in various times during the postcolonial period. Some are tied to the symbolic and embedded in the cultural, others are tied to local and national state-based institutions, and others derive from international norms. These different traditions emerged at different times in response to different circumstances and reflect different configurations of power and authority. Even if we take a more limited meaning of traditional justice as representing a particularly cultural form of justice based in ritual practice, the last chapter demonstrated that questions of justice and human rights are being negotiated on the very terrain of tradition, and thus it remains that there are multiple strands and understandings of traditional justice in this sense as well.

All these traditions can be drawn on now in order to deal with the legacy of the war. For this reason, it is better to speak not of traditional justice but of *traditions of justice* among the Acholi, where the Acholi are historicized, not essentialized, within precolonial, colonial, and postcolonial political and social processes. Following Hountondji, "African justice" itself is simply the debate that takes place in Africa and among Africans, drawing on these different traditions and positing new ones, in the search for what justice means for Africans today in response to the continent's unique historical experience.

Just as traditional justice as described by the ethnojustice discourse is not really traditional, so is it not really justice, because justice, like philosophy, by its nature must always be open, never closed, must always be plural and unfinished, and cannot be the preserve of a single group. Just as philosophy is "yet to come" for Hountondji, so is justice yet to come, in the sense that it is open to new voices, new opinions, new formulations and ideas into the indefinite future. There is no single true justice, for justice is a domain of ultimate uncertainty, a fact that ethnojustice rejects. Justice, spirituality, tradition, and society are all realms of internal contradiction and struggle, and only if that is recognized can justice be done to Acholi, and African, justice. The social order that can emerge from this process is democracy, within which justice is, not functional to the project of imposing an authoritarian social order, but rather the subject for deliberation, organization, and action in an inclusive, open, contentious social order.

In sum, the argument for ethnojustice ignores the fact that the resolution of the internal crisis of the Acholi must involve much more than just the reconstruction of chiefly authority. If chiefly authority is exclusively emphasized, it may, in fact, forestall this wider resolution, and many of the alternative processes and developments resulting from the current upheaval represent, not a deviation from a genuine Acholi traditional order, but rather opportunities for new forms of local democratization and political inclusion—forms that go beyond the reduction of the local to the customary. Times of violent upheaval—whether human-made or natural—represent opportunities for the emergence of new political and social orders. If the initiative in such situations falls into the hands of international donors, NGOs, and the state, then reconstruction may end up equivalent to discipline and coercion and may set the stage for future conflict. If the initiative is taken up by those in the midst of the conflict, however, then new forms of inclusive popular organization may emerge that reject the oppression of the past, demand that international intervention come into line with democracy, and lay the foundation for peace in the future.

6

The ICC and Human Rights Enforcement

Since the Rome Statute of the International Criminal Court (ICC) entered into force in 2002, the Court has been the subject, not only of a flood of books and articles, but also of popular movies and T-shirt campaigns. It has been celebrated as heralding the end of impunity, ushering in a new era of global accountability, and being the most important development in international order since the end of World War II. It has also been condemned as neocolonialist, a threat to peace, racist, or simply irrelevant. These controversies have focused on Africa, and often on Uganda, because all the ICC's cases as of early 2011 were on the continent, and in 2005 Uganda became the first case in which arrest warrants were issued.

As with other forms of human rights intervention, the ICC has been proclaimed by its supporters as addressing both the causes and consequences of violence, as helping to bring about both peace and justice. These justifications are often blurred together in ICC rhetoric, for example, when ICC supporters claim the Court fosters peace but, when faced with facts to the contrary, refuse to be held accountable for the consequences of intervention by invoking the absolute moral necessity of human rights and international law. In the face of this shifting rhetoric, claims that ICC interventions can realize peace and justice need to be disentangled and independently assessed, which this chapter does by evaluating the consequences of the ICC's intervention in northern Uganda against some of the sanguine declarations made by supporters of the intervention.

1. Sketching the Peace and Justice Debate

Arguments in favor of the ICC as an agent of peace can be broken into two groups. First, it is asserted that the ICC brings peace to the specific conflicts in which it intervenes. This is said to occur through a number of routes: criminal proceedings isolate or remove particularly violent or extreme actors, put pressure on armed

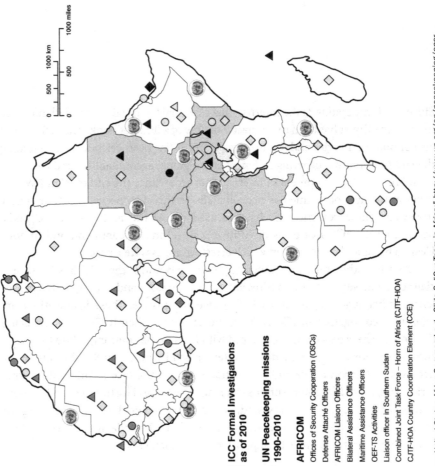

ICC Formal Investigations as of 2010

UN Peacekeeping missions 1990–2010

AFRICOM

○ Offices of Security Cooperation (OSCs)
◇ Defense Attaché Officers
△ AFRICOM Liaison Officers
● Bilateral Assistance Officers
◆ Maritime Assistance Officers
▲ OEF-TS Activities
● Liaison officer in Southern Sudan
◆ Combined Joint Task Force – Horn of Africa (CJTF-HOA)
▲ CJTF-HOA Country Coordination Element (CCE)

500   1000 km
0   500   1000 miles

Source: United States Africa Command n.d., Slide 6, "Our Team in Africa;" http://www.un.org/en/peacekeeping/operations/past.shtml; http://www.icc-cpi.int/Menus/ICC/Situations+and+Cases. Map prepared by Jonatan Alvarsson.

parties to come to the negotiating table, and mobilize international efforts, including the use of military force, to bring the worst offenders to justice. International criminal trials can also, it is argued—drawing on the transitional justice literature—play the role of rebuilding local and national communities shattered by violence, promoting healing, truth-telling, and reconciliation, giving a voice to the victims, and providing the normative foundations of a new, peaceful, era.

Second, it is asserted that the ICC brings peace by serving a broader prevention role beyond the specific intervention at hand, both through its pedagogical mechanism of spreading the rule of law and through deterrence. On the local level, it is argued that ICC prosecutions anywhere help empower the victims of massive human rights abuses everywhere by spreading a culture against impunity at the grassroots. On the national level, the ICC is said to promote, via its principle of complementarity, the domestication of international law so that states are encouraged—or intimidated—into carrying out their own prosecutions and building a culture of accountability nationally. Internationally, ICC prosecutions are said to send a message that "the old era of impunity is over," in the words of Ban Ki-moon,[1] because violent actors whom states are unwilling or unable to prosecute themselves will be brought to justice by the ICC. Its prosecutions, it is declared, are deterring those who would use extreme violence to further their political ends and sending the message that violence is no longer a legitimate tool for seizing power. According to its proponents, the ICC is the catalyst of a transnational legal infrastructure and a culture of accountability that will prevent atrocities from occurring, while also being prepared to prosecute in the exceptional cases that they still do. In this way, the ICC's practice embodies the total intervention agenda, bringing together interventions intended to promote societal empowerment and state-building, while reserving the right to use international coercion as a last resort.

Arguments proclaiming the ICC an instrument of justice can invoke both the shared universal values of humanity and the dignity and rights of the particular victims. As to the first, it is declared that ICC prosecutions realize justice because they are enforcing a universal law of humanity, which concerns human rights violations so grave that they brook no mitigating claims of cultural relativism or political expediency.[2] Punishing these crimes is a matter of defending humanity itself—they are categorically crimes against humanity. This claim that the ICC is the agent of universal law alternates with the claim that ICC intervention fulfills demands for justice coming from the victims themselves. Thus, ICC interventions can declare that they respond not only to a universal moral imperative but also to the particular moral claims embodied in the victims' demands for the fulfillment of their rights to justice and remedy.

I will argue that the ICC faces inherent dilemmas in trying to realize these lofty goals of peace and justice, which stem from the co-presence of the instrumental and administrative dimensions in ICC interventions. As to the first, ICC interventions inescapably take place in deeply political contexts within which it tends to be instrumentalized to unaccountable political power. As to the second, in pursuing its own form of justice, the ICC tends to depoliticize and silence political debate among those subject to it. The ICC's availability for political instrumentalization and its depoliticizing tendency are both enabled by the ICC's particular internal logic. This logic entails a specific framework employed to understand situations of violence—one that the ICC can end up imposing on those situations through its intervention. This framework is characterized by, to quote Makau Mutua, the "savage-victim-savior" structure.[3] The *savage* is the African violator of human rights, whether a state or nonstate entity. By the fact that it is a mechanism of criminal justice, the ICC must personalize political violence, reducing the etiology of violence to the criminal plots of a few individuals. The strong moral component of ICC criminalization means that those so criminalized are also demonized and considered to have put themselves outside the pale of politics, and even humanity, through their inhuman acts. As enemies of humanity, they and their supporters can become subject to violence itself unrestrained by human rights or humanitarian law.

The *victim* is individualized but anonymous, defined in terms of a universally applicable set of basic rights. It is toward this depoliticized victim image, in need of outside intervention for its redemption, that ICC intervention tends to normalize its subjects. Alternative ideas about what justice means in the wake of political violence are silenced as the ICC's own narrative, in which justice is equated with criminal justice through trials, is imposed and, often, is naturalized. The *savior* is the self-proclaimed enforcer of global law. The entwinement of global law with morality lends to those who claim to enforce it a certain sanctity, such that any action in the name of enforcing or upholding human rights is portrayed as inherently good and beyond contestation or accountability, dedicated to saving helpless innocents and eradicating incorrigibly savage criminals. International law enforcement is an attractive way for state and nonstate actors alike to justify their use of force, a characteristic of global law enforcement in general, but one that is particularly relevant to Africa, where the traditional image of the continent as a terrain without legitimate politics, the home of barbaric, irrational violence and helpless, trapped civilians, plays a key role in sanctifying and putting beyond question global law enforcement there.

This interpretive framework enables ICC interventions but also places a high burden on the Court, leaving it up to the ICC to save the victim and apprehend the savage. As more and more cases are referred to the ICC, this burden will only increase. Saving the victim requires victims who are willing to be saved and who define justice in the same way as the ICC does. This consent cannot be guaranteed, and so ICC interventions may provoke resistance, which it must either ignore or silence. The apprehension of the savage requires that the ICC undertake the impossible task of consistently enforcing human rights standards in a world rent by political inequalities and domination without an independent enforcement mechanism. Because it depends upon coercion to investigate and apprehend its savages and sometimes to silence recalcitrant victims, and because it depends on powerful states for its funding and existence, the ICC, in its quest for efficacy, ends up having to accommodate itself to political power instead of challenging it. Thus, global and local politics enter ICC decisions mediated by the Prosecutor's institutional self-interest. This is most clearly seen in the political selectivity with which the ICC Prosecutor pursues cases and suspects, a selectivity that is enabled by the significant prosecutorial discretion allowed by the Rome Statute. Indeed, the vast discretion afforded to the Office of the Prosecutor by the Rome Statute and the lack of transparency that characterizes the Prosecutor's decisions about whom to prosecute facilitate this type of politicization.

The ICC's need to accommodate itself to political power leads to serious problems with the kind of justice it can realize, but it also sets the stage for the instrumentalization of the ICC by those states whose cooperation the ICC needs in doing its work. Assuming the mantle of the savior, the enforcer of international law, becomes a convenient way for states or other political forces to justify their use of violence, often with the gratitude of the ICC. But even if the ICC is hesitant to sanction certain uses of force in its name, it lacks the capacity to regulate those uses of force, and so arrest warrants or even referrals can end up being employed as a carte blanche for military action, a fact that the Ugandan government, among others, has put to its advantage. The rest of this chapter will explore how these different possibilities played out in practice in Uganda.

2. Bringing Peace to Uganda?

With its 2003 "Referral of the Situation Concerning the Lord's Resistance Army" to the ICC, the Ugandan government launched a legal process that, it claimed, would bring peace and justice to war-torn northern Uganda. The ICC Prosecutor officially opened an investigation in response to the referral in July 2004, and in October 2005 the ICC unsealed arrest warrants, its historic first warrants, charging five of the top commanders of the rebel LRA with war crimes and crimes against humanity.[4] The Ugandan government explained its motivation for the referral as follows:

> Having exhausted every other means of bringing an end to this terrible suffering, the Republic of Uganda now turns to the newly established ICC and its promise of global justice. Uganda pledges its full cooperation to the Prosecutor in the investigation and prosecution of LRA crimes, achievement of which is vital not only for the future progress of the nation, but also for the suppression of the most serious crimes of concern to the international community as a whole.[5]

Payam Akhavan, a former legal adviser to the International Criminal Tribunal for Yugoslavia who advised the government of Uganda in the early stages of the case, went so far as to claim that, because of the ICC intervention, "the prospect of sustained national peace may finally be within Uganda's reach for the first time since its independence in 1961."[6]

Despite this lofty language, however, Uganda stood to gain very worldly benefits from ICC intervention, especially if it could ensure that the ICC would prosecute only the LRA—which is exactly what transpired. Indeed, the savage-victim-savior structure was applied to Uganda in perfect concordance with the official discourse on the conflict. The LRA, under the command of the master-mind Kony, was reduced to a criminal group, the Acholi peasantry seen as inno-cent, passive victims, and the ICC itself, aligned with the military force of the "responsible" Ugandan government and the West, cast itself as the interpreter and enforcer of justice. To understand the ICC's accommodation to political power in this case, it needs to be seen in the broader pattern of the Court's accommodation to power since its inception.

INSTRUMENTALIZING GLOBAL LAW

The ICC's accommodation to political power has been perhaps most apparent in the fact that it has, as of early 2011, opened investigations only in Africa and indicted only Africans. The ICC's defenders declare that this is because Africa is the site of situations of extreme violence that, due to Africa's lack of effective national judicial mechanisms, can be addressed only through international legal mechanisms. Africa is fortunate, they say, that the international community has finally decided to get involved in helping it end violence and impunity; as Moreno-Ocampo put it, ICC intervention is a welcome change from the inaction and ap-athy that had characterized the Western approach to Africa in the 1990s, with its tragic consequences.[7] The exclusive focus on Africa is the result, it is averred, of the universal, impartial application of global law and a new, long-overdue, moral commitment to Africa.

Some critics, however, maintain that the ICC's exclusive focus on Africa is not evidence of Africa's newfound good fortune, but rather is another symptom of the continent's longstanding historical domination. Indeed, the ICC's obsession with Africa should not be a surprise, they argue; Africa has traditionally been the ter-rain where the West experiments with new governing techniques, economic doc-trines, medicines, or weapons before it uses them on the rest of the world. To them, the ICC is simply the most recent manifestation of the West's civilizing mis-sion in Africa, the newest mode of criminalizing Africans and dismissing African sovereignty through the selective application of law and violence, possibly even as part of a project of recolonization.[8] This is a position that has been voiced not only by academic critics of the ICC, but also by African political leaders. As Jean Ping, the Chairperson of the Commission of the African Union, stated, "We are not for a justice with two speeds, a double standard justice—one for the poor, one for the rich,"[9] and President Paul Kagame of Rwanda condemned the ICC as "part of co-lonialism, slavery and imperialism."[10]

However, the fact is that not all ICC interventions have provoked opposition from African leaders—before the Omar al-Bashir case received the criticism it did, the Uganda case, for example, had been widely welcomed. Indeed, common interests have developed between the Court and leaders of certain African states, which both are keen to exploit. On the societal level, there has also been a surge of support voiced for the ICC by many African civil-society organizations in reaction against African leaders' intransigence over arrest warrants. The ICC's intervention in Africa, therefore, should be seen not as a uniform assault on African sovereignty nor as representing an anti-African conspiracy (though longstanding images of the continent can be seen as informing the way the ICC has intervened there). Instead, it should be seen more as a product of international power relations, which make Africa the only region weak enough so that international intervention can take place there without accountability, and unimportant enough so that the West will allow the ICC to act as its subcontractor there as a surrogate for more direct forms of intervention. It is also a product of the internal weakness of forces of political reform within African states: Kenya is an example of this, where the failure of political reform has led activists who are certainly no apologists for Western designs on the continent to welcome the ICC intervention.

The ICC's decision to focus exclusively on Africa is thus one expression of its accommodation to political power. Another such expression can be seen in the discretion practiced by the ICC in deciding where to intervene *within* Africa, prosecuting certain parties and investigating certain situations to the exclusion of others—a selectivity that also belies the idea of a conspiracy against African sovereignty, for the ICC has aligned itself *with* African state leaders more often than it has challenged those leaders. This selectivity makes sense when the ICC's need to conform to political power—whether global power configurations or configurations within Africa or within African states—in order to carry out viable prosecutions is taken into account.

The ICC's accommodation to U.S. power has perhaps been the most apparent form this has taken. It is ironic that it was precisely because of the Bush administration's early hostility to the ICC that the Court ended up accommodating itself to U.S. interests.[11] In its early days, the ICC appeared to have calculated that it could best protect its viability and relevance by showing the United States that it would not challenge it or its allies, since alienating the United States could easily spell disaster for the Court. Since its inception, therefore, the ICC has made clear its lack of interest in pursuing U.S. allies and its willingness to focus on U.S. enemies or enemies of U.S. allies, or simply to focus on issues that had little interest for the U.S. government. The Office of the Prosecutor has signaled that it sees alignment with U.S. interests as an acceptable price to pay for establishing its efficacy and has brought about that alignment by practicing a wide selectively in what cases it takes and whom it prosecutes. Even if the Prosecutor were to try to prosecute U.S. allies, the U.S. could exert its influence by threatening to revoke funding or support for the Court or by interfering with its internal workings, as it has done with other international tribunals.[12]

The ICC's need to accommodate itself to political power leads to a number of detrimental consequences for peace by setting the stage for the Court's instrumentalization. It can be instrumentalized by Western states, African states, or even non-state political forces such as rebel groups or local elites who seek to appropriate for themselves the mantle of savior so as to legitimate their violence. For Western states, law enforcement can provide a justification for the use of force or the threat of force against those whom the ICC has declared international criminals, because the ICC offers a convenient way to make military action "a totally legitimate operation, politically, legally," in the words of the Prosecutor's special advisor, and thus helps avoid having to locate other, more inflexible, sources of legitimacy.[13] Or, as with the Security Council Resolutions 1970 and 1973 on Libya in February and March 2011, an ICC referral can be used as one among a list of other rationales to justify the use of military force. As referrals and cases pile up for the ICC and it fails to capture suspects or successfully try those few it has in custody, perhaps this symbolic function of clearing the way for Western coercion will become the dominant role the ICC plays, its legal dimension marginalized.

The role of savior is also attractive for African states, who can obtain international legitimacy for their use of force by taking advantage of the ICC's need for effective local partners to pursue cases, in particular in situations of state self-referral. This ability to assume the role of human rights enforcer is typically the prerogative of states with the requisite international patronage—those states deemed responsible—and so global law enforcement can establish a certain link between the West and its allies, justifying militarized state-building in the name of building the capacity to enforce international justice. African states can also instrumentalize the ICC's resources in order to criminalize domestic or foreign opposition. The ICC, like other international interveners, finds an unaccountable elite at the core of African states—including Uganda—to be its natural ally in pursuing investigations and arrests.

It is not only states that can assume this role of international law enforcer and find international justification and impunity for their violence; nonstate actors and armed forces who claim to have the ICC behind them or who think they can rally the ICC to their side can also ignore domestic constituencies, escalating their violence under the cover of international sanction. It can help legitimate links between Western patrons and African rebel groups, but it can also be seized upon by rebels or other political forces independently of Western agendas. As Khalil Ibrahim, the leader of the Darfuri Justice and Equality Movement (JEM), told Al Jazeera: "They say the ICC does not have a mechanism to arrest him [al-Bashir]. But we say that JEM has its own great and powerful mechanism. . . . [There is] a mechanism by the Sudanese people, a mechanism of Justice and Equality, a mechanism of co-operation with the international community. We shall fully collaborate with the Security Council and the ICC." JEM's leaders seek to sanctify their violence in the name of international law enforcement, using it as a way to try to build their international support. And what would the ICC say if JEM launched an attack on Khartoum, captured President al-Bashir, and handed him over to the Court?

INSTRUMENTALIZING THE ICC IN UGANDA

Given the political pressures faced by the ICC, the 2003 Uganda referral came at an auspicious time for the fledgling court, because the ICC faced the urgent need to establish its efficacy through a viable first case. Such a case would have to be feasible on the local level, preferably by being conducted with the cooperation of a state or occupying force, and on the global level, by not stepping on the toes of any major powers. The Ugandan case fit the twofold requirement perfectly: it was a voluntary referral by a government that pledged its assistance, and it would prosecute a Sudanese ally and support an American ally. However, the condition the Ugandan government placed on its cooperation with the ICC appears to be that the ICC would only prosecute the LRA.

The Ugandan government made this apparent from the beginning: in the 2003 referral, the Ugandan government cited only LRA violence, reflected in the Referral's one-sided title. Despite Payam Akhavan's claim that the Ugandan government "was aware that in referring the LRA situation to the ICC, it was potentially exposing itself to international judicial scrutiny,"[14] the Ugandan government has consistently asserted that it would not be subject to ICC prosecution. The Ugandan government threatened several times to withdraw its referral to the Court, implying that it would cease cooperating if its own military became subject to prosecution. This is a concern for the ICC, since the termination of Ugandan cooperation could effectively close down the investigation. Further, Ugandan government and military officials have stated that they would not be subject to the Court's jurisdiction: Attorney General Amama Mbabazi has stated categorically that the UPDF is not guilty of crimes and will not be tried by the ICC.[15] This pressure came not only from Uganda, but from its Western allies: according to one analyst, in a closed-door meeting between ICC officials and the U.S. representative in charge of eastern Africa in the U.S. State Department, the U.S. representative expressed American support for the execution of the arrest warrants against the LRA, but reportedly warned the ICC Prosecutor not to pursue UPDF activities.[16]

In response, the Chief Prosecutor, despite occasional statements declaring his investigation open to Ugandan government crimes as well, has failed to issue arrest warrants for anyone but LRA commanders and has openly enjoyed a close relationship with the Ugandan government, especially President Museveni. This unashamed public support the ICC gives the Ugandan government has seen a number of highlights, from the initial joint press conference announcing the investigation between Luis Moreno-Ocampo and President Museveni, to ICC investigators occasionally being accompanied by UPDF officers, including the notorious divisional commander, when carrying out interviews with potential witnesses in Acholiland, to the 2010 ICC Review Conference held in Kampala and the tragi-comic spectacle of the War Victims' Day football match, held in the lead-up to the conference, in which President Museveni led a team of war victims named "Dignity" against a team led by Ban Ki-moon named "Justice."[17]

The ICC's involvement in Uganda clearly reveals the dilemma at the heart of ICC practice: in making decisions about what cases to accept and whom to prosecute, the Office of the Prosecutor responds to genuine episodes of egregious violence but must also respond to the ICC's need to be seen as effective. I would maintain, however, that the fact that the ICC must conform to powerful global and local political interests does not justify its doing so; instead, it illuminates the inherent limits of the ICC's capacity to realize justice or even abide by the rule of law.

The ICC has attempted to offer objective legal reasons for its decision to limit its focus to the LRA based upon the gravity of the crimes,[18] but the arguments typically boil down to categorical statements to the effect that, to quote ICC public relations adviser Christian Palme, "LRA crimes are far more serious than the crimes of the UPDF."[19] This reflects the Prosecutor's public acceptance of the official discourse on the conflict. Moreno-Ocampo's characterization of the situation simply assumes the absolute malevolence of the LRA and, by implication, the benevolence of the Ugandan government in combating the rebels: "Let me start with the conflict in northern Uganda. The Lord's Resistance Army, the LRA, is an armed rebel group, claiming to fight for the freedom of the Acholi people in northern Uganda. The LRA has mainly attacked the Acholis they claim to represent. For nineteen years the people of northern Uganda have been killed, abducted, enslaved and raped."[20] At another point, he refers simply to the "criminal campaign of the LRA."

Akhavan's defense of the ICC's intervention further demonstrates how the official discourse on the conflict has informed the ICC's intervention there and serves to silence any criticism of its one-sided character. He argues that Uganda's referral "was an attempt to engage an otherwise aloof international community by transforming the prosecution of LRA leaders into a litmus test for the much celebrated promise of global justice."[21] Up until the referral, he argues, the international community had ignored the conflict in the north because of "the absence of any vital national interests,"[22] echoing the familiar story that conflict in Africa is indigenous, allowed to continue through international apathy, and requires international intervention for its resolution. His account trumpets the most sensationalist aspects of the LRA, and declares their ranks "filled with ruthless warlords and slave masters who exercised power through terrorizing civilians."[23] "From its inception until the present," Akhavan declares, "the LRA has had no coherent ideology, rational political agenda, or popular support."[24] Akhavan's account moves from sensationalism to misrepresentation in the service of the Ugandan government when he states that, "hundreds of thousands of civilians have simply abandoned their homes and sought shelter in 'protected villages' where the UPDF provides security."[25] He argues that the Ugandan government has attempted good-faith peace negotiations on numerous occasions, but that the LRA has had the military capacity to be able to reject negotiations. It is the benevolent Ugandan government, abandoned by the international community to fight this barbaric terrorist group alone, that has demanded that the West make good on its lofty promises of global justice and help bring the war to an end. It is up to the international community to respond, to defeat this scourge on humanity, and bring its leaders to justice, according to Akhavan. However, this narrative and the ICC's exclusive focus on the LRA make little sense to many people who lived through the war or to many independent human rights and peace activists. Pressure mounted on the ICC to ensure that the Ugandan government too would face accountability for possible war crimes, or for the Court to show its impartiality and commitment to justice by prosecuting both sides, instead of taking sides, in the war.[26]

The Prosecutor found the perfect solution to these demands for impartiality not in prosecuting Ugandan government officials, but in invoking the complementarity principle and supporting the creation of a special division of the Ugandan High Court to deal with suspects not indicted by the ICC. In effect, the ICC declared the Ugandan government willing and able to carry out genuine prosecutions of its own officials—which many Ugandans took, not as a solution to the problem, but as further proof of the ICC's politicization and its mockery of justice. By giving its approval to the special division of the High Court, the ICC has declared legitimate a system in which the top commanders of the LRA will be tried by the ICC, while all Ugandan government officials will be tried by national courts. To many Ugandans, given the history of impunity that has plagued the process of finding justice for crimes by the Ugandan military in northern Uganda, and given the increasing politicization of the judiciary and the assaults upon its independence and integrity by the executive, national legal mechanisms appear dismally inadequate for finding justice in response to crimes committed by the state.[27] It appears that the ICC has effectively granted the Ugandan government impunity for its legacy of violence in northern Uganda in a case of double standards and the politicized use of complementarity, whereby international mechanisms are used to deal with the state's enemies, whereas the state is allowed to prosecute—and absolve—itself.

The Uganda case demonstrates that it is a viable strategy to take advantage of the ICC's need for cooperation by making voluntary state referrals that criminalize one's opposition, given the ICC's willingness to conduct one-sided prosecutions in return. It also shows how voluntary state referrals and the politicized deployment of complementarity can undermine, instead of strengthen, national judicial processes. The irony is that there may indeed be a place for international legal mechanisms in the pursuit of justice in northern Uganda, not so much to try the LRA, but rather to investigate and try those government and military officials who might otherwise enjoy impunity.

THE COST OF INSTRUMENTALIZATION

There has been significant controversy over the impact that the ICC arrest warrants have had on the peace process with the LRA and on the Ugandan conflict more generally. When the ICC launched its investigation, widespread accusations were heard that it would make peace negotiations impossible. Betty Bigombe, who was involved in a peace initiative at the time, condemned the ICC's involvement as harmful for peace, and Father Carlos Rodríguez of the Acholi Religious Leaders Peace Initiative declared, "Obviously, nobody can convince the leaders of a rebel movement to come to the negotiating table and at the same time tell them that they will appear in courts to be prosecuted."[28] But when the Juba peace talks between the LRA and the Ugandan government, hosted by the Government of South Sudan, began *after* the unsealing of the arrest warrants, many ICC supporters argued that the warrants had in fact brought the LRA to the negotiating table.[29] When the LRA moved from northern Uganda and southern Sudan to Democratic Republic of Congo and the Central African Republic (CAR), supporters argued that the ICC had brought peace to northern Uganda. When the peace talks broke down, with Kony announcing that he would rather die in the bush than end up in the hands of the Ugandan government or ICC and "be hanged,"[30] the critics again seemed tragically vindicated. As LRA atrocities escalated in their new locales, and the rebels threatened to return to South Sudan and disrupt the peace process there, it appeared that peace in northern Uganda had been purchased through increased conflict elsewhere, and the claim that the ICC's intervention had helped reduce violence rang increasingly hollow. If the military efforts being mobilized against the LRA with the help of ICC arrest warrants manage to capture Kony and other LRA commanders, the supporters will likely attempt to argue that the ICC deserves the credit; if those military operations backfire, as did Operation Lightning Thunder, and provoke even more violence, the critics will have more evidence for their argument that the ICC has made the conflict harder to resolve.

It is too early, and too little is still known, to pass final judgment on the impact of the ICC's involvement on peace in northern Uganda, because the ICC's impact is contingent upon the vagaries of history and politics. However, that contingency is just the point: the ICC's impact on peace where it intervenes is contingent upon the political context, a contingency that ICC supporters tend to deny, arguing categorically that international criminal prosecutions assist the cause of peace, that there can be "no peace without (criminal) justice." ICC supporters' blanket identification of peace with criminal justice gives rise to a self-serving reading of history, in which anything good that happens in situations where the ICC has intervened is caused by the ICC's intervention, while anything that goes wrong demonstrates the high cost of impunity and the need for further ICC intervention. This is how ICC supporters can, for example, give credit to the Court for driving the LRA out of northern Uganda and bringing peace there, while refusing responsibility for the violence used by the LRA against civilians in DRC, which instead is chalked up to continued impunity.

By denying the possibility of historical contingency and insisting that ICC interventions are uniformly and universally beneficial for peace, the Court's supporters can feel justified in condemning and even working against peace talks with war crimes suspects. This was evident in Uganda's case, where the Chief Prosecutor himself acted in ways that appeared to be intended to undermine and foreclose peace negotiations between the LRA and the Ugandan government, particularly through his repeated dismissals of the LRA's commitment to negotiations and accusations that the rebels were engaging in peace talks only to buy time and rearm so as to commit more atrocities—a strategy on the part of Moreno-Ocampo that can, if effective, become a self-fulfilling prophecy.[31] An Acholi colleague involved in the Juba peace talks complained to me in private that Moreno-Ocampo seemed to be keeping track of the developments in the negotiations and making statements specifically designed to defeat the efforts of the negotiators. If the ICC Prosecutor is going to actively work against peace negotiations, then the ICC is going to be a danger to peace wherever it intervenes and should be held accountable for the consequences of its actions.

Regardless of the impact that the ICC's one-sided prosecution has had on the peace process itself, it has had other consequences for Uganda that are incontrovertibly antithetical to long-term and sustainable peace. For one thing, the ICC intervention has led to increased militarization. As noted, arrest warrants can provide justification for the violence needed to carry them out, which Uganda took advantage of: the arrest warrants enabled the Ugandan government to focus attention on its "military solution" by deriving international legitimation for the military campaign from international law enforcement, a campaign that was redoubled after the breakdown of the Juba talks. Because Uganda is seen as a responsible state, this legitimation for the military campaign was widely seen as a positive development internationally. Because the LRA was already devoid of political legitimacy, Uganda was seen as waging a just war, and it was presumed that the ICC intervention would, by speeding the rebels' demise, serve everyone's interests in justice and peace.

However, the legitimacy for Uganda's militarization did not translate into military effectiveness against the LRA. Simultaneous with the announcement of the appointment of the investigation's prosecutor, the UPDF announced that it would re-enter Sudan to hunt down the LRA leadership.[32] Museveni has used the arrest warrants to justify the UPDF's reentry into eastern DRC, where their prior intervention led to massive looting and atrocities against Congolese civilians.[33] The UPDF now has a justification it uses for maintaining its troops in South Sudan and throughout central Africa with dangerous consequences for regional stability. The ICC intervention has also provided the justification for increased American militarization of Uganda and military involvement in central Africa. The most significant manifestation of this was the 2008 Operation Lighting Thunder, a military attack carried out by the UPDF with assistance from the U.S. military intended to capture the LRA command and bring them to justice. As will be discussed at length in the next chapter, this military involvement threatens to increase further with the passage of the LRA Disarmament Act.

The Ugandan government has also used the ICC intervention to justify its repression of domestic political dissent. Designating political opposition as international criminals helps legitimate the use of force against them. The ICC arrest warrants have provided the Ugandan government a tool to wield selectively against political opposition or to disqualify those calling for peace talks or for dialogue with the LRA. Given the utility of the arrest warrants to the Ugandan government, and given the interests that various parts of that government had in maintaining the war in the north, it is conceivable that the Ugandan government called in the ICC against the LRA not to help bring the war to an end but to entrench it and to obtain support for its military campaign. Even if the Ugandan government did not intend this instrumentalization when it first submitted its referral to the ICC, it quickly learned how to manipulate the Court to its advantage. Again, this is not to say that the ICC is acquiescent with all the violence used in its name; however, in this case the Ugandan government's actions, the ICC's statements, and powerful Western interests have indeed been tightly entwined.

The ICC intervention also has intensified the national political crises in Uganda, thus entrenching the conditions for possible future conflict. Akhavan claims that "International trials were also viewed as a depoliticized venue for justice that would be perceived as impartial. . . . in the face of the continuing distrust between Uganda's north and south, the ICC could also become an instrument for national reconciliation."[34] However, the politicized and partial manner in which the ICC intervened in Uganda gives the lie to the optimistic claim that ICC intervention will help bring about national reconciliation there by serving as an instrument of transitional justice. Instead, in Uganda, the international criminal legal process has only increased mistrust, as many Ugandans, especially in the north, see the ICC as thoroughly captured by the Ugandan government. In their eyes, instead of building trust, the ICC's involvement only further emphasizes the Ugandan government's refusal to be held accountable for its legacy of violence as well as the way in which the international community has consistently failed to hold the Ugandan government to account while providing it with extensive support. As the host of a call-in radio show on the ICC told me, the two questions that his Acholi callers consistently demanded answers to were, first, why the ICC would not deal with crimes before 2002, and, second, why the ICC was only pursuing the LRA—questions that are regularly raised in other forums as well. Through its accommodation to power, the ICC is imposing a solution that is based upon a narrative of the conflict that does not make sense to many Acholi, and so they reject that narrative and throw into question the model of justice that it informs. The Uganda case seems to confirm the doubts cast by many legal scholars on the possibility that international criminal trials can ever to serve the function of national reconciliation.[35]

A more fundamental problem is that the ICC cannot work as a mechanism of so-called transitional justice if there is no political transition. Without a political transition, without a change in the militarized, authoritarian power at the center of Uganda, any trials, whether by the ICC or by the Ugandan government, may well be seen as yet another attempt to impose antidemocratic and violent state power. For the Acholi, such trials could be seen as the continuation of war by legal means,[36] a reaffirmation of their victim status and their continued humiliation. The need for a political transition to underlie and provide meaning to justice mechanisms is sometimes ignored by the transitional justice industry, whose focus is on the implementation of technical solutions and whose only question is which specific mechanism—a truth commission, national trials, international trials, and so on—should be employed in any given case. This approach misses the fact that without a political transition, transitional justice can play only a managerial role.

It is ironic that the ICC has provoked this protest because of its own failure to meet the liberal standards of the rule of law and impartiality that it itself proclaims. Demands for impartiality may be impossible to meet, however, if the ICC Prosecutor sees a tacit guarantee of immunity to states as a necessary price to pay for ensuring their cooperation. If the ICC is willing to conform to the demands of abusive or antidemocratic states, the Court may find itself complicit with the very crimes it claims to prosecute and responsible for intensifying the violence it claims to resolve. With the Ugandan case under way, it has become evident that the problems relating to the ICC and state sovereignty in practice may end up being the opposite of what had been feared in the deliberations leading up to its creation. The overwhelming concern had been that the ICC, in imposing its jurisdiction, could run roughshod over the sovereignty of states. Instead, in the Ugandan case, the invocation of the ICC by President Museveni has only increased the discretionary power of his government, since the politicization of the ICC intervention serves the state's interests against those of the Ugandan people.[37] In this way, global criminal law, although premised upon overcoming sovereignty, can paradoxically end up promoting the most dangerous aspect of sovereignty: unaccountable state power over the population.

3. Peace through Prevention

Despite the negative consequences that ICC intervention has had for peace in Uganda, the argument might still be made that the ICC's intervention is nonetheless an important step on the way to building a transnational rule of law and culture of accountability and thus to establishing peace through law in the long term. This prevention argument is particularly attractive to ICC supporters because it is much harder to prove wrong—this way, the ICC can take credit based upon what does *not* happen, instead of staking its legitimacy on being able to prove that it has brought about specific positive developments. The Uganda case, however, throws these optimistic claims and the progress narrative they are based upon into doubt. The ICC intervention in Uganda shows that, instead of empowering victims, the ICC may silence and discipline them; instead of contributing to national reconciliation and democracy, it can undermine their possibility; and instead of contributing to international accountability, it can create a geography of impunity.

PROMOTING VICTIMS

Today, thanks to the Rome Statute, "victims are actors of international justice rather than its passive subjects," the Office of the ICC Prosecutor has triumphantly declared.[38] However, certain political critics of human rights might question this assertion. David Chandler, for one, has argued that international human rights do not enable "free, autonomous, and self-determined individual[s]," as do state-based constitutional rights.[39] Instead, according to Chandler, the human rights claimant, focusing his or her demands on the unaccountable "international community" instead of the state, is effectively divested of his or her quality as a legal rights-bearing subject and is steered away from making demands based upon the legal rights that the state must guarantee. Instead, he or she becomes an object of philanthropy, receiving only what is offered by the munificence of others. His argument draws on Hannah Arendt's withering criticism of international human rights, in particular of the "marginal figures—a few international jurists without political experience or professional philanthropists" who formed societies for the protection of human rights: "the groups they formed, the declarations they issued, showed an uncanny similarity in language and composition to that of societies for the prevention of cruelty to animals."[40] For those relying on human rights, she writes, the "prolongation of their lives is due to charity and not to right."[41] Chandler concludes, like Arendt, that "human rights can only imply dependency on others."[42]

Arendt and Chandler argue that the nation-state is the political form in which law defines the relation between the population and the decision-making locus, binding both. That is, the state is supposed to rule according to law and enforce the law, and the citizenry is to participate in making the law and is to hold the state accountable through the law. The idea of global law separates these instances, so that people are told to obey a law they did not make and that is enforced arbitrarily by agents with no accountability. Meanwhile, people's political claims, translated into human rights terms, become open-ended pleas for intervention to which the so-called international community does not have to listen or respond. People are diverted away from working towards the realization of enforceable rights within their own states by their pursuit of a chimerical global justice. As Chandler has consistently argued, the deployment of human rights by the putative subjects of global law can engender political incapacity. Children's rights are the paradigm of this reductive juridical order, as "rights" whose only entitlement is the vague hope for lobbying by foreign agents or name-and-shame campaigns. It ends up a barren human rights of the bare human; human rights merge with animal rights, as Slavoj Žižek puts it.[43]

This critique illuminates the significance of the disjuncture between the multitude of demands made for ICC intervention and those few instances in which the ICC does intervene, which occur not in response to the validity of specific demands for law enforcement, but in response to the ICC's own political and pragmatic exigencies. Although interventions do, indeed, sometimes occur in the name of enforcing international law, and claims are constantly being articulated in the language of international law, there is no necessary relationship between claim and enforcement, as there should be in a legal order. The provision of justice becomes attributed to an imaginary interventionist agent that conflates the ICC, the UN, the United States, and the international community.[44] At the same time, these claims provide a ready-made justification for those who seek to intervene out of their own self-interest: victims calling for intervention seem always to be found by those looking to intervene.

This disjuncture between hyperbolic claims and paltry reality creates an ambiguity that can be depoliticizing, as people simply do not know what to expect from different, supposedly legal, regimes. The ICC's failure to be universal and impartial can also lead to significant uncertainty among those trying to struggle for peace and justice themselves. States can take advantage of this multiplication of legal regimes so as to augment their own arbitrary power, as people lose their capacity to hold their states legally accountable. Privileging international human rights without regular enforcement can undermine enforceable citizen's rights, and it represents a dangerous assault on people's legal standing, protection, and potential for legal remedy. The ICC can promote a kind of political dependency among survivors, mediated by global law, in a context in which depending on the international community and awaiting its enforcement of human rights can be a thoroughly dangerous proposition.[45]

The mechanisms for victim participation in ICC prosecutions, the outreach by the ICC and its supporting organizations, as well as the work of international human rights organizations, can contribute to this depoliticization, as human rights practice becomes a practice of individual testimony among those identified as victims. These testimonies, made to investigators or human rights monitors, do not lead to the articulation and realization of common grievances, interests, and demands, but are divested of their capacity to produce meaningful collective action and are used in the production of international law or human rights reports for international elite consumption. This model of international human rights advocacy tries to reduce the survivor of violence to a victim, no more than raw material, another African natural resource. Their testimony and images are exported by Western human rights organizations and processed abroad into flashy human rights reports that advertise themselves with lurid titles—"Scars of Death," "Abducted and Abused," "Forgotten Voices," "State of Pain," "Suffering in Silence," to name a few international human rights reports on northern Uganda—and often with obscene photos of mutilated or suffering African bodies.

In Uganda's camps, the inefficacy of human rights claims against the state was compounded by the fact that, when donors *did* insist that the Ugandan government be held to human rights standards, it was not to the body of global criminal law that would be wielded against the LRA. Instead, as a "responsible" human rights protector, Uganda was not to be coerced but rather was to have its capacity built to promote the human rights of its IDPs through the Guiding Principles on Internal Displacement.[46] In 1998, in response to the apparent legal aporia faced by IDPs, the UN produced a set of principles comprising an extensive compilation of laws, norms, principles, and ideals culled from international legal instruments, conventions, declarations, and resolutions. However, the Guiding Principles fail to differentiate between hard international law and nonlegal aspirations or ideals;[47] indeed, in his introductory note, Francis Deng, the Representative of the Secretary-General on Internal Displacement, declares that the Principles "do not constitute a binding instrument."[48] The result is that all the norms expressed in the Guiding Principles are reduced to an equally nonlegal, unenforceable status, to a set of policy suggestions meant to "provide guidance" to "states when faced with the phenomenon of internal displacement."[49] Thus, the Ugandan government can fulfill its duties under the Principles, and supposedly fulfill its duties according to human rights and humanitarian law, by integrating its officials into committees to conduct sensitization campaigns, distributing booklets conveniently provided by the UN, holding workshops, and working in coordination with humanitarian NGOs. Human rights become a catalyst for the formation of administrative management networks incorporating Ugandan government officials and NGOs, as all become equal "stakeholders" in alleviating the suffering of IDPs through more efficient humanitarian activity.[50] By doing so, the Principles further depoliticize displacement and the response to it by ignoring the national legal aspects of displacement.

The camps were thus home to a multidimensional legal exceptionalism.[51] The localization of particular human rights discourses supplanted the normal legal order and took the camps out of the constitutional order of the state, despite the fact that they remained within the state's territorial bounds and subject to the state's power. This instantiation of human rights displays another aspect of the symbiosis between globally anchored human rights intervention and the violence of the state, a place where legal protections and entitlements are rendered uncertain by global law, and so the state is released to exercise arbitrary violence.

What was lost, between appeals for international intervention and human rights administration, was the fact that the state's policies, in particular the policy of forced displacement, could have been challenged through the law, starting with using constitutional and hard humanitarian law at the national level. Indeed, commentators and lawyers have argued that forced displacement could have comprised war crimes as well as violations of constitutional rights. Legal demands that forced internment be halted and that compensation be paid to the victims of that policy could possibly have played an important role in delegitimating the government's brutal counterinsurgency and helping to allow people to return home. Calls to that effect, however, let alone legal processes, never occurred, which was testament to the weakness of the human rights community in Uganda. Most larger human rights groups based in Kampala had almost no presence in the north and showed little concern with the war there, driven as they were by donor agendas and having bought into the official discourse on the war. In the north, those groups that did courageously document government human rights violations in forced displacement, in particular Human Rights Focus and Acholi Religious Leaders Peace Initiative, generally lacked the capacity or institutional alliances to do anything but try to publicize those violations. Those international human rights groups who did get involved in northern Uganda seem also to have accepted the official discourse at face value, and so spent most of their energy pursuing stories of LRA atrocities and child abductions instead of trying to end forced displacement by challenging the Ugandan government, the donors, or the complicity of the aid agencies.[52]

SILENCING DISSENT

ICC intervention can have a significant impact not only on people's legal standing, but also on their political autonomy, with deleterious consequences for peace and justice, as this section describes. ICC interventions can delegitimate, and its supporters can even seek to silence, any dissent from its model of justice-through-punishment or from the reductive narratives it imposes on the situations where it intervenes. This delegitimation, and its possibly counterproductive consequences, begins with the criminalized targets of ICC intervention themselves. Condemned as targets to be hunted down and captured, they are declared politically illegitimate, devoid of the possibility of political relevance, and their followers told to abandon them.[53] In situations in which the ICC targets political leaders with significant support, intervention may only lead to further radicalization or militarization, increase those targeted leaders' support, or disrupt potential political solutions.

When the ICC intervened against the LRA, it effectively declared the rebels politically irrelevant—a declaration that the Chief Prosecutor himself frequently and vociferously repeated. The ICC's narrative of the conflict also reduced the deep internal political crisis of the Acholi to a simple division between the criminal LRA and innocent civilians, a narrative that does not make sense to those who lived through the war. As Erin Baines has argued, this narrative, and the criminal justice it requires for the LRA, are inappropriate.[54] For one thing, the narrative fails to take into account the forcible conscription of many LRA, including even one of the men wanted by the ICC, Dominic Ongwen. It dehumanizes the LRA and denies the fact that many LRA members believe that they have legitimate political grievances and may continue fighting until they feel those grievances are addressed. The problems with this kind of delegitimation are recognized even by some LRA victims themselves: as Mareike Schomerus reports, Honorable Betty Ogwaro, a member of the Sudan Legislative Assembly for Magwi County (an area where the LRA operated for more than a decade), explained that, for the war to end, it is necessary that people "accept that they [the LRA] are human beings . . . We have to remember that the LRA have a reason to fight and that they deserve to be heard."[55] The irony is that it was during the Juba peace talks, after the ICC arrest warrants had been issued, that the LRA most explicitly and coherently voiced a political agenda, one that had resonance not only with the Acholi, but even elsewhere in Uganda. Finally, according to Baines, punishment through criminal trials is also inappropriate because it fails to "identify the overlapping layers of responsibility of national and international actors for failing to protect the Ugandan population in the first place."[56]

Those Acholi denominated victims were told not only to wait for the ICC to intervene to realize justice for their sake, but also found some of their own efforts to bring about justice shut down in the name of global justice. ICC intervention rejects the possibility that the realization of justice might be a project within which the Acholi community organizes and acts to bring about a more just social and political order. Instead, it turns the realization of justice into a demobilizing process, as Acholi are individualized into "witnesses," and testimony and people's experiences are reduced to the material for arrest warrants. The judgment about whether an individual's experience of suffering deserves reparation is removed from the individual and the community; it is not to be arrived at through common reflection, but through the ICC's nontransparent decision-making process. The responsibility for deciding what justice means and how it should be brought about is alienated from the hands of the community that has been subject to violence and put into the hands of an international body that is unaccountable to those it claims to serve.

The first major instance of the ICC silencing alternative approaches to justice was seen in its dismissal of the Ugandan Amnesty Act of 2000. There was a broad understanding in Acholiland that the war would not end until the LRA leadership abandoned the rebellion, which provided the impetus behind the mobilization for the act. At the insistence of Acholi peace activists and political leaders, and apparently over the preferences of President Museveni, the act granted a general amnesty to the LRA, including its top commanders.[57] Despite this popular support, however, the ICC demanded the Amnesty Act's amendment:

> In a bid to encourage members of the LRA to return to normal life, the Ugandan authorities have enacted an amnesty law. President Museveni has indicated to the Prosecutor his intention to amend this amnesty so as to exclude the leadership of the LRA, ensuring that those bearing the greatest responsibility for the crimes against humanity committed in northern Uganda are brought to justice.[58]

The ICC irresponsibly frames the Amnesty Act, not as the product of mobilization by the Acholi trying to find peace and duly promulgated by the Ugandan Parliament, but as a gift from the Ugandan executive, to be withdrawn by President Museveni at his convenience. Again, the reliance of the ICC on unaccountable state elites to facilitate its intervention, and those elites' readiness to take advantage of that intervention for their own interests, is put into relief.

The ICC's intervention was met by a variety of responses on the part of the Acholi, and its expansive promises of peace and justice, juxtaposed with its one-sided intervention, its collaboration with the Ugandan government, its dismissal of the Amnesty Act, and the apparent threat it posed to peace talks, sparked a significant debate within Acholi society over what justice would mean in the wake of the war. The last section will discuss this debate in more detail, but what I want to note now is how the ICC and its supporters, after sparking the debate, apparently proceeded to try to squash it and silence dissenting opinions. The ICC and its supporters denied the legitimacy of those who were calling for forms of justice other than criminal trials or who were calling for equal application of the law to the LRA and government. It launched a multipronged public relations campaign—"outreach"—to promote the benefits of ICC justice in northern Uganda. The inflow of funding tied to supporting the ICC has also helped create a cadre of agents paid by the ICC or its supporters drumming up consent and providing what was represented as authentic local support for the Court's work.

The putatively moral character of the use of force to uphold human rights in Africa places that force beyond legitimate challenge from those whose human rights are supposedly being fulfilled: Africans are told they cannot question the use of force for their own salvation, and those needing salvation must play the role of the helpless victim or risk being labeled criminal sympathizers themselves. Anyone questioning or proposing alternatives to the ICC may find their own legitimacy questioned and even themselves condemned with the criminals. For example, much African opposition to the ICC has been dismissed as coming from self-interested African leaders who fear their own prosecution or from academic apologists who have let their anti-Western zeal get in the way of their better judgment. As Kofi Annan voices this position, "One must begin by asking why African leaders shouldn't celebrate this focus on African victims. Do these leaders really want to side with the alleged perpetrators of mass atrocities rather than their victims?" The Chief Prosecutor is especially prone to this type of ad-hominem argument; for example, in a meeting between Luis Moreno-Ocampo and African and Africanist scholars in London in 2007, the Chief Prosecutor tried to silence those raising the possibility of Ugandan government war crimes with the outburst, "If you want to support the LRA, fine! But you should know they are a criminal organization."[59]

A more subtle illustration of this silencing can be found in the "Civil Society Declaration on Africa and the Review Conference of the Rome Statute of the International Criminal Court," circulated by a number of African and Western NGOs—in particular Human Rights Watch—in the lead-up to the 2010 ICC Review Conference. At the same time that the declaration asserts that "It is crucial that views from Africa be heard in these discussions and we encourage African states to make interventions on relevant stocktaking topics," it also condemns criticisms of the ICC "by some African leaders following the ICC arrest warrant for Sudanese President Omar al-Bashir" as "external attacks on the institution." Opinions by Africans that dare question the ICC are dismissed as "attacks," while opinions in support of the ICC are deemed "legitimate." As usual, the human rights industry prides itself on inviting African participation—but only as long as Africans say what they are supposed to say.

A GEOGRAPHY OF IMPUNITY IN AFRICA

Contrary to claims made by some ICC supporters that its interventions are spreading the rule of law and a culture of accountability globally, I argue that, as long as the ICC must accommodate itself to political power, its practice will have the tendency to expand impunity instead of accountability. The invocation of law enforcement to justify the use of force, although it endows itself with a vague legality, can end up fundamentally contradicting many of the basic tenets of the rule of law. Inherently flexible and undefined concepts, such as R2P or humanitarian intervention, are open to instrumentalization because of their ambiguity and lack of objective criteria. Along these lines, it might be thought that the ICC, with its greater level of formalization, would be less open to instrumentalization. Indeed, it was precisely this aspect that has made the United States wary of the ICC, even as it was willing to embrace more informal and flexible justifications such as R2P for its use of force. But the ICC's lack of flexibility is compensated for by the compelling legal mantle it provides and the Prosecutor's apparent willingness to conform to state interests. Through this route, those using force to execute ICC arrest warrants may claim legitimacy despite lacking Security Council authorization—they may seek to use the ICC to go outside *jus ad bellum*.

ICC warrants can also entrench impunity when they are used to justify violence in the name of capturing war criminals, violence that can claim to sanctified, released from the legal restrictions of *jus in bello*, and thus beyond accountability: this is Alex de Waal's "humanitarian impunity."[60] Any violence—whether the killing of civilians by errant drone strikes, the counterviolence provoked by military intervention, or the devastation caused in the course of targeting a regime—that is incurred as a result of military action carried out in the name of executing arrest warrants ends up excused in the name of international law enforcement. The presumed inherent beneficence of global law enforcement paradoxically puts the violence used in its service in a realm of morality outside the reach of law. In short, impunity is expanded as the use of force against Africans to enforce human rights tends to be effectively immune from legal limitation, whether *jus ad bellum* or *jus in bello*, and thus unaccountable to the very international law it claims to uphold.

Impunity can spread not only where the ICC does intervene, but also, and perhaps even more importantly, where it does not intervene. The ICC's increasing monopolization of the practice of international criminal justice in Africa means that those African states and actors not prosecuted by the ICC because of their international political alignment become effectively immune from any global law enforcement. The ICC becomes the de facto arbiter of criminal accountability and impunity in Africa, and those outside its scope end up effectively outside any international criminal law. This was most concretely instantiated in the bilateral immunity agreements between the United States and a number of African countries, but also takes on a much more powerful and insidious form in the informal understandings about who in Africa is subject to international law and who is immune. Ethiopian troops who, with U.S. support and complemented by U.S. air and land strikes, launched a bloody invasion and occupation of Somalia are apparently immune from human rights or international law standards, as appear to be the mostly Ugandan African Union (AU) forces who have replaced the Ethiopians—not to speak of the U.S. special forces operations and drone strikes that continue, targeting al Shabaab leaders. The ICC's politically selective enforcement of international law can thereby entrench impunity instead of spreading accountability.

This accommodation to power—particularly U.S. power—and its damaging consequences could increase further as the Court, in response to its perceived enforcement crisis, tries to convince the United States to lead the way in enforcing arrest warrants. The ICC has found that many states, even if willing to cooperate with it, lack the capacity to execute warrants, especially in cases of ongoing conflicts or when suspects can cross international borders. Moreover, the African Union's rejection of the ICC's arrest warrant for its most high-profile target, Sudanese President Omar al-Bashir, has led ICC supporters to worry that the AU will continue to challenge the Court's authority. Apparently having concluded that African states are either unwilling or unable to act quickly or forcefully enough to apprehend suspects, the Court has begun to seek increased support from the United States, as the one country that has shown itself willing and able to wield military force across the globe. That is, the ICC no longer is trying simply to avoid American censure, as it was in the early 2000s, but now may be actively courting the U.S. military for assistance. The result is that the United States may pose more of a threat to global justice, not by actively opposing the ICC, but by cynically engaging with it.[61]

The ICC's Office of the Prosecutor is leading this effort to encourage U.S. engagement. In June 2009 at a public event in the United States, Chief Prosecutor Moreno-Ocampo declared the need for "special forces" with "rare and expensive capabilities that regional armies don't have," and said that "coalitions of the willing," led by the United States, were needed to enforce ICC arrest warrants.[62] More recently, special adviser to the prosecutor Beatrice Le Fraper Du Hellen declared to CNN, "We have our shopping list ready of requests for assistance from the U.S. government," which, she asserted, "has to lead on one particular issue: the arrest of sought war criminals. President al-Bashir, Joseph Kony in Uganda, Bosco Ntaganda, the 'Terminator in Congo'—all those people have arrest warrants against them, arrest warrants issued by the ICC judges, and they need to be arrested now."[63] She said that the ICC needed American "operational support" for the DRC, Uganda, and CAR "to assist them in mounting an operation to arrest him [Kony]. They have the will—so it's a totally legitimate operation, politically, legally—but they need this kind of assistance. And the U.S. has to be the leader."[64]

The ICC's entreaties are a response to an apparent re-assessment of U.S.-ICC relations undertaken by the Obama administration and to the inception of a new U.S. policy of pragmatic, ad hoc engagement with the Court, as well as the creation of the new United States Africa Command (AFRICOM), discussed at length later. In the lead-up to the 2010 ICC Review Conference in Kampala, the U.S. government declared its interest in working more closely with the ICC, *not* with the intent of becoming a party to the ICC's Rome Statute, but to help execute arrest warrants. In late March, Stephen Rapp, U.S. Ambassador-at-Large for War Crimes, stated that "The United States is prepared to listen and to work with the ICC and go through requests that the Prosecutor has." He continued: "There may be obstacles under our law. But we're prepared to do what we can to bring justice to the victims in the Democratic Republic of Congo, in Uganda, and Sudan and in the Central African Republic."[65]

State Department Legal Adviser Harold Hongjuh Koh declared in March that the United States is seeking cooperation with the Court as a nonstate party observer:

> the Obama Administration has been actively looking at ways that the U.S. can, consistent with U.S. law, assist the ICC in fulfilling its historic charge of providing justice to those who have endured crimes of epic savagery. . . . We would like to meet with the Prosecutor at the ICC to examine whether there are specific ways that the United States might be able to support the particular prosecutions that are already underway.[66]

It appears that some within the U.S. government see the justification of force through the language of law enforcement, as well as the exemption of U.S. violence from the law, as playing a useful role in the U.S. attempt to project military power in Africa and establish a justification for intervening where and when it chooses. This was most recently seen in Security Council Resolutions 1970 and 1973 on Libya. The United States voted in favor of both the former, which referred the situation in Libya to the ICC, and the latter, which authorized the protection of civilians in Libya through military force. Resolution 1973, however, also explicitly declared that non-state parties to the ICC would exercise exclusive domestic jurisdiction over any war crimes that occurred in the course of the execution of the resolution—a guarantee of American immunity from human rights standards or the law of war.

If the ICC comes to rely on the military capacity of the United States as its enforcement arm, in particular when the United States continues to declare itself above the very law it claims to enforce, the ICC will end up trading what little independence it retains in return for access to coercive force, a Faustian bargain that will be made at the price of the Court's legitimacy, impartiality, and legality. However, the price paid by the ICC will be trivial compared to the very dangerous possibility that this alliance could help justify and expand U.S. militarization in Africa, in particular in conjunction with AFRICOM, at a dramatic cost to peace and justice. It is hard to imagine that the ICC, in its reliance on U.S. enforcement capacity, would be able to avoid politicization and not fall into the trap of prose-cuting only those the United States is willing to capture, regardless of crimes com-mitted. As a result, this proposed alliance deeply threatens the credibility of the ICC, because the Prosecutor's pandering to the U.S. military is an affront to all those around the world struggling to hold the U.S. military accountable or who have suffered at its hands.

As a result, the ICC's practice so far in Africa has already made it clear, and its potential alignment with U.S. military power would make it unquestionable, that the best way for an African state or armed force to be guaranteed immunity from criminal prosecution is not to avoid committing crimes, but to align oneself with U.S. security interests in Africa, by signing up to the War on Terror or by guaran-teeing oil supplies or other natural resources. The result is that the ICC, far from ushering in an expanding regime of justice in Africa, may be helping to create an expanding geography of violence and impunity there, following most closely the contours of American power.

NO PEACE WITHOUT JUSTICE

The political selectivity of ICC prosecutions and its counterproductive potential to to entrench impunity throw into doubt claims that the ICC can help prevent future acts of violence by deterring those considering such acts. This is despite assurances offered by the UN Secretary-General and the ICC Chief Prosecutor that the era of impunity is over and that an age of accountability has begun—assurances sup-ported at most by unverifiable anecdotes, such as Moreno-Ocampo's claim that the release of 3,000 child soldiers in Nepal was the result of the his prosecution of Timothy Lubanga.[67]

Even where political instrumentalization is not an issue, there are still signifi-cant doubts to be raised about the ICC's ability to deter future violence. Some legal scholars have argued that international criminal trials deal with a category of acts to which the deterrence argument simply does not apply.[68] Specifically, the attribu-tion of a deterrence function to the ICC ignores the fact that in many contexts where systematic and collective violence takes place—the very category of crimes subject to ICC jurisdiction—violence may not be seen as a deviation, but as normal or even politically or morally justified.[69] International criminalization may only reinforce that justification. Political scientists, for their part, have explained that empirical evidence also provides little support to the argument for deterrence.[70]

Furthermore, the deterrence argument presumes a highly reductive portrayal of the psychology behind atrocity: that mass violence is committed by nonpolitical, nonideological, self-interested, but risk-averse actors who are trying to maximize their personal gains and minimize losses. This does fit with one version of the image of African conflicts: greedy warlords engaging in perfectly rational, nonpolitical, behavior, and it is this image that the ICC frequently draws upon in constructing its narratives of violence. However, as many analysis have shown, this portrayal has little relation to reality in situations of mass violence. And in fact, deterrence makes no sense if violence is attributed to longstanding ethnic animosity or irrational barbarism, as many accounts of violence in Africa like to do.

ICC supporters may respond to these accusations with the mantra that there can be "no peace without justice"—this is even the name of one of the groups working most zealously in favor of ICC interventions.[71] This often repeated slogan is based upon a series of beliefs: that criminal trials are needed to remove the most violent actors and deter others from turning to violence; that without criminal trials punishing those responsible, violence may break out again as people are unsatisfied with amnesties; and that those who have used violence to seize power are inherently incapable of ruling peacefully—as Wangari Maathai has argued, "Surely such leaders who commit unspeakable acts of horror cannot be trusted to create peaceful societies? Not until those who perpetuate these gross violations of human rights are held accountable."[72]

Immi Tallgren puts these claims into perspective, however, explaining that,

> such broad arguments are impossible to verify by any empirical means. A quick random survey of historical examples of the evolution of different societies seems to suggest, however, that the argument of "no peace without justice" is as hollow as the promise of prevention. It seems to be the case that this slogan is only as valid as any other slogan, such as "peace without justice" and "justice without peace."[73]

Some of the most extreme claims in this vein—that "justice delayed is justice denied," for example—are obviously quite dangerous to peace if implemented categorically, for the insistence on immediate criminal trials would be a death warrant for almost any peace process. These categorical claims deny the simple fact that the impact of criminal prosecutions, including those of the ICC, on peace is dependent upon the political context in which those proceedings take place. This is not to say that political contexts never change—indeed, rejecting criminal prosecutions now because they are damaging to peace does not mean rejecting them in the future, when the political context may have changed and prosecutions can be part of a politically constructive process.[74]

Even the potential for ICC intervention can distort politics in ways that are harmful to peace and stability. This is because, when political actors invoke the ICC, they are not simply asking for legal remedy, but given the deeply political nature of the crimes the ICC has jurisdiction over, they are trying to enlist overwhelming external strength to their political cause. The mere existence of the ICC creates the permanent possibility of invoking it, and thereby the permanent possibility of raising the stakes of local, national, or regional politics immensely. At the same time, every demand for ICC intervention is a political demand that has been framed in the ICC's moral language, as so the existence of the ICC creates the permanent possibility of effecting a dangerous moralization of politics within African states and regions. Furthermore, the permanent possibility of ICC intervention, and the possibility of gaining external backing, leads individuals and groups to change their political strategies, seeking external intervention instead of building internal support. The terms in which politics take place become uncertain, since sudden external involvement can, at any point, sweep away expectations and establish a totally new political context.

The existence of the ICC and the ever-present possibility of its intervention lead political actors to moralize, polarize, and escalate political controversies and conflicts in ways that close politics to negotiation or compromise and may even undermine the possibility of meaningful politics itself. The ICC does not have to actually intervene in Africa for the Court's presence to have these distorting consequences for African politics. Law is supposed to stabilize expectations and take some of the unpredictability and discretion out of politics. The ICC can do the opposite of this, degrading law into a force that promotes political unpredictability and undermines political accountability.

In the face of missing evidence affirming the ICC's positive impact on peace, whether in specific cases or through a general prevention role, the typical rhetorical strategy by ICC supporters is to switch gears and to argue that the ICC is concerned solely with justice. As the Office of the Prosecutor puts it in a policy paper, "it would be misleading to equate the interests of justice with the interests of peace."[75] This assertion I consider next.

4. Justice through Global Law

Although supporters of the ICC may seek to pragmatically justify ICC interventions on the basis that they contribute to peace either today or in the future, there is often a point where the faith in "no peace without justice" runs up against inconvenient empirical evidence, and a shift is made to more forceful—and less falsifiable—arguments on the terrain of justice. However, given the limitations already noted that ICC prosecutions face, the claim that the ICC can be an agent of universal justice demands critical scrutiny. Arguments for the ICC on the basis of justice can be separated into two main themes: the ICC as enforcing a universal, moralized law of humanity; and the ICC as fulfilling specific victims' demands for and rights to justice and dignity.

ENFORCING THE LAW OF HUMANITY

The ICC claims to be the agent of universal justice, a claim that it will always fall short of in practice because of the selectivity it must exercise and the limitations placed upon its jurisdiction. Some critics dismiss the ICC on that basis, that it fails to enforce a global law impartially. Against these critics, however, ICC supporters may admit that considerations of pragmatic exigency enter into ICC decisions because it needs to go after accessible targets in order to ensure successful prosecutions.[76] The

ICC, however, is not delegitimated by that pragmatism, they assert, and it can be justified in one of two ways. The first way of justifying the ICC's pragmatic selectivity is through an evolutionary narrative that declares selective justice to be a step on the way to truly universal justice. The evolutionary claim translates the gap between the ICC's current—partial—practice and impartial justice into a temporal gap between the imperfect present and an inevitable future in which the ICC will overcome the political interests of weak and strong states alike. Universal global justice is *in statu nascendi*, so we should not expect it to be perfect yet. How long we will have to wait is uncertain—William Pace of the Coalition for the International Criminal Court declared that our grandchildren will live to see a universal system of global justice.[77] Invoking a future that none of us will live to see in order to justify obviously politicized justice now demands a faith that the ICC will, one day, redeem us all. Those focused on bringing justice to the world they live in now, however, may find this faith hard to afford and, as a result, alternatives to the ICC remain not only possible but necessary for those concerned with international justice today, even by the admission of its supporters.

The second mode for justifying the ICC's selectivity is to argue that it does not impugn those interventions that the ICC does carry out. Supporters of the ICC argue that some justice is better than no justice, and that the ICC's accommodation to political power is not a bad thing, but rather is simply the constitutive condition for the ICC to realize justice in specific cases. That is, bringing the LRA leadership to trial is still justice and still a worthy goal to be pursued, even if the Ugandan government is not being tried. Just because everyone is not tried does not mean that no one should be tried, some justice is better than no justice, and to wait for a time when everyone can be held accountable before holding anyone accountable is a recipe for paralysis and irresponsibility. As Gary Bass puts it, war crimes tribunals "have the clear potential to work," and so "if at first you don't succeed, try again."[78]

This argument, however, is flawed. First, from the perspective of the survivors of conflict or violence, criminal prosecutions of one side and not the other can appear a travesty of justice instead of its partial realization—"some justice" may not be justice at all, but may be interpreted instead as a provocation, a denial of justice, and itself a cause for grievance. However, more generally, the problem is that the assertion that some justice is better than no justice proclaims legitimate *any* politicization of justice, *any* instrumentalization of legal institutions to political interests, however unjust those interests may be. From this point of view, it simply does not matter if justice conforms completely to repressive, violent political power locally or globally. As long as certain cases are tried and some justice is done, the broader consequences of those interventions should not be questioned, because the interventions are fulfilling absolute moral imperatives. This is problematic morally and dangerous politically since it declares international justice available as a mantle to be draped at will over political interests by those with the power to do so. Indeed, how much can be justified in the name of bringing certain criminals to justice? How much injustice can legitimately be done in the name of "some justice"? The result is that the doctrine that some justice is better than no justice can end up, not only making justice conform unapologetically to power, but turning trials into an unaccountable tool of further violence and injustice. The selective prosecution of certain sides in certain conflicts ends up granting immunity to other actors in those conflicts and removing other situations from the realm of international justice. It entrenches impunity for most and justifies it by invoking the morality of prosecuting the few, selected on political grounds. If this is the price to be paid for "some justice," then some justice is incontestably worse than no justice.

VICTIMS' RIGHTS

In the face of such criticism, ICC supporters can remain on moral ground by switching gears: instead of celebrating the ICC as an instrument of impartial universal justice, the ICC is put forth as responding to the particular victims of injustice. This move is attractive, because it makes it possible to condemn any opposition to the ICC on the basis that, in Kofi Annan's words, it "demeans the yearning for human dignity that resides in every African heart."[79] This victim-centered argument claims that victims categorically demand justice through criminal trials, and that victims have a right to justice, to legal remedy through punishment. Like other forms of intervention described in previous chapters, this victim-centered approach depends on the abstract figure of the voiceless victim, which can be deployed in several ways. One approach is to define victims as those who have not received justice, which can be given a psychological framing by understanding peace as a kind of psychological peace of mind, which will not be established until the perpetrators are behind bars. Another approach is to assert the rights of victims and to declare that in order to fulfill victims' rights, perpetrators must be punished.

The victim-centered approach often goes beyond invoking the abstract victim categorically in need of justice and cites actual victims; anecdotes about people demanding justice through punishment often play an important role in justifying ICC interventions. In some cases, quantitative studies or consultations may be cited to provide evidence in favor of ICC intervention. Indeed, it is incontestable that, in many cases, empirical studies have demonstrated that those defined as victims do demand criminal prosecutions and welcome the ICC. The problem with such studies, however, is that sometimes, if the survey administers are not careful—and sometimes even if they are—the surveys may contradict what they had been intended to prove. People in many cases, especially in the midst of ongoing conflict, are not in favor of criminal prosecutions, and, for a host of reasons, may not be in favor of ICC intervention. Often it is peace, and thus a successful peace process, that is the most important thing for the affected communities. Or, people may want punishment, but see no need for trials and

would prefer summary executions to avoid the possibility that the guilty are ac-
quitted due to byzantine and capricious legal processes presided over by ignorant
and possibly compromised foreigners.

Those invoking the victims' perspective in order to provide support for ICC
intervention in northern Uganda face just these problems. There, much to the
ICC's surprise, the announcement of its intervention was met, not with celebration, but by opposition and resistance from many of the very victims they had
come to save. To date, the most vociferous criticism has come from groups who
reject justice through punishment on the grounds that it contradicts "traditional"
Acholi practices of justice through reconciliation, many of whom fall into the ethnojustice agenda discussed in chapter 5, and whose position had been given a dramatic boost as a result of the ICC's intervention. Others, as noted, have opposed
the ICC's involvement on different grounds, including because of its partiality,
politicization, and jurisdictional limitations. This opposition, and the self-serving
agendas motivating some of it, has led to a loud debate among researchers, international agencies, and donors over what "the Acholi truly want" in terms of justice.
Anthropologist Tim Allen points out that those promoting the traditional justice
agenda have often silenced the voices of those Acholi who would like to see the
LRA punished. He writes:

> There is, I conclude, no such thing as a unique Acholi justice system.
> People in northern Uganda require the same kinds of conventional
> legal mechanisms as everyone else living in modern states. Many of our
> informants are eager too to embrace international principles of human
> rights—for all their contradictions and imperfections. We found no
> widespread enthusiasm for *mato oput* ceremonies performed by the Par-
> amount Chief.

In conclusion, Allen writes, "there was no general rejection of international justice."[80] Although Allen recognizes the uncertainty over the question of justice
within the Acholi community, other studies, conducted by groups typically in
favor of justice through punishment, have tried to show that the Acholi are widely
supportive of punishment and of the ICC. However, these studies have, at times,
provided evidence that negates their own claims. According to one study, *only
three percent* of Acholi respondents named justice as being a priority for them,
whereas peace, health, security, food, land, return, money, and education were all
named by between 32 and 45 percent of people surveyed.[81] In 2007, a long-term
research project by Human Rights Focus found an overwhelming demand for
peace over the demand for criminal justice among displaced Acholi.[82]

This diversity of opinions among the victims is complicated further by uncertainty over the definition of *victim* itself. Practical questions, such as who gets to
be a victim and who makes that decision, do not have a self-evident answer, and
victimhood—like the identity of perpetrator—is a political designation, the result
of political negotiation, contestation, and decisions. The political contingency of

designations of victimhood is masked by asserting a "victim's perspective," which presumes perfectly self-evident categories of victims and perpetrators and a perfect correspondence between what is decided through the procedures of international criminal law and what the victims think is just.

When faced with victims who do not conform to the victim image and vociferously reject or demand alternatives to criminal trials for designated perpetrators, several other approaches can be taken by ICC supporters. One such approach is to blame such resistance on intimidation or propaganda by self-interested local elites. More commonly, however, recourse is taken to the universal moral argument: ICC interventions do not belong to the immediate victims, but belong to all of humanity, for it is all of humanity that is injured by the crimes the ICC prosecutes and it is all of humanity that will be redeemed through constructing the universal rule of law. In this argument, it is not the concrete, actual victims, or even the actual perpetrators, who matter—they are only sacrifices, required for the emergence of international law. This is the basis on which Judith Shklar condemns the American prosecutor's approach in the Tokyo Trials, in which, she said, he revealed that "metaphysics and the future of international law were his preoccupations,"[83] not the guilt or innocence of those on trial, who were to be "sacrificed" to help realize his preferred philosophy of history. In these cases, in which the demands made by those who have survived conflict are dismissed in the name of building the international rule of law, the truth of Koskenniemi's insight, that international criminal trials work to construct "a memory serving our personal and social projects [in the West], far removed from the events on trial—perhaps the construction of an 'international community' out of the tragedies of others," is starkly revealed.[84] It also raises the question of what measures those who feel they are being sacrificed for the future of international law may take to contest or prevent that fate.

These problems derive fundamentally from the very idea of a victim-centered approach. The idea that there is a victims' perspective that can be reached through consultations, quantitative research, and policy studies, and that justice interventions can be based upon it, is itself illegitimate. It is premised on the idea that there is an objectively measurable consensus among self-evident victims, and the only thing would-be agents of international justice have to do is to properly discern it and then intervene on that basis. This is founded upon the interventionist imaginary, in which "transitional justice" is just another deficit internal to Africa to be rectified through foreign intervention. Furthermore, it simply misses the point: what is important for justice is not finding the statistically most common opinion among victims and imposing it, but rather what is important is precisely the *lack* of consensus on any justice agenda. It is not up to foreign researchers to "determine victims' preferences" through surveys, but, rather, it is up to the political community itself, through its own organs and leaders, as a product of its own debates, to determine what is needed and to work to try to bring it about. Thus, it is not the debate among researchers and aid agencies that matters—for that debate is only over what kind of justice should be imposed—but rather it is the debate within Acholi society and Uganda more widely that should determine what justice will mean.

Indeed, the fact that more Acholi express support for punishing the LRA, or more express support for "traditional justice," does not make legitimate external interventions to support either one. Instead, what this co-existence of opinions demonstrates is the fundamental uncertainty and controversy among Acholi over what justice will mean in response to the LRA and the war and the need for the Acholi themselves to slowly, haltingly, and deliberatively decide what justice means for them. Indeed, both the ICC intervention and the ethnojustice agenda suffer from the same flaw: each claims incontestable legitimacy for its own ideal of justice—one by invoking a universal language of human rights and crimes against humanity, the other by invoking the particular language of custom—and attempts to impose that ideal upon all Acholi.

By taking what the survivors say seriously, and not simply assuming that everyone will or should support a certain kind of justice, it becomes apparent that, in every situation of mass violence, there will be some people who are demanding criminal justice, others who are not, others who are demanding different kinds of justice, others who would rather not get involved. There are political debates on justice and peace within every conflict-affected society—different concepts of justice between men and women, youth and the old, rebel and government sympathizers. It is this debate that researchers should pay attention to and, if invited, engage in, instead of seeking to determine a static set of preferences through surveys and basing intervention upon that. And it is this internal debate within conflict-affected societies that the ICC rejects. The ICC instead sees people as helpless, voiceless victims, sees the community as uniformly victimized and voiceless, and sees itself as representing the true interests of the victims, even if those designated as victims themselves reject the ICC.

This points to a deep political problem with the victim-centered perspective as it informs international criminal trials. A victim-centered approach might be appropriate for individual criminal procedures within an established national legal system. However, the ICC's interventions, and interventions in the wake of massive political violence in general, are inherently collective and political. No victim or perpetrator is an isolated individual, who can be taken out of their context for justice to be done. Legal interventions thus have collective political consequences that must be taken into account and according to which they must be judged. In this way, even if a victim's perspective is morally legitimate within an individualized rights-based approach, it will not be politically legitimate on that account. In situations in which acts of violence are truly individual deviations from an established norm of peace and are comprehended by an existing rule of law, then this individualized approach makes sense. However, in situations of massive violence, in which violence may become the norm, perpetrator and victim identities may be ambiguous and shifting, and responsibility may be widespread, this victim-centered approach is inapplicable. It values a particular kind of moral reasoning and a particular kind of political community, or non-community—one in which the individual, divorced from society, politics, history, and culture, needs to be redeemed and in which the moral claim of the individual victim, as interpreted by the ICC, trumps all other claims and projects.

Of course, this will never be the case in real political transitions or in the formation of real political communities. Designations of victim, perpetrator, and justice are all political phenomena, and in any such process some of those claiming victimhood will always find their claims trumped by claims made by others using similar language. Even more important and difficult is the fact that individual claims of victimhood may be trumped by the exigencies of peace or the formation of political communities. The focus on global justice, to be actualized through the abstract individual, ignores the real communities that are the key political and moral claimants and actors within a context of primarily national justice.[85] It is up to those who have survived violence to organize politically and demand the accountability they wish for, but it is also up to them to decide if justice includes accountability or instead involves political or social reforms that would address structural forms of injustice, not just the injustice of mass violence. However, this has to be done as part of the political process, so that the demand is itself made accountable and does not become simply a call for foreign intervention to tip the local political scales. It is political organization that ensures that political legitimacy align with moral legitimacy in the pursuit of justice. This result cannot be brought about through foreign intervention, which attempts to force politics to follow moral demands at the price of political disruption and possible further conflict. Supporters of the ICC seem to assume that justice through trials will always lead to the most advantageous form of political change and political community, which is rarely, if ever, the case in situations of mass violence.

So when the ICC intervenes, it is not a nonpolitical gesture of solidarity with voiceless victims. Rather, it is a political act, a political intervention into a community in significant upheaval, aligning with or refuting the interests of different political and social forces and actors. The ICC and those enforcing its justice need to be held responsible for the political consequences of their interventions and have to be judged according to those effects, a responsibility they cannot dodge by invoking the mantra of "no peace without justice," or the abstract figure of the voiceless victim, universal moral standards, or the development of international law. It needs to be asked if ICC intervention is helping to build sustainable, peaceful, just, and inclusive political communities, and my belief is that the political reforms necessary to build such political communities have to be driven chiefly from within, so that external ICC intervention will tend to interfere with this internal process of political change.

In Uganda, the pursuit of justice should help contribute to the resolution of the national and internal political crises of the Acholi, instead of further entrenching those crises as the interventions considered so far have tended to do. This would require freeing justice from its inscription in criminal liability for spectac-ular acts of violence, and understanding injustice and justice in broader terms. Justice in the wake of mass violence means reform towards a new social and polit-ical order, and it is this understanding that the ICC disciplines out of existence by equating justice with criminal justice. As the ICC's understanding of justice as criminal justice is imposed, disseminated, and naturalized, proposals for social and political justice are ignored, and the political and social reform that is the only thing that will prevent mass violence from recurring is precluded by the obsession over which handful of individuals will stand trial in the Hague.

RECLAIMING GLOBAL JUSTICE

At the civil society preparatory meeting for the 2010 ICC Review Conference in Kampala, the ICC representatives who attended faced questioning from two direc-tions.[86] First, the ICC was accused of employing double standards in its Uganda case, as was already discussed. A second accusation went further, however, and beyond the Uganda case itself to question the ICC's jurisdiction more broadly. As the representative from the Soroti Development Association and NGOs Network demanded to know, what about the "invisible perpetrators"—the Western donors, arms merchants, supporters of dictatorships, multinational corporations, and inter-national financial institutions who were deeply involved in African conflicts, but were ignored in favor of prosecuting a few Africans? The response from the Coali-tion for the International Criminal Court was that responsibility for such perpetra-tors is not the responsibility of the ICC, but rather, the responsibility of African states and societies.[87] That is, after a series of hyperbolic claims on behalf of the importance of the ICC, its power is disavowed and responsibility for bringing the biggest perpetrators to justice is handed off to Africa. Of course, this raises the ques-tion of why African states and societies would be able to hold to account perpetra-tors who are so politically insulated that they cannot be dealt with by the ICC, why it is left up to African states and societies to address crimes committed by the most powerful states and corporations that often wield far more power and violence than African states themselves, and why it is left up to the survivors to find justice on their own against forces far beyond their reach. In the name of complementarity and participation, the kind of justice demanded by survivors is declared impossible.

More important than this disavowal of responsibility on the part of ICC sup-porters, however, is what the line of questioning reveals about the inherent limita-tions on the "global justice" that the ICC can pursue. In this sense, the ICC imposes a form of discipline on the practice of global justice itself. The ICC is quickly estab-lishing a monopoly for international criminal justice as the primary form that global justice takes, as it and its supporters have defined global justice for Africa as a goal that is to be pursued exclusively through the ICC and other formal legal mechanisms, thus restricting those issues that can be addressed and those actors who can be held accountable.[88] Even the alternatives to the ICC are often framed in terms of postconflict legal accountability for the worst violence, thus effectively conceding the broader argument to the ICC and demonstrating how entrenched the criminal justice approach has become. In monopolizing the discourse of global justice in Africa, the ICC has placed certain fundamental issues outside the scope of what can be defined as unjust and thus subject to challenge and contestation through the pursuit of global justice. So even without overt political instrumental-ization, the ICC imposes a particular narrative of injustice and justice that very often does not make sense to the people who are supposed to be redeemed by the Court. This signals one reason why the distinction between so-called global and so-called local justice should be rejected: the justice of the ICC can be very partial, parochial, and politicized, restricting its scope to national or, at most, continental boundaries, and internalizing injustice to Africa; conversely, the justice demanded by supposedly local African victims may itself be truly global, going far beyond the narrow limits imposed by the ICC and defining injustice in ways that go far beyond national or continental boundaries.

The limitation upon the ICC's global justice becomes obvious when the ICC's subject-matter jurisdiction is considered: the forms of violence, repression, and in-equality that can be challenged as unjust are restricted to the most spectacular forms of overt violence within Africa. Less spectacular forms of domination, repression, and violence—such as economic exploitation, Western sponsorship of violent and antidemocratic political forces, internationally enforced disparities in access to medicines, trade regimes that undermine development and food security—none of these can be challenged through the pursuit of global justice when global justice is defined by the ICC. Global justice is exclusively associated with punishing the "most serious crimes of concern to the international community as a whole," conceived of as mass atrocities, but those crimes that *serve* the interests of the "international community" are conveniently outside the ICC's scope, and African citizenries are told that it is up to them to take care of such forms of injustice. Spec-tacular mass atrocity in Africa is made into the most pressing form of injustice globally, and its prevention and punishment is made into the most pressing issue for all those concerned with global justice, trumping all other concerns. The so-called international community is constructed as the agent of global justice, never as its object.[89]

Personal jurisdiction under the ICC is similarly restricted, focusing as it does on placing the entire blame for violence on a few particularly "savage" Africans—whether Omar al-Bashir or Kony—by misrepresenting situations and reducing the wide set of actors and structures involved in violence to just a few individuals. By focusing on those (Africans) with "greatest responsibility" and attributing to them vast conspiracies that perfectly account for episodes of violence, the ICC ignores the criminal responsibility of Western states, donors, aid agencies, and corpora-tions even in those episodes of violent atrocity that the Court is willing to investi-gate. Finally, the ICC's limited temporal jurisdiction excludes centuries of injustice, an entire history of Western violence in Africa.

If the ICC were conceived as simply a technical mechanism for use in specific, limited, circumstances, this would be less of a problem. The greater problem results from the ICC's tendency to monopolize the language of global justice in Africa. There is a vast regime of institutions and organizations engaged in a massive pedagogical project trying to build support for the ICC as the primary arbiter of global justice for Africa. It is precisely through those mechanisms that the ICC uses to promote victims' "participation" and "empowerment" that the experience of violence is made into the handle by which the ICC steers people to restrict their concepts of injustice and justice to those provided by the ICC and thus to put entire forms of national and international domination, violence, and inequality outside the scope of justice as unquestionable. This pedagogical, participatory, empowering project thus can further the legitimation of international domination and inequality *through* the very discourse of global justice. The irony is that the discourse of global justice is well positioned to challenge those forms of Western-imposed and supported domination and international inequality, and so the ICC ends up impoverishing what could be an emancipatory language of global justice. Taken together, the politicization of ICC interventions, the ICC's lack of universality, the limitations on its concept of global justice, and its monopolization of the global justice discourse force us to consider how to contest the disciplinary and depoliticizing tendencies of ICC interventions and reclaim the emancipatory potential of global justice.

First, in terms of ICC trials themselves, a trial-of-rupture strategy might be considered. As Martti Koskenniemi explains, describing the practice of French lawyer Jacques Vergès, "the defense is conducted entirely as an attack on the system represented by the prosecution case."[90] It is a matter of using the defendant's right to speak at the trial—that is, using the guarantees provided through formal legality—in order to contest the historical narrative embodied by the prosecution's case and to assert an alternative historical narrative, one that does not necessarily absolve the defendant of wrongdoing, but that places the defendant's violence in the context of the violence and crimes committed by those putting on and benefiting from the trial. In the case of Uganda, this would mean putting the LRA's violence in the context of the Ugandan government's violence, which would challenge the ICC's partiality within the Ugandan case and open the narrative of the "responsible," benevolent Ugandan government to scrutiny. It would also mean putting LRA violence in the context of the broader set of "invisible actors" who helped enable, intensify, and prolong the war over the years—the United States, the Western donors, the World Bank, the aid agencies. This would challenge the ICC's restrictive jurisdiction and as well as rupture the narrative of indigenous African conflicts in need of Western intervention in order to be resolved.

This strategy of rupture within ICC trials can be complemented with an effort to take back the discourse of criminal law and of global justice more generally. For one thing, justice needs to be refocused on the national level: the focus on global justice impoverishes movements toward finding justice on the national level and reduces justice to a matter of individuals finding redemption globally. Nevertheless, global justice still has a place. For example, criminal justice can be reclaimed through people's tribunals, following the lead of the people's tribunal on Iraq, or through the formation of an African criminal court, which would have the potential of avoiding some of the more blatant forms of political instrumentalization that the ICC is subject to. Beyond that, the very discourse of global justice needs to be taken back from the ICC, back from the focus on criminal justice and toward social and political justice, back from the obsession with spectacular atrocities committed by Africans, and instead toward contesting the massive transnational forms of inequality, oppression, and violence of which the West is the perpetrator and beneficiary, not the supposed redeemer.

7

AFRICOM: Militarizing Peace

Listening to some of its proponents, one would be forgiven for thinking that AFR-ICOM is some kind of a community-development NGO, not United States Africa Command, the new U.S. military command for Africa. General William Ward, its commander, declared AFRICOM's purpose to be to seek "African solutions to African problems," and President Bush announced that AFRICOM "will enhance our efforts to bring peace and security to the people of Africa" by promoting the "goals of development, health, education, democracy and economic growth."[1] AFRICOM will "help generate more indigenous and therefore more sustainable peace and security," and, according to another AFRICOM official, the new command is "a listening, growing and developing organization dedicated to partnering with African governments, African security organizations, and the international community to achieve the U.S. security goals by helping the people of Africa achieve the goals that they have set for themselves."[2] No longer will peace interventions be in variable and flexible relations with American power, AFRICOM declares, and no longer will the U.S. military struggle to use often-recalcitrant NGOs as "force multipliers," as Colin Powell put it,[3] but rather these interventions will be directly under the control of the U.S. military.

Although AFRICOM's emphasis on military means is a novel development, what it proposes to do with those means is not and, in fact, is familiar from the total intervention agenda: empowering societal interventions, state capacity building, and, as a last resort, direct coercion. AFRICOM, I argue, therefore displays intensified forms of the same political pathologies that have been seen with the forms of intervention considered already, pathologies that derive from the lack of accountability to so-called beneficiaries, but that are intensified by AFRICOM's direct access to military force. These problems are well-illustrated by AFRICOM's involvement in northern Uganda and its effort against the LRA.

AFRICOM became operational in 2008 in an attempt to respond adequately to Africa's increasing strategic importance to the United States. Until then, Africa had been divided between three different U.S. military commands, with United States European Command (EUCOM) being assigned most of the continent, and so AFRICOM brought under its area of responsibility all of Africa with the exception of Egypt.[4] This new command, however, would have a novel structure: it would represent a change from massive deployments of U.S. troops to smaller, more flexible deployments. It would have neither permanent combat troops assigned to it, nor even any permanent official bases housing U.S. troops in Africa, with the exception of Combined Joint Task Force-Horn of Africa (CJTF-HoA) at Camp Lemonier in Djibouti. Instead, its goal would be to put in place a "family" of established operating locations that would work together in a networked form of force projection.[5] To this end, AFRICOM is being built through informal base-sharing agreements with African states and through the establishment of "bare-bones" facilities, so-called "lily pads" or "Cooperative Security Locations," which can be converted into functioning U.S. military bases in 24–48 hours.[6]

AFRICOM's novelty relative to other U.S. military commands is also found in its unprecedented embrace of ideas of peacebuilding, participation, partnership, empowerment, cultural understanding, and human security, not only in its proponents' high-flown rhetoric, but also to some extent in its activities.[7] AFRICOM works in conjunction with African states, it carries out community humanitarian and development activities, and it tries to build relations with African civil society and engage in public dialogue with academics. Some critics dismiss AFRICOM's language of participation, capacity building, and human security as no more than empty rhetoric, a gloss over the U.S. military's real policy of "killing people and breaking things" in pursuit of U.S. economic and political self-interest. However, I argue that it is dangerous to dismiss AFRICOM's stated orientation toward human security. The command's adoption of a human security agenda, while at times no more than rhetoric, also presents the possibility that the U.S. military will become involved in far more expansive and intensive forms of intervention in Africa, militarized forms of intervention whose consequences are more subtle, but not necessarily any less damaging, than the massive, obvious destruction wreaked by traditional military intervention. Also a cause for concern is that the adoption of a human security agenda will allow AFRICOM's interventions to avoid much of the scrutiny from activists that would be provoked by the pursuit of traditional military intervention. Indeed, some activists have attempted to use the discourse of human security against AFRICOM, missing the fact that AFRICOM has already co-opted that discourse to a large extent.

Therefore, when we seek to understand the ways in which AFRICOM will "benefit the US military, US defense contractors, US oil companies," repressive African governments, and private security companies, as Catherine Besteman puts it,[8] we need to consider the novel ways in which AFRICOM will try to realize that role. We also need to consider the contradictions and incoherencies that are resulting from the adoption of a militarized peace-intervention agenda, for those may provide footholds for contesting this expanding militarization.

This chapter will detail how the United States arrived at a militarized peace-intervention agenda as a preferred mode of engagement with Africa, and what its consequences are for peace and democracy in the continent, with special attention to U.S. military involvement in Uganda. My conclusion will be that AFRICOM's militarization of peace presents a grave danger to Africa and threatens to even further degrade the very idea of peace itself.

Before continuing, a brief note: many of the arguments put forth in this chapter have been dismissed by those who maintain that I have taken future possibilities as present reality and created an imaginary, all-powerful AFRICOM, when in fact the organization is underfunded, understaffed, and basically just muddling through. These critics, including some AFRICOM staff themselves, argue that I base my criticism upon worst-case predictions and not upon what AFRICOM is actually doing—which, in actual fact, does not amount to much. I have two responses. First, AFRICOM is doing quite a bit right now, in particular through its security arrangements with African states, and stands ready to do quite a bit more. Moreover, the March, 2011 aerial bombardment of Libya under the command and control of AFRICOM Joint Task Force Odyssey Dawn shows how close to the surface the devastating use of American military force with total impunity against Africa remains, even for this flexible, "listening," organization. And second, even if AFRICOM today is generally the ineffective organization some make it out to be, the delineation of possible future scenarios remains important because, by bringing attention to the danger these scenarios pose, perhaps we can help prevent them from coming to pass.

1. American Security Policy in Africa

COMPETING AGENDAS

Since the launch of the so-called War on Terror, U.S. foreign policy toward Africa, and security policy in particular, has been oriented around a number of different, often conflicting, but also overlapping agendas that ultimately led to the establishment of AFRICOM in 2008. The first agenda was the War on Terror itself, with its antecedents in the U.S. policy of countering perceived Islamic extremism, for instance in its frontline states policy against Sudan and in the measures taken in the wake of the 1998 bombings of the U.S. embassies in Nairobi and Dar es Salaam. The counterterrorism agenda saw Africa, in particular the regions with significant Muslim populations, as a potential safe haven and breeding ground both for foreign terrorists, such as those expected to flee the American invasion of Afghanistan, as well as for indigenous African terrorists. This supposed terrorist threat was to be dealt with through a number of different tools, including building African state security capacity to establish control over borders and the "ungoverned spaces" thought to harbor terrorists—for example through the Pan-Sahel Initiative, which, it was claimed, would help "drain the swamp" of the Sahara.[9] Military strikes, in particular by special forces to eliminate specific terrorist threats, were also part of the agenda, as were "hearts and minds" campaigns, intended to build support for the United States, combat Islamic extremism, and alleviate some of the economic deprivation thought to provide the conditions for terrorist recruitment, as well to improve intelligence gathering.[10] The CJTF-HoA, established in 2002, has been a microcosm of this expansive counterterrorism agenda, carrying out activities in all these areas with its stated mission to "foster regional stability, build security capacity, and forge relationships using an indirect approach to counter violent extremism in the region."[11]

Counterterrorism, however, has not been the only security agenda competing for preeminence, and some analysts argue that it is, in fact, only a cover for the real interest driving American policy in Africa: access to Africa's resources, in particular oil and to a lesser extent natural gas and other forms of mineral wealth, of increased importance with China's rapid entry into the continent.[12] Much has been made of the increasing U.S. dependence on African oil, expected to reach 25 percent of U.S. imports by 2015, and of the subsequent revaluation of Africa's strategic importance for the United States.[13] The United States is pursuing Africa's oil through a diverse set of means, including building the security capacity of African states so that they can provide the needed security and stability to ensure access to resources with or without direct U.S. involvement; positioning U.S. forces in or around Africa in preparation for military contingency operations to counter extreme threats to oil supplies when African states fail to fulfill their security tasks; and even, at times, undertaking development projects in communities negatively affected by resource extraction to prevent them from disrupting access. The pursuit of oil is the dimension of U.S. interests in Africa that has evoked the most critical attention, with some arguing that the United States intends to use its "unprecedented military strength" to create a "full-spectrum dominance" in order to guarantee access to the resource.[14]

Third, there is a more diffuse agenda, reflecting concerns that emerged in the early 1990s but were given greater importance with the War on Terror, focused on countering the global security threats putatively emerging from Africa's weak and failing states, its "ungoverned spaces," its widespread poverty and disease, and its environmental crises.[15] Whether those threats are specified in terms of uncontrollable migration flows, global pandemics, armed conflict, mass atrocity, or terrorism, proponents argue that Africa's crises simply cannot be contained within Africa's borders in today's globalizing world and that they present a genuine threat to the West at the same time that they threaten Africa's peoples. In this widening human security agenda, a vast range of problems including "drugs, disease, terrorism, pollution, poverty, and environmental problems" create a "vicious circle of causes and effects,"[16] which, according to some of AFRICOM's proponents, demand a coordinated response from the U.S. military.[17] The focus on human security is supposed to be mutually beneficial to the United States and Africa, as Africa's and America's interests are said to coincide around a future of human rights, peace, and development.[18] As the U.S. National Security Strategy of 2002 frames this fortunate coincidence of interests, the United States should intervene in Africa for both moral and pragmatic reasons: "In Africa promise and opportunity sit side by side with disease, war and desperate poverty. This threatens both the core values of the United States—preserving human dignity—and our strategic priority—combating global terror."[19] These threats are to be addressed through a spectrum of policies, from state-building, peacekeeping, early-warning mechanisms, and security reform, to agricultural transformation, development, and anti-HIV/AIDS funding, to humanitarian military intervention. As the 2006 National Security Strategy puts it, Africa is a "high priority" and "our security depends upon partnering with Africans to strengthen fragile and failing states and bring ungoverned areas under the control of effective democracies."[20] This reflects the adoption of the expansive global governance agenda by sectors within the U.S. government, in which underdevelopment itself is imagined to be a security threat. The human-security agenda was given increased emphasis with the War on Terror, as the 2002 National Security Strategy makes clear: "Regional conflicts can arise from a wide variety of causes. . . . If left unaddressed, however, these different causes lead to the same ends: failed states, humanitarian disasters, and ungoverned areas that can become safe havens for terrorists."[21]

Almost any instance of U.S. foreign policy in Africa, therefore, can be seen within each of these frameworks—threatened U.S. intervention in Darfur, for example, has been variously explained as part of the War on Terror,[22] about securing oil supplies,[23] or about stopping genocide on ethical and human security grounds.[24] However, it is difficult to subsume all instances of U.S. policy in Africa within any one of these agendas. Indeed, American policy in the continent has, generally, not been characterized by the coherent pursuit of strategic objectives through rational means, but rather by inconsistent, incoherent, and often counterproductive interventions and policies reflecting the tensions between the various agendas driving U.S. policy, as well as reflecting the general obstacles to the U.S. capacity to realize its objectives, such as lack of regional expertise.[25] As Nicolas Van de Walle argues, the U.S. record in Africa suggests "a piecemeal approach in which different agencies pursued commercial, humanitarian, military, and diplomatic objectives, with little coordination or integration."[26] Each agenda is partially realized in different interventions in different African states with little coordination. This leads to glaring discrepancies between rhetoric and practice—such as the support provided to strategically important but authoritarian states despite the U.S. rhetoric of good governance and democracy—and to situations in which one U.S. government agency pursues policies against the interests of other agencies. Examples of the latter include the CIA's policy in the mid-2000s of supporting warlords in Somalia in the name of combating terrorism despite protest from the State Department, and the Bush administration's approach of simultaneously demonizing the Sudan government while depending on it for counterterrorism assistance. This uncertainty is also reflected in the diverse interpretations of U.S. policy arrived at by critics, some seeing the War on Terror as dominant, others seeing oil interests, some seeing U.S. policy as one of domination and brutal exploitation, others seeing it as focused on "policing global exclusion,"[27] crisis management and containment,[28] or integration.[29] However, the recognition of inconsistency on the part of U.S. policy in Africa should not be taken as an apology for U.S. power or as a denial of its negative consequences; rather, it is precisely this lack of coherence that, I argue, has led U.S. policy to converge on a multiform militarization culminating in AFRICOM, with damaging consequences for peace, justice, and democracy.

THE AFRICOM SOLUTION

In the mid-2000s, policy makers and analysts concerned with the lack of coherent strategic attention paid to Africa began to argue for institutional reform within the U.S. government that would help resolve the tensions between the different U.S. agendas and agencies and respond adequately to Africa's increasing relevance. This search for greater coherence and efficacy, however, took place in a context that limited the available options. First, there was the ongoing militarization of U.S. policy in Africa to contend with, occurring since the late 1990s when a concern with African oil and perceived Islamic extremism had come onto the U.S. radar.[30] At the same time, U.S. foreign policy, in general, was increasingly dependent on the military or military contractors as the Pentagon's budget expanded and the role of civilian agencies in U.S. foreign policy, particularly the State Department and USAID, lessened dramatically.[31] As Andrew Bacevich argues, this is part of a new militarism in which the U.S. military itself came to define the U.S. foreign policy agenda, and military dominance was seen as the solution to any potential problem.[32] In Africa, this has meant military spending (even without including funding through the State Department for military contractors) increasing between fivefold and tenfold over the 2000s,[33] and so by the end of the decade, a fifth of U.S. foreign aid to Africa was going through the Department of Defense.[34] However, this general expansion of the military was also qualified by the U.S. experiences in Iraq and Afghanistan, which had led military and civilian leaders alike to question the efficacy of "hard" military means alone for realizing national-security objectives, as reflected in shifts to ideas about counterinsurgency, "population-centric warfare," and stability operations in the Pentagon.[35] Dependence on the military was qualified further for Africa, because U.S. security policy there had to deal with a shortage of available troops due to its ongoing occupations in Iraq and Afghanistan and with the longstanding American reluctance to openly send troops to Africa.

In the face of these contradictory conditions, the U.S. solution for Africa was equally contradictory: AFRICOM was a new military command that would not have any permanent troops assigned to it, that would "focus on war prevention rather than war-fighting,"[36] and that would be partially staffed by civilians. Its task would be primarily conflict and crisis prevention, and, according to one official, it could count itself a success "if it keeps American troops *out* of Africa for the next 50 years,"[37] which it would strive to do by focusing on an all-encompassing "Phase Zero" of operations.[38] AFRICOM was fully within the sovereignty as responsibility discourse, in which Western intervention in Africa is to take place in order to empower Africa and thus avert the need for intervention in the future.

To achieve these novel ends, new tools were needed. According to Teresa Whelan, Deputy Assistant Secretary of Defense for African Affairs, AFRICOM would be more flexible, work through African partners, and support other U.S. government programs, thus taking a "more holistic and operationally efficient approach."[39] To this end, several programs previously undertaken by civilian agencies were placed under AFRICOM's command,[40] and, as a "listening" organization looking to "understand" the environments giving rise to insurgencies, AFRICOM has made an unprecedented push to engage with and recruit Africanist academics, following and expanding upon the interest in "Human Terrain Systems" forged by the Pentagon earlier in the decade.[41] For example, AFRICOM representatives are a constant presence at African Studies Association meetings, attending panels, asking questions, handing out cards, trying to defend the U.S. military when the good faith of AFRICOM's commitment to helping Africans is questioned.

The result has been that AFRICOM was burdened with a vast array of high expectations from its inception. One U.S. commentator declared it could "help weave many disparate elements of US foreign policy into one more-coherent package,"[42] and a South African analyst declared that "AFRICOM will result in informed, consistent, coherent, and sustained engagement by the United States in Africa."[43] In his encomium to AFRICOM in *Esquire* magazine, Thomas Barnett celebrated AFRICOM's commitment to "preemptive nation-building instead of preemptive regime change," its role as "a proving ground for the next generation of interagency cooperation that fuels America's eventual victory" in the war against radical Islam, as "Iraq done right."[44] However, the new centrality of stability, prevention, and human security has not been uniformly welcomed either within the U.S. government or within the military itself;[45] for example, an article by two Air Force insiders argues that "failed states are a non-problem getting too much attention" and that AFRICOM "is an indicator that US leaders take Barnett's call to intervention seriously," a call characterized as seriously misguided.[46]

Some critics outside the U.S. government have also focused on AFRICOM's stability and human security dimension, framing it as the newest phase in U.S. military strategy, one of prevention through limited but diversified intervention. As anthropologist Jan Bachmann puts it, through AFRICOM, "Africa is likely to become a testing site for new military activities that go beyond questions of (asymmetric, low scale, counterinsurgency) warfare inasmuch as the command proposes a long-term engagement of U.S. forces in spaces where violent conflict has not yet emerged, where crises have to be prevented."[47] Most critics on the left have dismissed the human security dimension of AFRICOM, arguing that it is meant only to hide the reality of AFRICOM's agenda, namely, oil, terrorism, and China.

Critics have been quick to point out that AFRICOM officials themselves seem to have admitted as much: Vice-Admiral Robert Moeller, General William Ward's military deputy, stated in 2008 that protecting "the free flow of natural resources from Africa to the global market was one of AFRICOM's "guiding principles," and described the challenges it faced as being, among others, "oil disruption," "terrorism," and China's "growing influence."[48] Many African commentators and political leaders have also been openly critical of AFRICOM, particularly around the issue of establishing permanent U.S. military bases on the continent, which will be discussed further later.[49]

Despite criticism, militarism has only intensified under President Obama: in 2009, the budget for AFRICOM was tripled, and a new military emphasis was seen in several ambassadorial appointments, including Uganda's. In 2010, $763 million was allotted to AFRICOM, whereas the State Department's Africa Bureau's operational budget had a $226 million allocation.[50] In response to criticism, in particular concerning the apparent militarization of U.S. Africa policy in ways detrimental to U.S. security interests[51] and concerning whether AFRICOM is even capable of carrying out a human-security agenda,[52] AFRICOM's supporters have recently attempted to argue that AFRICOM is not militarizing foreign policy, but will focus on military-to-military assistance and play a subordinate role to civilian agencies in other enterprises.[53] Regardless of the specific direction AFRICOM takes in coming years, signs suggest that the emphasis on militarization will remain.

MEANS BECOME ENDS

What is most significant about AFRICOM is not whether it is perfectly functional to any one security agenda—whether oil, counterterrorism, or human security— but rather the specific way in which it has tried to resolve the contradictions between the different U.S. agendas in Africa. It has done so by downplaying the divergent objectives of each agenda, emphasizing instead what all three agendas have in common, namely, the *means* that each relies on in order to realize its own ends, and proposing the military as the best agent for those means. These common means, employed by each agenda in different proportions and familiar from the interventions chronicled already, are to build the security capacity of African states, establish the ability for the United States to carry out direct military "contingency operations," and carry out politically geared development and humanitarian projects. Each of these could be best undertaken, it was maintained, through the power of the U.S. military.

AFRICOM's focus on means over ends therefore meant that a common agenda could be reached that focused on the U.S. military efficiently achieving certain tactical goals—such as building state military capacity, digging a well, setting up a base, carrying out a training exercise, or obtaining intelligence—even while the need to resolve the tensions between the different overall policy agendas, between the ends to which those means were to be directed, could be deferred. The focus on means over ends did away with the need to achieve, be accountable to, or even specify the ends toward which those means were directed, and so a joint military training exercise, for example, could be justified through an array of often contradictory assertions, including that it was to promote human security, improve disaster response, build state capacity, counter terrorism, or promote good governance. Critics could characterize the same exercise as strengthening undemocratic U.S. allies, laying the groundwork for military operations to secure oil supplies, or expanding the surveillance capacity and presence of the U.S. military.[54] In short, the tensions were not resolved by but were imported within AFRICOM and compounded due to its military character.

This displacement of ends by means has drawn critical scrutiny. According to one analyst, AFRICOM represents "a partial and inconsistent adjustment due to a conjunction of quite specific circumstances, rather than a paradigmatic shift in policy toward Africa."[55] The uncertainty and incoherence among different U.S. policy objectives that permeate AFRICOM as an organization, as many commentators have noted and many who have met AFRICOM staff have found, create situations where AFRICOM operations are themselves characterized by inefficiency, inefficacy, and counterproductivity. Commentators across the political spectrum have argued that AFRICOM's activities, whether developmental, state-building, or the deployment of military force, even when tactically effective—that is, even if they manage to dig a well, provide training to a military ally, or assassinate a suspected terrorist—are often counterproductive in terms of larger strategic goals, such as securing oil supplies in the long term. As one analyst puts it in a report published by the Strategic Studies Institute of the Army War College, the overall result of U.S. operations "has been a series of high-profile, marginally valuable kinetic strikes on suspected terrorists; affiliation with proxy forces inimical to U.S. policy goals; and the corrosion of African support for many truly valuable and well-intentioned U.S. endeavors."[56] And, as a recent Government Accountability Office report made clear, the "tactical" objectives are often far from effectively reached either.[57]

Again, however, this incoherence should not lead us to think that AFRICOM is innocuous, that is, so ineffective as to be irrelevant. Rather, the focus on moralized means in the absence of the ability to successfully and consistently realize specific ends, and the uncertainty concerning those ends, tends to help in the transformation of those means into an end in themselves. Because those means are military, the net effect of AFRICOM is a militarization of the U.S. presence in Africa, of African states, and of African societies, while further precluding the transparency or accountability of the transnational structures governing Africa. The expansion of the military becomes an end in itself, which can be deployed in the service of any of a number of agendas. Once underway, the process of militarization can begin to set the agenda itself, as interests and goals are limited and defined by available military means, leading to further expansion of militarized institutions and structures. As AFRICOM expands along with its associated blights, such as private military contractors, its own institutional self-interest, both governmental and private, will drive its expansion further. Militarization of previously civilian elements of U.S. presence—such as the embassies—only further strengthens the feedback loop. The strategic failure of AFRICOM to effectively realize any overarching agenda can set the stage for calls for its own reproduction and expansion and for the reproduction and expansion of militarization as a means without ends—and without end, without having to demonstrate success, its failure to realize its objectives taken to justify the need for even further expansion. AFRICOM takes its own expansion as its benchmark of success, and peace and security are equated with the presence of the U.S. military. Furthermore, AFRICOM's humanitarian moral justifications for intervention, in particular the War on Terror and human security, allow it to reject accountability or legal or political limitation.

2. AFRICOM in Practice

DENIABILITY

The U.S. decision to employ a flexible, often informal structure for AFRICOM around base-sharing agreements and without a significant concentrated troop presence reflects a number of different interests and conditions. It reflects the various interests behind AFRICOM: it can be explained as needed for rapid-response humanitarian deployments, counterterrorist operations against flexible terrorist networks, or "focused attacks, such as air strikes or airborne assaults against insurgents who threatened to interrupt oil supplies."[58] It can also be seen as reflecting the lack of overall strategic direction of U.S. policy, so that the determination of the actual shape and focus of AFRICOM is constantly being deferred.

As importantly, this flexibility and lack of permanent bases allows the United States and African states to avoid transparency and public opposition to Africa's militarization. The dependence on lily pads instead of formal bases allows U.S. officials and African governments to deny that the United States even has military bases in Africa. The controversy over AFRICOM's headquarters is symbolic of the U.S. approach: although at first, U.S. officials publicly sought a location in Africa to which to transfer AFRICOM's headquarters from Stuttgart, Germany, the resistance that proposal encountered led them to rethink their approach. They subsequently decided to retain the headquarters outside Africa while setting up Offices of Security Cooperation in a number of countries—what the Principal Deputy Under-Secretary of Defense for Policy termed "a distributed command," "networked" throughout Africa.[59] This informal approach has proved highly successful: regional bodies and African countries that were publicly opposed to AFRICOM have responded positively to the quieter approach and welcomed more discrete U.S. assistance.[60] General Ward has stated that AFRICOM has active programs in about 35 countries,[61] and at the end of 2009, AFRICOM had access to shared bases in at least a dozen African states, whereas few, if any, of those states would have allowed a permanent U.S. base on their soil.[62] These shared bases themselves represent only the most formal dimension of AFRICOM's flexible presence, which is further established through the widespread presence of U.S. advisers and trainers, development of surveillance systems, arrangement of regional security initiatives and task forces, and quiet forms of military assistance to states and non-state armed forces alike. This informality and lack of transparency is a direct threat to democracy in Africa—it reflects the mutual interest among the U.S. and the leadership of certain African states in increasing militarization while avoiding public scrutiny and democratic opposition. Once again, we see an alliance emerge between Western intervention and unaccountable African state elites as well as the tendency of intervention to increase those elites' lack of accountability. For this reason, sanguine claims that the American failure to find an African base for the command's headquarters represent a victory for resistance to AFRICOM need to be qualified by the recognition that the previous public approach of the United States has been replaced with an approach that is more dangerous precisely because it is less public and less subject to scrutiny.

Of particular importance to this informal, subcontracting approach is the expansion of the role of U.S. military contractors in American policy in Africa as the U.S. military tries to "reconcile the twin mandates of 'small footprint' with large mission."[63] Contractors, of course, allow U.S. interventions further flexibility, as well as even less transparency and accountability. The State Department in 2008 announced more than $1 billion worth of contracts in Africa for the next five years would go to up to four military contractors.[64] The absurdity of American-paid mercenaries being sent to teach Africans about human rights and good governance has not gone unnoticed, nor has the danger that their presence represents to democracy and peace.[65]

Given these conditions, this flexible, informal structure seems to be the path AFRICOM will take for some time to come. In what follows, I consider the political consequences of each of the three forms of intervention undertaken by AFRICOM, the three militarized means that the different policy agendas agree upon—building state security, humanitarian and development activities, and direct military action—even if they do not agree on the ends those means will serve.

MILITARIZED STATE-BUILDING

AFRICOM's objective of building state security capacity—whether in the name of helping states to control "ungoverned spaces," secure natural resources, fight terrorism, establish human security, or even capture war criminals—can be carried out under a wide range of different bilateral and regional military assistance and training programs and exercises. Some, like the East Africa Counter-Terrorism Initiative (EACTI), the Trans-Sahara Counter-Terrorism partnership, or the Operations Flintlock, are focused around fighting terrorism; some, like the Africa

Contingency Operations Training and Assistance Program (ACOTA), are focused around training for defensive and offensive military operations for peacekeeping; others, such as Operation Natural Fire 10 in Kitgum, are focused on humanitarian and natural disasters; and still others, such as the "presence operations" along the African coast, are focused on maritime security.[66] African states can also receive direct military aid, equipment, and training through a wide variety of programs implemented by AFRICOM. [67]

Critics have rightly noted that this form of aid can end up propping up dictatorships and undermining democracy.[68] Michael Klare and Daniel Volman point out that the types of multilateral and regional security training and capacity-building initiatives being carried out by the United States—"small unit manoeuvers, counter-insurgency, light infantry operations"—are perfectly suited for suppressing threats to oil installations and flow or in pacifying armed resistance to oil exploitation.[69] This militarized state-building, it is argued, also allows African states and militaries to easily instrumentalize U.S. assistance to their own interests.[70]

Uganda's relation to AFRICOM demonstrates the negative consequences that can stem from the various forms this militarized state-building program can take. Uganda has been the recipient of significant U.S. military assistance, which has waxed and waned but stands to increase further at present through three routes: first, U.S. funding for African-staffed peacekeeping operations, such as the mostly Ugandan AU deployment in Somalia; second, military support for African states to directly, without the mantle of the AU, pursue certain military objectives, such as the funding provided to Uganda to expand its presence throughout central Africa in pursuit of the LRA; and third, funding for humanitarian and disaster response operations, such as Uganda's Natural Fire 10.

First, U.S. assistance to African peacekeeping operations has often been framed as the most potentially beneficial dimension of AFRICOM, welcomed even by some commentators who are intensely critical of AFRICOM's other activities. The case of Somalia, however, reveals the problems with this form of U.S. support. It was an American-assisted Ethiopian invasion and occupation of Somalia in 2006 that drove out the Union of Islamic Courts, destroyed the modicum of stability they had established, and installed the extremely weak Somali Transitional Federal Government (TFG) in Mogadishu. As Ethiopia made clear its intention to depart, the African Union Mission in Somalia (AMISOM) gradually took over the duty of supporting the TFG, and since mid-2007, Ugandan troops have been upholding what little control is left to the TFG in the face of advances by al-Shabaab. In doing so, however, like the Ethiopian invasion before them, they have inflicted devastation on Somali civilians, provoking considerable resentment against their presence. The Obama administration has used AMISOM, and Ugandan forces in particular, to funnel arms to the TFG in contravention of the AU mandate and despite vociferous opposition from the Ugandan media and parliament.[71] The bombings in Kampala during the World Cup of 2010—apparently ordered by al-Shabaab—provided an opportunity for the Ugandan government to justify an expanded offensive military role in Somalia, and it was soon requesting U.S. support for 10,000 more Ugandan troops to be sent to Somalia as part of the erstwhile peacekeeping mission. Under the cover of supporting peacekeeping operations, the United States provides arms to the TFG, escalates the conflict, and pushes the U.S. military agenda, while the Ugandan government secures more U.S. military support and a firm justification for its own militarization. As usual, the price is paid by Ugandan and, especially, Somali civilians, and possible war crimes committed by Ugandan and Ethiopian troops with U.S. support are ignored or dismissed in the name of counterterrorism and peace. The United States promotes a cycle of militarization, radicalizing both its U.S. proxies and its enemies. The AU, meanwhile, sees its legitimacy diminished.

Second, the United States provides support to Uganda as part of the military effort against the LRA, whether in Southern Sudan, DRC, or CAR. This military funding is justified through a number of different claims, some moral and some political, including arresting Kony for the ICC, eliminating the LRA, rescuing abducted civilians, bringing Kony back to peace talks, and promoting regional stability and human security.[72] Some critics have identified hard U.S. interests behind this approach, namely, building Uganda's military in preparation for a possible return to war in Southern Sudan and securing access to DRC's natural resources. The most visible aspect of this support has been AFRICOM's involvement in Operation Lightning Thunder (OLT)—the December 2008 military operation carried out by the UPDF with U.S. assistance against LRA bases in DRC.[73]

The consequences of this form of militarized state-building can be devastating. African states can take advantage of the provision of external military support and step up violence against their own enemies. African militaries, with U.S. support, gain the incentive to polarize situations and provoke counterviolence so as to legitimate expanded militarization, while they lose the incentive to engage in negotiated solutions. AFRICOM also allows African states to moralize the violence they use under the cover of counterterrorism, peace, or even justice, releasing that violence from limitation. In the case of OLT, after the LRA escaped— evidently having been tipped off to the operation—it reacted by carrying out a series of brutal attacks on Congolese villages, killing hundreds of civilians and displacing tens of thousands. OLT led to further insecurity and instability in eastern DRC and South Sudan and to the militarization of communities in those areas, which, according to some commentators, made the LRA even stronger. However, because of the moralization of the use of force against Kony, these negative consequences are dismissed and neither the UPDF nor the U.S. government is held accountable.

AFRICOM can further avoid accountability by blaming its failures on its African partners, as it did in the wake of OLT. As significantly, AFRICOM's proponents take its failures as signaling the need for its expansion: instead of provoking a rethinking of militarization itself, the hundreds of dead Congolese, apparently representing the acceptable "collateral damage" of deepening U.S. military involvement, have been used to justify a call for a redoubled military effort to wipe out the LRA.[74] This was precisely the misguided lesson taken from OLT's failure by U.S. Senators Russ Feingold and Sam Brownback, egged on by American lobby groups such as Invisible Children, Resolve Uganda, and the ENOUGH Project, which will be discussed later.

The third mode through which AFRICOM provides military assistance to African states is joint humanitarian and disaster relief training exercises, such as Operation Natural Fire 10 hosted by the Ugandan government in Kitgum in October 2009. That operation included, according to an East African Community representative, training in humanitarian assistance, disaster-relief management, peace-support operations, counterterrorism operations, and crisis response, part of developing regional responses to "real and potential complex emergencies."[75] The U.S. Army web site was, as usual, even more vague about the purposes of the operation: "by building capacity within partner nations and increasing our ability to work together, US Army Africa will be better prepared for future engagements."[76] Although the U.S. government denied that Natural Fire was in preparation for possible operations against the LRA, critics and proponents alike presented that as Natural Fire's true motivation, pointing to the fact that the operation included live-fire training, crowd control, convoy security, and vehicle checkpoints.[77] Again, U.S. policy tends toward militarization at the international, national, and local levels, justified by multiple and ambiguous moral and political claims.

HUMANITARIAN AND DEVELOPMENT OPERATIONS

The humanitarian and development aspect of AFRICOM has taken center stage in its self-promotion, but thus far remains a limited part of its operations.[78] CJTF-HoA, for example, between 2003 and 2009 spent only $6.9 million on a total of 151 projects.[79] Nevertheless, the prominence of humanitarian and development activities and their potential to expand further, especially through crisis response training exercises, justify attention.

The importance of the humanitarian and development dimension of AFRICOM follows on wider trends within American military strategy. The Defense Department's 2005 Directive 3000.05, for example, termed "stability operations" "a core U.S. military mission that the Department of Defense shall be prepared to conduct and support. They shall be given priority comparable to combat operations." Stability operations were defined as activities "conducted to help establish order that advances U.S. interests and values. The immediate goal often is to provide the local populace with security, restore essential services, and meet humanitarian needs. The long-term goal is to help develop indigenous capacity for securing essential services, a viable market economy, rule of law, democratic institutions, and a robust civil society."[80] The expansive set of activities potentially falling under "stability operations"—such as economic development, human rights promotion, social capacity-building, state-building, peacebuilding, justice enforcement, gender protection, and rule of law promotion—are familiar from the total intervention agenda. Why this agenda should now come under the control of the U.S. military instead of being left to civilian agencies or NGOs is clarified by a proponent: "the military has an important role to play as a development actor. Its focus on countering threats to the United States makes it well-suited to performing development activities linked directly to security objectives, both in combat zones and in more permissive environments."[81] According to this argument, using the military allows development and humanitarian interventions to be closely tied to U.S. security concerns by way of AFRICOM's flexibility, lack of oversight, lack of accountability, significant resources, and ability to work in conflict zones. AFRICOM will normally work through and in conjunction with states, but it may also contract directly with "partners" at the substate level, where it is reported that "relevant communities are increasingly approached directly, as has become evident in new local participatory projects under the recent peace and security slogan."[82]

In northern Kenya, where such operations have been carried out by CJTF-HoA since the early 2000s, studies have questioned the success of these projects even on the most narrow, technical level, as it comes to appear that AFRICOM's military character—precisely what its proponents argue make it suitable for such projects—prevents it from having the expertise, capacity, or patience needed for successful community development. These projects have not led people to have better perceptions of the United States, nor have they established governance in ungoverned areas. Instead of building consent, the presence of the United States can provoke protest and resistance, often around fears about the U.S. military poisoning bore holes, using them to dump toxic waste, or poisoning animals.[83] Although many Kenyans evidently eventually adopted a pragmatic attitude toward the projects, they were under no illusion about whose interests had led the U.S. military there,[84] and they often declared that the U.S. presence was, if anything, making them less secure.[85] Once again, U.S. militarization, justified as bringing peace and stability, is perceived to fuel insecurity. The only strategic success CJTF-HoA did register was to help allow the U.S. military to establish a presence (in preparation for possible future "contingency operations") and gather some intelligence in those limited areas where resistance was not too great.[86]

In northern Uganda, for many years there was no open U.S. military presence. For almost the first two decades of the northern Uganda conflict, U.S. military involvement remained surreptitious, focused mainly on providing support through Uganda to the SPLA. However, by 2007 American marines were openly stationed in Kitgum, apparently with the cooperation of USAID, digging wells, vaccinating dogs, and undertaking other "humanitarian" activities. Many Acholi were confused over what the U.S. military was doing and why it was undertaking projects that NGOs could carry out more effectively. Many clearly understood, as a friend put it ironically, that U.S. marines vaccinating dogs in Kitgum illustrated the fact that some African dogs needed vaccinating more than others, and those roaming along the Uganda-Sudan border in the period leading up to the referendum in southern Sudan needed it the most.

Operation Natural Fire 10, conducted in Kitgum, exemplifies the dangerous consequences of the militarization of humanitarianism in Africa.[87] The operation had numerous purposes, among them getting Ugandans used to seeing and dealing with U.S. military. As a public relations officer at the American camp set up during the operation put it, "We want people to see the military as something other than soldiers. In the U.S. soldiers are seen as heroes. In Uganda they have much more fear, so we are trying to change that image. The intention is to blur the demarcations between civilian and military."[88] This is a frightening testament to the militarization of U.S. society, in which exporting American values now becomes equated with exporting the U.S. military. More immediately, it also shows how Natural Fire is conceived of as a public relations exercise both at the community level and at the international level, as a slew of human interest stories about the operation (including of an American nurse delivering a baby) were manufactured and disseminated. This normalization of the U.S. military presence may have a very immediate goal: according to reports, the United States is seeking tenders for a special-forces base in northern Uganda at present.

If its purpose really was, at least in part, to win hearts and minds, Operation Natural Fire appears to have been a failure. More extensive research is needed, but evidence provided by anthropologist Cecilie Lanken Verma shows the depth of resistance and anger that the militarization of services can provoke. She reports the military takeover of the Kitgum hospital, closing it off to regular patients so that people had to stand in line in the hot sun for hours or days—including those with serious illnesses, pregnant mothers, and so on—to get in. Of course, most did not. Verma reports people yelling at her and demanding answers, thinking she was part of the operation. In fact, the public relations officer Verma spoke to was particularly excited that AFRICOM had hit on the strategy of offering free health care in a devastated region as a way of creating the opportunity to practice crowd control techniques at the same time. Verma does not report open violence, but if people began protesting or rioting in reaction to the abuse being meted out on them by AFRICOM, it is clear that the military nature of the operation and its training in crowd control would quickly come to the fore.

Verma reports that the majority of comments she heard from Acholi were highly critical of the operation. As one person in Kitgum told her, "Whatever they say on the radio, I don't believe them. There is definitely something political which they are not telling. Bringing drugs to the people, no, it is not to be believed, really." An Acholi elder was thorough in his condemnation of the operation:

> I am holding the government responsible and I have asked the local coun-
> cilor to come and explain to us here how those people got permission to

use our homeland for their purposes. They have not explained that to us before they came and they have not asked for our permission, nor for our advice. It is very queer and I want them to explain. And if they are after our minerals, they should bring it out clearly. I don't trust our government and it is our government who invited the Americans. . . . If they want to bring medicine, why can't they bring it to our health centers and hospitals so that the services improve there? Why do they have to come and make a big show? Why must it be soldiers? Don't we have medical personnel from here? They come as if this is no man's land, ready for occupation. No, this is not no man's land. This is Acholiland!

The main consequence of these humanitarian and development operations, like much of U.S. policy in Africa, is militarization, this time of communities, services, and relief aid, with serious impacts on places where these militarized interventions take place. Even if the extent of these operations is limited, where they do take place AFRICOM directly incorporates administrative violence into its development and humanitarian activities, with the result that resistance becomes difficult and may be more likely to be met with violence. Protest against the destructive consequences of a U.S. military presence or against aid agencies working alongside the U.S. military can be seen as a challenge to the U.S. military, and peaceful civilian protest may become a target of administrative violence.[89] Whereas aid agencies can, if they see fit, refuse aid to uncooperative beneficiaries, or at most plead for external military support, military humanitarianism has its own guns to turn on recalcitrant "victims."

The militarization of relations between civilians and humanitarian or development actors can prevent political relations—let alone relations of accountability—from developing, which can set the stage for further violence.[90] The involvement of UN peacekeepers in prostitution rings and sexual exploitation enterprises in Kosovo, DRC, and elsewhere is only one of the more sensational aspects of this pathological disjuncture between humanitarian military forces and the populations they are supposed to serve. Former U.S. Army Colonel Ann Wright warned against deploying U.S. soldiers in the DRC, citing the high number of rape and violent sexual assault cases in the U.S. military and by U.S. military personnel against women and girls in areas around U.S. military bases.[91] As she stated, "If the women of the Congo should Google, 'U.S. military—sexual assault and rape,' I suspect they will decline the offer of assistance from the African Command." African gender-rights activists have also highlighted the potential for AFRICOM to undermine efforts to demilitarize African communities.[92]

AFRICOM's approach can militarize humanitarian and development interventions and the African communities where they take place. As Jeremy Keenan concludes, "While AFRICOM's commanders have been preaching 'security and development,' their operations on the ground have so far created insecurity and undermined democratic expressions of civil society."[93]

CONTINGENCY OPERATIONS

Direct military action by AFRICOM—what it terms "kinetic" or "contingency operations"—can take place under an array of moral and political justifications. Counterterrorism can be invoked in order to provide the use of force with a legitimacy beyond law. Peace is also a useful objective to claim: as a book published by the U.S. Institute of Peace explains, "defeating militant extremists" through a mix of "tried-and-true counterinsurgency methods with core principles derived from peace operations," in what it terms "fourth-generation peace implementation," can help "find, fix, and strike against the sources of violent obstruction to the peace process and to separate militant extremists from their popular support."[94] Human rights enforcement, either through the enforcement of ICC arrest warrants or through vague concepts like R2P, can also be used to justify the use of force, and these flexible justifications match AFRICOM's flexible militarization strategy well. Susan Rice, for example, has used R2P to argue for a U.S. bombing campaign against Sudan and the invasion of Darfur without Security Council approval. She admits, "some insist that, without the consent of the UN or a relevant regional body, we would be breaking international law. Perhaps, but the Security Council last year codified a new international norm prescribing 'the responsibility to protect.' It commits UN members to decisive action, including enforcement, when peaceful measures fail to halt genocide or crimes against humanity."[95] This ambiguity is seen even when Security Council authorization is obtained: Resolution 1973 of 2011, authorizing the attacks on Libya under the command and control of AFRICOM, invoked a hodge-podge of different justifications, including the "responsibility to protect," the need to end the "gross and systematic violation of human rights," and the demand that "those responsible for or complicit in attacks targeting the civilian population, including aerial and naval attacks, must be held to account" by the ICC, to which the Libya situation had been referred the previous month.

There are several specific situations in which AFRICOM may become more involved with direct military action in Africa. At the time of writing, the balance of forces that will emerge in North Africa remains to be seen, but AFRICOM's central role in the Libya campaign suggests that the direct use of military force may become more prominent there. CJTF-HoA provided assistance to the Ethiopian invasion of Somalia in 2006 via air strikes and special-forces attacks in the "kill zone" of southern Somalia and has been carrying out drone strikes and special-forces operations since, an effort that could increase further. Moreover, if war games are anything to go by, the Pentagon is making preparations for a potentially increased role in the Horn as well as in Nigeria.[96] The LRA Disarmament Act, depending on how it is implemented by the Obama administration, could also lead to AFRICOM's direct involvement in DRC, CAR, Uganda, and Sudan in the name of hunting down terrorists, protecting civilians' human rights, and enforcing ICC arrest warrants all at once.

One of the most dangerous aspects of this potentially increased use of force, whether justified in the name of human rights or counterterrorism, is that it will operate with impunity. Indeed, a certain affinity between counterterrorism and human rights enforcement becomes apparent when the consequences of employing them to justify military intervention are considered. Both terrorism and human rights violations are represented as being as threats to all humanity as well as threats to innocent civilians facing violence by absolute criminals, so both counterterrorism and human rights enforcement justify themselves as fulfilling universal moral values and as protecting civilians. Violence for the sake of eliminating terrorists or ending human rights violations claims a legitimacy beyond state sovereignty, and thus immunity from legal limitation. Security Council authorization may be deemed irrelevant to such force, as *jus ad bellum* restrictions are subverted by a discourse of the universal existential enemy who must be destroyed by whatever means are necessary.

Those who claim to use force against terrorists or human rights violators can thereby absolve themselves of responsibility for the consequences of that use of force. The humanitarian impunity that characterized UN intervention in Somalia in the early 1990s, where the UN claimed exemption from *jus in bello* and human rights standards and refused to be held accountable for its violence against civilians, could come to characterize AFRICOM's use of force as well.

The use of the absolute moral distinction between innocent, helpless victims, criminal predators, and sanctified intervener to justify the use of force leads to the disqualification and criminalization of any opposition to intervention.[97] Those resisting military intervention, even peacefully, may be seen as aligning themselves against the interveners and thus with the criminal predators, and so may find themselves targets of "legitimate" interventionist violence. This logic is seen at work when a UN official argued, concerning the UN's early-1990s Somalia intervention, "that it was illegal for Somalis to fire on UN troops, even in self-defense, because the latter were acting on behalf of the world's highest legal authority, the UN Security Council."[98] For their part, people who oppose, or even try or speak to, their self-appointed saviors find no channels for doing so—from their perspective, interveners cannot be reasoned with and only listen to the language of force. This corresponds to the situation described by Franz Fanon in which the colonizer, from the perspective of the colonized, understands only the language of violence.[99] So, when people rupture the victim identity in these highly militarized contexts, their only viable alternative may be to take up arms. That is, military intervention can leave civilians with the choice of demobilizing and playing the victim, or militarizing and joining armed factions. The ranks of armed groups can swell in response to military intervention as those who are to be "rescued" join the very groups they were to be rescued from and civilians act in the only way the interveners leave open to them in order to contest their self-proclaimed saviors. Nonmilitary power is degraded as military intervention militarizes politics.

This allows a *casus belli* to be built into the very use of force that occurs in the name of counterterrorism or human rights. By claiming to protect human life, either through abiding by certain humanitarian principles as part of population-centric warfare, or by purporting to protect the population from terrorists or human rights violators, intervening forces do away with the need to justify why they intervened in the first place because any resistance is categorically defined as terrorism or international crime. The *pro forma* criminalization of attacks on peacekeepers by the ICC, for example, means that any use of military force that claims to be for the sake of peacekeeping, by provoking resistance, will produce war criminals and thus its own supposed justification. Self-defense is criminalized and made into the justification for the original use of force being defended against. Similarly, resistance against American military aggression is defined categorically as terrorism and then used as proof that the invasion was needed in order to fight terrorism. In short, the consequences of violent intervention, the violence provoked by the intervention itself, paradoxically is used to provide a supposedly just cause for intervention. The result is a Catch-22 faced by those subject to military intervention: if they do not resist, they affirm the legitimacy of intervention through their supposed consent; if they do resist, they only prove that they are human rights violators, criminals, and terrorists, and thus were indeed in need of intervention. International military intervention—whether in the name of human rights, human security, or counterterrorism—can bootstrap itself into legitimacy as a just war, its supposed justice established through the criminalization of the resistance it gives rise to.

THE LRA ACT AND AMERICAN ACTIVISM

The potential for further direct U.S. military involvement has increased significantly with the LRA Disarmament and Northern Uganda Recovery Act, introduced in May 2009 and signed by President Obama on May 24, 2010. This act "Mandates President Obama to devise an interagency strategy within 180 days to prevent further LRA violence, which should include a multilateral plan to apprehend top LRA leaders, encourage defections of rebel commanders, demobilize child soldiers, and protect civilians from rebel attacks." The mandated strategy was revealed in late 2010, but did little to reveal precisely how that mandate would be implemented and whether direct U.S. military action, further military support to Uganda and other states, or alternative methods of eliminating the LRA would be pursued. If it does translate into increased direct or indirect military action, there are a number of potential dangers, in particular those concerning intervention's impact on peace and stability in the region. As African commentators and activists who will be directly affected themselves, including the Acholi Religious Leaders Peace Initiative and Riek Machar, the SPLA peace negotiator, have argued, military strikes will only further close off the possibility of a negotiated resolution to the conflict, lead to massive civilian casualties, and stand little chance of success even on their own terms.

As importantly, the LRA Act opens the way for increased, open-ended U.S. military involvement and further militarization of the region. After U.S. forces have set up bases or surveillance centers as part of an operation against the LRA, it will be easy for that military presence to remain long after the actual "enforcement" operation has ended. Once U.S. drones are circling overhead hunting terrorists or ICC suspects, these drones could easily keep circling, collecting intelligence and carrying out "targeted assassinations" when required. This danger is increased by the fact that these contingency operations may be carried out, not by uniformed U.S. soldiers, but by U.S.-contracted private security firms.

The LRA Act, as noted in the introduction to this book, represents the culmination of the Uganda conflict's ascendance in U.S. public consciousness and the consecration of the official discourse on the conflict at the highest levels. It also represents the tragic ascendance of militarism in the U.S. public consciousness.[100] The result is that the act fits in perfectly with AFRICOM's agenda, for, as Senator Feingold put it, the effort to stop the LRA is "exactly the kind of thing in which AFRICOM should be engaged."[101] President Obama's statement upon signing the act makes this even clearer:

> I signed this bill today recognizing that we must all renew our commitments and strengthen our capabilities to protect and assist civilians caught in the LRA's wake, to receive those that surrender, and to support efforts to bring the LRA leadership to justice.
>
> [...]
>
> I commend the Government of Uganda for its efforts to stabilize the northern part of the country, for actively supporting transitional and development assistance, and for pursuing reintegration programs for those who surrender and escape from the LRA ranks.
>
> I congratulate Congress for seizing on this important issue, and I congratulate the hundreds of thousands of Americans who have mobilized to respond to this unique crisis of conscience.
>
> We have heard from the advocacy organizations, non-governmental organizations, faith-based groups, humanitarian actors who lack access, and those who continue to work on this issue in our own government.
>
> We have seen your reporting, your websites, your blogs, and your video postcards—you have made the plight of the children visible to us all. Your action represents the very best of American leadership around the world, and we are committed to working with you in pursuit of the future of peace and dignity that the people who have suffered at the hands of the LRA deserve.

Two dimensions are worthy of note. First, Obama's statement reflects the typical jumble of different rationales used to justify military intervention, including bringing the LRA to justice for the ICC, rescuing child soldiers, ending the LRA's reign of terror against innocent victims, bringing peace and stability to central Africa, and assisting responsible states, such as Uganda, which is particularly commended for its efforts. If further U.S. military intervention fails to realize any one of the specific goals set out for it—say, it fails to usher in peace and stability—it has a number of other justifications to fall back on. Moreover, the moralization of the use of force against the LRA will be used to put that force beyond question or accountability.

The second dimension to be noted is Obama's praise for the advocacy and lobbying effort that went into getting the act passed—the "hundreds of thousands" of Americans who, according to him, have "made the plight of the children visible"—evidently a reference to the group Invisible Children. Indeed, the act could not have passed without significant lobbying, in particular by Invisible Children, Resolve Uganda, and the ENOUGH Project. These groups managed to build a significant movement mostly among American high school and college students, calling on the U.S. government to help end the war preferably by capturing, or perhaps killing, Joseph Kony. In the words of a joint statement by Resolve Uganda and the ENOUGH Project, "The United States military has strong ties to the Ugandan military and has assets based nearby at the U.S. military base in Djibouti. The incoming Obama administration should provide greater intelligence and logistical support and should consider direct support to, and collaboration with, Ugandan forces on the ground in direct action against the LRA."[102] This is an open invitation to AFRICOM.

The most prominent of these groups is Invisible Children, a group that grew up around a movie made by three young men from San Diego about Gulu's "night commuters." Invisible Children quickly became a significant national movement with a budget of millions of dollars, concentrated on high school and college campuses, and focused on "rescuing" the "invisible children" forcibly recruited by the LRA. Studies of Invisible Children are forthcoming, but a brief consideration of their mobilization strategy here is worthwhile for what it says about the popular U.S. approach to Africa and the militarization of that approach. According to a sociologist who has studied the movement, what has made Invisible Children so successful is the way it has created the opportunity for young, privileged, almost exclusively white, Americans to "do something" while also "feeling special."[103] Invisible Children's adherents are told that they are helping to solve one of the world's most pressing tragedies, that it is their personal responsibility to do so, and that they can do so with no sacrifice on their part beyond putting on parties and fund raisers with their friends. The hard work, patience, and frustration that accompany working for social or political change are forgotten in Invisible Children's slick, feel-good marketing videos. It invokes the ideology of the innocent child victim in need of white Americans for his or her redemption—and thus offers young privileged Americans, perhaps feeling guilty over their own consumerism, to redeem themselves as well, without having to substantively change their lifestyles—in fact, they can save Africa by indulging even further in consumerism and digital entertainment.

The group's focus on fund-raising among privileged young people has been extraordinarily successful, and the funds allow the group to produce ever more self-advertising. Invisible Children is thus characterized by a triumph of advertising over information,[104] and there is no effort made to recognize the politics or history of the Ugandan conflict. The original movie, *Invisible Children: Rough Cut*, provided no history, no reason about why people were living in camps and why children lacked protection and had to flee to town at night, reveling instead in decontextualized images of suffering and crying Acholi children.[105] In a particularly revealing moment, images of child soldiers from Sierra Leone are presented as being of child soldiers in Uganda.[106] Evidently, all African children look the same—they look like victims in need of rescue.

The Invisible Children movement would have remained simply another testament to the typical self-indulgent and irresponsible American approach to Africa, with little damage beyond steering a generation of white, privileged American youth away from recognizing their own responsibility for causing violence and suffering around the world, if the group had not decided to get directly involved in U.S. policy making. Together with the Washington, DC-based Resolve Uganda, and guided by key figures in the ENOUGH Project, Invisible Children decided to direct their massive youth base toward pressuring U.S. Congress to pass the LRA Disarmament Act (reportedly written by a former employee of Resolve Uganda, then on Senator Feingold's staff).

At this point, American activism around Uganda turned from farce to tragedy. Using militarized language and images, it took upon itself the task of pressuring the U.S. government to intervene militarily and help capture or kill Joseph Kony and the LRA leadership. In one of their videos, Invisible Children's Jason Russell and Laren Poole declare that the war can be ended by making "a plan to arrest Joseph Kony while limiting the casualties to the child soldiers. It's possible. We have the technology, we have the intelligence, we have the resources," while images flash on the screen of U.S. helicopter gunships and the CIA logo.[107] The history of the CIA in Congo is totally lost on these "activists," as is the possibility that some people may not see the CIA or U.S. helicopter gunships as forces for good. Invisible Children, like Save Darfur before it, is not a peace movement but a war movement—but it is not war *against* an African state that they demand, as does Save Darfur, but war *by* an African state, Uganda, in conjunction with international military assistance, to rescue child soldiers from the war criminal Joseph Kony's evil grasp. If Uganda cannot carry out the needed military operations on its own, then perhaps drone strikes and special-forces operations are required.

It is a tragedy that student mobilization, in the midst of ongoing violent U.S. occupations and militarization around the world, is itself calling for more violence, and that peace is thought to be possible only through more war. It is a tragedy that U.S. military power is being presented as the solution to Africa's problems, and that the horrible destruction wreaked by such thinking in Afghanistan and Iraq is being forgotten. And the greatest tragedy is that it is Africans who will pay the price for this American self-righteousness, even as many peace groups in northern Uganda call for an end to the military approach.[108] This U.S. activism ignores and silences those around the world calling for an end to devastating U.S. military interventions and mocks those victims of U.S. military violence so that self-righteous American youth can feel that they are saving helpless victims. The idea that a student "peace" movement takes as its goal further U.S. militarization shows just how dangerous the savior complex can be. It shows the danger of building activism around simplified moral narratives and decontextualized images of suffering, because that activism, having no critical perspective on the subject, can be easily manipulated toward violent and destructive ends by more savvy political operators. This type of activism is the antithesis of genuine solidarity, the possibility for which I explore in the next, and final, chapter.

8

Beyond Intervention

This book has argued that the dominant Western concept of human rights in Africa—Africa as a terrain of permanent human rights crises that require expansive and intensive interventions for their resolution—informs interventions that can lead to the entrenchment of antidemocratic states and political forces, depoliticize African citizenries, and facilitate and mediate international forms of inequality, domination, and violence, all with destructive consequences that may include enabling, prolonging, or intensifying the very conflicts, violence, and injustices the interventions claim to resolve. To contest this antidemocratic, interventionist, and often counterproductive deployment of human rights in Africa, I want to return to Issa Shivji's call, made over 20 years ago, for the development of concepts of human rights that will serve a politically emancipatory role in Africa's current historical and political context instead of helping to entrench injustice. Shivji himself emphasized the emancipatory potential of the rights to organization and self-determination in order to combat African authoritarianism and foreign interference through legitimating and mobilizing democratic, anti-imperialist political action.[1]

In today's neoliberal Africa, characterized by multiple forms of disciplinary depoliticization and militarization, Shivji's emphasis on the human rights to organization and self-determination as a route to justice and democracy still resonates. In this chapter, I first argue that a broadened right to organization can underpin processes of democratic politicization, even in the face of transnational administration and violence. From there, I argue that the right to organization implies the right to self-determination and requires a shift from sovereignty as responsibility to popular sovereignty. These anti-interventionist reconceptualizations of human rights and sovereignty also imply the need to reconceptualize peace. Peace is not a matter of imposing a static model of social, political, legal, or cultural order on Africa, of pacification and stabilization, but rather of opening up social, political, legal, and cultural orders to democratic determination. Social and political order are to be made subject to different demands for justice, and thus justice itself is realized through this ongoing process of inclusive mobilization and action.

Finally, violence needs to be reconceptualized. Just as interventionist human rights discourses are associated with a particular image of violence in Africa, in which that violence is indigenous and politically meaningless, the anti-interventionist concept of human rights developed here is associated with a transnational understanding that foregrounds existing Western responsibility for political violence instead of absolving the West of accountability. Based upon this, I argue that the dominant practice of the West toward Africa should be one of constructive disintervention, one of ending Western intervention, for the sake of human rights. I offer two qualifications to this agenda of disintervention, however. First, given the reality of episodes of extreme violence in Africa, during which questions of respecting self-determination and self-organization may become somewhat insignificant relative to the need to end mass violence, I leave space in this general disinterventionist agenda for a practice of humanitarian intervention focused on the cessation of hostilities—an Africanized practice within specific limits and made legally accountable. Second, given the reality of common political problems faced by Africa and the West, I leave open the possibility of a limited form of solidarity, what I call solidarity with consequences, which is based on the possibility of organizing and acting politically, but always self-critically, when faced with common struggles that bridge the Africa-West divide.

1. Human Rights and Popular Sovereignty

FROM INTERVENTIONIST TO DEMOCRATIC HUMAN RIGHTS

A foundation for a democratic, noninterventionist concept of human rights can be found in Claude Lefort's 1980 "Politics and Human Rights," which makes a strong argument for human rights as a foundation of democratic politics. Lefort attempts to refute Marx's classic denunciation of human rights as amounting to no more than the legal embodiment of egoistical, bourgeois man. Lefort, instead, argues that Marx ignores those rights that, rather than implying egoistical, monadic man, imply man's capacity to think, communicate, and act with others. That is, while Marx focuses his attack on the rights to private property and security, he ignores the rights to freedom of opinion, speech, assembly, and organization, essential to democratic politics. These latter rights, instead of isolating individuals, carve out a public space for collective opinion formation and action and "point to a sphere which is ineffaceably external to power."[2] They establish the legitimacy of and freedom for collective action and for thought itself in the face of power and have the capacity to bring people together as freely communicating individuals oriented toward common goals.[3]

Lefort expands on the importance of human rights for democratic politics, arguing that "Rights cannot be dissociated from the awareness of rights."[4] That is, human rights work by providing a language that allows people to understand themselves as rights-bearing agents, thus giving shape and legitimacy to their struggles. As people come to see themselves in this way, they begin a process of inclusive politicization that cannot be reversed. Lefort represents the struggle for human rights as a struggle over the preconditions for democratic politics. By demanding their rights, people are not only demanding the space in which they will be able to enjoy these freedoms, but, in the very act of making those demands, they are *doing* what is to be guaranteed by the right itself. Human rights become both form and content of democratic organization and action: the right to the freedom of speech is won through speaking freely; the right to organize is won through organization. The dissemination of the language of human rights not only catalyzes the struggle for those rights whose guarantee is the formal foundation of independent thought and action, and thus of democracy, but also leads, through the struggle itself, to the actualization of that independent thought and action which is the concrete foundation of democracy.

This democratic concept of human rights is characterized by a focus on rights that imply relationships among people, such that human rights are about collective deliberation and action, not about individual testimony or external provision of goods or protection. The agency for demanding rights comes from organized collectives whose rights are to be guaranteed in common, by the oppressed against their oppressors, and not "claimed" by those who take an interest, however genuine, in alleviating the suffering of others. Rights claims are not directed toward an unaccountable, ideologized "international community," but rather toward building political communities and then toward those institutionalized sites that retain a degree of responsiveness due to their dependence upon the people for legitimacy and authority. As long as international institutions have only a philanthropic relationship with people in the South, they are unaccountable politically and have no compulsion to respond, and so the nation-state remains the only political institution in which that compulsion can be found, however attenuated it may be as a result of states' reliance upon violence and donor support.

These rights can be effective even in the context of internment camps, where, despite disciplinary depoliticization and violence, rights can help create the conditions for inclusive political community. Where there is a radical depoliticization through violence and administration, civil and political rights may serve a transitional purpose and help construct the bridge from the human without political community to the human as part of a political community by bootstrapping legitimate political organization into existence. Human rights activists might help by making available noninterventionist human rights discourses that can find fertile ground among, for example, emergent youth groups or women's groups. It is perhaps counterintuitive that the very rights that seem least needed in conditions of war and displacement because they make no immediate promises as to physical well being—the rights to freedom of speech, assembly, and so on—may be the most effective in ultimately ensuring that security and well being. In northern

Uganda, this democratic human rights discourse may possibly help contribute to the democratization of Acholi society and the resolution of the internal crisis, the mobilization of political action on the national level, the accountability of the Ugandan state, and resolution of the national crisis, and to countering increasing transnational militarization. Those subject to intervention can also contest the experiments in social engineering being perpetrated upon them by foreign agencies by establishing alternatives legitimated in the language of human rights. This reorientation will encounter significant resistance from many sides, for these rights are not only inimical to insurgency and counterinsurgency, but are also inimical to the work of the interventionist organizations who want docile and disciplined populations to rescue or to reconstruct into "normal" subjects.

FROM SOVEREIGNTY AS RESPONSIBILITY TO POPULAR SOVEREIGNTY

The right to organization is important, but will have little meaning if that organization is subject to foreign interference or if the African state from which demands are made is insulated from democratic pressures by foreign support. This is where the right to self-determination comes in, offering the guarantee that these democratic processes of organization and action will be independent and will have at least a chance to be effective. As Michael Walzer explains, citing John Stuart Mill's argument against foreign intervention, self-determination is a necessary (but not sufficient) precondition for political freedom:

> We are to treat states as self-determining communities, he argues, whether or not their internal politics are free, whether or not the citizens choose their government and openly debate the policies carried out in their name. For self-determination and political freedom are not equivalent terms. The first is the more inclusive idea; it describes not only a particular institutional arrangement but also the process by which a community arrives at that arrangement—or does not. A state is self-determining even if its citizens struggle and fail to establish free institutions, but it has been deprived of self-determination if such institutions are established by an intrusive neighbor.[5]

The right to self-determination is the right to organize and act politically without outside interference, for a political community to win its own victories and make its own mistakes. It denies the idea that it is up to the West to decide when Africa needs intervention and when Africa can be safely left to practice politics on its own, which African states are responsible and can be allowed to reform internally and which are irresponsible and can only be reformed through external coercion. As such, self-determination is the precondition for a life of political and social dignity. To quote Walzer again, "the citizens of a sovereign state have a right, insofar as they are to be coerced and ravaged at all, to suffer only at one another's hands."[6]

Just as it is illegitimate to interfere with the political processes going on within a state, so is it illegitimate to interfere with states themselves, whether by supporting or coercing them. As Walzer puts it, "of course, not every independent state is free, but the recognition of sovereignty is the only way we have of establishing an arena within which freedom can be fought for and (sometimes) won."[7] Sovereign inviolability is, thus, essential for meaningful political life because it protects the most important formalized site—the state and its institutions— within which the people can express themselves in a meaningful way. Any foreign interference threatens the relevance of internal movements for political reform.

The concept of sovereignty as responsibility, therefore, should be replaced by popular sovereignty, which provides the best protection for these democratic processes. Popular sovereignty demands sovereign inviolability but also qualifies the prerogatives of the state over its own people by recognizing the people's constituent power to introduce reform or revolutionary change themselves, from within—exactly what sovereignty as responsibility denies. Boutros Boutros-Ghali was correct when he declared that the time of absolute sovereignty had passed—but it did not pass with the end of the Cold War and the inception of a new U.S.-led global interventionism; rather, it had passed over two centuries ago when peoples in different parts of the world declared that sovereignty was theirs and not the king's. In this spirit, sovereignty and political agency cannot be represented as the exclusive purview of the externally supported African state—and of the West when it deems the African state irresponsible. Instead, they reside in the people, in citizenries of African states. This would require the recognition that the state is not simply an administrator but is a political body, and that human rights abuses do not leave people agency-less victims but rather often spur people on to act politically.

Placing popular sovereignty at the center of the Western approach to Africa would help redress the dangers of human rights intervention. First, since popular sovereignty is a matter of the people having ultimate control over the state, it would reveal as antidemocratic and illegitimate those state-building interventions that proceed at the cost of democratic accountability or that create repressive security states, especially those that take place in the name of sovereignty and support unaccountable state elites. Second, because popular sovereignty requires state inviolability as its precondition—it is the terrain upon which popular sovereignty can be exercised—invoking popular sovereignty cannot provide a justification for coercive foreign interventions that violate African state sovereignty in the name of human rights. Finally, since popular sovereignty is founded upon and realized through the autonomous political organization and action of the people, the right to organize, those interventions that interfere with domestic politics, including those in the name of promoting democracy, human rights, or civil society, would be delegitimated, because popular sovereignty cannot and does not provide an excuse for interfering with internal politics, and the external promotion of political autonomy is a contradiction in terms.[8]

BEYOND AFRICA AS CRISIS

In order to develop a framework for a Western approach to Africa beyond intervention, based upon the rights to organization and self-determination, and regulated by the principle of popular sovereignty, there is a need for a new understanding of the causes of conflict and violence in Africa. This new understanding would break from the still-dominant post–Cold War image in which conflict in Africa is indigenous and politically meaningless, an image that implies that the West has withdrawn from Africa and is innocent of causing or contributing to conflict there, and, consequently, that the West only relates to Africa through a humanitarian model. According to this image, the West is a guiltless observer of suffering in Africa, but simultaneously is the only actor with the ability to resolve Africa's crises, which are too deep and paralyzing for Africa to resolve itself.

Instead of this image, there is the need to recognize how conflict in Africa has often been intensified, prolonged, and even caused, not by Western withdrawal and apathy, but by Western intervention itself. Much of the West's intervention in Africa today follows well-worn patterns, such as providing military aid to client regimes or engaging in the destructive exploitation of Africa's resources. At the same time, new forms of intervention have emerged in the post-Cold War period that go under the guise of peace and justice, the War on Terror, or structural adjustment, and that can take place in the name of the ICC or R2P. We must stop pretending that Western intervention in Africa is a practice of saving strangers in which action directed toward alleviating suffering caused by war is a sacrifice on the part of the globally privileged, a positive duty of assistance undertaken only because we deign to admit a shared humanity. Instead, we must understand historically how suffering and deprivation caused by war in Africa are being perpetuated and aggravated because of unjust political arrangements at the national level that are entwined with unjust structures and patterns of domination at the international and global levels—how Western intervention is *already* taking place. Rainer Forst emphasizes the multilayered nature of this "transnational injustice," in which the context of injustice is "a complex system of power and domination with a variety of powerful actors, from international institutions to transnational corporations, local elites, and so forth. Shifting perspective to that of the dominated, then, reveals that theirs is one of *multiple domination*."[9]

In northern Uganda, two areas can be delineated in which the decentralized global system of power, multiple domination, and transnational injustice upheld by states and citizenries in the West has prolonged and aggravated the war. This helps counter the dominant narrative, which maintains that the war in Uganda continued as long as it did because of Western neglect and apathy. First, the evisceration of democracy in Uganda and the consequent perpetuation of the war in the north have been driven on by international politics, within which the Ugandan government has been able to position itself so as to gain access to significant foreign support. This has occurred in particular through the dominance of neoliberal economics and the American War on Terror, but has also proceeded through the ICC and other forms of intervention. Neoliberalism and the War on Terror, mediated by national political structures, have produced patterns of domination and injustice within which the citizens of Uganda, especially in the north, were systematically divested of their ability to hold their state accountable. Second, as I have argued, the war in northern Uganda was able to continue, and the camps, in particular, were sustained, only due to extensive donor funding and the work done by Western nongovernmental and international agencies. These foreign interveners, including the Western aid workers running the interventions, donors who contribute, directly or indirectly, to those organizations, as well as the groups and individuals that propagate the dominant image of the conflict, all, directly or indirectly, helped to prolong the war and suffering in northern Uganda.

The Ugandan case is by no means an exception in this regard, since conflicts elsewhere have taken highly destructive forms precisely because of their deep interpenetration with international and global regimes and processes, some of which, ironically, are justified as helping to resolve conflict and alleviate suffering—or, in the past, to bring civilization and development. Thus, the West is not an innocent witness to the violence and suffering caused by the civil war in Uganda. Rather, the West's policies and the global political institutions the West has imposed—along with the history of domination and injustice—make us in the West causally and morally responsible for the perpetuation and aggravation of violence and its attendant suffering.[10] The West has been deeply involved in the conflict there for decades, despite Jan Egeland's declaration in 2003 that it was a "forgotten emergency." This understanding of the causes and politics of conflict in Africa allows us to draw different lessons from the signal event leading up to today's agenda of total interventionism—the Rwandan genocide. Instead of seeing the genocide as the product of the failure of the West to intervene, we should look at the Western interventions that were *already occurring* in Rwanda that helped set the stage for the genocide.[11] Therefore, the lesson of Rwanda for the West would not be that more Western intervention is needed in Africa, but, rather, that constructive Western disintervention is needed so that ongoing Western intervention does not unintentionally or intentionally set the stage for political violence.

2. Disintervention and Beyond

DISINTERVENTION

According to the dominant discourse on human rights in Africa, the West has a positive duty to intervene there to help resolve conflicts and end episodes of violence that are not of its making but that threaten everyone's shared humanity and security. However, given this alternative understanding of the causes of violent conflict in Africa, in which those conflicts are deeply imbricated with already existing Western intervention, the West's primary moral duty is not the positive moral duty to assist (indeed, I have pointed out the very counterproductivity of these efforts), but rather the *negative* moral duty to stop what we are doing now and to try to adjust international institutions and arrangements, formal and informal, so as to promote a more just global political order, one that values democracy and autonomy.

Western human rights practice in Africa should thus be premised upon a recasting of intervention itself toward a focus upon its negative duties. That is, instead of human rights practice being focused upon interventions intended to rescue humans from violence, it should be focused upon terminating existing contributions to the processes that are prolonging that violence and undermining the political autonomy of those living in situations of violence. Instead of a practice of human rights intervention, this would be a practice of human rights disintervention. The West first needs to look to itself and ask what it is already doing that is causing conflict in Africa, how it is already intervening in destructive ways, and then end those interventions instead of pretending that international intervention is the panacea for indigenous African conflict. The problem is not too little intervention as some proponents claim, but too much intervention that closes off the political space in which Africans can exercise their political agency in a meaningful way and in which democratic organization and action can have a fighting chance of having a political impact on the state. It is disintervention, not intervention, that can promote political accountability and responsibility.

Disintervention, I want to make clear, is not a call for an immediate and total withdrawal of all Western involvement, but rather a negotiated withdrawal based upon a delineation of the West's current responsibility for violence and suffering with an eye to the termination of harmful practices to which Western states and citizenries contribute. This embodies a cosmopolitan morality only in the thinnest sense, a recognition that those who cause harm to others, anywhere in the world, have a moral duty to cease doing so.[12] Beyond that, it is a call for the gradual political, legal, and moral delinking of Africa so as to provide to those experiencing injustice and violence the space needed for politics.[13] Disintervention should begin with an admission of already existing Western responsibility as a countermeasure to the dehistoricized, self-aggrandizing, and self-exculpating "responsibility" of such doctrines as the Responsibility to Protect.

The proposal for disintervention also allows the idea of prevention to be recast. Extreme violence in the future may well be prevented by demilitarizing and de-escalating Western involvement and ending destabilizing and distorting interventions. This approach to prevention can help avoid the problems inherent in trying to put forth a set of criteria that would determine when coercive intervention should occur to deal with extreme violence: the question, "What do 'we' do in case of genocide?" gives rise to dilemmas because it tries to provide a set of rules, whether based in morality or in objective criteria, to encompass the exception, but it cannot avoid leaving the decision on the exception open to politics. Therefore, instead of trying to prevent genocide by codifying a consistent set of objective criteria for humanitarian intervention—an impossibility—the exceptional can be dealt with by laying out practical policies applicable in normal times that prevent the exceptional from arising. These policies, however, would not comprise an attempt to place all of Africa under a totalizing regime of Western intervention, as the total intervention agenda claims to do, but would strive to prevent mass atrocity in the future by disintervening today.

Although I argue that disintervention should underpin the Western approach to Africa, I do not mean that sovereign inviolability should be held to be absolute. In the remaining pages, I argue that this disinterventionist concept of human rights provides space for two types of reconfigured interventionist practice in Africa: the first is a practice not of Western but of African intervention in cases where mass atrocity needs to be halted; and the second is a practice not of Western intervention but of tentative and self-critical solidarity between Africa and the West.

AFRICANIZING COERCIVE INTERVENTION

Michael Ignatieff argues that, although the tendency of human rights language to cast politics in non-negotiable and absolute terms makes it a poor tool for regular politics, in cases of genocide or other cases of mass atrocity the non-negotiable nature of human rights becomes a strength because it requires those with the ability to do so to refuse compromise and intervene forcefully.[14] That is, while the moralization and absolutization that human rights effects in the political realm are usually damaging, in certain truly exceptional cases, normal political concerns cease to matter and the political pathologies that coercive intervention may introduce are immaterial relative to the good it will do, at which point consequentialist reasoning has to be abandoned. Walzer is on similar ground when he argues that it is meaningless to talk about the political harm that a political community may incur as a result of intervention when the very existence of that political community is at stake.[15] In these cases, he argues, "it is their very incapacity that brings us in," and intervention can help salvage the precondition for politics itself.[16]

The problem, of course, is that Ignatieff's designation of situations in which a moral demand trumps politics, or Walzer's designation of situations in which the very existence of a political community is at stake, in practice will always be dependent upon a political decision, despite the fact that those decisions would have to be determined by formal moral or empirical criteria in order to be legitimate. No existing institution has shown itself to be a responsible guide to situations in which the time for politics, deliberation, and compromise is over—UN organs, the media, and various self-appointed representatives of global civil society or the conscience of mankind, including most recently the ICC, have all tried but instead demonstrated only their inescapable politicization and irresponsibility.

In cases of coercive interventions in Africa, some scholars and activists have argued that African institutions should make the decision to intervene and undertake the intervention, in particular through the AU. This might help address accusations of neocolonialism and the use of humanitarianism as a justification for Western aggression. Also, regionalizing the decision to intervene creates the possibility that interventions could become subject to a modicum of accountability to those in whose name they take place. This is because Africans in some way have to live with the consequences of their interventions in Africa, whereas the UN and the West do not, and so they avoid even the possibility of being accountable to Africans. According to Mamdani, the difference between the UN and the AU is that "practically every country in the African Union can see itself in Darfur's shoes, and that makes a world of difference."[17] AU interventions of course also need to be held accountable to the laws of war and human rights standards, so that the problem of humanitarian impunity can be addressed.

This proposal solves some problems but only displaces others. The most common accusation against the AU, that it is a "club of dictators" who will fail to intervene because they do not want to invite criticism of their own behavior, is based upon the questionable presumption that the Security Council's permanent five members or American "coalitions of the willing" would somehow arrive at more just decisions than would the AU concerning where and when to intervene in Africa. A more relevant critique is that the AU will lack independence and become a proxy for U.S. military intervention, much as the AU mission in Somalia and the numerous regional counterterrorism security arrangements appear to be. Indeed, AU security bodies stand little chance of being effective without Western (or perhaps increasingly Chinese) aid, and that aid will not be provided without conditions. Ultimately, these problems can be addressed only through the democratization of the AU and its member states, and so, in the interim, there is no guarantee that the AU will be more effective or accountable than other options. Nevertheless, I would emphasize the point that at least the possibility exists that AU intervention can be made accountable to Africans, whereas even the possibility of accountability is absent from military intervention originating from outside the continent.

TRANSNATIONAL JUSTICE: SOLIDARITY WITH CONSEQUENCES

Finally, there is the question of the possibility of solidarity between Africa and the West replacing Western intervention in Africa. Solidarity, I argue, is a means toward transnational justice, where justice is rescued from the international criminal justice model, disaggregated from depoliticizing notions of "global justice" or "local justice," and embodied instead in coordinated political action by citizens struggling in their own states against common forms of transnational injustice.

The foundation for this solidarity between Africa and the West, this acting together, is by no means clear. Cosmopolitans might assert a solidarity among all humanity and argue that the "human community" is thick enough so as to equalize individuals and enable solidarity across global divides. However, as I have argued throughout this book, the insistence on a universal human community as the basis for intervention only obscures the existing imbalance between intervener and subject of intervention, absolves the intervener of responsibility for causing or perpetuating suffering, and gives a carte blanche to the intervener to act however he or she sees fit in "solidarity" with the suffering human. Some writers on global governmentality have claimed that both intervener and subjects of intervention face equivalent forms of globalized biopower or sovereign power and, thus, all can participate equally in a global "struggle for and on behalf of alterity."[18] Mark Duffield argues for "the rediscovery of politics in the practical solidarity of the governed," based upon the claim that "We are all governed and therefore in solidarity."[19] However, the assertion of an abstract community of "the governed" or, in Hardt and Negri's term, the "multitude," provides no more purchase for political organization and action than does the equally thin category of "humanity." To argue that the West intervenes "in solidarity" with Africans based on common humanity or subjection to governmental or sovereign power only effaces the history of Western violence in Africa and the foundation of Western privilege upon that history.

None of these forms of proclaimed community between intervener and those subject to intervention can escape the fact that the interventionist encounter itself inherently prevents the development of relations between equals because of the fundamental unaccountability that characterizes the role of the intervener. The Western intervener can afford to be unaccountable because the consequences of intervention are borne unequally—that is, the consequences are all borne by Africans. That is the core of the intervener's privilege, the privilege not to have to face any consequences for one's actions. Some have argued that this relation of inequality can be overcome by instituting genuine, non-instrumental communication between the parties.[20] However, this non-instrumental communication is inherently impossible within the interventionist encounter, because that encounter necessarily involves an instrumental relation between the two parties: the intervener engages in dialogue with the subject of intervention instrumentally in order to realize strategic objectives, that is, a more effective form of intervention, thus rendering impossible encounters oriented purely toward gaining mutual understanding.

Therefore, solidarity between citizens of African states and Western states would require both undoing the Westerner's lack of accountability and creating noninstrumental encounters, encounters that are, paradoxically, nevertheless motivated by political commitment and instrumental to achieving the political objective of solidarity. Westerners' privilege in Africa can be remedied to some extent if they work to ensure that they *do* have to live with the consequences of their actions. This can be achieved not by increasing the risk one faces "in the field," because that only leads to masochistic adventurism and does not address the fundamental issue that one can still go home.[21] Rather, this privilege can be partially remedied by working on issues that *have consequences at home*—consequences that one has to live with and that make it impossible simply to run away. By addressing specific forms of transnational political injustice to which citizens in the West are also subject, a concrete grounding for solidarity may be found to replace the patronizing reference to a common humanity that tends to inform intervention today. This grounding can be found in actually existing, concrete problems that Westerners and Africans both face. By working on those mutual concerns, Westerners in Africa would come to have to live with the consequences of their actions and be somewhat accountable for what they do in the name of Africa, because they would also be doing it in their own name within their own political communities.

This reorientation would help remove the instrumental dimension from the encounter between Westerners and Africans, while maintaining the political commitment that motivates it, because Western activists would be engaging with African activists and trying to understand their situation, *not* so as to act strategically upon those African interlocutors, but precisely so as to understand what they all have in common, to understand common problems and struggles. If that encounter is oriented only toward finding common ground, toward establishing mutual understanding so that Westerners can then go home and work on those common problems, then "responding to the appeal of the other" in a noninstrumental manner at least becomes a possibility.[22]

The War on Terror, and, more broadly, militarization, provide an exemplar of these common concerns. The consequences of the War on Terror have been similar for Africans and those in the West: illegal and destructive wars, securitization of the state, criminalization and persecution of certain ethnic and religious groups, arbitrary detentions, criminalization of dissent, evisceration of civil liberties, and the expansion of unaccountable, arbitrary state power. Americans, in particular, who want to help promote peace and justice in northern Uganda should work to end the War on Terror, specifically by challenging the legitimacy of the actions taken in the name of combating terrorism. In doing so, Americans also challenge the political repression they and their fellow citizens face from their own government, challenging their own government at home. The consequences of this kind of solidarity cannot be escaped through a plane flight back to the United States—in fact, the risks may increase once back home where, instead of deportation, prosecution under vague and far-reaching material support provisions may loom.

Human rights can help provide a transnational language for this solidarity, drawing on a model of human rights proposed by Malcolm X in his speech, "The Ballot or the Bullet."[23] Human rights can provide a link, he said, to bring together those working on common problems across global divides, bringing together people of color across the globe facing American imperialism and capitalism. Perhaps today, given the massive, immediate threats to human life posed by transnational violence and global capitalism, new human rights discourses may develop to provide a basic shared content for new forms of politics. Human rights may provide one common language linking struggles transnationally so that citizens can demand national reform more effectively. This pursuit of transnational justice based in a democratic human rights discourse could ground a practice of *solidarity with consequences*, which refuses the unaccountability that defines the dominant model of Western human rights practice in Africa.

Indeed, these proposals for solidarity fly in the face of the dominant model of Western intervention, a model that has behind it billions of dollars, an enormous administrative apparatus, significant international political interests, military force, and endless promises of peace, justice, prosperity, and salvation, both for Africans and for Westerners. As such, it is no surprise that the dominant model appeals powerfully to people's desires in the West and in Africa. However, this dominant model is also founded upon a basic lie—the lie that says that Africans are helpless victims who can be saved only through Western intervention. The alternative proposed here rejects this lie and demands instead the recognition of people's capacity to act for themselves. As such, it offers the possibility—but only the possibility and never the guarantee—of peace, but only through people's own organization and action. It is one attempt to navigate the question of realizing justice in a global order that denies large parts of the world the fundamental dignity that makes us truly human.

ACRONYMS

AFRICOM	United States Africa Command
AMISOM	African Union Mission in Somalia
ARLPI	Acholi Religious Leaders Peace Initiative
AU	African Union
CAR	Central African Republic
CJTF-HoA	Combined Joint Task Force-Horn of Africa
DP	Democratic Party
DRC	Democratic Republic of Congo
HSM	Holy Spirit Movement
HSMF	Holy Spirit Mobile Forces
HURIFO	Human Rights Focus (Gulu)
ICC	International Criminal Court
IDP	Internally Displaced Person
IMF	International Monetary Fund
KKA	Ker Kwaro Acholi
LDU	Local Defense Unit
LRA/M	Lord's Resistance Army/Movement
MSF	Médecins Sans Frontières
NGO	Non-governmental Organization
NRA/M	National Resistance Army/Movement
NRC	Norwegian Refugee Council
NURP	Northern Uganda Reconstruction Program
NUSAF	Northern Uganda Social Action Fund
OLT	Operation Lightning Thunder
R2P	Responsibility to Protect
RC/LC	Resistance Council/Local Council
SPC	Special Police Constable
SPLA/M	Sudan People's Liberation Army/Movement
TFG	Transitional Federal Government (Somalia)
UN OCHA	United Nations Office for the Coordination of Humanitarian Affairs
UNC	Uganda National Congress
UNHCR	United Nations High Commissioner for Refugees
UNICEF	United Nations Children's Fund
UNLA	Uganda National Liberation Army
UPC	Uganda People's Congress
UPDA	Uganda People's Democratic Army
UPDF	Uganda People's Defence Force
WFP	World Food Program

NOTES

Introduction

1. Finnström 2008.
2. Mudimbe 1988; Lindqvist 1997.
3. Bauman 2004.
4. Dolan 2009.
5. Atkinson 2010; for an account that puts more emphasis on changing politics among the donors, see Perrot (2010).

Chapter 1

1. Shivji 1989.
2. For an exposition of this new understanding of the state, see Chandler (2006, ch. 2).
3. Deng and Zartman 1991.
4. Deng et al. 1996, vii.
5. Ibid., 211.
6. Furley 1995; Harbeson and Rothchild 1995.
7. Annan 1998, para. 10.
8. Collier and Hoeffler 2000.
9. The New Partnership for African Development (NEPAD) is perhaps the most important African expression of the connection between the exclusion from globalization and poverty.
10. Castells 2000, 164–65.
11. Ibid., 82–83.
12. This conception is critiqued forcefully in Zeleza (2003, 3).
13. Annan 1998, para. 12.
14. Ibid.
15. Furley 1995, 1.
16. Deng et al. 1996, xiii.
17. Boutros-Ghali 1995, para. 10.
18. Ibid., para. 13.
19. Ibid., para. 12.
20. Annan 1998, para. 3.
21. The most prominent American example is the film *Invisible Children: Rough Cut* (Jason Russell, Bobby Bailey, and Laren Poole, directors. United States, 2003).
22. Kaplan 1994. An antidote to this discourse on the LRA is provided by Chris Dolan, who argues that the rebels were in fact *un*exceptional (2009, 92–97).
23. Collier and Hoeffler 2002.
24. Keen 1998, 47; see also Keen (1997).

25. Annan 1998, para. 3.
26. Ibid., para. 29.
27. Ibid., para. 5.
28. Deng et al. 1996, 27.
29. Ibid., 222.
30. Quoted in Boutros-Ghali (1996, 33).
31. Chopra and Weiss 1992.
32. Thakur 1995, 22.
33. Chopra and Weiss 1992, 116–17.
34. Ibid., 110.
35. Weiss and Minear 1993a, vii.
36. Weiss and Minear 1993b, 61. See also Minear, Weiss, and Campbell (1991, 36–42), and Bettati (1991).
37. Chopra and Weiss 1992, 108.
38. Ibid., 95.
39. Ibid., 117.
40. For a discussion of the context and importance of *Agenda for Peace*, see Burgess (2001).
41. Boutros-Ghali 1995, para. 17.
42. Ibid., para. 3.
43. Quoted in Patman 1995, 92.
44. Kaldor 1999, 111.
45. Mamdani 2009, 296.
46. For an early critique, see Lewis, Maksoud, and Johansen (1991). See also Chomsky (2000).
47. Chomsky 1993/1994; Falk 1993/1994.
48. Slim 2002, 14.
49. Douzinas 2007, 189.
50. Ibid., 190.
51. Schmitt 1996, 54. See also the account provided of this position in Pugh (2002).
52. Calhoun 2004.
53. Hirsch and Oakley 1995, 35–47; de Waal 1997a, 159–204; Clarke and Herbst 1997.
54. UNSC Resolution 794 (1992), preambular para. 3, para. 12.
55. United States Department of State 1994.
56. Ibid., 813.
57. Power 2002, ch. 10.
58. Annan 1998, para. 11.
59. Boutros Ghali 1995, para. 13–17.
60. Ibid.
61. Annan 1998, para. 48.
62. Ibid., para. 47.
63. Ibid., para. 2.
64. Deng et al. 1996, 194.
65. Lund 2001, 16. For the key critical accounts of this expansion, see Chandler (2002), Duffield (2001a), and Richmond (2002, 2005).
66. For an account of intervention's expanding focus on all forms of instability, see Duffield (2007, 24–27).

67. For contemporary versions of the idea of a "trap," see Collier et al. (2003), and Sachs (2006).

68. Deng et al. 1996, 194.

69. Ibid., 223.

70. Chandler 2006; Kennedy 2005.

71. For a collection exploring the connections between human rights and conflict, see Mertus (2006).

72. For the "right to peace," see Said and Lerche (2006).

73. Slim 2002, 14.

74. Quoted in Fox (2002, 30).

75. Quoted in Fox 2001, 278.

76. Some analysts have characterized this as a shift from "traditional" humanitarianism to "new" humanitarianism; see Fox (2001), and Macrae and Leader (2001).

77. Curtis 2001, 15–16; see also Fox (2001, 2002).

78. Duffield 2001, 317. For an example of this tendency, see the "Key Performance Indicators" listed by the World Bank for NUSAF (World Bank 2002, 2–3).

79. Confidential interviews with NGO employees by author, Gulu District, February–March 2003.

80. Boutros-Ghali 1995, para. 89.

81. Annan 1998, para. 70.

82. Deng et al. 1996, xii.

83. Mamdani 2009, 300.

84. Duffield 2001a; Hardt and Negri 2000.

85. Duffield 2007, 158.

86. Bouris 2007.

87. de Waal 1997a, 136.

88. Marriage 2006; Maren 1997.

89. My understanding of this dimension draws on the approach of James Ferguson in the *Anti-Politics Machine* (1994).

90. For descriptions of these kinds of networks emerging through intervention, see the edited collection by Callaghy, Kassimir, and Latham (2001).

91. Chandler 2002, ch 4.

92. de Waal 1997a, 138.

93. For "governance states," see Harrison (2004). For proponents of such state-forms in state-building see Ghani and Lockhart (2008), and Call (2008); for critical approaches, see Chandler (2006), and Bickerton, Cunliffe, and Gourevitch (2007).

94. For the former, see Kaldor (1999), and Paris (2004); for the latter, see Hardt and Negri (2000). Chandler (2009) exposes the common ground between these supposedly opposed accounts.

95. Paris 2004, 209–10; see also Chopra and Hohe (2004).

96. Duffield 2007, 34.

97. Rahnema 1992; see the extended discussion in chapter 4 below.

98. Abrahamsen 2004a.

99. This radical politics of participatory development is articulated by Hickey and Mohan (2004); it is applied to refugees in Doná (2007).

100. White 1996, 9.

101. Paris 2004, 209.

102. Deng et al. 1996; for the emphasis on market democracies, see Call (2008).

103. Some argue that the state still has not been brought back in enough; Ghani and Lockhart, for example, argue that intervention today, despite its commitment to state capacity building, still "tends to undermine rather than support state institutions" (Ghani and Lockhart 2008, 98).

104. Deng et al. 1996, xiii, 213.

105. Ibid., 221.

106. Ibid., xviii.

107. Ibid., 28.

108. The presumption of this failure is made clear in ibid. (xii–xiii).

109. Mamdani 2009, 296.

110. Chatterjee 2004.

111. Speed 2008.

112. Malkki 1995, 237.

113. Comaroff 2007.

114. Fassin 2007; Robbins 2009.

Chapter 2

1. Mamdani 1996, 103.

2. Ibid., 24.

3. Ibid., 43.

4. Ibid., 41. For an account of the colonial order in Lango and its relation to pre-colonial order, see Tosh (1973).

5. Behrend 1999, 14–19; Atkinson 1999, 269–70.

6. Among classic accounts, see Girling (1960), p'Bitek (1971), and Crazzolara (1937).

7. *Moo* is an Acholi word meaning, in this case, oil, referring to the oil with which the *rwodi* were anointed, to distinguish them from the chiefs appointed by the British. See Finnström (2008, 42).

8. Atkinson 1999, 75–78.

9. Girling 1960, 100.

10. Ingham 1958, 120–21. Girling concurs, writing that the Acholi *rwodi* were unable or unwilling "to act as chiefs in the Government's sense of the word" (1960, 111). Although Atkinson attributes significant powers to the *rwodi*, he too describes in detail the limitations on the power of the *rwodi* and the system of balanced powers and counterpowers that existed among the region's chiefdoms (Atkinson 1999, 103, 84–95).

11. Kabwegyere 1995, 63–67.

12. Behrend 1999, 15.

13. Finnström 2008, 40–42; Girling 1960, 84–85.

14. Girling 1960, 9; Finnström 2008, 67.

15. Adimola 1954.

16. Gray (1951–52) provides a general history of this period.

17. For the history of legal instruments of native administrations, see Burke (1964, 36–41), Richards (1960, chs. 7 and 10), and Mamdani (1996, ch. 3). For post-colonial history, see Robertson (1982).

18. Sathymurthy 1986, 343.
19. Atkinson 1999, 262; Bere 1955.
20. Girling 1960, 9.
21. Kabwegyere 1995, 40; see the discussion in Finnström (2008, 37–61).
22. Burke 1964, 143; Gertzel 1974, 17.
23. Mitchell 1939; quoted in Sathyamurthy (1986, 339).
24. Girling 1960, 84; Gertzel 1974, 17; Bere 1955, 50–51.
25. Quoted in Sathyamurthy (1986, 339).
26. Mamdani 1976, 192–95.
27. Sathyamurthy 1986, 343. See also Hailey (1957, 292–98), and Gertzel (1974, 15–23).
28. Mamdani 1976, 52.
29. Ibid., 133.
30. Gertzel 1976, 12.
31. Mamdani 1976, 154; Leys 1967, 50.
32. Mamdani 1976, 46.
33. Quoted in Gertzel (1976, 12).
34. Leys 1967, 49; Sathyamurthy 1986, 341.
35. Leys 1967, 49.
36. Kasfir 1976, 110.
37. Leys 1967, 93.
38. Mamdani 1976, 208–9.
39. Ibid., 151, 154.
40. Ibid., 205.
41. Kasfir 1976, 183, 185; Finnström 2008, 91.
42. Mamdani 1996, 105.
43. Gertzel 1976, 60.
44. Ibid., 22.
45. Ibid., 23.
46. Leys 1967, 29–30.
47. Ibid., 11.
48. Gertzel 1976, 62.
49. Ibid., 67.
50. Ibid., 66.
51. Ibid., 68.
52. Sathyamurthy 1986, 344.
53. Ibid., 395.
54. Bere 1955, 8; see also Finnström (2008, 83).
55. Political party lines cut across clan lines, and often trumped clan (Leys 1967, 16). See also Kayunga (1995, 81–89), Gingyera-Pinycwa (1972), and Low (1962).
56. Gingyera-Pinycwa 1978, 195–214. See also Robertson (1982, 29).
57. Mudoola 1996, 105; Finnström 2008, 99.
58. Sathyamurthy 1986, 451.
59. Richards 1982, 33–34.
60. Kasfir 1976, 212.
61. Leys 1967, 31.
62. Sathyamurthy 1986, 429–35.

63. Ibid., 441.
64. Mamdani 1976, 273, 291.
65. Karugire 1980, 196.
66. Mamdani 1976, 270.
67. Omara-Otunnu 1987, 51.
68. Ibid., 81–85.
69. Mudoola 1996, 97.
70. Sathyamurthy 1986, 449.
71. Ibid., 535–43.
72. Omara-Otunnu 1987, 87–91.
73. Omara-Otunnu 1987, 87–91; Mutibwa 1992, 71–72; Mudoola 1996, 103.
74. Omara-Otunnu 1987, 104, 133–36; Mamdani 1976, 303; Mamdani 1984, 42–43; Mutibwa 1992, 88; Sathyamurthy 1986, 615.
75. Mutibwa 1992, 108; Sathyamurthy 1986, 613, 644–45.
76. Mamdani, 1984, 45.
77. Omara-Otunnu 1987, 110.
78. Ibid., 125–26.
79. Mutibwa 1992, 88.
80. Kasozi 1994, 121.
81. Mutibwa 1992, 153.
82. Omara-Otunnu 1987, 149–51.
83. Mutibwa 1992, 137; Kasozi 1994, 176–79.
84. Mutibwa 1992, 161.
85. Museveni 1997, 123.
86. Ibid., 125–32.
87. Kuperman 2004, 66. For a history of Tutsi refugees in Uganda, see Watson (1991), and Mamdani (2001, 160–66).
88. Mamdani 1996, 200.
89. Ibid., 200–201; Museveni 1997, 134.
90. Mamdani 1996, 208.
91. Ibid., 209.
92. Gingyera-Pinycwa 1989, 53. The idea that the NRA, and Museveni in particular, were primarily motivated by anti-Northern, and especially anti-Acholi, sentiment in launching their rebellion is an article of faith among many Acholi political leaders in Uganda and those in the diaspora. This can also mesh with the idea of a Bahima/Tutsi conspiracy led by Museveni, the object of which is to re-create an empire across central Africa, and whose obstacle was the pre-1986 Northern domination of the Ugandan state and army. Much has been made of Museveni's November, 1985 interview with Nairobi-based *Drum* magazine, where he stated that the "political mess" in Uganda was a result of misrule by northerners and called for unity among Bantu speakers in response; in Museveni's words, "The problem in Uganda is that the leadership has mainly been from the north. The southerners who are mainly Bantu have played a peripheral role all these years since independence in 1962" (*Drum Magazine [East]*, October 9, 1985). Dani Nabudere (2003) is one such critic. Kampala-based Refugee Law Project plays down the relevance of this interview, pointing out that it is invoked so frequently by critics because it is the *only* instance where Museveni made this claim so explicitly (Refugee Law Project 2004). The

supposed existence of an anti-Northern agenda among the NRA has been hotly contested by its supporters (Museveni 1997; Museveni 1986; Mutibwa 1992, 154–55; Amaza 1998, 23–38; Ngoga 1998, 91–106; Prunier 1998). For academic treatments, see Clark (2001) and Jackson (2002).

93. For the importance of anti-Northern sentiment in the mobilization of the Baganda peasantry, see Finnström (2008, ch. 2), Okuku (2002, 23), and Omara-Otunnu (1987, 176).

94. Finnström 2008, 74.

95. Mamdani 1996, 208–9.

96. Ibid.

97. Mutibwa 1992, 161.

98. "NRA, Okello Forces fight for Karuma Falls," *Weekly Focus*, February 7, 1986.

99. "Bazirio, [*sic*] forces evacuate Kitgum, Arua Towns," *Weekly Focus*, March 11, 1986.

100. "NRA completes liberation struggle," *Weekly Focus*, March 27, 1986.

101. Behrend 1999, 24, 28.

102. Behrend 1998, 109; Pain 1997, 48; Amaza 1998, 62; "War gets rough in the North," *Weekly Focus*, February 18, 1986.

103. Gingyera-Pinycwa 1989, 1992.

104. Omara-Otunnu 1987, 177.

105. Ibid., 178.

106. Confidential interviews by author, Gulu Town, November 2005.

107. For an early reference to the RC system in Acholiland, see "Crisis in the North: Government Officials also to Blame," *Weekly Topic*, September 17, 1986.

108. Museveni 1997, 177.

109. "Gulu: The Legacy of War," *Financial Times*, August 23, 1986; "NRA soldier goes on shooting spree," *Weekly Focus*, April 18, 1986.

110. Behrend 1999, 25; Doom and Vlassenroot 1999, 13–14.

111. "Four NRA killed in Kitgum," *Financial Times*, July 8, 1986.

112. "Insecurity grips Gulu, Kitgum," *Financial Times*, August 14, 1986.

113. "Rebels harass NRA," *The Citizen*, [n.d.] August 1986; "Thugs Terrorise Gulu, Kitgum," *Financial Times*, June 19, 1986.

114. Gersony 1997, 21–23; Amnesty International 1989, 1991.

115. "Museveni explains situation in Northern Uganda," *Focus*, February 27, 1987; "NRA Sweeps North," *New Vision*, September 16, 1986.

116. For the idea of the NRA representing an external enemy, see Behrend (1999, 23–26).

117. "Violation of Human Rights: Govt's credibility is at stake," *Citizen*, September 26, 1986; see also "Amnesty complains of NRA atrocities," *Weekly Topic*, November 4, 1987; "Atrocities shake N. Uganda," *Citizen*, September 5, 1986.

118. "Govt. troops intensify operations," *Focus*, December 19, 1986.

119. "N. Uganda: Okeny petitions Museveni," *Citizen*, December 7, 1988; Gersony, 12; "People kill, burn rebels in the North," *Star*, March 25, 1987.

120. "Gulu witnesses brutality and atrocity," *Weekly Topic*, December 2, 1987; Dolan 2000; Finnström 2008, 71–74.

121. Confidential interviews by author in internment camps in Gulu District, March 2003; "Horror in Gulu: A personal account," *Weekly Topic*, February 25, 1987; "Govt. troops close Catholic Mission in Northern Uganda," *Focus*, December 5, 1986.

122. "Gulu: The Legacy of War," *Financial Times*, August 23, 1986.

123. See the communiqué released by the Uganda Goodwill Mission after their trip to Sudan to consult with the UPDA in "Why Gulu–Kitgum rebels are fighting," *Weekly Topic*, May 13, 1987; see also "Allimadi is imposter," *New Vision*, April 7, 1987.

124. In February, according to one account, there were ten major rebel groups ("Horror in Gulu: A personal account," *Weekly Topic*, February 25, 1987).

125. "Northern rebels now turn against each other," *Focus*, January 30, 1987.

126. Allen 1991, 378.

127. Omara-Otunnu 1992.

128. "Fighting continues in Lira and Apac," *New Vision*, March 21, 1987; Behrend 1999, 67–71.

129. Ibid., 85.

130. "Rebels launch attack on Gulu," *Focus*, July 17, 1987; Allen 1991, 372–73.

131. Behrend 1999, 85–87; "Kenya becomes rebels' rear base," *Weekly Topic*, August 26, 1987.

132. Tim Allen characterizes the HSM's violence against civilians as widespread (Allen 1991, 373).

133. Behrend 1999, 67–68.

134. Ibid., 70; "Rebel Alice Lakwena sends warning to Mbale," *Focus*, September 4, 1987.

135. "Tororo people take up arms against Lakwena," *Weekly Topic*, October 14, 1987; "Rebels from Lakwena-Otai meeting cause panic in Tororo town," *Focus*, October 16, 1987; "Rebel Lakwena forces regroup for counterattack," *Focus*, October 6, 1987.

136. See "Lakwena attacks Magamaga," "Foreign press meets Lakwena," "Interview with a rebel," and "Lakwena not a military threat," *New Vision*, October 26, 1987; "Lakwena affair proved that people are the best soldiers," *Weekly Topic*, February 3, 1988; Behrend, 1999, 92–93; Mamdani 1995, 50–52.

137. This is subject to much speculation; for the most comprehensive treatment, see Finnström (2008).

138. "A footnote to Lakwena debacle," *Weekly Topic*, January 27, 1988.

139. "Was NRM taken for a ride in N. Uganda?" *Citizen*, August 29, 1988.

140. Lamwaka 2002, 31; see also Dolan (2009, 97–102) on the government's tendency to provoke the LRA. On negotiations between Kony's forces and the NRA in Gulu, see "Holy Spirit talks continue," *New Vision*, April 16, 1988; and "NRA, UPDA in final talks," *New Vision*, April 11, 1988.

141. Behrend 1999, 173–74.

142. Lamwaka 2002, 32–33.

143. Ddungu 1989; Salyaga 1986; Mamdani 1995, 32–62; Oloka-Onyango 2000.

144. Etori 1987.

145. More rebels respond to amnesty," *Focus*, January 12, 1988; "Army, RCs relations deteriorate in Gulu," *Guide*, May 10, 1990; "'Anti-Lakwena' dismissals hit Gulu," *Citizen*, June 14, 1989.

146. "Holy Spirit smashed in Kitgum, Latek flees to Sudan," *New Vision*, November 22, 1988.

147. For an explication of this dilemma, see Branch (2005b).

148. "Holy Spirit smashed in Kitgum, Latek flees to Sudan," *New Vision*, November 22, 1988.

149. "Bloody 'battle' at Koch Goma: Peace disrupted again," *Weekly Topic*, March 9, 1988.

150. Allen 1991, 378; Dolan 2009, 86; Titeca 2010.

151. "Kony still in Kitgum," *New Vision*, July 5, 1991.

152. Finnström 2008, ch. 3; Dolan 2009, 83–85; "Gulu in big panic: Kony fights for multipartyism," *New Vision*, March 6, 1996; "Kony rebels hold political rallies," *Sunday Vision*, April 14, 1996; "Kony rallies OK, says Ssemogerere," *New Vision*, April 16, 1996; "Kony rebels vow to take part in May elections," *Monitor*, April 22, 1996.

153. "Civilians escape Gulu rebels," *New Vision*, February 19, 1991.

154. Editorial, *Weekly Topic*, January 11, 1991.

155. "Rebels promote Latek," *New Vision*, November 1, 1988. For reports on NRA violence, see "Amnesty concerned at reports of killings in the North," *Weekly Topic*, December 14, 1988; for the failure to protect the Acholi civilians, see "100,000 displaced in Gulu," *New Vision*, November 14, 1988; and "NRM officials narrowly escape rebel attack," *Citizen*, May 3, 1989. See also "NRA mops up in the North," *New Vision*, March 18, 1989, which reports that the NRA troops in the area want the war to continue because of "operational allowances" and because they see it as intra-Acholi violence. For genocide, see "N. Uganda: Okeny petitions Museveni," *Citizen*, December 7, 1988, where Okeny states that the NRA's "scorched earth policy" in Acholiland appears to many Acholi civilians to be "the implementation of the often publicly uttered statements by high ranking NRM officials to exterminate a people." The fact that the NRA felt it had to defend itself against these accusations speaks to the accusations' broad appeal: see "Holy Spirit enters Kitgum," *New Vision*, November 16, 1988, where an NRA officer argues that, "The government troops are not out to wipe the Acholi. Some civilians believe that the government troops are in a sort of campaign to wipe them out."

156. "Calm restored in Gulu," *New Vision*, July 21, 1989; "Peace returns to Gulu: What next?," *Weekly Topic*, September 20, 1989.

157. "Rebels in Kitgum hack 43 to death," *New Vision*, April 11, 1990; "Over 300 feared killed in Gulu crossfire," *The Guide*, April 27, 1990; "NRA, DA accused of rights violation in Gulu," *Guide*, August 2, 1990; "Of civilians trapped between the army and rebels," *Weekly Topic*, December 13, 1990; "Civilians escape Gulu rebels," *New Vision*, February 19, 1991.

158. Behrend 1999, 188.

159. "NRA mops up in the North," *New Vision*, March 18, 1991; "NRA launches search operation in the North," *New Vision*, April 3, 1991.

160. "Lira radios seized," *New Vision*, April 4, 1991.

161. "Kitgum DA replaced," *New Vision*, April 6, 1991; "Atubo arrested," *New Vision*, April 17, 1991.

162. "Gulu gets Easter 'panda gari,'" *Weekly Topic*, April 12, 1991.

163. *Citizen*, April 24, 1991, gives details abuses of detainees, dozens killed, scores tortured, looting, and rapes by the NRA.

164. "Museveni refutes brutality claims," *New Vision*, May 14, 1991; see also "Minister, CMs in court for treason," *New Vision*, May 6, 1991.

165. "3000 rebels netted in Kitgum," *New Vision*, May 14, 1991.

166. "Tinyefuza welcomes Red Cross," *New Vision*, May 15, 1991.

167. "Kitgum forms peoples' battalions," *New Vision*, May 17, 1991; "Gulu forms 'arrow' battalions," *The Economy*, June 4, 1991.

168. Behrend 1999, 189; "Kitgum stabilizes," *New Vision*, July 30, 1991.

169. "Kitgum rebels burn 14 in hut," *New Vision*, June 4, 1991.

170. "Kony still in Kitgum," *New Vision*, July 5, 1991.

171. "Gulu assured of unity, peace," *New Vision*, June 12, 1991.

172. "Over 1500 rebels killed," *Weekly Topic*, August 9, 1991.

173. "Tinyefuza ends Operation North," *New Vision*, July 30, 1991; "Word of advice to Betty Bigombe," *Weekly Topic*, July 26, 1991.

174. "Rebels massacre over 60 civilians," *Guide*, October 24, 1991.

175. "Where tears and pain never seem to end," *Weekly Topic*, September 20, 1991.

176. "Rebels massacre over 60 civilians," *Guide*, October 24, 1991.

177. Confidential interviews by author, Kampala, February 2003; Gulu District, April 2003.

178. "Kony rules revealed," *New Vision*, February 14, 1992.

179. O'Kadameri 2002. See also Dolan (2009, ch. 4).

180. "Kony wants UN role," *New Vision*, February 22, 1994.

181. "Bigombe, rebels meet in forest," *New Vision*, December 1, 1993; "Spirits give green light: Kony to meet Museveni," *Daily Topic*, January 13, 1994; "Museveni and Kony, make peace," *Monitor*, February 25, 1994; "Kony rebels reject Museveni's ultimatum?," *Monitor*, February 18, 1994.

182. "Kony rebels minor problem—Museveni," *New Vision*, February 25, 1994.

183. "Atrocities in Northern fighting: Secrets of NRA-Kony war exposed," *Monitor*, March 11, 1994; see also "Blood, tears flow in Gulu war," *Monitor*, March 29, 1994.

184. Johnson 2003.

185. "Museveni and Kony, make peace," *Monitor*, February 25, 1994; Amaza 1998, 136.

186. "Kony intransigent," *New Vision*, March 23, 1994; "Kony gets new foreign arms supply," *Monitor*, July 15, 1994; "Sudan disowns Kony," *Daily Topic*, August 3, 1994.

187. "Five civilians killed," *New Vision*, March 15, 1994.

188. "Kony rebels get better weapons," *Sunday Vision*, March 20, 1994.

189. "Kony abducts boys for Sudan military camps," *Monitor*, October 19, 1994; "Kony flees to Sudan confirms Brig Shef Ali," *New Vision*, November 3, 1994.

190. "SPLA executes Kony prisoners," *New Vision*, January 18, 1995; "Terror as rebel mines blow up 23," *Monitor*, February 15, 1995.

191. "Disband Kony rebels, Museveni tells Sudan," *New Vision*, May 3, 1995; "Why has NRA failed to finish off Kony," *Monitor*, May 12, 1995; see also "Let someone take Kony as cheap labour," *Monitor*, May 8, 1995, in which Museveni blames the war on Sudan's intention to export Islam throughout the continent.

192. Slavery was a popular theme among American supporters of the SPLA, and the Ugandan government perhaps hoped to tap further into American support; see "Kony abducts Children," *New Vision*, February 20, 1995; "Slavery returns: Sudanese dealers buy 110 Ugandan kids," *New Vision*, February 7, 1995.

193. "Gulu attacks spread," *Daily Topic*, February 23, 1994; "Kony rebels burn minister's Pajero," *New Vision*, February 23, 1994; "Fighting erupts in Gulu," *Daily Topic*, February 21, 1994; "Rebels abduct women," *New Vision*, May 13, 1994; "Kony abducts 50," *New Vision*, May 14, 1994; "Havoc as Kony goes for RCs," *Daily Topic*, May 25, 1994.

194. "Kony rebels burn minister's Pajero," *New Vision*, February 23, 1994; "Kony rebels play soccer," June 18, 1994.

195. Finnström 2008, ch. 3; Dolan 2009, ch. 4.

196. "LRA rebels to honour ceasefire—spokesman," *New Vision*, April 28, 1996.

197. "Gulu in big panic: Kony fights for multipartyism," *New Vision*, March 6, 1996; "Kony rebels hold political rallies," *Sunday Vision*, April 14, 1996; "Kony rallies OK, says Ssemogerere," *New Vision*, April 16, 1996; "Kony rebels vow to take part in May elections," *Monitor*, April 22, 1996.

198. Finnström 2008, 162.

199. "SPLA fighters kill 36 Kony rebels," *New Vision*, November 3, 1995; "SPLA rescues 100 children," *New Vision*, November 7, 1995.

200. "Kony supporters are demoralized—Bigombe," *New Vision*, December 12, 1995; "Itongwa, Kony finished says Maj. Gen. Mugisha Muntu," *Monitor*, December 8–11, 1995.

201. "Kony rebels enter Uganda," *New Vision*, February 13, 1996; "Kony attacks Kitgum," *New Vision*, February 15, 1996.

202. "Kony wants to disrupt elections," *New Vision*, February 17, 1996.

203. "Museveni telling lies about Kony?," *Crusader*, February 23, 1996; "Can Shefe Ali bring peace to Acholiland?," *The People*, February 21, 1996; "Sifting truth from hollow lies on Kony," *Monitor*, February 23, 1996.

204. "Kony rebels hit Gulu," *New Vision*, March 30, 1996; "Museveni rejects Kony peace talks," *New Vision*, March 15, 1996.

205. "Huge demos planned against Govt, Kony," *Monitor*, March 13, 1996.

206. "Kony rebels plan attack," *New Vision*, May 29, 1996; "200 rebels on rampage as PM Kintu enters Gulu," *Monitor*, June 7, 1996.

207. "Saleh announces North offensive," *New Vision*, June 20, 1996; "No more talks with Kony—Saleh," *Crusader*, July 18, 1996.

208. Museveni's official decree ordering the creation of the camps came out in September 27, and wide-scale forcible displacement began on October 2 (Human Rights Focus 2002, 11).

209. World Food Program (WFP), Emergency Report no. 41, October 8, 2004.

210. Acholi Religious Leaders Peace Initiative 2001, 8–10; Human Rights Focus 2002, 16–24; "Leave Protected Villages—Lagony," *Monitor*, November 20, 1996.

211. Senior Presidential Adviser Major Kakooza Mutale, quoted in Human Rights Focus (2002, 18).

212. Dolan 2009, 144–150.

213. Reno 2002, 422–425.

214. Refugee Law Project 2004, 30.

215. "9000 homeguards to counter Kony," *Sunday Vision*, October 23, 1994; "EC envoys assess Sudan-Kony threat," *New Vision*, December 1, 1994.

216. "Scores killed as NRA hits back," *Monitor*, January 25, 1995; "Slavery returns: Sudanese dealers buy 110 Ugandan kids," *New Vision*, February 7, 1995.

217. Confidential interviews by author, Gulu District, May 2003.

218. Human Rights Focus 2002, 29.

219. Acholi Religious Leaders Peace Initiative 2001, 12; Finnström 2008, 140–145; Amnesty International 1999.

220. Human Rights Focus 2002, 10.

221. "Kony rebels massacre 82," *New Vision*, April 22, 1995; "Kony toll rises," *New Vision*, April 24, 1995; "Atiak's longest day of the bullet," *Sunday Vision*, April 30, 1995.

222. "Homeguards kill six Kony rebels," *New Vision*, April 28, 1995; "Govt to be sued over Atiak massacre," *Monitor*, May 19, 1995.

223. Confidential interviews by author, Gulu District, March-April 2003.

224. Tripp 2004; Kasfir 1998.

225. Finnström 2009, 69.

226. Oloka-Onyango 2000.

227. Major Shaban Bantariza, UPDF Spokesman, interview by author, Kampala, October 23, 2004. See also Van Acker (2004, 352–53).

228. ICG 2004, 13–18; see also Van Acker (2004, 353).

229. This idea was expressed by Acholi political and cultural leaders in interviews by author (Gulu and Kampala, March 2003).

230. Mwenda 2010, 54.

231. ICG 2004, 11.

232. Ibid., 11–12.

233. One example is President Museveni's speech at Kaunda Grounds, Gulu Town, 8 March 2003, at which the author was present.

234. "Uganda's Besigye Denies Treason," BBC News On-line, April 4, 2006.

235. Sjögren (2007) explains how militarization is expanding to become the hallmark of government presence in the south as well.

236. Refugee Law Project 2004, 28; Van Acker 2004, 353; ICG 2004, 17–18.

237. MP Reagan Okumu, interview by author, Kampala, October 28, 2004; confidential interviews with human rights activists, community leaders by author, Gulu District, October-December 2004. See also Refugee Law Project (2004, 27), and ICG 2004, 11.

238. Doom and Vlassenroot 1999, 31.

239. Mwenda 2010.

240. For a particularly dramatic portrayal of donors' willingness to support the northern conflict, see Peter Chappell's documentary film, *Our Friends at the Bank* (France, 1997). I was told by a European defense analyst that the Ugandan government consistently purchased military equipment earmarked for the war in the north that was irrelevant to that conflict and was in fact much more appropriate to the war in Congo (European defense analyst confidential interview by author, Kampala, April 2003).

241. Finnström 2008, 127–30; for more extensive documentation, see note 278.

242. Mwenda 2010.

243. Reno 2002.

244. Easterly 2010.

245. "Ugandan government could collapse without donor aid, say experts," *Monitor*, May 8, 2005.

246. Williams 2000, 572.

247. Mwenda 2010.

248. Tripp 2004; Mwenda 2007.

249. Ayittey 2002.

250. "Uganda's bright star dims: Critics say president corrupted by 18 years in power," *Chicago Tribune*, December 13, 2004.

251. Some of this support has come by means of his links to the ultraright American Christian group, "The Family" (Kaoma 2009/2010); see also "The Secret Political Reach of the Family," National Public Radio, November 24, 2009.

252. USAID website, http://www.usaid.gov/locations/sub-saharan_africa/countries/uganda.

253. Finnström 2008, 108–12.
254. "Girls Escape Ugandan Rebels," BBC News On-line, June 25, 2003.
255. For more on these conditionalities, see Bibangambah (2001, 120–21).
256. Ibid.
257. Economist Intelligence Unit 2005, 25.
258. Bibangambah 2001, 128.
259. World Bank 2000, 15.
260. Economist Intelligence Unit 2005, 36.
261. Ibid., 34.
262. Ibid.
263. Reno 2002, 426.
264. Ibid., 426, 428.
265. Bibangambah 2001, 128–129.
266. UNECA 2003, 85–86.
267. Reno 2002, 430.
268. Quoted in Christian Aid (UK) 2004, 35.
269. Mwenda 2010, 50–51.
270. Ibid.
271. Reno 2002, 431. Today, donors may be shifting their positions on Uganda and, instead of continuing to trumpet its movement towards good governance and democracy, espousing instead the idea of "good enough governance," in which Western donors forgive abuses by externally-sponsored African states in the name of pragmatism. For a critique of "good enough governance," see Duffield (2007, 178).
272. "Uganda Military Allocated $200m as Donors Protest," *East African* (Nairobi), June 20, 2005.
273. Reno 2002, 428.
274. Information from World Bank website for Uganda, http://go.worldbank.org/FBNY7UVIF0.
275. "Cautious Welcome for G8 Debt Deal," BBC News On-line, June 12, 2005.
276. Statement made by Anthony Lake at a conference organized by Center for Strategic Studies, February 15, 1995.
277. Available at http://frwebgate.access.gpo.gov/cgi-bin/getdoc.cgi?dbname=1997_register&docid=fr05no97–126.pdf.
278. For an extensive list of sources documenting U.S. aid to the SPLA through Uganda, see Nafeez Mosaddeq Ahmed, "United States Terrorism in the Sudan: The Bombing of Al-Shifa and its Strategic Role in U.S.-Sudan Relations," Media Monitors Network, October 22, 2001; available at http://www.mediamonitors.net/mosaddeq16.html#_edn38. I reproduce some of those citations here: *Africa Confidential* reported the SPLA "has already received U.S. help via Uganda," and that U.S. special forces are on "open-ended deployment" with the rebels (*Africa Confidential*, November 15, 1996); "To the peril of regional stability, the Clinton Administration has used northern Uganda as a military training ground for southern Sudanese rebels fighting the Muslim government of Khartoum" (*Boston Globe*, December 8, 1999); "The Clinton administration has launched a covert campaign to destabilise the government of Sudan . . . More than $20m of military equipment, including radios, uniforms and tents will be shipped to Eritrea, Ethiopia and Uganda in the next few weeks. Although the equipment is earmarked for the armed forces of those countries,

much of it will be passed on to the Sudan People's Liberation Army (SPLA), which is preparing an offensive against the government in Khartoum" (*Sunday Times*, November 17, 1996); "Nearly $20 million in surplus U.S. military equipment will be sent to Ethiopia, Eritrea and Uganda, the officials said, adding that the three countries support Sudanese opposition groups [particularly the SPLA] preparing a joint offensive to topple the government of Sudan" ("Wielding Aid, The US Targets Sudan," *Washington Post*, November 10, 1996); "The United States pretends the aid is to help the governments concerned . . . to protect themselves from Sudan. It is clear the aid is for Sudan's armed opposition" (*Africa Confidential*, November 15, 1996).

279. According to a State Department spokesperson, "To further protect the safety of the US and its citizens, Secretary of State Colin L. Powell, in consultation with the attorney general, on 6 December designated 39 groups as Terrorist Exclusion List organizations under section 212 of the Immigration and Nationality Act" ("US Lists ADF, LRA as Terrorists," *New Vision*, December 8, 2001).

280. "Uganda pledges to support USA in combating terrorism," *New Vision*, December 12, 2001; Ambassador Brennan termed an LRA attack a "pure terrorist act against humanity" ("US Ambassador Condemns LRA Rebel Attack in the North," Radio Uganda, Kampala, 1000 gmt., March 21, 2002).

281. "USA Gives $3M to Fight Kony," *New Vision*, January 10, 2003.

282. Christian Aid (UK) 2004, 29.

283. Interview with General Wald, BBC News On-line, March 23, 2004; quoted in Christian Aid (UK) 2004, 29.

284. "Ugandan fury over UN report into Congo 'war crimes,'" BBC News On-line, September 30, 2010.

285. Mwenda and Tangri 2005.

286. World Bank 1981, 8. This opinion continues to have its adherents; see, for example, Collier (2007).

287. Harrison 2004.

288. Mwenda and Tangri 2005, 451.

Chapter 3

1. Rieff 2002.
2. Ignatieff 1998, 23.
3. Kaldor 1999.
4. Chandler 2002, 21–52.
5. Marriage provides a detailed account of aid to the RPF (2006, 71–93).
6. See for example Lobel (2000), and Woodward 2001.
7. This complicity has been alluded to but not thoroughly theorized: Agamben mentions a "secret solidarity" between humanitarianism and state violence (1998, 133–34); and, from a less metaphysical angle, Dillon and Reid (2000, 118) state that "the radical and continuous transformation of societies that global liberal governance so assiduously seeks must constitute a significant contribution to the very violence that it equally also deplores."
8. Anderson 1999; Terry 2002.
9. de Waal 1997a, 136. See also Karim et al. (1996), Minear (1991), African Rights (1997), and Keen (1994).

10. For a devastating critique of this phenomenon, see Marriage (2006).

11. For the most extensive academic account of the camps, see Dolan (2009).

12. "1,000 displaced die every week in war-torn north," U.N. Integrated Regional Information Networks (IRIN), August 29, 2005. Jan Egeland, the Under-Secretary General for Humanitarian Affairs and Emergency Relief Coordinator, famously called the situation in northern Uganda the world's worst neglected humanitarian crisis ("War in Northern Uganda World's Worst Forgotten Crisis: UN," Agence France-Presse, November 11, 2003).

13. "12 Die in UPDF Protected Villages," *Monitor*, October 30, 1996.

14. UNDHA 1996.

15. WFP 1996.

16. For example, until late 1996 Uganda was generally mentioned in WFP Weekly Reports only in the context of the conflicts in neighboring countries, but from late 1996 onward it appeared in those reports every week due to internal displacement (see the reports at http://iys.cidi.org/humanitarian//wfp/). This was confirmed through confidential interviews with NGO national staff by author, Gulu Town, May 2003.

17. There is a brief mention of the debate in Gersony (1997, 34–36). See also UNDHA (1997).

18. See, for example, UNDHA (1997), and WFP (1997a). WFP had established a suboffice in Gulu Town by March, 1997 (WFP 1997b).

19. UNDHA 1997.

20. UNOCHA 2005a.

21. Ibid. For a comprehensive list of the projects and their budgets, see UNOCHA (2005b).

22. WFP 2004.

23. "IDPs cost donors $200 million annually," *Daily Monitor (Kampala)*, March 27, 2007.

24. For an account of these moral dilemmas, see Slim (1997).

25. Stockton 1998, 356.

26. WFP 1999, quoted in Dolan (2009, 230–231).

27. Ibid., quoted in Dolan (2009, 230).

28. Ibid., quoted in Dolan (2009, 230–231).

29. Ibid.

30. Ibid., quoted in Dolan (2005, 307).

31. Dolan 2009, 1–2.

32. Ibid., ch. 6.

33. Ibid., 128.

34. Ibid., 129.

35. Confidential interviews by author, Gulu District, March, May 2003.

36. Acholi Religious Leaders Peace Initiative 2001, 12; Finnström 2008.

37. Confidential interviews by author, Gulu District, March–April 2003.

38. Ibid.

39. Ibid.

40. World Bank official, confidential interview by author, May 2003.

41. Human Rights Watch 2004.

42. The idea of "security corridors" was mentioned to the author in a discussion with Walter Ochora (Local Council V Chairman, Gulu District), May 20, 2003; see also the discussion in ICG (2004, 22–23).

43. This strategy, which I have sometimes found myself subject to, is a good example of the "fabricated clarity" described by Marriage (2006, 188–89).

44. See the discussion of the development of the IDP discourse in Dubernet (2001, ch. 1).

45. Foucault 1991, 102; see also Dillon (1995), and Fassin and Pandolfi (2010).

46. For other approaches to transnational governmentality, see Ferguson and Gupta (2002), and Moulin and Nyers (2007).

47. See Calhoun (2004); Duffield also examines the centrality of the discourse of emergency (2007, ch. 2); see also Nyers (2006, 4–8).

48. This argument is similar to that of Alex de Waal concerning the technicization of famine (1997a, 23–25).

49. See also Edkins (2003, 253–58).

50. For a laudatory account of this macro-surveillance function, see Steele and Amoureux (2005).

51. Bjorgo 2002.

52. Davies and Gurr 1998.

53. Much of the effort around the so-called Responsibility to Protect can also be seen as part of this trend; see Bellamy (2009).

54. See Dubernet (2001), and Hyndman (2000).

55. Malkki 1995, 236.

56. Local Council I Pabbo members, interview by author, Pabbo internment camp, March 2003.

57. Interviews by author, Gulu District, November 2005.

58. For details on this relationship, see Komakech (2005).

59. Harrell-Bond 1986, 11.

60. Malkki 1996, 388.

61. Ibid., 388–90.

62. Pouligny 2006, 67. See also Hyndman (2000, xxii).

63. Harrell-Bond 2002, 52.

64. Ibid., 60.

65. Ibid., 61.

66. Hyndman 2000, 127–31.

67. Malkki 1995, 235; Nyers 2006, 114.

68. Harrell-Bond 1986, 90–91.

69. de Waal 1997, 138.

70. Allen and Turton 1996.

71. This information is from interviews conducted by a team of researchers and myself in May–August 2007; see the introduction to this book for details and see the full report in Human Rights Focus (2007).

72. Hyndman 2000, 128.

73. Confidential interviews by author, Pabbo internment camp, Gulu District, Uganda, November 2004.

74. For a detailed treatment of the importance of rumors and conspiracies, see Finnström (2008, ch. 5).

75. Confidential interviews by author, Gulu Town, November 2005.

76. Harrell-Bond 1986, 26.

77. Singer 2003.
78. de Waal 1997, 189.
79. WFP 1999, quoted in Dolan 2009, 231.
80. Finnström 2008, 158–59.
81. "Two Aid Workers Killed in LRA Attacks in Northern Uganda," Agence France-Presse, English Edition, October 26, 2005; "LRA Kill British National," *New Vision*, November 7, 2005.
82. Dolan 2009, 84.
83. Pandolfi 2003, 370. For critique from within anthropology, see Fassin (2007) and Robins (2009).
84. Edkins 2000, 13–14. See also Douzinas (2007, 108).
85. Edkins 2000, 19.
86. Nyers 2006, 199. See also Edkins and Pin-Fat (2005).
87. Amnesty International, in an early treatment of forced displacement from a human rights and humanitarian law perspective, stated that: "In the context of gross human rights abuses by the LRA against unarmed civilians, Amnesty International does not believe that the creation of camps for internally displaced people, or a policy of moving people into camps by the authorities, is intrinsically a violation of international human rights or humanitarian law by the Uganda Government" (1999, 3). Of course, a policy of forced displacement would not "intrinsically" be a violation of human rights or humanitarian law, since, under specific circumstances, it is allowed by the Geneva Conventions. Amnesty International ignores the important point, however, which is that it was precisely the way in which displacement and internment were carried out in Uganda which qualify those policies as violations of human rights and humanitarian law.
88. Protocol Additional to the Geneva Conventions of 12 August 1949, and Relating to the Protection of Victims of Non-International Armed Conflicts (Protocol II), June 8, 1977, Art. 17.
89. Ibid.
90. Stein 2008, 138.
91. See the Humanitarian Accountability Project website, http://www.hapinternational.org/. See also the discussion from the perspective of international law in Clapham (2006, 310–16).
92. de Waal 2000, 228.
93. Ibid., 229.
94. Groupe URD 2008, 7.
95. Duffield and Prendergast 1994, 6.
96. Ibid., 16.
97. Ibid., 170.
98. Smillie 2001.
99. Kaiser 2004, 187.
100. Herson 2003; see also Stein (2008, 132).
101. Herson 2003.
102. Davis 2003.
103. Ibid.
104. Terry 2002, 54–55.
105. Ibid., 10.

106. See for example McIvor (2004).

107. Alex de Waal found that in one context, "famine victims" only derived 10 percent of their domestic income from relief aid (2004). See also Stockton (2006).

Chapter 4

1. Barnett et al. 2007.

2. The literature on this is extensive; for the best and most economically rigorous independent assessment of the first 20 years of structural adjustment in Africa, see Mkandawire and Soludo (1999). See also MacEwan (1999) and, on Uganda in particular, Bibangambah (2001, 129–33).

3. For critical overviews of this agenda, see Orford and Beard (1998), and Moore (1999).

4. Williams 2008; Harrison 2004; Moore 1999.

5. See especially Harrison (2004, ch. 4).

6. Gathii 1999.

7. This relates to Duffield's discussion of "non-material development" in Mozambique (2007, ch. 4).

8. World Bank 2000, 39.

9. This is a dimension downplayed by Harrison in his study of Uganda and the World Bank (2004); the duality, however, is emphasized by Sjögren (2007). See also Tangri and Mwenda (2006).

10. Golooba-Mutebi and Hickey 2010.

11. World Bank 2000, 57.

12. Ibid., 3.

13. Ibid., 2; emphasis in original.

14. Ibid., 49.

15. The first stirrings of this neostatism can be seen in World Bank (1997); see also Mkandawire (2001, 307).

16. World Bank 2000, 27.

17. Ibid., xi.

18. Ibid., 66.

19. Ibid., 62.

20. World Bank Group 2002. It explains that NUSAF will "directly respond to the needs of vulnerable community members, especially those created by past conditions of war and insecurity. All of the five sub-regions in the North are in a under post conflict situation although, three have had a rather longer spell and are just emerging from war been affected by war and are in the post-war reconstruction phase" (2). See also World Bank (2002).

21. Confidential interviews by author, Gulu District, Kampala, March-April 2003. See also Office of the Prime Minister (2003).

22. Christian Aid (UK) 2004, 35.

23. For the connection between NURP I and Operation North, see Behrend (1999, 188).

24. Harrison 2004, ch 7.

25. World Bank 2000, 62.

26. See the discussion of this agenda in Moore (2000).

27. World Bank 2000, 62.

28. Agard Didi, Minister of State in charge of Rehabilitation of Northern Uganda, Interview, *East African* (Nairobi), July 22, 2002; see also Kreimer (2000).

29. This trend is illustrated by World Bank (2002).

30. Ibid., 2.

31. Ibid.

32. Ibid., 4.

33. Office of the Prime Minister 2002, 5–6.

34. World Bank 2002, 3–4.

35. Office of the Prime Minister 2002, 6.

36. John J. Oloya, Rural Development Specialist, World Bank, interview by author, Kampala, March 5, 2003; he was the principal designer and coordinator of two of the components; see also Golooba-Mutebi and Hickey (2010, 1223).

37. World Bank 2002, 3.

38. Office of the Prime Minister 2002, 5.

39. World Bank 2000, 72.

40. Ibid., 67.

41. World Bank 2002, 28.

42. Ibid., 7.

43. World Bank 1989, 84. See the genealogy of NGOs in Manji and O'Coill (2002).

44. Mamdani 1993, 6; for the depoliticizing tendencies of NGOs, see Shivji (2007). See also Weiss and Gordenker (1996), and Hudock (1999). Tvedt (1998) stresses the strategic promotion of NGOs against the ideology of their spontaneous generation.

45. Brigg 2001.

46. John J. Oloya, interview by author, Kampala, March 5, 2004.

47. Golooba-Mutebi and Hickey 2010, 1233.

48. Ibid., 1232.

49. Confidential interviews by author, Gulu District, October 2004.

50. I attended a five-day workshop on conflict resolution funded by the Ford Foundation and conducted by a UK-based conflict resolution organization, Kasese Town, Uganda, March 29–April 2, 2003.

51. Secondary school justice and peace club, interview by author, Gulu District, March 2003.

52. In the NGO directory provided by the Gulu District NGO Forum, there were over 30 NGOs that included nontraditional conflict resolution among their activities (photocopy, June 26, 2006, on file with author).

53. UNICEF 2005.

54. Ibid., iii.

55. Ibid., 20–21.

56. The 2006 Gulu District NGO Forum Directory included almost a dozen organizations that include children's rights promotion in their mandates.

57. On the ascendance of children's rights, see Pupavac (2002), and for children's rights in the Uganda case, see Dolan (2002).

58. Foreign NGO employees interviews by author, Gulu Town, April-May 2003.

59. Teachers, interviews by author, Atiak Camp, March 2003.

60. "Peace Concert On," *The New Vision*, April 30, 2008.

61. Edmondson 2005.

62. Baines 2009.

63. Edmondson 2005, 469.

64. Amnesty Commission officer, Kitgum Town, February 27, 2003. Meanwhile, on the government side, many young men, some as young as ten, but mostly in their midteens, are joining the Homeguard as it is the only way they can protect themselves and possibly their families (interviews by author, Atiak Camp, March 2003).

65. See in particular Blattman and Annan (2010).

66. Mergelsberg 2010, 167.

67. UNICEF Public Relations Officer, interview by author, Kampala, October 27, 2004.

68. Dolan 2002.

69. Quoted in Bradbury (1999, 24). See also Pupavac (2001).

70. The 2006 Gulu District NGO Forum Directory included over 40 NGOs that list psychosocial support, psychotherapy, or counseling among their activities.

71. Blattman 2009.

72. Mergelsberg 2010, 175.

73. Thanks to Adrian Yen for this point.

74. The quotations in this section are drawn from interviews conducted by the author and the research team he led in Gulu Town in mid-2007; see the introduction for details. For the first major assessment of this question, see Allen and Schomerus (2006); for more recent work, see the publications by the Survey of War Affected Youth (SWAY) project (http://chrisblattman.com/projects/sway/).

75. See the trenchant critique of World Vision child sponsorship programs in Jefferess (2002).

76. Justice and Reconciliation Project and Quaker Peace and Social Witness 2008.

77. Dolan (2009, ch. 7) provides an indispensable analysis of the politics of gender in the camps.

78. Experiences of the displaced in camps was significantly worse than the experiences of those in Gulu Town; see Branch (2008b). All the quotations from this section are drawn from interviews conducted by the author and the two research teams he led, one in the camps and one in Gulu Town, during mid-2007; see the introduction for details.

79. Dolan 2009, ch. 7.

80. See the discussion of similar phenomena in Koyama and Myrttinen (2007).

81. This is not to say that these practices are "traditional"—see Tamale's (2008) discussion of the gendered construction of present understandings of traditional practices.

82. For important discussions of this issue, see Speed (2008), and Merry (2006).

83. This phenomenon is not unique to northern Uganda, but is part of an explosion of such organizations throughout the country since the mid-1990s; see Dicklitch (1998).

84. Cohen and Arato 1992, ix.

85. Mamdani 1993, 6.

86. The following interviews were conducted mid-2007 in Gulu Town by the author's research team; it draws upon material published in Branch (2008b) and Human Rights Focus (2007).

87. Marriage 2006, 222.

88. Cohen and Arato 1992, 19; emphasis in original.

89. Interviews by author with job seekers outside NGOs that had posted openings, personal communications with NGO employers, Gulu Town, November 2004.

90. Finnström 2008.

91. Pouligny 2002, 215.

92. Ibid., 208, 203.

93. Spivak 1988.

94. Mosse 1994; Cooke and Kothari 2001.

95. Cleaver 1999.

96. Kaiser 2004, 196.

97. Jok 1996.

98. Pouligny 2006, ch. 5.

99. Mamdani 1993; Tvedt 1998.

100. White 1996, 13–15.

101. Rahnema 1992, 120.

Chapter 5

1. Gregory 2008.

2. MacGinty 2008, 140.

3. The need for traditional or indigenous forms of participation in peace and conflict resolution is put forth by Chopra and Hohe (2004) and Richmond (2008). For an early articulation of this agenda, see Zartman (2000). For a positive assessment of traditional peacebuilding in Somaliland, often represented as the exemplar of traditional conflict resolution, see Farah (2001). For the most developed recent treatment of the questions around "local justice," see Shaw and Waldorf (2010).

4. Scholars have drawn attention to the collaboration between neoliberal governance and the instrumental articulation of cultural difference; the most significant body of work concerns the revival of indigenous identity as a strategy of promoting popular self-management by neoliberalizing Latin American states (Speed 2008). The juxtaposition of neoliberalism and the Ugandan government's strategy of tribalizing national politics certainly merits further attention in this context.

5. Pain 1997.

6. Liu Institute for Global Issues 2005.

7. Pain 1997; for the early debate around traditional reconciliation in northern Uganda, see the critical work by Dolan (2000) and Bradbury (1999), and also the work of Afako (2001) and Hovil and Quinn (2005).

8. Dolan 2000, 12. Several ideas expressed in Dolan's incisive critique are echoed in this chapter.

9. Pain 1997, 56.

10. Ibid., 54.

11. Ibid., 2.

12. Ibid., 54.

13. Ibid.

14. Ibid., 51.

15. This internalization is recognized by Mark Bradbury, who points out that "celebrating Acholi culture and identity expresses Acholi separateness or difference from the rest

of Uganda, and holds the danger of reformulating the war as an 'internal' intra-Acholi conflict" (1999, 20).

16. Pain 1997, 56.

17. Ibid.

18. Office of the Prime Minister 2002, 8.

19. Ibid., 4.

20. John J. Oloya, interview by author, Kampala, March 5, 2003.

21. Confidential interviews by author, Gulu District, November 2004.

22. Hountondji 1996. Subsequent parenthetical citations in the text are to this book.

23. Liu Institute for Global Issues 2005. Subsequent parenthetical citations in the text are to this report.

24. Allen 2006, 2010.

25. Allen 2010, 253.

26. Allen has done the most to document this disruptive power (1991, 2006).

27. Thanks to Adrian Yen for making this point to me.

28. See Titeca (2010) and Mergelsberg (2010) for accounts of the spiritual practices of the LRA.

29. Pain 1997, 53.

30. Timothy Lubanga, Project Coordinator, Office of the Prime Minister, interview by author, Kampala, March 5, 2003.

31. NUSAF Program Officer, interview by author, Gulu Town, March 2003.

32. Ibid.

33. Baines 2009, 184.

34. Branch 2008b. Interviews were conducted mid-2007 by the camp-based and Gulu Town–based research teams; see the introduction for details.

35. Baines 2007.

36. Allen 2010, 257–60.

37. Ibid., 253.

Chapter 6

1. Ban 2010.

2. Ruti Teitel chronicles the emergence and rise to dominance of this new "humanitarian legal regime," which she terms "humanity's law," and which "is largely directed at managing systemic political violence" (2002, 376). See also Meron (2000).

3. Mutua 2001. See also Foucault (1980, 8–9).

4. UN IRIN 2005.

5. Government of Uganda 2003, para. 6. This referral was handed out to participants at the Uganda Human Rights Commission's conference on "The Implications of the ICC Investigations on Human Rights and the Peace Process in Uganda," Kampala, October 5, 2004, at which the author was present.

6. Akhavan 2005, 421.

7. Moreno-Ocampo 2010.

8. Mamdani 2009.

9. "Darfur: Bashir Genocide Charges to be Reconsidered," *BBC News On-line*, February 3, 2010.

10. Kimani 2009.

11. Mamdani 2008.

12. See del Ponte and Sudetic (2009) for details on U.S. meddling in the International Criminal Tribunal for Yugoslavia.

13. "Ambassador: U.S. moving to support international court," CNN U.S. On-line, March 24, 2010.

14. Akhavan 2005, 411.

15. Public statement at Uganda Human Rights Commission's conference on "The Implications of the ICC Investigations on Human Rights and the Peace Process in Uganda," Kampala, October 5, 2004, at which the author was present.

16. Perrot 2010, 199.

17. It seemed to be lost on the Secretary-General, the ICC, and the group "No Peace without Justice," which provided technical assistance for the match, that President Museveni, given the UPDF's record of extreme violence in northern Uganda and eastern DRC, and given his own use of child soldiers in the Bush War of the early 1980s, might not be the most appropriate captain for a team of war victims from those very areas (for photos and more information, see http://www.victimsfootballday.org).

18. Moreno-Ocampo 2005.

19. "UN Criminal Court to Target Uganda Rebels, DR Congo Militia," Agence France-Presse, February 8, 2005.

20. Moreno-Ocampo 2005.

21. Akhavan 2005, 404.

22. Ibid.

23. Ibid., 407.

24. Ibid.

25. Ibid., 409.

26. James Otto, Director, Human Rights Focus, interview by author, Gulu Town, November 5, 2005; see also UN IRIN (2004).

27. Allen 2006, Baines 2007.

28. Quoted in Branch (2004, 24).

29. Brubacher 2010.

30. Atkinson 2010, 220.

31. Moreno-Ocampo's claims that the LRA was using the peace talks to rearm and regroup have been refuted by recent studies (Atkinson 2009, 16).

32. "U.S. Lawyer to Probe Kony," *Monitor*, February 5, 2004.

33. An early suggestion that the UPDF could enter DRC to hunt the LRA is found in "Museveni Wants to Hunt LRA in Congo," *New Vision*, June 19, 2006.

34. Akhavan 2005, 410–11.

35. Koskenniemi 2002.

36. This was Hans Kelsen's accusation against the Nuremberg trials; quoted in Zolo (2009).

37. The Ugandan case puts into doubt the general validity of the claim that the ICC will promote democracy and democratic institutions made by Mayerfeld (2004, 147).

38. Office of the Prosecutor of the International Criminal Court 2010, 1.

39. Chandler 2002, 100–101.

40. Arendt 1968, 172.

41. Ibid., 176.

42. Chandler 2002, 109.

43. Žižek 1997.

44. One question that was going around in northern Uganda ask in the wake of the issuance of the ICC arrest warrant was, "Is America going to come and catch Kony?" My answer was, "I don't know, but I wouldn't depend on it."

45. de Waal 1997b.

46. "Guiding Principles on Internal Displacement," U.N. Doc.# E/CN.4/1998/53/ Add.2.

47. Alex de Waal draws attention to the substitution of humanitarian principles for hard international law (2000, 211–16).

48. Deng 1998b.

49. "Guiding Principles on Internal Displacement," Introduction, para. 3.

50. The final report from one training workshop on the Guiding Principles in November 2003 in Gulu and Kitgum districts conducted by Francis Deng is available at http://www.reliefweb.int/idp/docs/reports/TrainUgandaexannexNov03.pdf.

51. Giorgio Agamben discusses "the paradoxical status of the camp as a space of exception" (Agamben 1998, 170).

52. See Amnesty International (1999) for a typically ambivalent analysis of forced displacement and internment.

53. The ICG at one time went so far as to propose a bounty be put on Kony's head—although "it would have to be small enough not to attract mercenary elements," they reassure their gentle readers (ICG 2006, 11).

54. Baines 2007, 2009.

55. Schomerus 2010, 100.

56. Baines 2009, 186.

57. For more on the Amnesty Act, see Hovil and Lomo (2005).

58. ICC 2004.

59. Meeting of academics with Chief Prosecutor Moreno-Ocampo, London School of Economics, March 3, 2007, at which the author was present.

60. de Waal 1997a, 182–88.

61. See Al-Bulushi and Branch (2010) for this argument; I thank Samar Al-Bulushi for allowing me to use parts of our piece here.

62. Video Clip, Invisible Children Website, http://www.invisiblechildren.com/videos/5429085.

63. "Ambassador: U.S. moving to support international court," CNN U.S. On-line, March 24, 2010.

64. Ibid.

65. Ibid.

66. Koh 2010.

67. Moreno-Ocampo 2010.

68. See Arendt (1963) for the classic exposition of the dilemmas of legal justice for mass crimes.

69. Koskenniemi argues that international criminalization may only further legitimate violence by political leaders in the eyes of their supporters (2002, 8).

70. Snyder and Vinjamuri 2003.

71. See their website at http://www.npwj.org.

72. Maathai 2010.

73. Tallgren 2002, 592.

74. For an interesting assessment of the potential political meanings of trials in Burundi, see Nee and Uvin (2010).

75. Quoted in Brubacher (2010, 267).

76. This is what Jonathan Graubart (2010) terms "pragmatic legalism." This section is informed by discussions with him.

77. William Pace, public statement at "Enhancing Civil Society Participation in the ICC Review Conference: International Symposium on Stocktaking Processes," May 27–28, 2010, Hotel Africana, Kampala. The author participated as a delegate of Human Rights Focus (Gulu).

78. Bass 2000, 310.

79. Annan 2009.

80. Allen 2006, 83. However, I would point out that the legal processes carried out by the ICC are not "conventional" and do not correspond to the modern state. Indeed, ICC interventions reject and suppress conventional, modern state-based legal mechanisms in favor of tenuous global mechanisms, thus bringing into question the very foundation of the modern state—namely, the concept of sovereignty. In this sense, the ICC intervention is just as inimical to the "conventional legal mechanisms [required by] everyone else living in modern states" as is the practice of "traditional" justice.

81. International Center for Transitional Justice 2005.

82. Human Rights Focus 2007.

83. Shklar 1964, 181.

84. Koskenniemi 2002, 34.

85. See the discussion in Drumbl (2007).

86. "Enhancing Civil Society Participation in the ICC Review Conference: International Symposium on Stocktaking Processes," May 27–28, 2010, Hotel Africana, Kampala.

87. William Pace, public statement at "Enhancing Civil Society Participation in the ICC Review Conference."

88. See Clarke's (2009) discussion of the "tribunalization of African violence."

89. Tallgren 2002.

90. Koskenniemi 2002, 26. See also the discussion in Simpson (2007).

Chapter 7

1. Glover and Lee 2007.

2. "AfriCom Partners with African Nations to Promote Stability, Security," American Forces Press Service, July 15, 2008.

3. Powell 2001.

4. For background, see Ploch (2009). The arrogance entailed by the idea that the United States has the right to divide the world between its military commands, and that it somehow dignifies Africa to receive its very own command, has not gone unnoticed by critics.

5. This approach draws on the Pan-Sahel Initiative; see Ellis (2004). For more on this flexible, networked mode of U.S. power, see Biel (2003).

6. Volman 2010b, 87.

7. Bachmann 2010, 571–73.

8. Besteman 2008, 20.

9. A representative piece describing the connection of terrorism with failed states is Rotberg (2002). For a critical account of the development of this discourse, see Kraxberger (2005).

10. Bachmann and Hönke 2009, 112.

11. Quoted in Burket (2010).

12. Abramovici 2004; Klare and Volman 2006a; Volman 2008b.

13. Ploch 2009, 14.

14. Foster 2006.

15. This line of thinking was apparently influenced by Barnett (2004). See also Lyman and Dorff (2007).

16. This characterization of the agenda is provided by Chandler (2009, 102).

17. Barnett 2004.

18. McFate 2008, 120.

19. Quoted in Abrahamsen (2004b, 678).

20. Quoted in Ploch (2009, 13).

21. Ibid., 16.

22. Mamdani 2009.

23. Fake and Funk 2009.

24. Rice 2007.

25. Van de Walle 2010; Kraxberger 2005. See in general Chandler (2009) on this subject.

26. Van de Walle 2010, 11.

27. Carmody 2005, 102.

28. Abrahamsen 2004b, 681.

29. Bialasiewicz et al. 2007.

30. Volman 2010b.

31. See the accounts in Ploch (2009) and Bachmann (2010).

32. Bacevich 2005.

33. Volman 2010b, 85.

34. Van de Walle 2010, 13.

35. See Bachmann (2010) for the best account of the impact of these shifts on AFRICOM.

36. Quoted in Keenan (2008, 18).

37. Quoted in Ploch (2009, 5).

38. McFate 2008.

39. "AfriCom Partners with African Nations to Promote Stability, Security," American Forces Press Service, July 15, 2008.

40. Volman 2008a.

41. Network of Concerned Anthropologists 2009.

42. Munson 2008, 99.

43. Esterhuyse 2008, 119.

44. Barnett 2007. See also Kaplan (2007).

45. Dickinson 2009.

46. Forsyth and Saltzman 2009, 5.

47. Bachmann 2010, 565.

48. Minter and Volman 2009.

49. Africa Action 2008.

50. "Africa: US Military Edging Out Diplomacy," *East African* (Nairobi), August 17, 2010. To put this amount in perspective, $350 million is spent in Iraq every day.

51. Marks 2009.

52. Isike, Okeke-Uzodike, and Gilbert 2008.

53. Yates 2009; Moeller 2010; Bachmann 2010, 569–70.

54. Bah and Aning 2008; Volman and Tuckey 2008.

55. Van de Walle 2010, 3. David Chandler would probably characterize AFRICOM as "better grasped as reflecting a sense of weakness and lack of capacity," and so "rather than a security agenda of control, management and strategic intervention, this is one of *ad hoc* reactions and damage limitation" (2009, 102–3).

56. Berschinski 2007, 2.

57. GAO 2010.

58. Klare and Volman 2006b, 302.

59. Volman 2008a.

60. Esterhuyse 2008. The benefit of pursuing private cooperation with African governments in the War on Terror in order to overcome the difficulties of more public cooperation is discussed in Whitaker (2008).

61. Transcript: Ward Testifies Before the House Armed Services Committee, Washington DC, March 18, 2009, http://www.africom.mil/getArticle.asp?art=2832.

62. Ploch 2009, 9.

63. McFate 2008, 118; TransAfrica Forum n.d.

64. Volman 2009a; see also (Falconer and Schulman (2009).

65. Aning, Jaye, and Atuobi 2008.

66. Volman 2010b, 86–87.

67. Foreign Policy in Focus 2010.

68. Bachmann 2008.

69. Klare and Volman 2006b, 299.

70. Keenan 2009.

71. Volman 2010a.

72. This account is taken largely from Schomerus and Tumutegyereize (2009), Atkinson (2009), and van Puilenbroek and Ploojer (2009).

73. AFRICOM's support for OLT was reported in "US Aided a Failed Plan to Rout Ugandan Rebels," *New York Times,* February 7, 2009. See also Atkinson (2009, 16–17).

74. For example, see Spiegel and Atama (2009).

75. UN IRIN 2009.

76. Quoted in Ibid.

77. Kelley 2009.

78. Bachmann 2010.

79. Bradbury and Kleinman 2010, 9.

80. Brigety 2008, 8–9.

81. Ibid., 4.

82. Bachmann and Hönke 2009, 99.

83. Bradbury and Kleinman 2010.

84. Ibid., 52–55.

85. Ibid., 47–48.

86. Ibid., 72.

87. I am grateful to Cecilie Lanken Verma for sharing her first-hand experiences of the operation and interviews with me.

88. This and other quotations are provided by Verma, e-mail communication, November 8, 2010.

89. de Waal 1997a, 186.

90. Pouligny (2006) provides the most comprehensive discussion of the relations between international troops and the people to whom they are supposed to bring peace.

91. Wright 2009.

92. Mama and Okazawa-Rey 2008.

93. Keenan 2008, 20.

94. Covey, Dziedzic, and Hawley 2005, 17–19.

95. Rice 2007.

96. Volman 2009b.

97. My discussion draws on discussions in Simpson (2007), Zolo (2009), and Kennedy (2005).

98. de Waal 1997a, 188.

99. Fanon 1965.

100. For more on this, see Network of Concerned Anthropologists (2009) and Bacevich (2005).

101. Al-Bulushi 2010.

102. Quoted in Al-Bulushi 2010.

103. Amy Finnegan, e-mail communication, September 14, 2010. Finnegan is currently finishing her PhD dissertation in sociology at Boston College on this topic.

104. See Mamdani's account of the Save Darfur movement (2009).

105. See Jefferess (2002) and Edmondson (2005) for incisive assessments of the marketing of images of suffering.

106. Finnström (2008, 111) also draws attention to this scene.

107. "Why We Want Obama." http://www.invisiblechildren.com/videos/7272280.

108. See the open letter by the Acholi Religious Leaders Peace Initiative to Barack Obama, "Regarding the 'Lord's Resistance Army Disarmament and Northern Uganda Recovery Act of 2009,'" June 15, 2010. http://www.arlpi.org/draft-pen.

Chapter 8

1. Shivji 1989.

2. Lefort 1986, 251.

3. Ibid., 250.

4. Ibid., 260.

5. Walzer 1977, 87.

6. Ibid., 86.

7. Ibid., 89.

8. Claims that popular sovereignty should itself be construed as a human right and can, upon that basis, legitimate foreign intervention (Franck 1992) should be dismissed; to

quote Jean Cohen, "To construe popular sovereignty or democracy as a human right is to make a category mistake: it collapses political into moral categories, reducing the citizen to 'person' and confusing collective political action of a citizenry with the citizen's legal standing" (2004, 17).

9. Forst 2001, 170–73.

10. This is a transposition of Thomas Pogge's dictum that "our economic policies and the global economic institutions we impose make us causally and morally responsible for the perpetuation—even aggravation—of world hunger" into the realm of political justice (2001, 15).

11. Mamdani 2009, 67–68; Uvin 1998.

12. This should not be confused with the "give war a chance" position (Luttwak 1999), which refuses to recognize the responsibility and negative duty that informs the practice of disintervention.

13. Amin 1990.

14. Ignatieff 2003, 20.

15. Walzer 1977, 101.

16. Ibid., 106.

17. Mamdani 2009, 300.

18. Campbell 1998, 520. See also Edkins (2003).

19. Duffield 2007, 232.

20. See the discussion in Kapoor (2004, 2008).

21. A call for this kind of self-sacrifice can be found in Davis (2007).

22. Kapoor 2004, 641–42.

23. Malcolm X 1994.

REFERENCES

Abrahamsen, Rita. 2004a. The Power of Partnerships in Global Governance. *Third World Quarterly* 25(8): 1453–67.

Abrahamsen, Rita. 2004b. A Breeding Ground for Terrorists? Africa & Britain's "War on Terrorism." *Review of African Political Economy* 31(102): 677–84.

Abramovici, Pierre. 2004. United States: The New Scramble for Africa. *Review of African Political Economy* 31(102): 685–90.

Acholi Religious Leaders Peace Initiative (ARLPI). 2001. *Let My People Go: The Forgotten Plight of the People in the Displaced Camps in Acholi.* Gulu Town: Gulu Archdiocese.

Adimola, A. B. 1954. The Lamogi Rebellion, 1911–12. *Uganda Journal* 18(2): 166–77.

Afako, Barney. 2001. *Seeking Alternatives in Justice: The Experience of Northern Uganda.* London: African Rights.

Africa Action. 2008. African Voices on AFRICOM, February 22. http://www.pambazuka.org/en/category/comment/47047.

African Rights. 1997. *Food and Power in Sudan: A Critique of Humanitarianism.* London.

Agamben, Giorgio. 1998. *Homo Sacer: Sovereign Power and Bare Life.* Stanford, CA: Stanford University Press.

Ahmed, Nafeez Mosaddeq. 2001. United States Terrorism in the Sudan: The Bombing of Al-Shifa and its Strategic Role in U.S.-Sudan Relations. Media Monitors Network, October 22. http://www.mediamonitors.net/mosaddeq16.html#_edn38.

Akhavan, Payam. 2005. The Lord's Resistance Army Case: Uganda's Submission of the First State Referral to the International Criminal Court. *American Journal of International Law* 99(2): 403–21.

Al-Bulushi, Samar. 2010. US Legislation Authorizes Military Action Against the LRA in Uganda. *Pambazuka News* 475, March 25. http://www.pambazuka.org/en/category/features/63283.

Al-Bulushi, Samar, and Adam Branch. 2010. AFRICOM and the ICC: Enforcing International Justice in Africa? *Pambazuka News* 483, May 27. http://www.pambazuka.org/en/category/features/64752.

Allen, Tim. 1991. Understanding Alice: Uganda's Holy Spirit Movement in Context. *Africa* 61(3): 370–99.

Allen, Tim. 2006. *Trial Justice: The International Criminal Court and the Lord's Resistance Army.* London: Zed Books.

Allen, Tim. 2010. Bitter Roots: The "Invention" of Acholi Traditional Justice. In *The Lord's Resistance Army: Myth and Reality,* edited by Tim Allen and Koen Vlassenroot, 242–61. London: Zed Books.

Allen, Tim, and Mareike Schomerus. 2006. *A Hard Homecoming: Lessons Learned from the Reception Centre Process in Northern Uganda—An Independent Study.* Kampala: Management Systems International.

285

Allen, Tim, and David Turton. 1996. Introduction. In *In Search of Cool Ground: War, Flight, and Homecoming in Northeast Africa*, edited by Tim Allen, 1–22. Trenton, NJ: Africa World Press.

Amaza, Odonga Ori. 1998. *Museveni's Long March from Guerrilla to Statesman*. Kampala: Fountain Publishers.

Amin, Samir. 1990. *De-linking: Towards a Polycentric World*. London: Zed Books.

Amnesty International. 1989. *Uganda: The Human Rights Record (1986–1989)*. London.

Amnesty International. 1991. *Uganda—Human Rights Violations by the National Resistance Army*. London.

Amnesty International. 1999. *Breaking the Circle: Protecting Human Rights in the Northern War Zone*. London.

Anderson, Mary B. 1999. *Do No Harm: How Aid Support Peace—or War*. Boulder, CO: Lynne Rienner Publishers.

Aning, Kwesi, Thomas Jaye, and Samuel Atuobi. 2008. The Role of Private Military Companies in US-Africa Policy. *Review of African Political Economy* 35(118): 613–28.

Annan, Kofi. 1998. The Causes of Conflict and the Promotion of Durable Peace and Sustainable Development in Africa. Secretary-General's Report to the United Nations Security Council, April 16.

Annan, Kofi. 2009. Africa and the International Court. *New York Times*, June 30. http://www.nytimes.com/2009/06/30/opinion/30iht-edannan.html?_r=1.

Arendt, Hannah. 1963. *Eichmann in Jerusalem*. New York: Penguin.

Arendt, Hannah. 1968. *Imperialism*. New York: Harcourt Brace & Company.

Atkinson, Ronald R. 1999. *The Roots of Ethnicity: The Origins of the Acholi of Uganda before 1800*. Kampala: Fountain Publishers.

Atkinson, Ronald R. 2009. *From Uganda to the Congo and Beyond: Pursuing the Lord's Resistance Army*. Washington, DC: International Peace Institute.

Atkinson, Ronald R. 2010. "The Realists in Juba"? An Analysis of the Juba Peace Talks. In *The Lord's Resistance Army: Myth and Reality*, edited by Tim Allen and Koen Vlassenroot, 205–22. London: Zed Books.

Ayittey, George B. N. 2002. Revamping U.S.-Africa Policy. http://freeafrica.org/commentaries11.html.

Bacevich, Andrew J. 2005. *The New American Militarism: How Americans Are Seduced by War*. New York: Oxford University Press.

Bachmann, Jan. 2008. The Danger of "Ungoverned" Spaces: The "War on Terror" and its Effects on the Sahel Region. In *The Social Life of Anti-Terrorism Laws: The War on Terror and the Classifications of the "Dangerous Other,"* edited by Julia M. Eckert, 131–61. New Brunswick, NJ: Transaction Publishers.

Bachmann, Jan. 2010. "Kick Down the Door, Clean up the Mess, and Rebuild the House"—The Africa Command and Transformation of the US Military. *Geopolitics* 15(3): 564–85.

Bachmann, Jan, and Jana Hönke. 2009. "Peace and Security" as Counterterrorism? The Political Effects of Liberal Interventions in Kenya. *African Affairs* 109(434): 97–114.

Bah, A. Sarjoh, and Kwesi Aning. 2008. US Peace Operations Policy in Africa: From ACRI to AFRICOM. *International Peacekeeping* 15(1): 118–32.

Baines, Erin. 2007. The Haunting of Alice: Local Approaches to Transitional Justice in Northern Uganda. *International Journal of Transitional Justice* 1(1): 91–114.

Baines, Erin. 2009. Complex Political Perpetrators: Reflections on Dominic Ongwen. *Journal of Modern African Studies* 47(2): 163–91.

Ban Ki-moon. 2010. The Age of Accountability. May 27. http://www.un.org:80/wcm/content/site/chronicle/home/archive/webarticles2010/The_Age_of_Accountability.

Barnett, Michael, Hunjoon Kim, Madalene O'Donnell, and Laura Sitea. 2007. Peacebuilding: What Is in a Name? *Global Governance* 13(1): 35–58.

Barnett, Thomas P. M. 2004. *The Pentagon's New Map: War and Peace in the 21st Century.* New York: Putnam Publishing Group.

Barnett, Thomas P. M. 2007. The Americans Have Landed. *Esquire*, July. http://www.esquire.com/features/africacommando707.

Bass, Gary. 2000. *Stay the Hand of Vengeance: The Politics of War Crimes Tribunals.* Princeton, NJ: Princeton University Press.

Bauman, Zigmunt. 2004. *Wasted Lives: Modernity and Its Outcasts.* Malden, MA: Polity Press.

Behrend, Heike. 1998. War in Northern Uganda: The Holy Spirit Movements of Alice Lakwena, Severino Lukoya, and Joseph Kony (1987–1997). In *African Guerrillas*, edited by Christopher Clapham, 107–18. Oxford: James Currey.

Behrend, Heike. 1999. *Alice Lakwena and the Holy Spirits: War in Northern Uganda, 1985–97.* Kampala: Fountain Publishers.

Bellamy, Alex. 2009. *Responsibility to Protect: The Global Effort to End Mass Atrocities.* London: Polity.

Bere, R. M. 1955. Land and Chieftainship among the Acholi. *Uganda Journal* 19(1): 49–56.

Berschinski, Robert G. 2007. AFRICOM's Dilemma: The "Global War on Terrorism," "Capacity Building," Humanitarianism, and the Future of U.S. Security Policy in Africa. Carlisle, PA: Strategic Studies Institute, U.S. Army War College.

Besteman, Catherine. 2008. "Beware of Those Bearing Gifts": An Anthropologist's View of AFRICOM. *Anthropology Today* 24(5): 20–21.

Bettati, Mario. 1991. The Right to Interfere. *The Washington Post.* April 14.

Bialasiewicz, Luiza, David Campbell, Stuart Elden, Stephen Graham, Alex Jeffrey and Alison J. Williams. 2007. Performing Security: The Imaginative Geographies of Current US Strategy. *Political Geography* 26(4): 405–22.

Bibangambah, Jossy R. 2001. *Africa's Quest for Economic Development: Uganda's Experience.* Kampala: Fountain Publishers.

Bickerton, Christopher J., Philip Cunliffe, and Alexander Gourevitch, eds. 2007. *Politics Without Sovereignty: A Critique of Contemporary International Relations.* London: University College London Press.

Biel, Robert. 2003. Imperialism and International Governance: The Case of US Policy towards Africa. *Review of African Political Economy* 30(95): 77–88.

Bjorgo, Einar. 2002. *Space Aid: Current and Potential Uses of Satellite Imagery in U.N. Humanitarian Organizations.* Washington, DC: U.S. Institute of Peace.

Blattman, Christopher. 2009. From Violence to Voting: War and Political Participation in Uganda. *American Political Science Review* 103(2): 231–47.

Blattman, Christopher, and Jeannie Annan. 2010. On the Nature and Causes of LRA Abduction: What the Abductees Say. In *The Lord's Resistance Army: Myth and Reality*, edited by Tim Allen and Koen Vlassenroot, 132–55. London: Zed Books.

Bouris, Erica. 2007. *Complex Political Victims.* Bloomfield, CT: Kumarian Press.

Boutros-Ghali, Boutros. 1995. *An Agenda for Peace, 1995: With the New Supplement and Related UN Documents*. New York: United Nations Publications.

Boutros-Ghali, Boutros. 1996. Introduction. In *The United Nations and the Iraq-Kuwait Conflict, 1990–1996*, edited by Boutros Boutros-Ghali. New York: United Nations Publications.

Bradbury, Mark. 1999. *Reflecting on Peace Practice: An Overview of Initiatives for Peace in Acholi, Northern Uganda*. Cambridge, MA.: Collaborative for Development Action.

Bradbury, Mark, and Michael Kleinman. 2010. *Winning Hearts and Minds? Examining the Relationship between Aid and Security in Kenya*. Boston: Feinstein International Center, Tufts University.

Branch, Adam. 2004. International Justice, Local Injustice. *Dissent* 51(3): 22–26.

Branch, Adam. 2005a. American Morality over International Law: Origins in UN Military Interventions, 1991–1995. *Constellations* 12(1): 103–27.

Branch, Adam. 2005b. Neither Peace nor Justice: Political Violence and the Peasantry in Northern Uganda, 1986–1998. *African Studies Quarterly* 8(2). http://www.africa.ufl.edu/asq/v8/v8i2a1.htm.

Branch, Adam. 2007. Uganda's Civil War and the Politics of ICC Intervention. *Ethics and International Affairs* 21(2): 179–98.

Branch, Adam. 2008a. Against Humanitarian Impunity: Rethinking Responsibility for Displacement and Disaster in Northern Uganda. *Journal of Intervention and Statebuilding* 2(2): 151–73.

Branch, Adam. 2008b. Gulu Town in War . . . and Peace? Displacement, Humanitarianism, and Post-War Crisis. Working Paper No. 36, Cities and Fragile States. London: Crisis States Research Centre, London School of Economics.

Branch, Adam. 2009. Humanitarianism, Violence, and the Camp in Northern Uganda. *Civil Wars* 11(4): 477–501.

Branch, Adam. 2010. Exploring the Roots of LRA Violence: Political Crisis and Ethnic Politics in Acholiland. In *The Lord's Resistance Army: Myth and Reality*, edited by Tim Allen and Koen Vlassenroot, 25–44. London: Zed Books.

Brigety, Reuben E., II. 2008. *Humanity as a Weapon of War: Sustainable Security and the Role of the U.S. Military*. Washington, DC: Center for American Progress.

Brigg, Morgan. 2001. Empowering NGOs: The Microcredit Movement through Foucault's Notion of Dispositif. *Alternatives* 26(3): 233–58.

Brubacher, Matthew. 2010. The ICC Investigation of the Lord's Resistance Army: An Insider's View. In *The Lord's Resistance Army: Myth and Reality*, edited by Tim Allen and Koen Vlassenroot, 262–77. London: Zed Books.

Burgess, Stephen Franklin. 2001. *The United Nations under Boutros Boutros-Ghali, 1992–1997*. Lanham, MD: Scarecrow Press.

Burke, Fred. 1964. *Local Government and Politics in Uganda*. Syracuse, NY: Syracuse University Press.

Burket, Alison. 2010. AFRICOM on the Horn of Africa: The Military's Fumbling Humanitarian Foot Forward. Africa Faith and Justice Network, June 9. http://afjn.org/focus-campaigns/militarization-us-africa-policy/105-commentary/830-africom-on-the-horn-of-africa-the-militarys-fumbling-humanitarian-foot-forward.html.

Calhoun, Craig. 2004. A World of Emergencies: Fear, Intervention, and the Limits of Cosmopolitan Order. *Canadian Review of Sociology and Anthropology* 41(4): 373–95.

Call, Charles T., ed. 2008. *Building States to Build Peace.* Boulder, CO: Lynne Rienner Publishers.

Callaghy, Thomas, Ronald Kassimir and Robert Latham, eds. 2001. *Intervention and Transnationalism in Africa: Global-Local Networks of Power.* Cambridge: Cambridge University Press.

Campbell, David. 1998. Why Fight? Humanitarianism, Principles, and Post-structuralism. *Millennium* 27(3): 497–521.

Carmody, Pádraig. 2005. Transforming Globalization and Security: Africa and America Post-9/11. *Africa Today* 51(2): 97–120.

Castells, Manuel. 2000. *End of Millennium.* Oxford: Blackwell.

Chandler, David. 2002. *From Kosovo to Kabul: Human Rights and International Intervention.* London: Pluto Press.

Chandler, David. 2006. *Empire in Denial: The Politics of Statebuilding.* London: Pluto Press.

Chandler, David. 2009. *Hollow Hegemony: Rethinking Global Politics, Power and Resistance.* London: Pluto Press.

Chatterjee, Partha. 2004. *The Politics of the Governed: Reflections on Popular Politics in Most of the World.* New York: Columbia University Press.

Chomsky, Noam. 1993/1994. Humanitarian Intervention. *Boston Review* 18(6). http://bostonreview.net/BR18.6/chomsky.html.

Chomsky, Noam. 2000. *Rogue States: The Rule of Force in World Affairs.* Cambridge, MA: South End Press.

Chopra, Jarat, and Tanja Hohe. 2004. Participatory Intervention. *Global Governance* 10(3): 289–305.

Chopra, Jarat, and Thomas G. Weiss. 1992. Sovereignty Is No Longer Sacrosanct: Codifying Humanitarian Intervention. *Ethics & International Affairs* 6(1): 95–117.

Christian Aid. 2004. *Politics of Poverty: Aid in the New Cold War.* London.

Clapham, Andrew. 2006. *Human Rights Obligations of Non-State Actors.* Oxford: Oxford University Press.

Clark, John F. 2001. Explaining Ugandan Intervention in Congo: Evidence and Interpretations. *Journal of Modern African Studies* 39(2): 261–87.

Clarke, Kamari. 2009. *Fictions of Justice: The International Criminal Court and the Challenge of Legal Pluralism in Sub-Saharan Africa.* New York: Cambridge University Press.

Clarke, Walter S., and Jeffrey Ira Herbst, eds. 1997. *Learning from Somalia: The Lessons of Armed Humanitarian Intervention.* Boulder, CO: Westview Press.

Cleaver, Francis. 1999. Paradoxes of Participation: Questioning Participatory Approaches to Development. *Journal of International Development* 11(4): 597–612.

Cohen, Jean L. 2004. Whose Sovereignty? Empire versus International Law. *Ethics and International Affairs* 18(3): 1–24.

Cohen, Jean L., and Andrew Arato. 1992. *Civil Society and Political Theory.* Cambridge, MA: MIT Press.

Collier, Paul. 2007. *The Bottom Billion: Why the Poorest Countries Are Failing and What Can Be Done about It.* New York: Oxford University Press.

Collier, Paul, and Anke Hoeffler. 2000. *On the Incidence of Civil War in Africa.* Washington, DC: World Bank.

Collier, Paul, and Anke Hoeffler. 2002. *Greed and Grievance in Civil War.* Working Paper No. 2002–01, Centre for the Study of African Economies, Oxford University.

Collier, Paul, V.L. Elliott, Håvard Hegre, Anke Hoeffler, Marta Reynal-Querol, and Nicholas Sambanis. 2003. *Breaking the Conflict Trap: Civil War and Development Policy.* Washington, DC: World Bank and Oxford University Press.

Comaroff, Jean. 2007. Beyond the Politics of Bare Life: AIDS and the Global Order. *Public Culture* 19(1): 197–219.

Cooke, Bill, and Uma Kothari, eds. 2001. *Participation: The New Tyranny?* London: Zed Books.

Covey, Jock, Michael J. Dziedzic, and Leonard R. Hawley, eds. 2005. *International Intervention and Strategies for Conflict Transformation.* Washington, DC: United States Institute of Peace Press.

Crazzolara, J.P. 1937. The Lwoo People. *Uganda Journal* 5(1): 1–21.

Curtis, Devon. 2001. Politics and Humanitarian Aid: Debates, Dilemmas and Dissension. Report of a conference organized by ODI, POLIS at the University of Leeds and CAFOD. London: Overseas Development Institute.

Davies, John L., and Ted Robert Gurr, eds. 1998. *Preventive Measures: Building Risk Assessment and Crisis Early Warning Systems.* Lanham, MD: Rowman & Littlefield.

Davis, Austen. 2003. Accountability and Humanitarian Actors: Speculations and Questions. *Humanitarian Exchange Magazine* 24: 16–18.

Davis, Austen. 2007. *Concerning Accountability of Humanitarian Action.* Humanitarian Practice Network Paper No. 58. London: Overseas Development Institute.

Ddungu, Expedit. 1989. *Popular Forms and the Question of Democracy: The Case of Resistance Councils in Uganda.* Working Paper No. 14. Kampala: Centre for Basic Research.

de Waal, Alex. 1997a. *Famine Crimes: Politics and the Disaster Relief Industry in Africa.* Oxford: James Currey.

de Waal, Alex. 1997b. Becoming Shameless: The Failure of Human Rights Organizations in Rwanda. *Times Literary Supplement*, February 21, 3–4.

de Waal, Alex, ed. 2000. *Who Fights, Who Cares? War and Humanitarian Action in Africa.* Trenton, NJ: Africa World Press.

de Waal, Alex. 2004. *The Famine that Kills: Darfur, Sudan*, Revised Edition. New York: Oxford University Press.

del Ponte, Carla, and Chuck Sudetic. 2009. *Madame Prosecutor: Confrontations with Humanity's Worst Criminals and the Culture of Impunity.* New York: Other Press.

Deng, Francis. 1998a. *Internally Displaced Persons: Compilation and Analysis of Legal Norms.* New York, Geneva: United Nations.

Deng, Francis. 1998b. Introductory Note to the Guiding Principles on Internal Displacement. U.N. Doc.# E/CN.4/1998/53/Add.2.

Deng, Francis Mading, Sadikiel Kimaro, Terrence Lyons, Donald Rothchild, and I. William Zartman. 1996. *Sovereignty as Responsibility: Conflict Management in Africa.* Washington, DC: Brookings Institution Press.

Deng, Francis M., and I. William Zartman, eds. 1991. *Conflict Resolution in Africa.* Washington, DC: Brookings Institution Press.

Dickinson, Elizabeth. 2009. Think Again: Africom. *Foreign Policy*, November 17. http://www.foreignpolicy.com/articles/2009/11/17/think_again_africom.

Dicklitch, Susan. 1998. *The Elusive Promise of NGOs in Africa: Lessons from Uganda*. New York: St. Martin's Press.

Dillon, Michael. 1995. Sovereignty and Governmentality: From the Problematics of the "New World Order" to the Ethical Problematic of World Order. *Alternatives* 20(3): 323–68.

Dillon, Michael, and Julian Reid. 2000. Global Governance, Liberal Peace, and Complex Emergency. *Alternatives* 25(1): 118.

Dolan, Chris. 2000. "Bending the Spears": Notes on Dennis Pain's report to International Alert. COPE Working Paper No. 31. London: ACORD.

Dolan, Chris. 2002. Which Children Count? The Politics of Children's Rights in Northern Uganda. *Accord: Protracted Conflict, Elusive Peace: Initiatives to End the War in Northern Uganda* 11: 68–71.

Dolan, Chris. 2005. *Understanding War and Its Continuation: The Case of Northern Uganda*. PhD diss., Development Studies Institute, London School of Economics and Political Science, University of London.

Dolan, Chris. 2009. *Social Torture: The Case of Northern Uganda, 1986–2006*. New York: Berghahn Books.

Doná, Giorgia. 2007. The Microphysics of Participation in Refugee Research. *Journal of Refugee Studies* 20(2): 210–29.

Doom, Ruddy, and Koen Vlassenroot. 1999. Kony's Message: A New Koine? The Lord's Resistance Army in Northern Uganda. *African Affairs* 98(390): 5–36.

Douzinas, Costas. 2007. *Human Rights and Empire: The Political Philosophy of Cosmopolitanism*. New York: Routledge-Cavendish.

Drumbl, Mark. 2007. *Atrocity, Punishment, and International Law*. Cambridge: Cambridge University Press.

Dubernet, Cécile. 2001. *The International Containment of Displaced Persons: Humanitarian Spaces without Exit*. Aldershot, UK: Ashgate.

Duffield, Mark. 2001a. *Global Governance and the New Wars: The Merging of Development and Security*. London: Zed Books.

Duffield, Mark. 2001b. Governing the Borderlands: Decoding the Power of Aid. *Disasters* 25(4): 308–20.

Duffield, Mark. 2007. *Development, Security, and Unending War: Governing the World of Peoples*. Cambridge: Polity.

Duffield, Mark, and John Prendergast. 1994. *Without Troops and Tanks: The Emergency Relief Desk and the Cross Border Operation into Eritrea and Tigray*. Lawrenceville, NJ: Red Sea Press.

Easterly, William. 2010. Foreign Aid for Scoundrels. *The New York Review of Books* 57(18). http://www.nybooks.com/articles/archives/2010/nov/25/foreign-aid-scoundrels/.

Economist Intelligence Unit. 2005. Country Profile: Uganda. London.

Edkins, Jenny. 2000. Sovereign Power, Zones of Indistinction, and the Camp. *Alternatives* 25(1): 3–25.

Edkins, Jenny. 2003. Humanitarianism, Humanity, Human. *Journal of Human Rights* 2(2): 253–58.

Edkins, Jenny, and Véronique Pin-Fat. 2005. Through the Wire: Relations of Power and Relations of Violence. *Millennium* 34(1): 1–24.

Edmondson, Laura. 2005. Marketing Trauma and the Theatre of War in Northern Uganda. *Theatre Journal* 57: 451–74.

Ellis, Stephen. 2004. Briefing: The Pan-Sahel Initiative. *African Affairs* 103(412): 459–64.

Esterhuyse, Abel. 2008. The Iraqization of Africa? Looking at AFRICOM from a South African Perspective. *Strategic Studies Quarterly* 2(1): 111–30.

Etori, F. E. 1987. War Problem of Democracy. *Weekly Topic.* September 9.

Fake, Steven and Kevin Funk. 2009. *The Scramble for Africa: Darfur—Intervention and the USA.* Montreal: Black Rose Books.

Falconer, Bruce, and Daniel Schulman. 2009. Blackwater's New Frontier: Their Own Private Africa. *Mother Jones*, March/April. http://motherjones.com/politics/2009/03/blackwaters-new-frontier-their-own-private-africa.

Falk, Richard. 1993/1994. Intervention and Resistance. *Boston Review* 18(4). http://bostonreview.net/BR18.6/interresist.html.

Fanon, Franz. 1965. *Wretched of the Earth.* New York: Grove Press.

Farah, Ahmed Yusuf. 2001. Roots of Reconciliation in Somaliland. In *Peacebuilding: A Field Guide,* edited by Luc Reychler and Thania Paffenholz, 138–44. Boulder, CO: Lynne Rienner.

Fassin, Didier. 2007. Humanitarianism as a Politics of Life. *Public Culture.* 19(3): 499–520.

Fassin, Didier, and Mariella Pandolfi. 2010. *Contemporary States of Emergency: The Politics of Military and Humanitarian Interventions.* Cambridge: Zone Books.

Ferguson, James. 1994. *The Anti-Politics Machine: "Development," Depoliticization, and Bureaucratic Power in Lesotho.* Minneapolis: University of Minnesota Press.

Ferguson, James, and Akhil Gupta. 2002. Spatializing States: Toward an Ethnography of Neoliberal Governmentality. *American Ethnologist* 29(4): 981–1002.

Finnström, Sverker. 2008. *Living with Bad Surroundings: War, History and Everyday Moments in Northern Uganda.* Durham, NC: Duke University Press.

Foreign Policy in Focus. 2010. Africa Policy Outlook 2010. http://www.fpif.org/articles/africa_policy_outlook_2010.

Forst, Rainer. 2001. A Critical Theory of Transnational Justice. *Metaphilosophy* 32(1–2): 160–79.

Forsyth, James Wood Jr., and B. Chance Saltzman. 2009. Stay Out: Why Intervention Should Not Be America's Policy. *Strategic Studies Quarterly* 3(2): 3–12.

Foster, John Bellamy. 2006. A Warning to Africa: The New U.S. Imperial Grand Strategy. *Monthly Review* 58(2): 1–12.

Foucault, Michel. 1980. On Popular Justice: A Discussion with Maoists. In *Power/Knowledge: Selected Interviews and Other Writings, 1972–1977,* edited by Colin Gordon. New York: Pantheon.

Foucault, Michel. 1991. Governmentality. In *The Foucault Effect: Studies in Governmentality,* edited by Graham Burchill, Colin Gordon, and Peter Miller, 87–104. London: Harvester Wheatsheaf.

Fox, Fiona. 2001. New Humanitarianism: Does it Provide a Moral Banner for the 21st Century? *Disasters* 25(4): 275–89.

Fox, Fiona. 2002. Conditioning the Right to Humanitarian Aid? In *Rethinking Human Rights: Critical Approaches to International Politics,* edited by David Chandler, 29–37. New York: Palgrave Macmillan.

Franck, Thomas. 1992. The Emerging Right to Democratic Governance. *American Journal of International Law* 86(1): 46–91.

Furley, Oliver, ed. 1995. *Conflict in Africa.* New York: St. Martin's Press.

Gathii, James Thuo. 1999. Good Governance as a Counterinsurgency Agenda to Opposi-tional and Transformative Social Projects in International Law. *Buffalo Human Rights Law Review* 5: 107–74.

Gersony, Robert. 1997. *The Anguish of Northern Uganda: Results of a Field-based Assessment of the Civil Conflicts in Northern Uganda*. Kampala: USAID Mission.

Gertzel, Cherry. 1974. *Party and Locality in Northern Uganda, 1945–1962*. London: Athlone Press.

Ghani, Ashraf, and Claire Lockhart. 2008. *Fixing Failed States: A Framework for Rebuilding a Fractured World*. New York: Oxford University Press.

Gingyera-Pinycwa, A. G. G. 1972. *Some Dimensions of Pre-Independence Politics in Uganda, 1952–1962: A Case Study Based in the Catholic Church and Politics in Northern Uganda in the Decade 1952–1962*. PhD Diss., University of Chicago.

Gingyera-Pinycwa, A. G. G. 1978. *Apolo Milton Obote and His Times*. New York: NOK Publishers.

Gingyera-Pinycwa, A. G. G. 1989. Is There a "Northern Question"? In *Conflict Resolution in Uganda*, edited by Kumar Rupesinghe. London: James Currey.

Gingyera-Pinycwa, A. G. G. 1992. *Northern Uganda in National Politics*. Kampala: Fountain Publishers.

Girling, F. K. 1960. *The Acholi of Uganda*. Colonial Research Studies No. 30. London: Her Majesty's Stationery Office.

Glover, Danny, and Nicole C. Lee. 2007. Say No to Africom. *The Nation*, November 19. http://www.thenation.com/article/say-no-africom.

Golooba-Mutebi, Frederick and Sam Hickey. 2010. Governing Chronic Poverty under Inclusive Neoliberalism: The Case of the Northern Uganda Social Action Fund. *Journal of Development Studies* 46(7): 1216–39.

Government Accountability Office (GAO). 2010. *Improved Planning, Training, and Inter-agency Collaboration Could Strengthen DOD's Efforts in Africa*. GAO-10-794.

Government of Uganda. 2003. *Referral of the Situation Concerning the Lord's Resistance Army*. Kampala. On file with author.

Graubart, Jonathan. 2010. Rendering Global Criminal Law an Instrument of Power: Prag-matic Legalism and Global Tribunals. *Journal of Human Rights* 9 (4): 409–26.

Gray, John Milner. 1951–1952. Acholi History 1860–1901. Part I, *Uganda Journal* 15(2): 121–43; Part II, *Uganda Journal* 16(1): 32–50; Part III, *Uganda Journal* 16(2): 132–44.

Gregory, Derek. 2008. "The Rush to the Intimate": Counterinsurgency and the Cultural Turn. *Radical Philosophy* (150): 8–23.

Groupe URD. 2008, Policy Paper on Principle 7 of Good Humanitarian Donorship Initia-tive. Plaisians, France.

United Nations. 1998. Guiding Principles on Internal Displacement. U.N. Doc.# E/CN.4/1998/53/Add.2.

Hailey, William Malcolm. 1957. *An African Survey, Revised 1956: A Study of Problems Arising in Africa South of the Sahara*. London: Oxford University Press.

Harbeson, John W., and Donald Rothchild, eds. 1995. *Africa in World Politics: Post-Cold War Challenges*, Second Edition. Boulder, CO: Westview Press.

Hardt, Michael, and Antonio Negri. 2000. *Empire*. Cambridge, MA: Harvard University Press.

Harrell-Bond, Barbara. 1986. *Imposing Aid: Emergency Assistance to Refugees*. Oxford: Oxford University Press.

Harrell-Bond, Barbara. 2002. Can Humanitarian Work with Refugees be Humane? *Human Rights Quarterly* 24(1): 51–85.

Harrison, Graham. 2004. *The World Bank and Africa: The Construction of Governance States*. New York: Routledge.

Herson, Maurice. 2003. Putting the "H" Back into Humanitarian Accountability. *Humanitarian Exchange Magazine* 24: 4–6.

Hickey, Samuel, and Giles Mohan. 2005. *Participation: From Tyranny to Transformation?* London: Zed Books.

Hirsch, John L., and Robert B. Oakley. 1995. *Somalia and Operation Restore Hope: Reflections on Peacemaking and Peacekeeping*. Washington, DC: United States Institute of Peace Press.

Hountondji, Paulin J. 1996. *African Philosophy: Myth and Reality*, Second Edition. Bloomington: Indiana University Press.

Hovil, Lucy, and Zachary Lomo. 2005. *Whose Justice? Perceptions of Uganda's Amnesty Act 2000: The Potential for Conflict Resolution and Long-Term Reconciliation*. Refugee Law Project Working Paper No. 15. Kampala: Refugee Law Project.

Hovil, Lucy, and Joanna R. Quinn. 2005. *Peace First, Justice Later: Traditional Justice in Northern Uganda*. Working Paper No. 17. Kampala: Refugee Law Project.

Hudock, Ann. 1999. *NGOs and Civil Society: Democracy by Proxy?* Malden, MA: Polity Press.

Human Rights Focus (HURIFO). 2002. *Between Two Fires: The Plight of IDPs in Northern Uganda*. Gulu Town.

Human Rights Focus (HURIFO). 2007. *Fostering the Transition in Acholiland: From War to Peace, from Camps to Home*. Gulu Town.

Human Rights Watch. 2004. *Human Rights Overview: Uganda*. New York.

Hyndman, Jennifer. 2000. *Managing Displacement: Refugees and the Politics of Humanitarianism*. Minneapolis: University of Minnesota Press.

Ignatieff, Michael. 1998. *Warrior's Honor: Ethnic War and the Modern Conscience*. New York: Metropolitan Books.

Ignatieff, Michael. 2003. *Human Rights as Politics and Idolatry*. Princeton, NJ: Princeton University Press.

Ingham, Kenneth. 1958. *The Making of Modern Uganda*. London: Allen and Unwin Ltd.

International Center for Transitional Justice. 2005. *Forgotten Voices: A Population-based Survey on Attitudes about Peace and Justice in Northern Uganda*. New York.

International Criminal Court. 2004. President of Uganda Refers Situation Concerning the Lord's Resistance Army (LRA) to the ICC. Press Release. The Hague, January 29.

International Crisis Group. 2004. *Northern Uganda: Understanding and Solving the Conflict*. ICG Africa Report No. 77. Nairobi/Brussels.

International Crisis Group. 2006. *A Strategy for Ending Northern Uganda's Crisis*. Africa Briefing No. 35. Nairobi/Brussels.

Isike, Christopher, Ufo Okeke-Uzodike, and Lysias Gilbert. 2008. The United States Africa Command: Enhancing American Security or Fostering African Development? *African Security Review* 17(1): 20–38.s

Jackson, Stephen. 2002. *Regional Conflict Formation and the "Bantu/Nilotic" Mythology in the Great Lakes*. New York: Center on International Cooperation Report, New York University.

Jefferess, David. 2002. For Sale—Peace of Mind: (Neo-) Colonial Discourse and the Commodification of Third World Poverty in World Vision's "Telethons." *Critical Arts: A Journal of North-South Cultural Studies* 16(1): 1–21.

Johnson, Douglas. 2003. *The Root Causes of Sudan's Civil Wars*. Oxford: James Currey.

Jok, Jok Madut. 1996. Information Exchange in the Disaster Zone: Interaction between Aid Workers and Recipients in South Sudan. *Disasters* 20(3): 206–15.

Justice and Reconciliation Project and Quaker Peace and Social Witness. 2008. *Sharing the Burden of the Past: Peer Support and Self Help amongst Former Lord's Resistance Army Youth*. Gulu Town.

Kabwegyere, Tarsis. 1995. *The Politics of State Formation and Destruction in Uganda*. Kampala: Fountain Publishers.

Kaiser, Tania. 2004. Participation or Consultation? Reflections on a "Beneficiary Based" Evaluation of UNHCR's Programme for Sierra Leonean and Liberian Refugees in Guinea, June-July 2000. *Journal of Refugee Studies* 17(2): 185–204.

Kaldor, Mary. 1999. *New and Old Wars: Organized Violence in a Global Era*. Cambridge: Polity Press.

Kaoma, Kapya. 2009/2010. The U.S. Christian Right and the Attack on Gays in Africa. *The Public Eye Magazine*, Winter/Spring. http://www.publiceye.org/magazine/v24n4/us-christian-right-attack-on-gays-in-africa.html.

Kaplan, Robert D. 1994. The Coming Anarchy. *Atlantic Monthly*, February. http://www.theatlantic.com/magazine/archive/1994/02/the-coming-anarchy/4670/.

Kaplan, Robert. 2007. The Next Frontier. *The Atlantic*, November 1. http://www.theatlantic.com/magazine/archive/2007/11/the-next-frontier/6453/.

Kapoor, Ilan. 2004. Hyper-self-reflexive Development? Spivak on Representing the Third World "Other." *Third World Quarterly* 25(4): 627–47.

Kapoor, Ilan. 2008. *The Postcolonial Politics of Development*. New York: Routledge.

Karim, Ataul, Mark Duffield, Susanne Jaspars, Aldo Benini, Joanna Macrae, Mark Bradbury, Douglas Johnson, George Larbi, Barbara Hendrie. 1996. *Operation Lifeline Sudan: A Review*. Nairobi: UN.

Karugire, Samwiri Rubaraza. 1980. *A Political History of Uganda*. Nairobi: Heinemann Educational Books.

Kasfir, Nelson. 1976. *The Shrinking Political Arena: Participation and Ethnicity in African Politics, with a Case Study of Uganda*. Berkeley: University of California Press.

Kasfir, Nelson. 1998. "No-party Democracy" in Uganda. *Journal of Democracy* 9(1): 49–63.

Kasozi, A. B. K. 1994. *The Social Origins of Violence in Uganda: 1964–1985*. Montréal: McGill-Queen's University Press.

Kayunga, Sallie Simba. 1995. *Uganda National Congress and the Struggle for Democracy: 1952–1962*. Working Paper No. 14. Kampala: Centre for Basic Research.

Keen, David. 1994. *The Benefits of Famine: A Political Economy of Famine and Relief in Southwestern Sudan, 1983–1989*. Princeton, NJ: Princeton University Press.

Keen, David. 1997. A Rational Kind of Madness. *Oxford Development Studies* 25:1.

Keen, David. 1998. *The Economic Functions of Violence in Civil Wars*. Adelphi Papers No. 320. Oxford: Oxford University Press.

Keenan, Jeremy. 2008. US Militarization in Africa: What Anthropologists Should Know about AFRICOM. *Anthropology Today* 24(5): 16–20.

Keenan, Jeremy. 2009. *The Dark Sahara: America's War on Terror in Africa*. London: Pluto Press.

Kelley, Kevin. 2009. Uganda: Big U.S. Military Exercise for Northern Region. *The East African*, October 12. http://www.theeastafrican.co.ke/news/-/2558/670850/-/qxs6erz/-/index.html.

Kennedy, David. 2005. *The Dark Sides of Virtue: Reassessing International Humanitarianism*. Princeton, NJ: Princeton University Press.

Kimani, Mary. 2009. Pursuit of Justice or Western Plot? International Indictments Stir Angry Debate in Africa. *Africa Renewal*, October. http://www.un.org/ecosocdev/geninfo/afrec/vol23no3/233-icc.html.

Klare, Michael, and Daniel Volman. 2006a. The African "Oil Rush" and US National Security. *Third World Quarterly* 27(4): 609–28.

Klare, Michael, and Daniel Volman. 2006b. America, China, and the Scramble for Africa's Oil. *Review of African Political Economy* 33(108): 297–309.

Koh, Harold Hongju. 2010. The Obama Administration and International Law. Keynote Speech at the Annual Meeting of the American Society of International Law, March 26. http://www.state.gov/s/l/releases/remarks/139119.htm.

Komakech, Martin. 2005. The Internal Displacement Phenomenon in the Internal Armed Conflict within Acholi sub-region of Northern Uganda: The Challenge to Provide Protection. Masters Thesis, the European Inter-University Council, Ruhr University Bochum.

Koskenniemi, Martti. 2002. Between Impunity and Show Trials. *Max Planck Yearbook of United Nations Law* (6): 1–35.

Koyama, Shukuko, and Henri Myrttinen. 2007. Unintended Consequences of Peace Operations on Timor Leste from a Gender Perspective. In *Unintended Consequences of Peacekeeping Operations*, edited by Chiyuki Aoi, Cedric de Coning, and Ramesh Thakur, 23–43. Tokyo: United Nations University Press.

Kraxberger, Brennan M. 2005. The United States and Africa: Shifting Geopolitics in an "Age of Terror." *Africa Today* 51(1): 46–68.

Kreimer, Alcira. 2000. *Uganda: Post-Conflict Reconstruction: Country Case Evaluation*. Washington, DC: World Bank.

Kuperman, Alan J. 2004. Provoking Genocide: A Revised History of the Rwandan Patriotic Front. *Journal of Genocide Research* 6(1): 61–84.

Lamwaka, Caroline. 2002. The Peace Process in Northern Uganda, 1986–1990. *Accord: Protracted Conflict, Elusive Peace: Initiatives to End the War in Northern Uganda* 11: 28–33.

Lefort, Claude. 1986. *The Political Forms of Modern Society: Bureaucracy, Democracy, Totalitarianism*, edited by John B. Thompson. Cambridge, MA: MIT Press.

Lewis, Stephen, Clovis Maksoud, and Robert C. Johansen. 1991. The United Nations after the Gulf War. *World Policy Journal* 8(3): 539–74.

Leys, Colin. 1967. *Politicians and Policies: An Essay on Politics in Acholi, Uganda, 1962–65*. Nairobi: East African Publishing House.

Lindqvist, Sven. 1997. *Exterminate all the Brutes*. New York: The New Press.

Liu Institute for Global Issues and Gulu District NGO Forum. 2005. *Roco Wat I Acholi: Restoring Relationships in Acholi-land: Traditional Approaches to Justice and Reintegration*. Vancouver: University of British Columbia.

Lobel, Jules. 2000. American Hegemony and International Law: Benign Hegemony? Kosovo and Article 2(4) of the U.N. Charter. *Chicago Journal of International Law* 1(1): 19–36.

Low, D.A. 1962. *Political Parties in Uganda: 1949–1962*. London: Athlone Press.

Lund, Michael. 2001. A Toolbox for Responding to Conflicts and Building Peace. In *Peacebuilding: A Field Guide*, edited by Luc Reychler and Thania Paffenholz, 16–20. Boulder, CO: Lynne Rienner.

Luttwak, Edward. 1999. Give War a Chance. *Foreign Affairs* 78(4): 36–45.

Lyman, Princeton N., and Patricia Dorff, eds. 2007. *Beyond Humanitarianism: What You Need to Know about Africa and Why It Matters*. New York: Council on Foreign Relations.

Maathai, Wangari. 2010. International Criminal Court Belongs to Us Africans. *The East African*, May 24–30. http://www.theeastafrican.co.ke/news/International%20Criminal%20Court%20belongs%20to%20us%20Africans/-/2558/924060/-/item/1/-/l5uwcuz/-/index.html.

MacEwan, Arthur. 1999. *Neoliberalism or Democracy?* London: Zed Books.

MacGinty, Roger. 2008. Indigenous Peace-Making versus the Liberal Peace. *Cooperation and Conflict* 43(2): 139–63.

Macrae, Joanna, and Nicholas Leader. 2001. Apples, Pears and Porridge: The Origins and Impact of the Search for "Coherence" between Humanitarian and Political Responses to Chronic Political Emergencies. *Disasters* 25(4): 290–307.

Malkki, Liisa H. 1995. *Purity and Exile: Violence, Memory, and National Cosmology among Hutu Refugees in Tanzania*. Chicago: University of Chicago Press.

Malkki, Liisa H. 1996. Speechless Emissaries: Refugees, Humanitarianism, and Dehistoricization. *Cultural Anthropology* 11(3): 377–404.

Mama, Amina, and Margo Okazawa-Rey. 2008. Editorial: Militarism, Conflict and Women's Activism. *Feminist Africa* (10): 1–8.

Mamdani, Mahmood. 1976. *Politics and Class Formation in Uganda*. Kampala: Fountain Publishers.

Mamdani, Mahmood. 1984. *Imperialism and Fascism in Uganda*. Trenton, NJ: Africa World Press.

Mamdani, Mahmood. 1993. *Pluralism and the Right of Association*. Working Paper No. 29. Kampala: Centre for Basic Research.

Mamdani, Mahmood. 1995. *And Fire Does Not Always Beget Ash: Critical Reflections on the NRM*. Monitor Publications: Kampala.

Mamdani, Mahmood. 1996. *Citizen and Subject: Contemporary Africa and the Legacy of Late Colonialism*. Princeton, NJ: Princeton University Press.

Mamdani, Mahmood. 2001. *When Victims Become Killers: Colonialism, Nativism, and the Genocide in Rwanda*. Princeton, NJ: Princeton University Press.

Mamdani, Mahmood. 2008. The New Humanitarian Order. *The Nation*, September 29. http://www.thenation.com/article/new-humanitarian-order.

Mamdani, Mahmood. 2009. *Saviors and Survivors: Darfur, Politics, and the War on Terror*. New York: Pantheon.

Manji, Firoze and Carol O'Coill. The Missionary Position: NGOs and Development in Africa. *International Affairs* 78(3): 567–83.

Maren, Michael. 1997. *The Road to Hell: The Ravaging Effects of Foreign Aid and International Charity*. New York: The Free Press.

Marks, Edward. 2009. Why USAFRICOM? *Joint Forces Quarterly* 52(1): 148–52.

Marriage, Zoë. 2006. *Not Breaking the Rules, Not Playing the Game: International Assistance to Countries at War.* London: Hurst & Company.

Mayerfeld, Jamie. 2004. The Democratic Legacy of the International Criminal Court. *Fletcher Forum of World Affairs* 28(2): 147–56.

McFate, Sean. 2008. US Africa Command: Next Step or Next Stumble? *African Affairs* 107(426): 111–20.

McIvor, Chris. 2004. Children's Feedback Committees in Zimbabwe: An Experiment in Accountability. *Humanitarian Exchange Magazine* 27: 30–33.

Mergelsberg, Ben. 2010. Between Two Worlds: Former LRA Soldiers in Northern Uganda. In *The Lord's Resistance Army: Myth and Reality*, edited by Tim Allen and Koen Vlassenroot, 156–76. London: Zed Books.

Meron, Theodor. 2000. The Humanization of Humanitarian Law. *American Journal of International Law* 94(2): 239–78.

Merry, Sally Engle. 2006. *Human Rights and Gender Violence: Translating International Law into Local Justice.* Chicago: University of Chicago Press.

Mertus, Julie, and Jeffrey W. Helsing, eds. 2006. *Human Rights and Conflict: Exploring the Links between Rights, Law, and Peacebuilding.* Washington, DC: United States Institute of Peace.

Minear, Larry. 1991. *Humanitarianism under Siege: A Critical Review of Operation Lifeline Sudan.* Trenton, NJ: Red Sea Press.

Minear, Larry, Thomas G. Weiss, and Kurt M. Campbell. 1991. *Humanitarianism and War: Learning the Lessons from Recent Armed Conflicts.* Occasional Paper No. 8. Providence, RI: Thomas J. Watson Jr. Institute for International Studies.

Minter, William, and Daniel Volman. 2009. Making Peace or Fueling War in Africa. Foreign Policy in Focus, March 13. http://fpif.org/fpiftxt/5960.

Mitchell, P. E. 1939. *Native Administration: Note by the Governor.* Entebbe: Government Printer.

Mkandawire, Thandika. 2001. Thinking about Developmental States in Africa. *Cambridge Journal of Economics* 25(3): 289–313.

Mkandawire, Thandika, and Charles Soludo. 1999. *Our Continent, Our Future: African Perspectives on Structural Adjustment.* Dakar: CODESRIA.

Moeller, Robert. 2010. The Truth about AFRICOM. *Foreign Policy*, July 21. http://www.foreignpolicy.com/articles/2010/07/21/the_truth_about_africom.

Moore, David. 1999. "Sail on, O Ship of State": Neo-Liberalism, Globalisation, and the Governance of Africa. *Journal of Peasant Studies* 27(1): 61–96.

Moore, David. 2000. Leveling the Playing Fields and Embedding Illusions: "Post-conflict" Discourse and Neo-Liberal "Development" in War-Torn Africa. *Review of African Political Economy* 27(83): 11–28.

Moreno-Ocampo, Luis. 2005. Statement of the Chief Prosecutor on the Uganda Arrest Warrants. The Hague, October 14.

Moreno-Ocampo, Luis. 2010. Review Conference—General Debate, Statement. Kampala, May 31.

Mosse, David. 1994. Authority, Gender and Knowledge: Theoretical Reflections on the Practice of Participatory Rural Appraisal. *Development and Change* 25: 497–526.

Moulin, Carolina, and Peter Nyers. 2007. "We Live in a Country of UNHCR"—Refugee Protests and Global Political Society. *International Political Sociology* 1(4): 356–72.

Mudimbe, V. Y. 1988. *The Invention of Africa: Gnosis, Philosophy, and the Order of Knowledge*. Bloomington: Indiana University Press.

Mudoola, Dan. 1996. *Religion, Ethnicity and Politics in Uganda*. Kampala: Fountain Publishers.

Munson, Robert. 2008. Do We Want to "Kill People and Break Things" in Africa? *Strategic Studies Quarterly* 2(1): 97–110.

Museveni, Yoweri. 1986. *Selected Articles on the Uganda Resistance War*. Kampala: NRM Publications.

Museveni, Yoweri. 1997. *Sowing the Mustard Seed: The Struggle for Freedom and Democracy in Uganda*. London: Macmillan.

Mutibwa, Phares Mukasa. 1992. *Uganda since Independence: A Story of Unfulfilled Hopes*. London: Hurst.

Mutua, Makau wa. 2001. Savages, Victims, and Saviors: The Metaphor of Human Rights. *Harvard International Law Journal* 42(1): 201–45.

Mwenda, Andrew. 2007. Personalizing Power in Uganda. *Journal of Democracy* 18(3): 23–37.

Mwenda, Andrew. 2010. Uganda's Politics of Foreign Aid and Violent Conflict: The Political Uses of the LRA Rebellion. In *The Lord's Resistance Army: Myth and Reality*, edited by Tim Allen and Koen Vlassenroot, 45–58. London: Zed Books.

Mwenda, Andrew, and Roger Tangri. 2005. Patronage Politics, Donor Reforms, and Regime Consolidation in Uganda. *African Affairs* 104(416): 449–67.

Nabudere, Dani. 2003. *The Hidden War, the Forgotten People*. Kampala: Makerere University Human Rights and Peace Centre.

Nee, Ann, and Peter Uvin. 2010. Silence and Dialogue: Burundians' Alternatives to Transitional Justice. In *Localizing Transitional Justice*, edited by Rosalind Shaw, 157–82. Stanford, CA: Stanford University Press.

Network of Concerned Anthropologists. 2009. *The Counter-Counterinsurgency Manual*. Chicago: Prickly Paradigm Press.

Ngoga, Pascal. 1998. Uganda: The National Resistance Army. In *African Guerrillas*, edited by Christopher Clapham, 91–106. Oxford: James Currey.

Nyers, Peter. 2006. *Rethinking Refugees: Beyond States of Emergency*. New York: Routledge.

Office of the Prime Minister. 2002. *Community Reconciliation and Conflict Management Handbook*. Kampala: Northern Uganda Social Action Fund.

Office of the Prime Minister. 2003. Post-Conflict Reconstruction: The Case of Northern Uganda. Discussion Paper No. 7. Kampala: Ministry of Finance, Planning, and Economic Development.

Office of the Prosecutor of the International Criminal Court. 2010. Policy Paper on Victims' Participation. The Hague.

O'Kadameri, Billie. 2002. LRA/Government Negotiations 1993–1994. *Accord: Protracted Conflict, Elusive Peace: Initiatives to End the War in Northern Uganda* 11: 34–41.

Okuku, Juma. 2002. *Ethnicity, State Power, and the Democratization Process in Uganda*. Discussion Paper No. 17. Uppsala: The Nordic Africa Institute.

Oloka-Onyango, Joseph. 2000. New Wine or Old Bottles? Movement Politics and One-partyism in Uganda. In *No-Party Democracy in Uganda: Myths and Realities*, edited by Justus Mugaju and Joseph Oloka-Onyango, 40–59. Kampala: Fountain Publishers.

Omara-Otunnu, Amii. 1987. *Politics and the Military in Uganda, 1890–1985*. Basingstoke, Hampshire: Macmillan.

Omara-Otunnu, Amii. 1992. The Struggle for Democracy in Uganda. *Journal of Modern African Studies* 30(3): 443–63.

Orford, Anne, and Jennifer Beard. 1998. Making the State Safe for the Market: The World Bank's World Development Report 1997. *Melbourne University Law Review* 22(1): 195–216.

Pain, Dennis. 1997. *"The Bending of the Spears": Producing Consensus for Peace and Development in Northern Uganda.* London: International Alert/Kacoke Madit.

Pandolfi, Mariella. 2003. Contract of Mutual (In)Difference: Governance and the Humanitarian Apparatus in Contemporary Albania and Kosovo. *Indiana Journal of Global Legal Studies* 10(1): 369–81.

Paris, Roland. 2004. *At War's End: Building Peace after Civil Conflict.* Cambridge: Cambridge University Press.

Patman, Robert G. 1995. The UN Operation in Somalia. In *A Crisis of Expectations: UN Peacekeeping in the 1990s*, edited by Ramesh Chandra Thakur and Carlyle A. Thayer, 85–104. Boulder, CO: Westview Press.

p'Bitek, Okot. 1971. *Religion of the Central Luo.* Nairobi: East African Literature Bureau.

Perrot, Sandrine. 2010. Northern Uganda: A "Forgotten Conflict," Again? The Impact of the Internationalization of the Resolution Process. In *The Lord's Resistance Army: Myth and Reality*, edited by Tim Allen and Koen Vlassenroot, 187–204. London: Zed Books.

Ploch, Lauren. 2009. *Africa Command: U.S. Strategic Interests and the Role of the U.S. Military in Africa.* Congressional Research Service, October 2.

Pogge, Thomas. 2001. Properties of Global Justice. In *Global Justice*, edited by Thomas Pogge, 6–23. Malden, MA: Blackwell.

Pouligny, Béatrice. 2002. Building Peace in Situations of Post-Mass Crimes. *International Peacekeeping* 9(2): 181–201.

Pouligny, Béatrice. 2006. *Peace Operations Seen from Below: UN Missions and Local People.* London: Hurst & Company.

Powell, Colin. 2001. Remarks to the National Foreign Policy Conference for Leaders of Nongovernmental Organizations. US Department of State, October 26.

Power, Samantha. 2002. *"A Problem from Hell": America and the Age of Genocide.* New York: Basic Books.

Prunier, Gérard. 1998. Uganda, Nearly a Miracle. *Le Monde Diplomatique*, English Edition, February. http://mondediplo.com/1998/02/10uganda.

Pugh, Michael. 2002. Maintaining Peace and Security. In *Governing Globalization: Power, Authority and Global Governance*, edited by David Held and Anthony McGrew, 209–33. Malden, MA: Polity Press.

Pupavac, Vanessa. 2001. Therapeutic Governance: Psycho-social Intervention and Trauma Risk Management. *Disasters* 25(4): 358–72.

Pupavac, Vanessa. 2002. The International Children's Rights Regime. In *Rethinking Human Rights: Critical Approaches to International Politics*, edited by David Chandler, 57–75. New York: Palgrave Macmillan.

Rahnema, Majid. 1992. Participation. In *The Development Dictionary: A Guide to Knowledge as Power*, edited by Wolfgang Sachs, 116–31. London: Zed Books.

Refugee Law Project. 2004. *Behind the Violence: Causes, Consequences and the Search for Solutions to the War in Northern Uganda.* Working Paper No. 11. Kampala.

Reno, William. 2002. Uganda's Politics of War and Debt Relief. *Review of International Political Economy* 9(3): 415–35.

Rice, Susan. 2007. The Escalating Crisis in Darfur. Speech before the Spring Africa Speaker Series, SAIS, February 21, Johns Hopkins University, Baltimore.

Richards, Audrey, ed. 1960. *East African Chiefs*. London: Faber and Faber.

Richards, Audrey. 1982. Changing Local Government Policy: 1950–1970. In *Uganda's First Republic: Chiefs, Administrators and Politicians, 1967–1971*, edited by A. F. Robertson, 8–52. Cambridge: African Studies Centre, Cambridge University.

Richmond, Oliver. 2002. *Maintaining Order, Making Peace*. London: Palgrave Macmillan.

Richmond, Oliver. 2005. *The Transformation of Peace*. London: Palgrave Macmillan.

Richmond, Oliver. 2008. *Peace in International Relations*. London: Routledge.

Rieff, David. 2002. *A Bed for the Night: Humanitarianism in Crisis*. New York: Simon & Schuster.

Robertson, A. F., ed. 1982. *Uganda's First Republic: Chiefs, Administrators, and Politicians 1967–1971*. Cambridge: African Studies Centre, Cambridge University.

Robins, Steven. 2009. Humanitarian Aid beyond "Bare Survival": Social Movement Responses to Xenophobic Violence in South Africa. *American Ethnologist* 36(4): 637–50.

Rotberg, Robert I. 2002. Failed States in a World of Terror. *Foreign Affairs* 81(4): 127–40.

Sachs, Jeffrey D. 2006. *The End of Poverty*. New York: Penguin Books.

Said, Abdul Aziz, and Charles O. Lerche. 2006. Peace as a Human Right: Toward an Integrated Understanding. In *Human Rights and Conflict*, edited by Julie Mertus and Jeffrey W. Helsing, 129–50. Washington, DC: United States Institute of Peace.

Salyaga, S. 1986. RCs: A Path for Democracy? *Forward Magazine* 9(2).

Sathyamurthy, T. V. 1986. *The Political Development of Uganda, 1900–1986*. Aldershot, Hants, UK: Gower.

Schmitt, Carl. 1996. *The Concept of the Political*, translated by George Schwab. Chicago: University of Chicago Press.

Schomerus, Mareike. 2010. Chasing the Kony Story. In *The Lord's Resistance Army: Myth and Reality*, edited by Tim Allen and Koen Vlassenroot, 93–112. London: Zed Books.

Schomerus, Mareike, and Kennedy Tumutegyereize. 2009. *After Lightning Thunder: Protecting Communities and Building Peace*. London: Conciliation Resources.

Shaw, Rosalind, Lars Waldorf, and Pierre Hazan, eds. 2010. *Localizing Transitional Justice: Interventions and Priorities after Mass Atrocities*. Stanford, CA: Stanford University Press.

Shivji, Issa. 1989. *The Concept of Human Rights in Africa*. London: CODESRIA Book Series.

Shivji, Issa. 2007. *Silences in NGO Discourse: The Role and Future of NGOs in Africa*. Oxford: Fahamu Books, Pambazuka Press.

Shklar, Judith. 1964. *Legalism*. Cambridge, MA: Harvard University Press.

Simpson, Gerry. 2007. *Law, War and Crime: War Crimes Trials and the Reinvention of International Law*. Cambridge: Polity.

Singer, P. W. 2003. *Corporate Warriors: The Rise of the Privatized Military Industry*. Ithaca, NY: Cornell University Press.

Sjögren, Anders. 2007. Global Power Relations and State Formation in Uganda. In *Globalization, Imperialism and Resistance*, edited by Lars Lindström, Mats Wärn, and Björn Beckman, 35–58. Stockholm: PODSU.

Slim, Hugo. 1997. Doing the Right Thing: Relief Agencies, Moral Dilemmas and Moral Responsibility in Political Emergencies and War. *Disasters* 21(3): 244–57.

Slim, Hugo. 2002. Not Philanthropy but Rights: The Proper Politicisation of Humanitarian Philosophy. *International Journal of Human Rights* 6(2): 1–22.

Smillie, Ian, ed. 2001. *Patronage or Partnership: Local Capacity Building in Humanitarian Crises*. Bloomfield, CT: Kumarian Press.

Snyder, Jack, and Leslie Vinjamuri. 2003. Trials and Errors: Principle and Pragmatism in Strategies of International Justice. *International Security* 28(3): 5–44.

Speed, Shannon. 2008. *Rights in Rebellion: Indigenous Struggle and Human Rights in Chiapas*. Stanford, CA: Stanford University Press.

Spiegel, Julia, and Noel Atama. 2009. Finishing the Fight against the LRA. Strategy Paper. Washington, DC: ENOUGH Project. http://www.enoughproject.org/files/publications/lra_strategy_paper_051209.pdf.

Spivak, Gayatri Chakravorty. 1988. Can the Subaltern Speak? In *Marxism and the Interpretation of Culture*, edited by Cary Nelson and Lawrence Grossberg, 271–313. Urbana: University of Illinois Press.

Steele, Brent J., and Jacque L. Amoureux. 2005. NGOs and Monitoring Genocide: The Benefits and Limits to Human Rights Panopticism. *Millennium* 34(2): 403–32.

Stein, Janice Gross. 2008. Humanitarian Organizations: Accountable—Why, to Whom, for What, and How? In *Humanitarianism in Question: Politics, Power, Ethics*, edited by Michael Barnett and Thomas G. Weiss, 124–42. Ithaca, NY: Cornell University Press.

Stockton, Nicholas. 1998. In Defence of Humanitarianism. *Disasters* 22(4): 352–60.

Stockton, Nicholas. 2006. The Accountability Alibi. *Humanitarian Exchange Magazine* 34: 34–35.

Summerfield, Derek. 1999. A Critique of Seven Assumptions behind Psychological Trauma Programmes in War-affected Areas. *Social Science and Medicine* 48(10): 1449–62.

Tallgren, Immi. 2002. The Sensibility and Sense of International Criminal Law. *European Journal of International Law* 13(3): 561–95.

Tamale, Sylvia. 2008. Law, Sexuality, and Politics in Uganda: Challenges for Women's Human Rights NGOs. In *Human Rights NGOs in East Africa: Political and Normative Tensions*, edited by Makau Mutua, 51–74. Philadelphia: University of Pennsylvania Press.

Tangri, Roger, and Andrew Mwenda. 2006. Politics, Donors and the Ineffectiveness of Anti-Corruption Institutions in Uganda. *Journal of Modern African Studies* 44(1): 101–24.

Teitel, Ruti. 2002. Humanity's Law: Rule of Law for the New Global Politics. *Cornell International Law Journal* 35(2): 355–87.

Terry, Fiona. 2000. The Limits and Risks of Regulation Mechanisms for Humanitarian Action. *Humanitarian Exchange Magazine* 17: 20–21.

Terry, Fiona. 2002. *Condemned to Repeat? The Paradox of Humanitarian Action*. Ithaca, NY: Cornell University Press.

Thakur, Ramesh Chandra. 1995. UN Peacekeeping in the New World Disorder. In *A Crisis of Expectations: UN Peacekeeping in the 1990s*, edited by Ramesh Chandra Thakur and Carlyle A. Thayer, 3–22. Boulder, CO: Westview Press.

Titeca, Kristof. 2010. The Spiritual Order of the LRA. In *The Lord's Resistance Army: Myth and Reality*, edited by Tim Allen and Koen Vlassenroot, 59–73. London: Zed Books.

Tosh, John. 1973. Colonial Chiefs in a Stateless Society: A Case-Study from Northern Uganda. *Journal of African History* 14(3): 473–90.

TransAfrica Forum. n.d. AFRICOM: A New Military for Hire? http://www.transafricaforum.org/files/AFRICOM%20-PMC%20factsheet.doc.

Tripp, Aili Mari. 2004. The Changing Face of Authoritarianism in Africa: The Case of Uganda. *Africa Today* 50(3): 3–26.

Tvedt, Terje. 1998. *Angels of Mercy or Development Diplomats? NGOs and Foreign Aid.* Trenton, NJ: Africa World Press.

United Nations Children's Fund (UNICEF). 2005. *Suffering in Silence: A Study of Sexual and Gender-based Violence (SGBV) in Pabbo Camp, Gulu District, Northern Uganda.* New York.

United Nations Department of Humanitarian Affairs (UNDHA). 1996. Humanitarian Situation Report on Uganda. December 4. http://www.africa.upenn.edu/Hornet/irin_120496.html.

United Nations Department of Humanitarian Affairs (UNDHA). 1997. Humanitarian Situation Report on Uganda. March 15. http://www.africa.upenn.edu/Hornet/irin_31597.html.

United Nations Economic Commission for Africa (UNECA). 2003. *Economic Report on Africa 2003: Accelerating the Pace of Development.* Addis Ababa.

UN Integrated Regional Information Networks (UN IRIN). 2004. Amnesty and Peace Groups Urge ICC to Probe Government Army Too. February 3.

UN Integrated Regional Information Networks (UN IRIN). 2005. Uganda: ICC Issues Arrest Warrants for LRA Leaders. October 7.

UN Integrated Regional Information Networks (UN IRIN). 2009. East Africa: US Troops Help Build Disaster Response Capacity. October 21.

United Nations Office for the Coordination of Humanitarian Affairs (UNOCHA). 2005a. *Consolidated Appeal Process: Uganda 2005.* Geneva.

United Nations Office for the Coordination of Humanitarian Affairs (UNOCHA). 2005b. *Consolidated Appeal Process: Uganda 2005: Projects.* Geneva.

United States Africa Command. n.d. Command Overview. PowerPoint presentation by Major General Mike Snodgrass, Chief of Staff. http://www.au.af.mil/awc/africom/documents/awc_briefing_snodgrass.ppt.

United States Department of State. 1994. Administration Policy on Reforming Multilateral Peace Operations. Publication 10161. Washington DC: Department of State, Bureau of International Organizational Affairs. May. Reprinted in *International Legal Materials* 33 (May 1994): 795–813.

Uvin, Peter. 1998. *Aiding Violence: The Development Enterprise in Rwanda.* Bloomfield, CT: Kumarian Press.

Van Acker, Frank. 2004. Uganda and the Lord's Resistance Army: The New Order No One Ordered. *African Affairs* 103(412): 335–57.

van de Walle, Nicolas. 2010. US Policy towards Africa: The Bush Legacy and the Obama Administration. *African Affairs* 109(434): 1–21.

van Puilenbroek, Joost, and Nico Ploojer. 2009. *How EnLightning Is the Thunder?* Utrecht: IKV Pax Christi.

Volman, Daniel. 2008a. AFRICOM: The New U.S. Military Command for Africa. African Security Research Project, June 27. http://concernedafricascholars.org/african-security-research-project/?p=12.

Volman, Daniel. 2008b. The Military Dimensions of Africa's New Status in Global Geopolitics. http://concernedafricascholars.org/african-security-research-project/?p=49.

Volman, Daniel. 2009a. AFRICOM and the Obama Administration. African Security Research Project, April 1. http://concernedafricascholars.org/african-security-research-project/?p=43.

Volman, Daniel. 2009b. Full Report on US Army Wargames for Future Military Intervention in Nigeria and Somalia. African Security Research Project, August. http://concernedafricascholars.org/african-security-research-project/?p=77.

Volman, Daniel. 2010a. Obama's National Security Policy towards Africa: The First Year. *Pambazuka News*, January 20. http://www.pambazuka.org/en/category/features/61614.

Volman, Daniel. 2010b. The Origins of AFRICOM: The Obama Administration, the Sahara-Sahel and US Militarization of Africa. *Concerned Africa Scholars Bulletin* 85: 85–88.

Volman, Daniel, and Beth Tuckey. 2008. Militarizing Africa (again). Foreign Policy in Focus, February 20. http://www.fpif.org/articles/militarizing_africa_again.

Walzer, Michael. 1977. *Just and Unjust Wars*. New York: Basic Books.

Watson, Catherine. 1991. *Exile from Rwanda: Background to an Invasion*. Washington, DC: US Committee for Refugees.

Weiss, Thomas, and Leon Gordenker, eds. 1996. *NGOs, the U.N., and Global Governance*. Boulder, CO: Lynne Rienner.

Weiss, Thomas, and Larry Minear. 1993a. Preface. In *Humanitarianism across Borders: Sustaining Civilians in Times of War*, edited by Thomas Weiss and Larry Minear, vi–xi. Boulder, CO: Lynne Rienner.

Weiss, Thomas, and Larry Minear. 1993b. Force and Action: Commentary. In *Humanitarianism across Borders: Sustaining Civilians in Times of War*, edited by Thomas Weiss and Larry Minear, 57–68. Boulder, CO: Lynne Rienner.

Whitaker, Beth Elise. 2008. Reluctant Partners: Fighting Terrorism and Promoting Democracy in Kenya. *International Studies Perspectives* 9(3): 254–71.

White, Sarah. 1996. Depoliticising Development: The Uses and Abuses of Participation. *Development in Practice* 6(1): 6–15.

Williams, David. 2000. Aid and Sovereignty: Quasi-states and the International Financial Institutions. *Review of International Studies* 26(4): 557–73.

Williams, David. 2008. *The World Bank and Social Transformation in International Politics: Liberalism, Governance and Sovereignty*. New York: Routledge.

Woodward, Susan L. 2001. Humanitarian War: A New Consensus? *Disasters* 25(4): 331–44.

World Bank. 1981. *Accelerated Development in Sub-Saharan Africa*. Washington, DC.

World Bank. 1989. *Sub-Saharan Africa: From Crisis to Sustainable Growth*. Washington, DC.

World Bank. 1997. *World Development Report 1997: The State in a Changing World*. Washington, DC .

World Bank. 2000. *Can Africa Claim the 21st Century?* Washington, DC.

World Bank. 2002. Project Appraisal Document on a Proposed Credit in the Amount of SDR 80.1 Million (US$100 Million Equivalent) to the Republic of Uganda for a Northern Uganda Social Action Fund. Report No. 23885-UG, June 7. http://www-wds.worldbank.org/external/default/WDSContentServer/IW3P/IB/2002/07/26/000094946_02071004024056/Rendered/PDF/multiopage.pdf.

World Bank Group. 2002. Integrated Safeguards Data Sheet (Updated), July 31. wds.world-bank.org/external/default/WDSContentServer/IW3P/IB/2002/08/27/000094946_02080604013327/Rendered/PDF/multiopage.pdf.

World Food Program (WFP). 1996. Weekly Review, Report No. 47 of 1996, November 29. http://iys.cidi.org/humanitarian//wfp/96b/0021.html.

World Food Program (WFP). 1997a. Weekly Review, Report No. 6 of 1997, February 7. http://iys.cidi.org/humanitarian//wfp/97a/0005.html.

World Food Program (WFP). 1997b. Weekly Review, Report No. 12 of 1997, March 21. http://iys.cidi.org/humanitarian//wfp/97a/0011.html.

World Food Program (WFP). 1999. *WFP Assistance to Internally Displaced Persons: Country Case Study of Internal Displacement. Uganda: Displacement in the Northern and Western Districts*. Rome. http://www.internal-displacement.org/8025708F004CE90B/%28httpDocuments%29/611FAD994328DB04802570B7005A55B3/$file/WFP+REPORT%28September%29.pdf.

World Food Program (WFP). 2004. Emergency Report No. 41, October 8. http://www.reliefweb.int/rw/RWB.NSF/db900SID/JCDR-65KT9Y?OpenDocument.

Wright, Ann. 2009. With Its Record of Rape, Don't Send the U.S. Military to the Congo. *Huffington Post*, August 21. http://www.huffingtonpost.com/ann-wright/with-its-record-of-rape-d_b_264980.html.

X, Malcolm. 1994. The Ballot or the Bullet. In *Malcolm X Speaks: Selected Speeches and Statements*, edited by George Breitman. New York: Grove Press.

Yates, Mary C. 2009. U.S. Africa Command: Value Added. *Joint Forces Quarterly* 52(1): 152.

Zartman, I. William, ed. 2000. *Traditional Cures for Modern Conflicts: African Conflict "Medicine."* Boulder, CO: Lynne Rienner.

Zeleza, Paul T. 2003. *Rethinking Africa's Globalization*. Trenton, NJ: Africa World Press.

Žižek, Slavoj. 1997. Repeating Lenin. http://lacan.com/replenin.htm.

Zolo, Danilo. 2009. *Victors' Justice: From Nuremberg to Baghdad*. London: Verso.

INDEX

Abrahamsen, Rita, 38
Acana II, Rwot, 158–59
accountability
　and AFRICOM, 216, 222–37
　democratic, 114–18
　through disintervention, 241, 244, 247, 249–52
　and the ICC, 179–213
　and humanitarianism, 104, 111, 111–18
　legal, 112–13, 196–97
　and peacebuilding, 145, 151
　and the Ugandan government, 65, 69, 146, 243–44
　and Western intervention, 7, 27, 31–32, 36–37, 87
ACF. See Action against Hunger
Acholi, political order among
　and Acholi exclusion from NRM government, 63–66
　and its changes in the camps, 137–40
　crisis of, 57, 61–71, 88–89, 120, 148–49
　and its devastation under Amin, 57–58
　and its development during Obote I, 55–56
　under early colonial rule, 47–49
　and its image in ethnojustice, 165–66
　and need for local political reform, 74
　and non-political civil society, 142–49
　pre-colonial, 48, 165–66
　and the resolution of its crisis, 178
　See also traditional leadership
Acholiland
　AFRICOM presence in, 230–32
　civil society in, 142–49
　colonial economy in, 49–50
　humanitarian economy in, 144–47
　massacres by Idi Amin in, 57
　occupation by NRA of, 62
　in pre-colonial period, 47
Acholi matar, 176
Acholi political identity
　attempts by rebels to assert, 65, 66–67, 69–71
　and its consolidation under colonialism, 52–53
　and ethnojustice, 164–65
　origins of, 47–49
Acholi Religious Leaders Peace Initiative, 150, 190, 197, 235
Action against Hunger, 95
activism, American, 235–39

administration
　and civil society, 143, 146
　and ethnojustice, 155
　and human rights enforcement, 196
　and humanitarianism, 90, 99–104, 107, 109
　and ICC, 181
　and peacebuilding, 29, 42–43, 120, 129
　and state-building, 8, 29, 39, 41, 122
　and total intervention, 33, 35–39, 240, 242, 252
　See also discipline; violence, administrative
Afghanistan, 218, 221, 238
Africa, image of
　in human rights discourse, 195
　in ICC intervention, 182
　post–Cold War, 16–20
　Western, 5–7, 154–55, 245–46
Africa Contingency Operations Training and Assistance Program (ACOTA), 227
African criminal court, 215
African exclusion, 17–18
African Philosophy: Myth and Reality, 159
African state, crisis of, 17–19
African Studies Association, 222
African Union (AU), 86, 184, 201, 227–28, 249
African Union Mission in Somalia (AMISOM), 86–87, 227–28
AFRICOM, 13, 86, 120, 153, 202, 216–39
　and administrative violence, 232
　and contingency operations, 233–35
　criminalization of resistance to, 234–35
　as form of total intervention, 216
　and human security, 216–28, 235
　humanitarian and development agenda of, 229–32
　and military bases in Africa, 217, 223, 225–26
　as networked, 225
　in northern Uganda, 230–32
　as participatory, 216–17
　and prevention, 221–22
　and stability operations, 221, 229
　as reflecting U.S. weakness, 281n55
　and U.S. agendas in Africa, 218–21
　and U.S. militarization in Africa, 224–25
　and use of contractors, 217, 221, 225–26
　and violence against women, 232
　and the War on Terror, 218–21